INSIDERS' GUIDE®
North Carolina's
Outer Banks

INSIDERS'GUIDE® to
North Carolina's Outer Banks

THIRTY-THIRD EDITION

REVISED BY KIP TABB

Globe
Pequot
GUILFORD, CONNECTICUT

All the information in this guidebook is subject to change. Hurricane Dorian caused significant damage to the region in September 2019, especially Hatteras and Ocracoke Islands. At press time, recovery efforts were underway, but we recommend that you call ahead to obtain current information before traveling.

Globe Pequot

An imprint of The Rowman & Littlefield Publishing Group, Inc.
4501 Forbes Blvd., Ste. 200
Lanham, MD 20706
www.rowman.com

Distributed by NATIONAL BOOK NETWORK

Title page image © AlpamayoPhoto/GettyImages
Images by the author unless otherwise noted.

British Library Cataloguing in Publication Information available

Library of Congress Cataloging-in-Publication Data available

ISBN 978-1-4930-4400-9 (paper : alk. paper)
ISBN 978-1-4930-4401-6 (electronic)

∞™ The paper used in this publication meets the minimum requirements of American National Standard for Information Sciences—Permanence of Paper for Printed Library Materials, ANSI/NISO Z39.48-1992.

Contents

How to Use This Book

Celebrating the 33rd edition of the *Insiders' Guide to North Carolina's Outer Banks*, we've updated, changed, and revised our extensive collection of favorite restaurants, shops, attractions, events, getaways, activities, and much more.

Besides introducing you to the area's fascinating history and hidden treasures, we provide practical information on camping, real estate, vacation rentals, ferry schedules, fishing sites, and other areas of interest. Also discover valuable tips—look for the ⓘ—that you could get only from an insider. We've designed the *Insiders' Guide to North Carolina's Outer Banks* as a handy reference for all aspects of life here. Keep it in hand, and let us accompany and guide you along every step of your Outer Banks journey.

We begin with colorful overviews of each area along the barrier islands, from the sand-tail villages of Carova (at the Virginia–North Carolina border) to the windswept shores of Ocracoke Island; after that you'll find a chapter on the various ways to get to and around the Outer Banks and sections on our history. Comprehensive chapters tailored to meet your personal needs follow. If you're looking for a cozy dinner spot, browse through the **Dining** chapter. If you want to spend the afternoon in search of a special souvenir, turn to **Shopping**. If you've always wanted to try scuba diving, parasailing, or surfing, all the information you'll need is in **Water Sports**.

SCOUTGIRL/GETTYIMAGES

We've arranged this book so you can read it bit by bit, opening to those particular pages that pique your interest while breezing by those that don't. But please go back and thumb through any parts you may have skipped at first. We bet you'll learn something interesting and maybe even discover some new favorite sports or pastimes along the way. To guide you along your adventure, a passel of excellent maps is tucked in at the book's beginning as well.

Scattered throughout the various chapters are special Insiders' tips (as noted earlier they're indicated by an "i") for quick insights, and Close-ups profiling truly unique aspects of the area's lifestyle and culture.

You'll also find listings accompanied by the ★ symbol—these are our top picks for attractions, restaurants, accommodations, and everything in between that you shouldn't miss while you're in the area. You want the best this region has to offer? Go with our Insiders' Choice.

Finally, if you're moving to the Outer Banks or already live here, be sure to check out pages at the back of the book. There you will find the **Living Here** appendix that offers sections on relocation and retirement.

North Carolina's Outer Banks

The Outer Banks is a world unto itself, made of islands linked to the rest of civilization only by a few bridges and ferries. This fact lends a separatist character to the Outer Banks. A little bit isolated, this is a place where generations have lived and others residents who are proud to have escaped have come to escape the trappings of the mainland. Here vacationers come to put aside the crush city life and the daily pressure of a job. Days go by in the indescribable realm of "island time," becoming more surreal the farther south you and life on a sandbar.

Cultural traditions and norms seem to fall by the wayside once one has crossed over onto one of the islands. Whether visiting or living here lifestyle changes inevitably occur. Suddenly it's perfectly acceptable to go barefoot all day, to wear your bathing suit to the grocery store, to take a book to the beach and never read a word, to spend hours on the porch staring at the water, or to stop to watch the sun set.

The area is a chain of several islands, most little more than sandbars— Roanoke, Colington, Bodie, Hatteras, and Ocracoke. Stretching more than 100 miles along the North Carolina coast, the largest landmass of the Outer Banks, Bodie Island, encompasses the land from the north side of Oregon Inlet through Carova on the Virginia border. Physically it's connected to Virginia, technically it's no longer an island, is actually a very long and thin peninsula. However, since the state border is closed to land crossings, Bodie is, in many minds, an island.

AREA OVERVIEW

The Outer Banks extends from the Virginia border through Ocracoke. There are also some wonderful beaches south of Ocracoke and wonderful places to visit. For information about the best spots in those areas check out our *Insiders' Guide to North Carolina's Central Coast and New Bern* and *Insiders' Guide to North Carolina's Southern Coast and Wilmington*.

Bodie, Hatteras, and Ocracoke Islands are barrier islands, separated from the mainland by a system of wide, shallow sounds. The barrier islands are reefs of sand protecting the mainland from the ravages of the Atlantic Ocean. What keeps the barrier islands from washing away in the face of all that power is their ability to shift and move, to go with the flow of nature. There are other forces at work; vegetation plays a huge part in the stabilization of the islands and residents and government have worked to keep the shoreline intact, making them fit for human occupation.

Made up of 3,000 square miles of surface water and 30,000 square miles of watershed, The Albemarle–Pamlico Sounds system that separates the Outer Banks from the mainland is the second largest estuary in the United States, second only to the Chesapeake Bay. The system consists of seven sounds—Albemarle, Pamlico, Currituck, Croatan, Roanoke, Bogue, and Core. The individual sounds are fed by inlets, cuts of water that slice through the skinny islands from the ocean, and by five major rivers. The Albemarle–Pamlico system is one of the most biologically productive estuaries in the United States, supporting a huge variety of wildlife, fish, shellfish, and plants.

Three North Carolina counties lay claim to these barrier islands—Currituck, Dare, and Hyde. Dare is the largest county with 383 square miles of land and almost 1,200 square miles of water. Dare County stretches from Duck on the north end to the tip of Hatteras Island, including Roanoke Island and a mass of mainland. Currituck County encompasses 255 square miles of land, most of it on the mainland and a small portion of barrier island from north of Duck to the Virginia border. Geographically divided, Currituck County has a population of more than 24,000; around 500 reside on Currituck's northern beaches year-round. Hyde County's Outer Banks portion is Ocracoke Island, a 9-square-mile island with around 900 residents.

The 37,000 or so year-round residents of the Outer Banks host more than 7 million visitors a year. Due to bridges and air travel, the Outer Banks islands are now more easily accessible than ever, leading to rapid development and a dramatic increase in the availability of goods and services. Residents have all the accoutrements needed for a comfortable way of life, including a thriving economy with low unemployment, affordable housing, retail stores offering almost everything, and an abundance of restaurants, arts and entertainment, medical care, and recreational opportunities. With all this, however, no one will deny that the pulse of life on these barrier islands is still set by wind and water. The weather and the natural world play intimate and demanding roles in the lives of barrier island residents.

Much of what keeps the Outer Banks so special is Cape Hatteras National Seashore, which encompasses more than 75 miles of rugged, undeveloped beaches, dunes, marshes, and flatlands. With commercial and residential development continually increasing on the barrier islands, Cape Hatteras National Seashore—the first national seashore in the nation—is treasured and appreciated more than ever. Three national wildlife refuges further protect portions of the Outer Banks from development.

Whether it's the sunrise, the sunset, or what goes on between, the Outer Banks offers the most extraordinary of what island life has to offer. "The sunsets here are the prettiest I have ever seen," Orville Wright wrote to his sister in 1900. "The clouds light up with all colors, in the background, with deep clouds of various shapes fringed with gold before. The moon rises in much the same style, and lights up the pile of sand almost like day." We have more than just good looks and personality, though: We have history. We have drama. We have lots of good stories to tell.

In this chapter we offer overviews of the areas that make up the Outer Banks, taking you on a north-to-south tour of Corolla and Currituck beaches, Duck, Southern Shores, Kitty Hawk, Kill Devil Hills, Colington Island, Nags Head, Roanoke Island, Hatteras Island, and Ocracoke Island.

Hurricane Dorian caused significant damage to the region in September 2019, especially Hatteras and Ocracoke Islands. At press time, recovery efforts were underway, but we recommend that you call ahead to obtain current information before traveling.

> **i** The US Army Corps of Engineers research pier north of Duck is the only oceanographic research pier of its kind in the world. No tours are available; however, you can view the pier from along the shore.

COROLLA & CURRITUCK BEACHES

Just a little bit remote, the Currituck Outer Banks extend north from the town of Duck to the Virginia state line. The whole area is often called Corolla, but that is not quite correct. Corolla is the area north of the Currituck County line to the end of the paved road. To be very technical, Corolla is only the tiny, old village that sits at the base of the lighthouse. The Currituck Outer Banks has no incorporated towns and consists of several planned developments. From north to south, these are Ocean Hill, Corolla Light, Monterey Shores, Whalehead Beach, Buck Island, Crown Point, Ocean Sands, Ocean Sands South, and Pine Island.

The village of Corolla has retained many of its original buildings. What was once a home to fishermen and hunting guides is now a quaint shopping district perfect for an afternoon stroll.

Away from the village of Corolla there has been a building boom. From these barren dunes harboring a few fishing shacks and a handful of private homes, thousands of upscale houses, including 7,000-square-foot mansions, have sprung up on miles of recently paved subdivision roads. A family-owned convenience store that once supplied the only local goods for fewer than 100 permanent residents has been overshadowed by two chain grocery stores. A lighthouse completed in 1875 has become more important as a landmark for tourists than as a guide for sailors. Dozens of eateries offer a variety of cuisines, and several quality resort shopping plazas are available to serve the hundreds of thousands of visitors who flock to the northernmost Outer Banks each summer.

The tiny community where everyone knew everyone else has undergone enormous change with its transformation into a favorite travel destination, but development has been tasteful and aesthetically pleasing. (Local residents still know almost all of the year-rounders by first name.)

North of Sanderling, Palmer's Island is a 35-acre development with 15 oceanfront 1-acre lots, 8 of which have estates ranging from 6,000 to 10,000 square feet each. The homes are engineered to withstand 120 mph winds. Signature architectural embellishments are scaled to match the grandeur of the natural environment.

How Corolla Got its Name

Nestled at the base of Currituck Beach Lighthouse, the cluster of homes did not have a name until 1895 when the US Postal Service provided one. The Postal Service asked residents what name they wanted. Currituck Beach was rejected because there was already a Currituck post office in the county. Jones Hill, the name of the Coast Guard station at that location was rejected—no one is quite sure why but it was.

Finally someone suggested the name of petals of a flower—corolla—and that name was accepted.

CAROVA, AN ISOLATED OUTPOST

After NC 12 ends north of the Village of Corolla, there are no paved roads to the Virginia border. Although remote and accessible only by 4WD vehicles, the area has undergone a building boom over the past five years. On summer afternoons more than a thousand four-wheel-drive vehicles create their own paths on the beach as they drive into and around a community called Carova—where North Carolina meets Virginia. Note that Carova's name is a melding of both states.

Where once lonely homes stood watch over the Corolla Wild Horses and the rhythm of waves beating upon the beach, now 24-bedroom event homes dot the landscape. Yet there is still magic here. Much of the land is protected and paved roads are prohibited. The wild horses still wander at will among the homes, stopping from time to time to graze on a tasty morsel of grass. The sea still rolls to the beach, where a common summer sight is a stallion and his harem cooling off in the surf.

It takes a special kind of person to live away from the paved road. There are no stores, no restaurants, no gas stations—just a few hundred homes, open vistas and wild horses. Residents must negotiate tides and the beach in off-road and four-wheel-drive vehicles, often timing trips to "civilization" around storms and abnormally high tides.

Although relatively protected from civilization, the area is patrolled by county, state, and federal officers. A system of dirt roads behind the dune line allows residents access to their homes. Most residents and visitors to Swan Beach, Carova, North Swan Beach, and the Seagull subdivisions drive on the beach above the waterline or on well-trodden tracks at the base of the dune line. The speed limit on the beach is 35 MPH and 15 MPH on all other roads. Citations are issued for exceeding the speed limit.

Without a four-wheel-drive vehicle, you should not drive on the beach. Watch out for tree stumps, though. An ancient forest that historians say grew along the sound more than 800 years ago still thrusts its sea-withered trunks through the waves at an area known as Wash Woods. Local guides gladly show visitors around in off-road vehicles. Guided tours of the area are available (see the **Recreation** chapter).

Whether you're staying in one of Currituck Beach's exclusive rental homes or camping somewhere on the southern Outer Banks, Corolla and the four-wheel-drive area are well worth exploring.

Carova Permits

There is an ordinance requiring permits to drive all-terrain vehicles (ATVs) in Carova. Drivers must prove ownership of property in Currituck to gain a free permit.

Currituck County also requires a daily use permit for the beach in Carova. This permit applies to the Carova area only, and does not apply to any area in the county south of the end of NC12.

Guests renting homes in Carova, should have permits available to them at no additional charge.

The permit is for beach use only. If you are planning on surf fishing or swimming in Carova, a permit is required. If your family is planning on driving a 4WD vehicle in the area in search of wild mustangs, no permit is required.

DUCK

What makes Duck unique is its village-like atmosphere and the incredible water and sunset vistas. Stroll along the town's mile-long soundside boardwalk and sample gourmet foods for lunch or dinner or stop by the many superb businesses the line the sound.

In this upscale resort community, you'll find wonderful waterfront boutiques, art galleries, and a variety of fine restaurants and casual eateries within easy strolling distance of one another and within walking or biking distance of many of Duck's neighborhoods. The village has been working hard to create a pedestrian- and bike-friendly downtown, and the work is paying off. Duck is probably the most pedal- and foot-friendly town on the Outer Banks.

In the busy season Duck teems with visitors, and traffic crawls along the two-lane highway that runs north to Corolla. But even if you're staying elsewhere, it's worth a special trip.

Tourism was slow to find Duck. It began to catch hold in the early 1980s, but once it did the town grew rapidly (too rapidly, according to many locals). Two decades ago, T-shirts that read "Stuck in Duck" seemed to speak for a lot of the young people who craved more excitement than could be found in this sleepy town. Today it is affluent, busy, and thriving, and around 450 residents call Duck their year-round home. In the quaint shops nestled throughout this village, you can find some real treasures, authentic and one-of-a-kind items to bring home as souvenirs. Plan to enjoy at least one meal here: Duck boasts many outstanding restaurants, and some offer outdoor tables. Don't expect to find strings of motels. Almost every visitor to Duck rents a vacation home.

Duck makes an excellent jumping-off point for the full range of water sports. You'll find places to rent kayaks, canoes, windsurfing equipment, sailboats, Jet Skis, and WaveRunners, and you can launch very close to restaurants and shops. For extra exhilaration try a few hours of stand-up paddleboarding (SUP) followed by lunch or dinner at a soundside table.

The town grew up on one of the most slender strips of sand on the Outer Banks. The ocean and the sound are close enough here so that many cottages offer extraordinary views of both. The neighborhoods in and around Duck are a pleasing mixture of graceful older cottages and luxurious new homes. The gently rolling terrain contrasts with the flatter areas of the Outer Banks. This is the place if you crave a shady, tree-lined escape or a hilltop retreat where you can watch the sun rise and set from two sides of the same home.

Beyond the US Army Corps of Engineers Field Research Facility and the Duck Pier, heading toward Corolla, you'll find the Duck Volunteer Fire Department, the Dare County Sheriff's Office northern beach station, and the Duck Recycling Center.

About five miles north of the Village of Duck, Sanderling is the northernmost community on Dare County's beaches—an isolated, exclusive enclave with 300 acres stretching from sound to sea.

The community itself was started in 1978, setting a precedent for excellence among vacation destinations. These neighborhoods, barely visible from the road, approach land planning sensitively, preserving as much natural vegetation as possible and always aiming for architectural excellence. They are well worth searching out.

In 1985 the Sanderling Inn and Restaurant (now known as Sanderling Inn Resort) opened in the restored Caffey's Inlet Lifesaving Station, built in 1874. With cedar-shake siding, natural wood interiors, and English country antiques, it has the appearance of turn-of-the-20th-century Nags Head resorts and the ambience of a European escape. It's large and airy, with wide porches offering plenty of room for conversation, drinks, and soaking in the sunrise while rocking in wooden chairs (see the **Accommodations** and **Dining** chapters for details).

SOUTHERN SHORES

Stretching from sound to sea, Southern Shores is heralded as one of the most beautiful, well-thought-out developments on the Outer Banks. Interwoven with canals, maritime hardwood forests, dunes, and private beaches, its scenic beauty is hard to match. Real estate agents call Southern Shores property one of the best Outer Banks values for long-term investment.

Southern Shores is south of Duck and north of Kitty Hawk. You can enter this community from the south via NC 12; by South Dogwood Trail, which runs alongside Kitty Hawk School; or by Juniper Trail, which runs perpendicular to the Marketplace shopping center.

A Haven of Solitude

Comprising mostly single-family homes, Southern Shores is predominantly a residential town uncluttered by the commercial aspects of other Outer Banks areas, making it the perfect place to seek solitude.

Founded in 1947 when artist Frank Stick purchased 2,600 acres of beach, marsh and maritime forest, the town was envisioned as a haven for families from the beginning. With his son, David, author of a number of histories of the Outer Banks including *Graveyard of the Atlantic*, he designed the Southern Shores flat top vacation homes that are considered outstanding examples of "a mid-20th century modernist home."

Needing to drain the marsh on the sound side of the town, the Sticks also created a network of canals. Residents still enjoy canoeing or kayaking in the canal system that connects interior properties to Jean Guite Bay and Currituck Sound.

The community includes two private marinas, soundside picnic and bathing areas, and ocean beach accesses situated every 600 feet. The accesses are available only to residents and vacationers staying in the area (make sure you display the proper permit), affording every beachgoer enough elbow room to comfortably spread a blanket or throw a Frisbee. A soundside wading beach on North Dogwood Trail is a favorite spot for families because the shallow sound water is a safer place for children to swim than the ocean. In the summer the picnic area has toilet facilities. Paved and unpaved bike trails meander through the town. Anyone can use the facilities, but to park you must belong to the civic association or get a town sticker. In either case, you have to be a property owner or guest to park in Southern Shores.

The golf course at Duck Woods Country Club winds its way through a residential neighborhood of Southern Shores, offering outstanding play in a pristine setting among tall pines, dogwoods, and other foliage. The 18-hole course is the oldest on the Outer Banks and accepts public play year-round (see the **Recreation** chapter).

The 40 original families who inhabited Southern Shores formed the town's first civic association. The Southern Shores Civic Association acts like a parks and recreation department. It owns, operates, and maintains the marinas, playgrounds, beach accesses, and crossovers for residents, property owners, and guests. Membership dues cover costs, but most of the physical upkeep is done by volunteers in the community.

Today the population has expanded to more than 2,600 year-round residents, swelling to 10,000 in the summer months. Until recently most residents were retirees, but now Southern Shores has an equal number of young families living within its boundaries.

It's been more than 70 years since Frank Stick first purchased Southern Shores, but the slow pace of development means there is still real estate available. Raw land on the oceanfront or soundfront is hard to come by these days, but those wanting to purchase property can obtain homes or land in the beach zone, dunes, or woods. Due to careful planning, Southern Shores has land reserved for a future civic center and several plots to be developed for other town needs.

One of the town's two retail establishments, the Marketplace, includes Food Lion and a multitude of smaller shops (see the Shopping chapter). This complex sits at the edge of Southern Shores, just east of the base of the Wright Memorial Bridge. Southern Shores Crossing, situated behind Southern Shores Realty, offers more small shops, a specialty market, a day spa, and an upscale restaurant.

Southern Shores was incorporated in 1979 and growth has occurred in the development since Frank Stick's purchase, but the developers' spirit of conservation is felt with every bike ride, sunset, and tour of the waterways that weave together flora, fauna, and humankind. The town continues to be environmentally conscious and was the first Outer Banks community to offer curbside recycling.

KITTY HAWK

If you access the Outer Banks from North Carolina's Currituck County mainland, the first town you'll reach is Kitty Hawk. This beach municipality begins at the eastern end of the Wright Memorial Bridge over the Currituck Sound and stretches sound to sea for about 4 miles. Within its town limits are a maritime forest, a fishing pier, a golf course, condominiums, and a historic, secluded village.

Southern Shores forms the northern boundary of Kitty Hawk, and Kill Devil Hills is to the south. Milepost (MP) markers offer the best means of finding your destination. Most rental cottages, shops, restaurants, attractions, and resorts in this area can be located by green milepost markers along US 158,

Soft sand and bright sunshine make for a perfect beach day in Kitty Hawk.

Croatan Highway (insiders call this the Bypass) and NC 12, Virginia Dare Trail (insiders call this the Beach Road). The first milepost marker (MP 1) is in Kitty Hawk, where the highway splits near the Aycock Brown Welcome Center.

Much of its 4 miles of beachfront is more developed than any other place on the barrier islands with many of the homes and businesses built in the 1930s, 1940s and 1950s. Kitty Hawk offers a great vacation getaway with lots of family-oriented activities, a fishing pier, some great eateries, convenient shopping, and all the fun you could want on a clean beach.

Cruising south along the beach, you'll notice some weather-beaten houses perched on the shoreline. At high tide and in stormy weather, waves crash under the house pilings and wash out truckloads of sand. In the past, ocean played chicken with these beach cottages, and just about every year a cottage would cry uncle and collapse into the surf. However, the Kitty Hawk beach has been nourished, and the result is been a wider, better beach that offers protection to the classic beach cottages.

Kitty Hawk's name will forever be bound to the history of aviation and the Wright Brothers. It was in the Village of Kitty Hawk that Wilbur first set foot on the Outer Banks. His brother, Orville, joined him 11 days later. They stayed at the home of town's Postmasters, Bill and Addie Tate, and it was Bill Tate's letter to an inquiry from the brothers that brought them to his home.

"This in my opinion would be a fine place; our winds are always steady, generally from 10 to 20 miles velocity per hour," he wrote, adding the Kitty Hawk residents were "...a hospitable people when you come among us."

The Tate house was on Moor Shore Road. The house no longer exists, but a monument, paid for by the citizens of Kitty Hawk was placed on the site in 1928. The monument is still there.

The brothers flew their experimental kites at Kitty Hawk in 1900, but the following year set up a permanent camp in a series of high dunes out of the town called Kill Devil Hills. At the time it was part of Kitty Hawk, but is now the town of Kill Devil Hills.

By one popular version of the story, Kitty Hawk owes its colorful name to a derivation of local Indians' references to goose hunting season as "killy honker" or "killy honk." Eighteenth-century documents record this beach community as "Chickahauk," a name adopted by the prestigious southeastern section of Southern Shores. Other theories say the name evolved from "skeeter hawk," mosquito hawks that were prolific in the area, or from ospreys or similar raptors preying on the area's kitty wren.

The Transition to Vacation Destination

Unlike Nags Head, which has been a thriving summer resort since before the Civil War, Kitty Hawk didn't become a vacation destination until about 75 years ago. A group of Elizabeth City businessmen bought 7 miles of beach north of Kitty Hawk Village in the late 1920s and formed the Wright Memorial Bridge Company. By 1930 they had built a 3-mile wooden span across the Currituck Sound from Point Harbor to the Outer Banks. Travelers could finally arrive at island beaches by car from the mainland. Kitty Hawk land became popular—and a lot more pricey. Summer visitors streamed across the new bridge, paying $1 per car for the privilege.

With the sudden boom in tourism, development shifted from the protected soundside hammocks to the open, windswept beaches. Small wooden cottages sprung from behind dunes on the oceanfront. As the beach eroded over the years, wind and water had their way with many of the beachfront homes. Houses were swept away during hurricanes and nor'easters, providing newfound ocean frontage for the neighbor cottage across the street. In 2003 Hurricane Isabel took an additional seven homes.

Even the original Kitty Hawk Lifesaving Station had to be jacked up and moved to a more protected site on the west side of the Beach Road to prevent tides from carrying it to a watery grave. The station is now a private residence, but travelers can still recognize the original Outer Banks gabled architecture of this historic structure.

In the western reaches of this community, the maritime forest of Kitty Hawk Woods winds for miles over tall ridges and blackwater swamps. Primarily year-round residents make their homes here on private plots and in new subdivisions. Some lots are much larger than in other central beach communities. The twisting vines, dripping Spanish moss, and abundant tall trees offer seclusion and shelter from the storms not found in the expansive, open oceanfront areas. On summer days locals often ride horses around the shady lanes of old Kitty Hawk Village, reminiscent of the days before bridges.

Although you'll find some businesses tucked back in the trees of Kitty Hawk Village at the western end of Kitty Hawk Road near the sound, most of this town's commercial outposts are along the Bypass and the Beach Road. The Shoreside Center near the end of the Wright Memorial Bridge is anchored by a Walmart and Harris Teeter. Other shopping plazas include the Dune's Shops with its eclectic collection of eateries and Buccaneers Shops anchored on the end by the iconic Captain Franks.

If you're headed for the beach, you'll find a public bathhouse at MP 4½. There is also a number of public parking areas for beachgoers throughout the town. The public is also welcome to use the Dare County boat launch at the end of Bob Perry Road, where locals and visitors can set sail on a hot summer day and watch the dolphins frolic in Kitty Hawk Bay.

From fishing, to surfing to kayaking, Kitty Hawk offers exceptional recreational possibilities. With all the water fun rounded out with a fine selection of dining establishments, convenient shopping, and medical services, along with history and natural beauty, it's obvious why Kitty Hawk is a favorite beach retreat for families, retirees, and college students.

KILL DEVIL HILLS

Even among all the other romantic and striking names of Outer Banks communities, Kill Devil Hills swirls a little longer in the imagination. One legend has it that Kill Devil Hill, the sand dune where the Wright brothers revolutionized transportation, was named after the wretched-tasting kill-devil rum that may have washed up in barrels from shipwrecks in early colonial days. According to another tale these hills were named after a rogue called Devil Ike, who blamed the theft of shipwrecked cargo on the devil, whom he claimed to have chased to the hills and killed. Other local lore tells of an Outer Banker who, atop one of the dunes, tried to kill the devil he had traded his soul to for a bag of gold.

A wonderful attraction away from the beach is the **Nags Head Woods Ecological Preserve**. The parking lot and information center are actually located in Kill Devil Hills, although much of the park crosses into Nags Head. Hikers, birders, and nature lovers delight in this wooded anomaly, where diverse flora and fauna can be enjoyed in stunning silence.

The Outer Banks' first incorporated and most populous town, Kill Devil Hills is bookended by Kitty Hawk and Nags Head. Spanning the barrier island from sound to sea, this beach community is the geographic center of Dare County, with a little over 7,000 permanent residents. Hundreds of thousands of tourists visit this bustling beach town each summer. Indeed, the intersection of Ocean Bay Boulevard and Colington Road—where the Wright Memorial, a

Held on Veterans Day Weekend every year, the Outer Banks Marathon begins in Kitty Hawk Woods finds its way to the hard packed dirt roads of Nags Head Woods and finally ends in Manteo.

beach bathhouse, the post office, the town municipal center, the county chamber of commerce, the library, a school complex, and the entrance to the only road to Colington Island are grouped—is the busiest junction in the county and possibly the busiest secondary road in North Carolina. Bottlenecks are common in the morning and midafternoon hours.

Despite the trend toward bigger and more exclusive resort homes and amenities elsewhere on the Outer Banks, Kill Devil Hills remains a family-oriented beach for visitors and a centrally located town of moderately priced housing for the permanent population. Kite flying, surfing, sea kayaking, windsurfing, sunbathing, shopping, restaurants, motels, churches, and schools combine to make this town a top choice for many, as it has been for more than a 60 years.

Condominiums and franchise hotels dot the 5 miles of once-barren dunes. More than 41 miles of paved roads have replaced sandy pathways. Fast food restaurants have sprung up along the five-lane US 158, forming the Outer Banks' commercial hub, known locally as French Fry Alley.

COLINGTON ISLAND

In 1633, Colington Island became the first land in Carolina to be deeded to an individual. Today this 2-mile-long, 2.5-mile-wide island, although developing rapidly, is one of the last of the Outer Banks communities to experience growth. Around 3,500 people make Colington their year-round home.

The east end of Colington Island lies a mile west of the Wright Brothers National Memorial, linked by a bridge over Colington Creek, which separates the island from Kill Devil Hills and Dare County beaches. Colington's other borders are surrounded by open water. Kitty Hawk Bay is to the north and Buzzard Bay is to the south. The mouths of four sounds (Currituck, Albemarle, Croatan, and Roanoke) converge on the west side of this family community.

Colington, named after its first proprietor, Sir John Colleton, was originally tilled to grow grapes for a winery shortly after settlers in 1664 founded the first Outer Banks community. The grapes, along with crops of tobacco, fruits, and vegetables, failed after three successive hurricanes, but by the early 1800s, a thriving fishing community had grown on two halves of the island: Great Colenton and Little Colenton, cleaved in 1769 by the Dividing Creek. Fishing, crabbing, and hunting sustained islanders generation after generation. Eventually, years after the rest of the barrier islands, Colington natives got paved roads, telephones, and electric service.

Now they have tourism as well. Just like the four- or five-generation families that live here, Colington Island has its own unique Outer Banks identity. High, uneven dunes meet dank, brackish swamplands. Thick groves of pine, dogwood, live oak, beech, and holly drip Spanish moss over expanses of sandy shoreline. Thin creeks widen to unexpected harbors and bays. In summer months soft-shell crab holding pens illuminate strips of scrubby yard along the sounds at night, the naked light bulbs glaring out of the darkness like a Reno casino. Advertisements for waterfront property in pricey new subdivisions are posted not far from where trailers and campgrounds line the twisting road. Mansions are barely evident, perched on their sandy shelves overlooking Colington Road, the most heavily traveled secondary road in Dare County.

Colington Harbour, the island's first subdivision, was built in 1965. Since then numerous other subdivisions have been constructed along canals, marshlands, and soundfronts and in woodlands throughout Colington Island. After a year of weighing benefits and risks, newcomers and natives hammered out a reasonable zoning plan. Several restaurants, a storage garage, and a go-kart track mingling with crab shedders and fish houses along the road illustrate the conflict and challenges this sheltered community faced over dramatic change. With new development approved every year, residents have accepted the inevitability of growth. The future face of Colington will be determined by the strength of the zoning plan and the people who molded it.

NAGS HEAD

Home of the Outer Banks' first resort, the community of Nags Head is south of Kill Devil Hills and north of Oregon Inlet. It stretches from the Atlantic

Ocean to the Roanoke Sound and has remained a popular vacation destination for almost 200 years. Many first-time vacationers mistakenly refer to the whole middle-Banks area as "Nags Head," lumping the town together with neighboring Kill Devil Hills and Kitty Hawk. Most likely this is historically based, due to the fact that at one time Nags Head was the only true destination on the middle Banks.

The booming summer scene was once anchored by cottages towering over the shallow sound, elaborate hotels facing the mainland, and calm—water canoeing, crabbing, and conversation. This relaxed style of soundside vacationing has long since been altered by shifting sands and changing values.

The Story Behind the Name

The primary resort destination on these barrier islands for more than a century, Nags Head has been the official name of the area since at least 1738, when it first appeared on maps. Historians say the beach town got its name from the horses that once roamed throughout the islands. The much more colorful legend we insiders prefer is that Nags Head was derived from a custom locals used to lure ships to the shores. Securing a lantern from a Banker pony's neck, residents would drive the horse up and down the beach, the light swinging with the same motion as a sailboat. The unsuspecting offshore vessel would steer toward the light and proceed to get grounded on the shoals. The locals would then promptly ransack the hapless ship.

Nags Head Today

Today Nags Head is home around 3,000 residents. Hotels, restaurants, piers, rambling residences, and luxurious vacation cottages line Nags Head's oceanfront, which remains predominantly vacation oriented. Local residents live in the middle and on the west side of the island, away from the harsh elements of the sea. The sound shores are filled with private cottages, except one portion of lower Nags Head that features water-sports outfitters, go-kart tracks, and mini golf galore. South Nags Head, stretching from MP 17 to MP 21, is an exclusively residential area with no commercial development.

Jockey's Ridge State Park is Nags Head's most popular attraction aside from the beach. The best kite flying, hang gliding, and sunset views are found atop this natural phenomenon, which is the largest sand dune on the East Coast. Every summer day the sprawling dune is dotted with hundreds of people who climb to the top for recreation and for the expansive views of sea and sound.

Nags Head is well known for its recreational opportunities. The Outer Banks has expanded its bike and multi-use paths and there are interconnected bike paths from the Currituck County line on the north End of Duck to South Nags Head. A Scottish links–style golf course, **Nags Head Golf Links**, is one of the area's most beautiful and challenging courses. It stretches along the Roanoke Sound, offering sound views and the opportunity to see a variety of waterbirds and wildlife. Dolphin tours, airboat rides, boat rentals, Jet Ski rentals, kiteboarding lessons, windsurfing, and sailing are all offered on the sound in lower Nags Head, around MP 16 and on the Nags Head–Manteo Causeway. Miniature golf and go-kart tracks also cluster in this area. Nags Head has the YMCA complex and the area's only bowling alley.

Shoppers flock to Nags Head's name-brand outlet stores and to its several strip malls and grocery stores. Nags Head is home to many art galleries, including an artists' enclave known as Gallery Row (see the **Arts & Culture** chapter). Restaurants and nightspots lure diners and revelers to Nags Head. Owens' Restaurant has been a Nags Head institution for more than 50 years. Pamlico Jack's offers some of the best sunset views on the Outer Banks.

Since it's centrally located on the Outer Banks, Nags Head is a favorite destination of people who want to take day trips to Hatteras Island and Corolla. If you don't want to get back in the car once you've arrived at your vacation destination, you can get everything you want within walking distance of most Nags Head hotels and cottages.

Whether you're looking to escape the bustle of the beach by taking a quiet hike through the Nature Conservancy's Nags Head Woods Ecological Preserve or dance the night away at a beachside tavern, this Outer Banks town remains one of the area's most popular resorts.

ROANOKE ISLAND

Nestled between the Outer Banks and the North Carolina mainland, Roanoke Island is one of the most historic places in America. Roanoke Island is the site of England's first attempt to establish a permanent colony in the New World. Beginning in 1584, Sir Walter Raleigh dispatched a series of voyages carrying courageous souls to settle in the New World. These journeys culminated in a colony of 117 men, women, and children, sent in 1587, only to disappear mysteriously." The Lost Colony of Roanoke Island remains a puzzle. Theories concerning the colonists' fate abound, but until archaeologists dig up some real proof, we'll continue to wonder what really happened to these early settlers.

For those who appreciate concrete links to the past, relics have been retrieved from the waters surrounding Roanoke Island—artifacts that may provide clues to centuries-old puzzles. Numerous locals and archaeologists alike have combed the island for treasures from the Native American culture, earliest English settlements, and Civil War times. Old English coins, a powder horn, a vial of quicksilver, weapons, bottles, iron fragments, pottery, and arrowheads have been discovered here.

Roanoke Island tends to bring out the nature lover in all of us. In the spring, summer, and fall, early mornings and late afternoons find marsh rabbits nibbling roadside grasses. Red-winged blackbirds, looking much like holiday ornaments, adorn the bushes alongside the road. They really stand out in winter, when the leaves have left trees barren. Scan the creeks in the warm months, just before entering Roanoke Island from the west, and you can see turtles lined like soldiers on half-sunken logs and along the banks. Crossing the Washington Baum Bridge from the east, we regularly spot osprey flying overhead, clutching dangling snakes or fish in their claws. A wide variety of fish, such as spot, croaker, pigfish, sea mullet, sheepshead, and stripers, inhabit the surrounding waters. Boats and recreational water vehicles of all sorts share the sounds and bays in fair weather.

By land you can walk back in time at **Roanoke Island Festival Park**. Docked at the Park is the *Elizabeth II*, a 69-foot replica of the typical British ship plying the seas in 1584. The *Elizabeth II* was christened in 1984 to mark the 400th anniversary of the first expedition to Roanoke Island.

You can also examine history at **Fort Raleigh**. Make sure to explore the park's nature path, the Thomas Hariot Trail. Hariot, a 16th-century author, wrote the first book about the New World in Elizabethan English. His book is a study of the Native Americans and a survey of the area's natural resources. Only six copies of his literary treatise are said to exist.

Island Economy & Tourism

At the heart of Roanoke Island life is the inhabitants' desire to preserve a small-town feeling while finding ways to make a living. Islanders mostly work in tourist- and service-oriented businesses, at fishing-related jobs, as writers and artists, in local government, and in the public school system.

Roanoke Island has history to market. The **Attractions** chapter describes the island's top sites: the Elizabethan Gardens, the North Carolina Aquarium, Fort Raleigh National Historic Site, the Outer Banks History Center, Roanoke Island Festival Park, the North Carolina Maritime Museum, and *The Lost Colony* outdoor drama.

The Outer Banks History Center, housed at Roanoke Island Festival Park (see the **Attractions** chapter), is a fount of Roanoke Island lore and has old photos and area maps on display.

The main branch of the Dare County Library on US 64, just across from Manteo Elementary School, is another good source for more island information. For overall Outer Banks information, such as maps, brochures, and other local data, stop in at the Outer Banks Visitors Bureau on US 64/264. The staff is friendly and helpful.

Talk with some of our old-timers for some really entertaining inside information. Conversation with lifelong locals is bound to reveal a colorful tale or two. Pick up a copy of *Memories of Manteo and Roanoke Island, NC*, by Suzanne Tate as told by the late Cora Mae Basnight, if you're unable to make a

Entrance and main building of the Elizabethan Gardens on Roanoke Island.
TerryHealy/GettyImages

personal connection. This oral history, from the mouth of a much-loved native (and late mother of the former president *pro tem* of the North Carolina Senate, Marc Basnight), is a delightful book accented with interesting photographs. Ms. Basnight, according to Tate's book, held the record for playing the same role longer than any actor in American theater, that of Agona, a Native American woman, in *The Lost Colony*. Many consider her the quintessential Agona. Another fantastic, more thorough history of the town and island is *Manteo, A Roanoke Island Town*, by Angel Ellis Khoury. It's filled with fascinating stories, anecdotes, and facts about this area.

Lots of exciting tales revolve around *The Lost Colony*, the historic outdoor drama that outlines the story of the first English settlement and its disappearance. Pulitzer Prize–winning playwright Paul Green wrote the drama, which debuted in 1937. It has played a major role in the lives of local folk ever since (see the **Arts & Culture** chapter). The production celebrated its 80th anniversary in 2019.

Generations of families grew up acting in the annual play. From representing the infant Virginia Dare to playing the role of Gov. John White or Chief Manteo, many a Roanoke Island resident nurtured a love of history through the play and a love of theater as a result. Andy Griffith, who played Sir Walter Raleigh in his first acting stint, became a permanent Roanoke Island resident.

Among other notable veterans of the play are William Ivey Long, Terrance Mann, Chris Elliott, and Eileen Fulton.

William S. Powell's *Paradise Preserved* is the definitive source for the history of the Roanoke Island Historical Association, perpetuators of the historic play. Powell offers an exciting account of the creative endeavors of Mrs. Mabel Evans Jones, the author and producer of local pageants on Roanoke Island that predate Green's play. Evans Jones, the former superintendent of schools in Dare County, ran a summer arts camp on the island in the early 1920s. As it is with an archaeologist, the more you dig, the more you're likely to uncover something concerning Roanoke Island's roots and tales of the people who called the island home.

Boatbuilding

A description of Roanoke Island would be incomplete without a nod to a very special livelihood shared by many native islanders. Boatbuilding was and continues to be a major part of life on Roanoke Island. From the small bateau put together in a backyard shed to the 100-foot yachts constructed at major boatbuilding operations, Manteo and Wanchese share in this rich heritage.

The North Carolina Maritime Museum operates in the old **George Washington Creef Boathouse** on the Manteo waterfront. The museum pays tribute to the area's boatbuilding heritage. Here you can watch old crafts being restored and view a variety of boat exhibits.

George and Benjamin Creef operated the facility as the Manteo Machine Shop and Railways in the 19th century. The shop was built in 1884. Boats were hauled out of the water and serviced there. At this location "Uncle Wash" Creef built the first shad boat, designated the Official State Historic Boat of North Carolina in 1987. One of the most important fishing vessels of its time, its design allowed it to effectively work nets and carry weight yet still ride well in the water.

Boats are still built on Roanoke Island—huge, sleek vessels with their hulls buffed to a sun-splintering shine. Each spring these brand-new, 50-foot-plus boats emerge from private building barns and are tugged slowly down the highway to Wanchese to be put in the water for the first time. On board the boat, members of the construction crew carefully lift power lines as their vessel moves down the road, invariably delaying traffic. Smiles wreathe the faces of the crew: After six to eight months of hammering, sanding, and painting, they are ready to christen the fruit of their labor. It is a tense time, too, for no one really relaxes until everyone sees that the boat sits and moves "just right" in the water.

HATTERAS ISLAND

The sea is a strong tonic that humans often crave at the expense of security. Nowhere is this desire more obvious than on this little stretch of sand that juts precariously out into the Atlantic Ocean just off North Carolina's coast. Hatteras Island residents accept the stresses of living with a seasonal economy, storm damage, and cultural isolation as part of life in the shifting sand. The decision to live on the threshold of land and sea forges an intimate relationship with nature. Hearty islanders pulled together to rebuild hard hit areas after 2011's Hurricane Irene wreaked havoc upon northern sections of Hatteras Island.

South of Nags Head and north of Ocracoke Island, Hatteras Island measures 60 miles from Oregon Inlet to Hatteras Inlet and consists of seven small towns with a total year-round population of about 4,000 residents. Running north to south they are Rodanthe, Waves, Salvo, Avon, Buxton, Frisco, and Hatteras Village. You can enter the island from the north by car via NC 12 after crossing the Marc Basnight Bridge or from the south by ferry via Ocracoke Island. As with other townships and islands of the Outer Banks, you can also reach the area by air—setting down on a small airstrip in Frisco—or by boat. (See the **Getting Here, Getting Around** and **Recreation** chapters for airfield, marina, and ferry information.)

Island Living, Economy & Tourism

Overall, Hatteras Island's residents live and work supported mostly by tourism, fishing, real estate, teaching, and government employment. Because of the seasonal economy, weather-related economic setbacks, and lack of corporations and industries that hire mass amounts of people, it's not unusual for residents to have more than one job. Cleaning rental cottages on the side provides extra money, and you may find that your waiter during the summer months is a professional from another trade altogether. Necessity also provokes creativity, and many locals sell their carvings or paintings in local shops and galleries.

Families thrive despite typical inconveniences to be expected in village living on a remote island. They pattern their living styles accordingly. You won't find a Walmart on the island, but mail—order companies get their share of business. A sense of community is evident in the packed stands at the Cape Hatteras High School basketball games (even folks with no kids attend).

It's only been during recent years that Hatteras residents have left the island in large numbers during county-mandated hurricane evacuations. More nonnatives who now live here are less likely to ride out a storm. Storm danger and damage has increased due to development and tighter living quarters.

Weather plays a regular role in Hatteras life. When the island is evacuated during a hurricane warning, local businesses may lose up to a week's worth of revenue. With their annual income primarily made during the 12 weeks of summer, evacuations cause financial hardship for businesses and their employees.

Despite the imposing hold nature can cast over the barrier island, visitors flock here annually to enjoy its beauty and seclusion. Today there are enough conveniences, restaurants, and diversions within reach to entertain even sophisticated vacationers. The Cape Hatteras School, with help from the Dare County Arts Council and the Bryan Cultural Series brings in cultural events for residents. There are also several noteworthy art galleries on the island (see the **Arts & Culture** chapter).

History tells us, though, that even without these modern additions, folks would still come to relax Hatteras-style, away from the busier pace of the towns farther up the barrier islands, to do a little crabbing, clamming, fishing, beach walking, bird watching, or chatting with the anglers who relax at the docks. Many a modern-day adult vacationer has been coming to the Outer Banks since childhood. In fact, generations of families can call Hatteras Island their summer home.

The island has two obvious drawing cards: the sea and unique landscape. Some of the best windsurfing, kiteboarding and surfing in North America can be done in the waters along Hatteras Island (see the **Attractions** and **Recreation** chapters). Surfers from all over the East Coast come to Hatteras Island to surf the breakers, especially during strong nor'easters. Surfers look forward to hurricane season from June through November, when big northern swells can push wave heights to 8 feet or more.

Hatteras Island is famous as an East Coast fishing hot spot. About 40 miles offshore are the Gulf Stream, a shelf current, and the Deep Western Boundary Current, all of which cross near the continental shelf's edge. The influence of this convergence is both positive and negative. These crossing currents spawned Diamond Shoals, creating the groundwork for danger but also supplying a rich habitat for sport fish. A wide variety of fish travel up the Gulf Stream, giving this area the reputation for being the "Billfish Capital of the World." World-record fish have been caught both offshore and in the surf at Cape Hatteras Point, where red drum and many other fish come to feed. Much of the tip of Hatteras is lined with marinas where recreational charter boats take visitors to inshore and offshore waters (see the **Recreation** chapter). Full-service tackle shops, staffed with knowledgeable insiders, speckle the barrier island.

North of Rodanthe and just south of Oregon Inlet is **Pea Island National Wildlife Refuge**, where birding is popular and rewarding. A unique maritime forest lies farther south in Buxton, with a nature trail and informative signs (see the **Attractions** chapter for descriptions of both).

There are three National Park Service campgrounds on Hatteras Island (at Oregon Inlet, Frisco, and Cape Point) offering more laid-back and less expensive camping than the rest of the Outer Banks' camping facilities. Several private campgrounds also are established in the island communities (see the **Accommodations** chapter).

If nature hasn't sold you on Hatteras Island's wild, raw beauty, check out the **Recreation** chapter for other amusements that can be enjoyed by the whole family.

The Tri-Villages

Rodanthe is Hatteras Island's northernmost village, situated about 12 miles from the northern tip of the island. Rodanthe blends seamlessly with Waves and Salvo to form what is sometimes referred to as the Tri-Village area.

Rodanthe and Waves were once one, called Chicamacomico north and south. In 1874 the US Postal Service decided the area needed a post office. Concerned that the name Chicamacomico would be too hard to spell or recognize, a different name was selected, and the area became Rodanthe. Although there are no records indicating why the name was chosen, a non-native cactus-like plant, the *Rodantha*, seems a possible source. Waves was named in 1939 when the Postal Service decided to create a new post office south of Rodanthe. Postmistress Anna Midgette, with an eye toward tourism, suggested Waves.

The story of how Salvo got its name includes a quick journey back to the Civil War. In 1861, Union forces seized forts at Ocracoke and Hatteras Inlet. Confederate forces moved south to contest the loss of the inlets. Northern warships were ordered to shell the area. According to USPS records, when the USS *Monticello* fired one last salvo, "Salvo" was marked on the map where the village is today. In 1901, the post office was officially named Salvo. Before that it was Clark-Betheny.

Rodanthe is home to the restored 1874 Chicamacomico Lifesaving Station, a historic tourist attraction that offers many activities. The village also boasts a popular fishing pier.

It's hard to know when you actually enter Waves because there are no signs welcoming you. Surfers stole those so many times that the villagers finally gave up installing them. Salvo also has nebulous village boundaries. The locals know them, though, and that's all that matters. Salvo is vacation-oriented, although there aren't many commercial enterprises. At the south end of the village is a NPS day-use area that's great for soundside picnicking, swimming, windsurfing, and kitesurfing.

Over the past ten years, the Tri-Villages, Rodanthe and Waves in particular, have seen a significant amount of development. They have managed to retain much of their Outer Banks village feel, but with two kitesurfing resorts, Kitty Hawk Kites in Rodanthe and Real Sports in Waves, a number of businesses have opened to serve the increase in visitors.

There are no supermarkets in the Tri-Villages although there are two well-stocked convenience stores that should be able to take care of most needs. Island Convenience is on the north end of Rodanthe and should have all the basics needed for a vacation stay. It has a very old-time Outer Banks feel to it.

In the St. Waves Plaza in Waves, the Waves Deli Market has killer sandwiches basic groceries and produce.

Avon

Avon is about 10 miles south of Salvo, separated from the northern villages by a long, beautiful stretch of undeveloped NPS property. Originally called Kinakeet, a name that is still used by many old-timers, the name changed when the village got a post office in 1883.

Avon is as close to the middle of Hatteras Island as any town and consequently there is more commercial development, including the island's only large chain grocery store. The Village also has many shops, restaurants, watersports rentals, a fishing pier, and a medical facility. One of the best-known windsurfing spots in the world, **Canadian Hole**, is on the south end of Avon.

Old Avon Village, on the west side of the island, offers a chance to see local life. Turn toward the sound at the stoplight by Sunrise Seafood to see the old cottages, fishing gear, boats, and villagers.

Buxton and Frisco

Buxton is at the widest part of the island, on a point of land that juts into the sea and is known as Cape Point. Hotels, restaurants, shops, and a locally owned supermarket line the highway. Tackle shops are abundant here because fishing at Cape Point is rightly famous, as is surfing.

The black-and-white candy-striped vertical lines of **Cape Hatteras Lighthouse** dominate the skyline. Completed in 1870, the 198-foot lighthouse is

The tallest brick lighthouse in the nation, Cape Hatteras Lighthouse has stood vigil over the dangers of Diamond Shoals since 1870.

the tallest brick lighthouse in the country. At its base **Buxton Woods**, a rare maritime forest, provides protection for the village. When Buxton got its post office in 1873, it was called simply The Cape. The name changed in 1882.

Frisco, the next town heading south, is the perfect place to get away from it all, with many vacation rental homes, a couple of art galleries, some shops and restaurants, and a Native American museum. Frisco is also the location of Billy Mitchell Ariport, a 3,000-foot long runway, owned by the National Park Service and maintained by the state.

But mostly it's the fishing, uncrowded beaches, and solitude which attract people to Frisco.

Hatteras Village

Hatteras Village, at the southernmost end of the island, is a picture-book fishing village and the ferry embarkation point for Ocracoke Island. When people say they're going to Hatteras, they mean the village, not the lighthouse, the cape, or the inlet.

With its proximity to the Gulf Stream, Hatteras Village has the second largest commercial fishery on the Outer Banks and is a world-class sport fishing locale, especially renowned for its bluefin tuna and marlin fishing in winter. Several marinas and charter fishing vessels call Hatteras Village home.

The village has always had a quaint, homespun appeal, with independently run restaurants and shops, small motels geared to anglers, and simple homes. In recent years Hatteras Village has seen the addition of upscale oceanfront homes, a fancy shopping complex, and the first chain hotel on the island, a Holiday Inn.

The **Graveyard of the Atlantic Museum**, at the southernmost point of the village is a must-see part of the Outer Banks experience. Exhibits include the history of sport fishing, information about the USS *Monitor* and historic boats of the Outer Banks.

OCRACOKE ISLAND

One of the oldest settled areas of the Outer Banks, this quaint homey village was once the gateway to the sounds and interior ports of North Carolina. It was here in 1719 that Blackbeard the Pirate met his fate at the hands of Lt. Robert Maynard of the British Royal Navy.

Insiders generally see Ocracoke as a tourist attraction during the warm months and romantic hideaway during the off-season, but this is a wonderful place to visit any time of the year. There's just no place like this quaint island with its pristine beaches and homey atmosphere.

Nearly all development on the island surrounds Silver Lake in Ocracoke Village. The island is but a slender strip of sand, geographically much like the other Outer Banks islands. At its widest, the 16-mile-long island is only about

2 miles across, narrowing in some sections to a half mile, where sound and sea are both visible from the two-lane road.

Island Economy & Tourism

Vacationers flock to Ocracoke during the warm months. Once a simple fishing village where islanders primarily lived off the sea, Ocracoke now operates as a vacation resort nine months out of the year. Tourism and traffic have changed the pace of this traditional fishing village, but the influx of visitors is necessary to maintain a healthy economy.

While many Ocracokers work at tourist-related businesses, year-round residents also are employed by the National Park Service, in the local school, in the building industry, or as commercial and recreational fishermen. The island's natural beauty and easy pace act as a magnet for artists, craftspeople, and writers.

You can park your vehicle after arriving on the island and not use it again until you leave. Make sure to stroll through the village, which surrounds Silver Lake. Wander the back roads: Specialty shops, galleries, and old island cottages are waiting to be discovered. Casually elegant restaurants and come-as-you-are eateries offer several meal choices, and friendly islanders will make recommendations, pointing you in the right direction (we outline more than a dozen spots in the **Dining** chapter).

Sailboats moor in the protected cove of Silver Lake, and charter and commercial fishing boats fill the downtown docks. You can book half- and full-day fishing excursions year-round. All accommodations—including bed-and-breakfast inns, hotels, rental cottages, and private campgrounds—are close to the island's activity (see the **Shopping**, **Fishing**, and **Accommodations** chapters for details).

On the oceanside about halfway to the village from the Hatteras ferry dock, tents and camping trailers dot the secondary dunes. This popular NPS campground is open from late spring to early fall and requires advance reservations (see the **Accommodations** chapter). The **Attractions** chapter describes the island's historic sites in detail. Make sure you take in the British Cemetery and the stately Ocracoke Inlet Lighthouse. Come January the flow of visitors subsides, and islanders take a break from long, seven-day workweeks. Off-season tourists still can find accommodations.

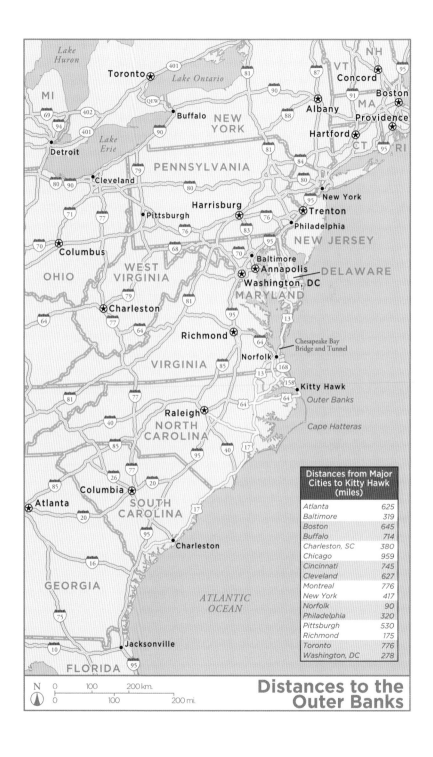

Distances from Major Cities to Kitty Hawk (miles)

Atlanta	625
Baltimore	319
Boston	645
Buffalo	714
Charleston, SC	380
Chicago	959
Cincinnati	745
Cleveland	627
Montreal	776
New York	417
Norfolk	90
Philadelphia	320
Pittsburgh	530
Richmond	175
Toronto	776
Washington, DC	278

Distances to the Outer Banks

N   0   100   200 km.
    0   100   200 mi.

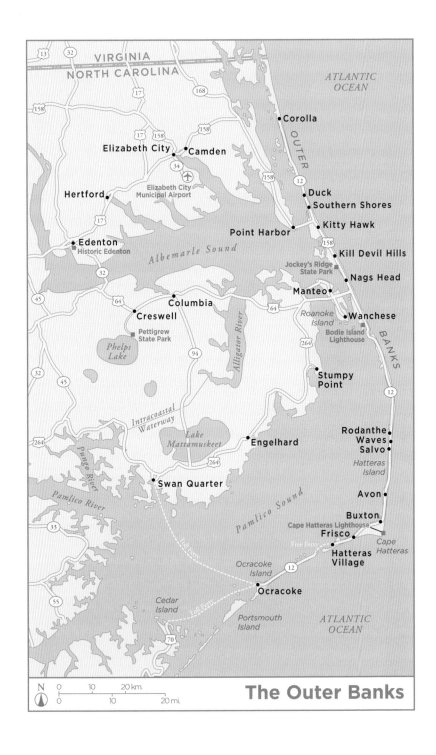

The Outer Banks

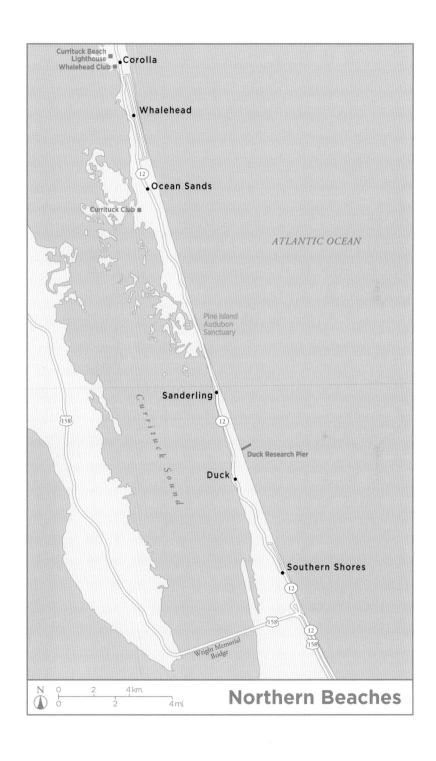

Currituck Beach
Lighthouse ■
Whalehead Club ■ • Corolla

• Whalehead

⑫
• Ocean Sands

Currituck Club ■

ATLANTIC OCEAN

Pine Island
Audubon
Sanctuary

C u r r i t u c k   S o u n d

Sanderling •

⑫

▬ Duck Research Pier

Duck •

⒅

Southern Shores •

⑫

⒅

⑫
⒅

*Wright Memorial
Bridge*

N   0   2   4 km.
Ⓝ 0   2   4 mi.

Northern Beaches

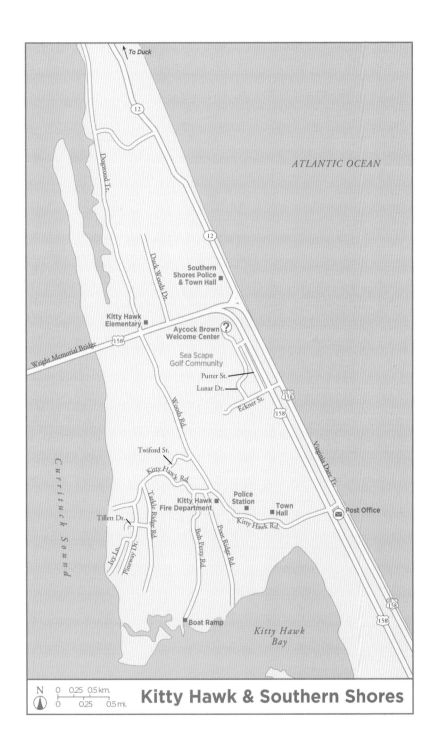

Kitty Hawk & Southern Shores

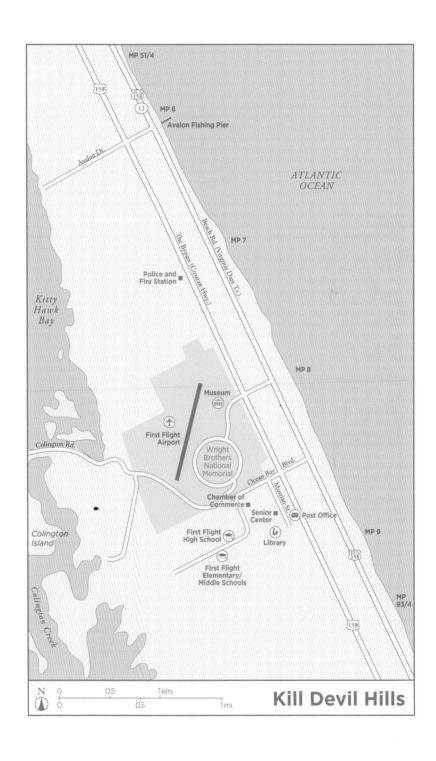

MP 51/4

158

BUS 158

12

MP 6
Avalon Fishing Pier

Avalon Dr.

ATLANTIC OCEAN

The Bypass (Croatan Hwy.)

Beach Rd. (Virginia Dare Tr.)

MP 7

Police and
Fire Station

Kitty
Hawk
Bay

MP 8

Museum

First Flight
Airport

Wright
Brothers
National
Memorial

Colington Rd.

Ocean Bay Blvd.

Mustian St.

Chamber of
Commerce

Senior
Center

Post Office

First Flight
High School

Library

MP 9

BUS 158

Colington
Island

First Flight
Elementary/
Middle Schools

Colington Creek

MP 93/4

158

N

0   0.5   1km.
0   0.5   1mi.

Kill Devil Hills

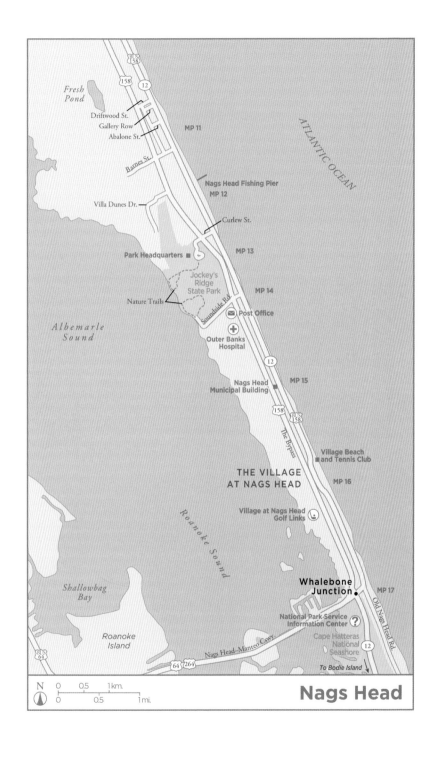

Nags Head

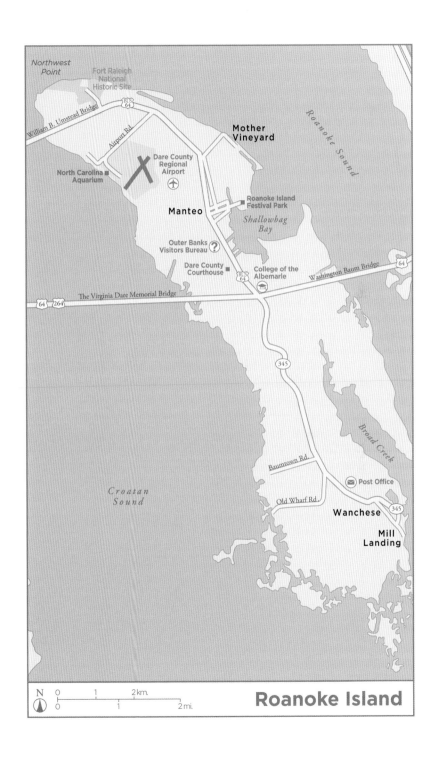

Northwest
Point

Fort Raleigh
National
Historic Site

64

William B. Umstead Bridge

Airport Rd.

North Carolina
Aquarium ■

Dare County
Regional
Airport ✈

Manteo

**Mother
Vineyard**

■ Roanoke Island
Festival Park

*Shallowbag
Bay*

Outer Banks
Visitors Bureau ?

Dare County
Courthouse ■

64

College of the
Albemarle

Roanoke Sound

64

Washington Baum Bridge

The Virginia Dare Memorial Bridge

64 264

*Croatan
Sound*

345

Baumtown Rd.

✉ Post Office

Old Wharf Rd.

Wanchese

345

**Mill
Landing**

Broad Creek

N 0   1   2 km.
  0   1   2 mi.

Roanoke Island

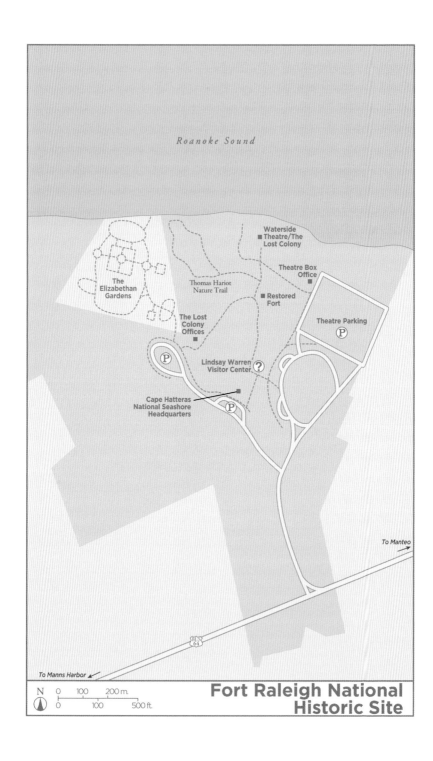

Roanoke Sound

Waterside
■ Theatre/The
Lost Colony

Theatre Box
Office ■

The
Elizabethan
Gardens

Thomas Hariot
Nature Trail

■ Restored
Fort

Theatre Parking
Ⓟ

The Lost
Colony
Offices ■

Ⓟ

Lindsay Warren
Visitor Center Ⓠ

Cape Hatteras
National Seashore
Headquarters

Ⓟ

To Manteo

BUS
64

To Manns Harbor

N   0   100   200 m.
     0   100   500 ft.

Fort Raleigh National
Historic Site

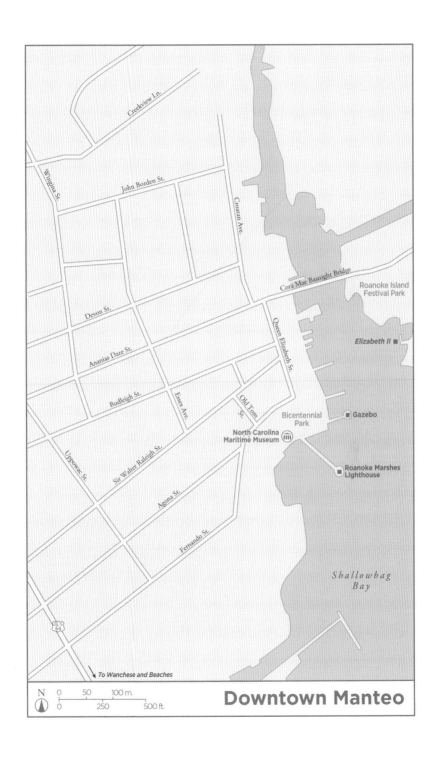

Creekview Ln.

Wingina St.

John Borden St.

Chovan Ave.

Cora Mae Basnight Bridge

Roanoke Island
Festival Park

Devon St.

Elizabeth II ■

Queen Elizabeth St.

Ananias Dare St.

Budleigh St.

Essex Ave.

Old Tom St.

Gazebo ■

Bicentennial
Park

North Carolina
Maritime Museum

Roanoke Marshes
Lighthouse ■

Uppowoc St.

Sir Walter Raleigh St.

Agona St.

Fernando St.

*Shallowbag
Bay*

US 64

→ *To Wanchese and Beaches*

N

| 0 | 50 | 100 m. |
| 0 | 250 | 500 ft. |

Downtown Manteo

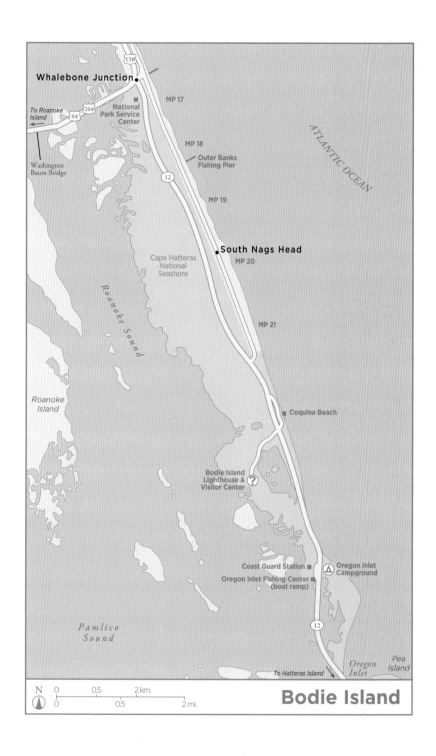

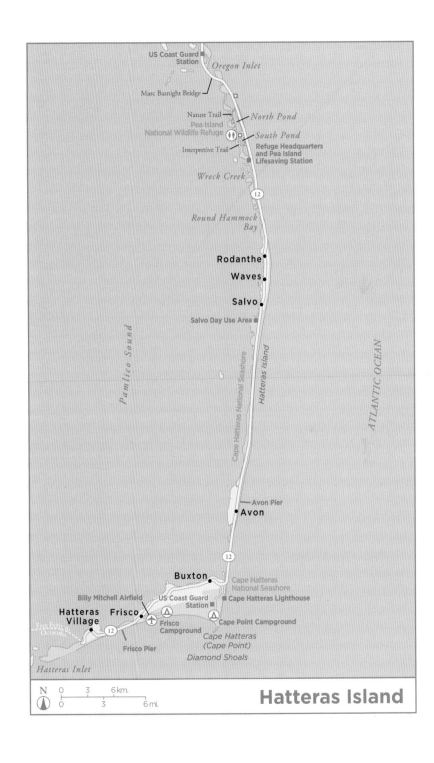

US Coast Guard
Station

Oregon Inlet

Marc Basnight Bridge

Nature Trail
Pea Island
National Wildlife Refuge

North Pond

South Pond

Interpretive Trail

Refuge Headquarters
and Pea Island
Lifesaving Station

Wreck Creek

12

*Round Hammock
Bay*

Rodanthe

Waves

Salvo

Salvo Day Use Area

Pamlico Sound

Cape Hatteras National Seashore

Hatteras Island

ATLANTIC OCEAN

Avon Pier

Avon

12

Buxton

Cape Hatteras
National Seashore

Billy Mitchell Airfield

US Coast Guard
Station

Cape Hatteras Lighthouse

**Hatteras
Village**

Frisco

Frisco
Campground

Cape Point Campground

First Pond Ocracoke

12

Frisco Pier

*Cape Hatteras
(Cape Point)*

Diamond Shoals

Hatteras Inlet

N   0   3   6 km.

0   3   6 mi.

Hatteras Island

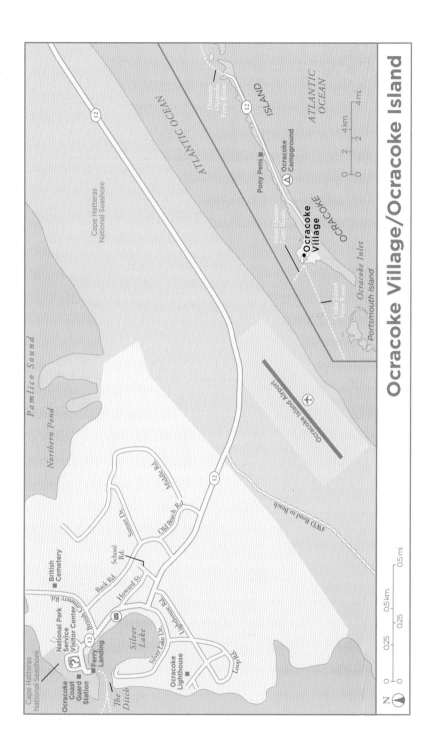

Ocracoke Village/Ocracoke Island

Getting Here, Getting Around

When the original Wright Memorial Bridge opened in 1930, it was the first bridge connecting the Outer Banks with the outside world. A wooden toll road, it barely rose above the waters of the Albemarle Sound and there are numerous accounts of the terror of crossing the bridge during wind events as the waves of the sound splashed across the wooden planks. In 1966 NCDOT opened the new Wright Brother Bridge and built a parallel bridge in 1995.

Before the bridges were built, most visitors reached these barrier islands by ferry from Elizabeth City. Others came from Virginia Beach by driving along the coast. There are now two bridge access points, one in Kitty Hawk, used mostly by travelers from the north, and one from Roanoke Island to Nags Head, used mostly by visitors from the south and west. North Carolina's Department of Transportation has spent considerable time and money improving state routes, making it increasingly easier to get to the bridges.

Another way to get to the Outer Banks is via long ferry rides from the North Carolina mainland to Ocracoke Island. In fact, ferry travel is still the only way to reach Ocracoke Island—outside of private motorboat or private plane—and no change is foreseeable.

Other than the state-run ferries to Ocracoke, there is no public transportation to the Outer Banks. The nearest Amtrak station is in Newport News, Virginia, and the nearest bus stations are in Elizabeth City, North Carolina, and Norfolk, Virginia. The nearest commercial airport is in Norfolk. Bus, train, or plane will get you closer, but you must either rent a car and drive to the Outer Banks or hire a private plane or shuttle service.

This chapter outlines the best routes for getting here by land, sea, and sky. Once you arrive, however, know that you will need some form of transportation—a motorcycle, a car, a bicycle, a scooter, or at least enough money for a cab or ride service—if you plan to venture around a bit. Don't even think of complaining about the lack of public bus transportation. Instead, while you're still unwinding from your trip, venture on down to the beach. Remove your shoes, take off your socks, and walk in the tideline. Now, are you really concerned about bus transportation? If so, you haven't walked far enough.

By Land

You can't get to any islands without spanning water, and thankfully we have several bridges. In a state of emergency, such as a hurricane evacuation, bridges are the only way off the island. During such mass exits local officials usually close the bridges to incoming traffic and use all the lanes to expedite evacuation. In peak travel times (summer weekends), the bridges, especially the Wright Memorial Bridge, bottleneck, so drive cautiously.

Arriving from the North: To the Wright Memorial Bridge

Since so many visitors are from Pennsylvania, New York, New Jersey, Connecticut, and Washington, DC, we begin this section with directions from Richmond, Virginia, which from the north can be reached on I-95 south. If you're coming from north of the Outer Banks but south of Richmond, read through the directions and select the route nearest your location.

From Richmond, follow I-64 east to I-664 east at Hampton/Newport News and take the Monitor-Merrimac Bridge/Tunnel across the James River to I-64. The VA 168 Bypass allows you to skirt the traffic lights and congestion on Battlefield Boulevard in Chesapeake, thus easing your drive to and from the Outer Banks. From I-64, take exit 291B to VA 168 south. VA 168 becomes US 158 in North Carolina; don't worry, both names refer to the same road.

There are two options for traveling on VA 168, but both get you to the same place. The VA 168, linking I-64 in Chesapeake with US 158 to the Outer Banks, is known as the Chesapeake Expressway and is a faster, four-lane option, although there is a toll to use it. The second choice is to take Battlefield Boulevard. Past Chesapeake on VA 168, it's a straight shot to the Wright Memorial Bridge, which crosses the Currituck Sound to Kitty Hawk on the Outer Banks. The drive from the Virginia/North Carolina border takes about an hour, though you may wish to stop at the many antiques shops, thrift stores, and produce stands. You'll pass Mel's Diner, a 1950s-style diner in Grandy that thrives on tourism and has a loyal local following as well. If you just can't wait for some Carolina barbecue, stop at locally famous Currituck BBQ on 158 in Coinjock where you can dine in their open-air pavilion, indoors, or get take-out.

Another option coming from the north is to take US 17 south from I-64 in Virginia. This span of highway flanks the Intracoastal Waterway through the aptly named Great Dismal Swamp. Follow US 17 south to South Mills, where you take NC 343 to Camden, following signs to US 158 and the Outer Banks.

Arriving from the West: To the Washington Baum Bridge

From I-95 in North Carolina, take US 64 east toward Rocky Mount, passing through Williamston, Jamesville, Plymouth, Creswell, Columbia, over the Alligator River, and through East Lake and Manns Harbor to Roanoke Island.

The bridge over the Alligator River, part of the Intracoastal Waterway, is an old-fashioned drawbridge, opened as needed by an on-site bridge tender. If you're lucky enough to get caught by a bridge opening, get out of the car and enjoy the unique vantage of peering over the railings into the water. Yes, alligators do live in the water here. Generally, Alligator River is the northernmost waterway where these creatures reside.

It is a sparse area with few stops between Plymouth and the Outer Banks, so fuel up, especially if you're traveling at night. If you have to pull off the road, do so carefully and choose a wide shoulder if possible. Along this route watch for deer, black bears, red wolves, and a wide variety of birds. You'll spot an occasional blue heron wading in the roadside creeks. The state adorns the byways with colorful poppies and other wildflowers. It's tempting to pick the lush beauties, but it's illegal.

Continuing east on US 64, you'll cross The Virginia Dare Memorial Bridge (known as "the New Bridge" to locals) stretching from the mainland at Manns Harbor to the Nags Head–Manteo Head Causeway, completely bypassing Manteo. This 5.2-mile bridge, the longest in the state, shaves 20 minutes or so from the trip to the beaches because it avoids the two-lane bottleneck through Manteo. An Outer Banks Visitors Bureau welcome center and rest area is located at the bridge's eastern terminus. However, the old Manns Harbor Bridge remains open and can be used if you want to visit the attractions, restaurants, and shops of Roanoke Island and Manteo.

To get to the Old Manns Harbor Bridge, turn left at the flashing warning light just before the Virginia Dare Bridge. Follow old US 64 through the sparsely populated village of Manns Harbor to the William Umstead Bridge. During the summer somewhere around 100,000 purple martins use the bridge as a nesting site and the speed limit on the bridge is reduced to 20 mph to protect birds and drivers.

Old US 64 and the Manteo bypass intersect about a mile west of the Virginia Dare Bridge. If the plan is to go to the fishing village of Wanchese, turn right onto NC 345 if coming from the Virginia Dare Bridge.

However, after a few hours of driving to get to the Outer Banks, most people opt to go straight to their destination. For Outer Banks beaches, Cape Hatteras, Nags Head, and points north just keep going straight. Overhead signs make getting lost unlikely, but if you find yourself off your intended route, blame it on the scenery and turn back. You can't get too lost here on these islands and peninsulas! US 64 will take you across the Nags Head–Manteo Causeway and the Washington Baum Bridge.

Arriving from the West: To the Wright Memorial Bridge
Backtrack to Williamston for an alternate route to the Outer Banks. Instead of traveling on US 64 along the southern route, you can choose to take US 17 to Elizabeth City. Both routes take about the same traveling time. From Elizabeth

City follow signs on US 158 to Nags Head and Manteo, and arrive on the island from the north, crossing the Wright Memorial Bridge. US 17 seems to be the route preferred by most visiting Virginians.

Arriving from the South: To the Ocracoke Ferries

From points south, take I-95 north to Rocky Mount, North Carolina, then US 64 east to Williamston, following the directions given earlier for arriving from the west. For an alternate southern route, follow the coastline north to Morehead City and Cedar Island, where you board a toll ferry to Ocracoke Island. Another option is to take US 17 north from Wilmington, North Carolina, through Jacksonville and New Bern to Washington. From Washington, take US 264 east to Swan Quarter and follow signs to the Swan Quarter toll ferry, which brings you to Ocracoke Island. The route goes through the Swan Quarter National Wildlife Refuge, with gracious old cedars lining the way. From Ocracoke follow NC 12 to the Ocracoke–Hatteras ferry for passage to Hatteras Island and points north. For ferry schedules and further information, see the Ferries section of this chapter.

> **i** The Bypass (US 158) and the Beach Road (NC 12) are marked by mileposts that originate at the Wright Memorial Bridge in Kitty Hawk and continue through MP 21 in South Nags Head. An address that reads "MP 7, Beach Road, Kill Devil Hills" is located 7 miles south of the Wright Memorial Bridge.

Crossing the Wright Memorial Bridge

No matter which route you choose, the destination is well worth the journey. Because the Wright Memorial Bridge is the main thoroughfare to and from the Outer Banks, bear in mind that summer season peak travel time (going to the island) is from noon to 6 p.m. on Saturday and Sunday. This is rush-hour traffic, Outer Banks–style. Peak travel time leaving the island is from about 8 a.m. to noon on the same days. Delays are possible from Memorial Day to Labor Day; for your convenience, travel advisories are posted on a flashing sign at the bridge.

Once you cross the bridge into Kitty Hawk, you can't miss the bigger-than-life signs that lead you to your destinations. To get to Southern Shores, Duck, Sanderling, Corolla, or Carova, turn left on NC 12 and head north. For destinations Kitty Hawk and south, continue on US 158 to Kill Devil Hills and Nags Head. Just past 16 miles south of the bridge, the road veers right toward Roanoke Island and Manteo and branches left toward Oregon Inlet and the Cape Hatteras National Seashore. Follow NC 12 on Hatteras Island to the communities of Rodanthe, Waves, Salvo, Avon, Buxton, Frisco, and Hatteras. In Hatteras Village a ferry provides free transport to Ocracoke Island.

At the junction of US 158 and NC 12 in Kitty Hawk is the Aycock Brown Welcome Center, which offers a wealth of information to visitors. Another great information stop is the Outer Banks Chamber of Commerce, located on 101 Town Hall Dr. about 1 block west of US 158 in Kill Devil Hills.

Crossing the Washington Baum Bridge

The Washington Baum Bridge from Roanoke Island leads to South Nags Head, where you can choose to travel north toward Nags Head, Kill Devil Hills, Kitty Hawk, Duck, and Corolla or south to Hatteras Island and Ocracoke Island. The Cape Hatteras turnoff is on the right, about a mile from the bridge's eastern terminus. At this intersection—referred to as Whalebone Junction—you bear left onto US 158 in Nags Head or go straight to connect with the Beach Road (NC 12), either of which takes you north from Nags Head through Kitty Hawk. (Note that South Nags Head is accessed in this area via Old Nags Head Road.) A right turn at Whalebone Junction puts you on NC 12 toward Bodie Island, the Oregon Inlet Fishing Center, and points south. If you continue on NC 12 across the Marc Basnight Bridge onto Hatteras Island, the road goes through Rodanthe, Waves, Salvo, Avon, Buxton, Frisco, and Hatteras Village. A ferry in Hatteras Village goes to Ocracoke Island.

By Air

Airports & Airstrips

Note to pilots: Several Outer Banks airstrips are unattended, as explained in this section. Call the state Division of Aviation at (919) 840-0112 for information not covered in the following entries.

BILLY MITCHELL HATTERAS ISLAND AIRSTRIP, NC 12, Frisco. Also known as Hatteras Mitchell Field, this Hatteras Island airport is on National Park Service land. The airport is unattended. Billy Mitchell Airstrip's unlighted runway is approximately 3,000 feet long, and fuel is not available. There is a parking lot. A shelter on the premises has a phone and toilets.

DARE COUNTY REGIONAL AIRPORT, Airport Road, Roanoke Island; (252) 475-5570; ncdot.gov/travel/airports. If you'd like to fly your own plane to the Outer Banks, this is the airport to call. Dare County Regional Airport's two runways measure 3,300 feet and 4,300 feet, and both are lighted. Jet-A and 100 LL fuels are available. Operating hours are 8 a.m. to 7 p.m. daily. This airport is manned, has a terminal VOR, DME, and NDB, plus automated weather updates through AWOS, which you can access at radio frequency 128.275 or by calling (252) 473-2826.

FIRST FLIGHT AIRSTRIP, Wright Brothers National Memorial; US 158, MP 8, Kill Devil Hills; (252) 473-2111. Every pilot visiting the Outer Banks should sign in at least once at this historic location. At First Flight your stay is limited to 24 hours. This unattended 3,000-foot strip is maintained by the National Park Service. Since there are no lights, takeoffs and landings are permitted during daylight hours only. Reservations are not necessary, and a sign-up book is on premises. No fuel is available.

NORFOLK INTERNATIONAL AIRPORT, 2200 Norview Ave., Norfolk, VA; (757) 857-3351; norfolkairport.com. Open 24 hours a day, Norfolk International Airport offers air service on American, Continental, Delta, Northwest, United, US Airways, and Southwest Airlines. Major rental car companies have offices at the airport. For main passenger information call the airport. For private charter information see the following entries.

OCRACOKE ISLAND AIRSTRIP, NC 12, Ocracoke Island; (252) 928-9901. Another airstrip maintained by the National Park Service, this unattended facility has a 3,000-foot-long runway and no lights. There is a parking lot and a pay telephone. The runway has brush and 25-foot sand dunes at either end. Listen to the weather radio or call for weather updates.

Air Service

BARRIER ISLAND AVIATION, (252) 473-4247; barrierislandaviation .com; Outer Banks Air Charters, (252) 256-2322; outerbanksaircharters.com. Both offer charter service to and from Dare County Regional Airport. Car rentals are available at the airport; call in advance.

BURRUS FLYING SERVICE, (252) 986-2679; obxflightseeing.com. Burrus Flying Service, operating from the Billy Mitchell Airport, offers air tours and aerial photography for the Outer Banks.

By Water

The best way to beat the traffic—and to see some incredible scenery while you're at it—is to arrive at the Outer Banks by boat. Only very experienced boaters should attempt to navigate these tricky waters, and only with proper equipment in the best weather. Discuss your trip with a local sailor or captain while making your plans, and be sure to pick up a copy of the *Mid-Atlantic Waterway Guide*; it provides the most detailed information available about the area's waterways. Current chart numbers from the Intracoastal Waterway (ICW) to Manteo on Roanoke Island are 12204 and 12205. Chart 12204 is a large map of the North River, and chart 12205 is a strip map that includes both the Alligator and North Rivers. Both charts cover the inlet, although 12205 provides more detail.

For navigating the southern Outer Banks NOAA charts 11550 Ocracoke and Part of Core Sound and 11555 Cape Hatteras, Wimble Shoals to Ocracoke Inlet will be needed.

From the North

If you're boating from points north, you can enter the ICW in Norfolk, Virginia. The trip from Norfolk to Manteo is about 80 nautical miles. In fair weather and with a fast boat, you can make it to the Outer Banks in five to six hours; if you're sailing you may wish to spend your first night at the Coinjock Marina. Be prepared for wind, chop, and shallow waters in the Albemarle Sound. As long as you remain within the ICW markers, you won't have to worry about depth.

Any of the following three routes lead you to the Outer Banks. One takes you from Norfolk, Virginia, across the Currituck Sound to Coinjock, North Carolina, the North River, and the Albemarle Sound. From the ICW mid-sound marker, head east and look for day markers leading to the waterfront town of Manteo on Roanoke Island.

An alternate route from Norfolk leads to Deep Creek, Virginia, through the Great Dismal Swamp to Lake Drummond, North Carolina. From there, travel through South Mills to the Pasquotank River, where the ICW—locally known as the Ditch—joins the Albemarle Sound. Refer to your charts for navigating across the Albemarle Sound to the Alligator River, and then travel either the Croatan Sound or the Roanoke Sound to Manteo.

The third—and probably the easiest—route takes you from the end of the North River into the Albemarle Sound. Look for marker number 173, then bear left and follow the day markers leading behind Powell's Point. The first marker you'll come to is number 4; from there look for number 2 and then MG (the middle-ground marker). From MG head nearly due south. Look for another number 2 day marker, which takes you from the north end of East Lake toward Manns Harbor Channel, where day markers lead to the Roanoke Island Channel. (All of these markers are noted on the charts.)

From the South

If you are boating to the Outer Banks from the south, pick up the ICW between Beaufort and Morehead City, North Carolina, and follow it to the Neuse River. Take the ICW north from the Neuse River across the Pamlico River to Belhaven on the Pungo River. You may want to stop in Belhaven at the River Forest Manor, a country inn, restaurant, marina, and shipyard, where you can fuel up while touring the century-old southern plantation mansion or getting a bite to eat in its historic restaurant. Sunday brunch alone is worth the trip. An alternative stop is the new Dowry Creek Marina, with slips and fuel. After you leave Belhaven, continue north on the ICW to the Alligator River, then travel east until you spot the Roanoke Sound day markers, which lead to Manteo on Roanoke Island.

If seas aren't rough, the fastest route from the south is to go through the Pamlico Sound from either the Pamlico or Neuse River. After you pass under the Manns Harbor Bridge, look for the Roanoke Sound day markers leading to Manteo.

Roanoke Island Marinas

Manteo has several docks within walking distance to restaurants and attractions. Locations and amenities are as follows. Also see the Boating section of the **Water Sports** chapter.

PIRATE'S COVE MARINA, Roanoke Sound, between Manteo and Nags Head; (252) 473-3906; fishpiratescove.com. Open year-round, Pirate's Cove can accommodate boats from 25- to 110-feet in 195 slips. Transients are welcome, and many slips are rented year-round. Call or check the website rates, as prices vary. Slip rental includes water and electricity, showers, cable TV hookup, and laundry facilities. Pirate's Cove offers one courtesy car that boaters can use on a limited basis to fetch supplies or other necessities. Boaters can use the tennis courts, pool, and other on-site facilities.

The on-site ship's store and restaurant are open to the public, as is the fuel dock. On the top deck of the on-site restaurant, you can have a cold drink and some steamed shrimp while getting a bird's-eye view of one of the area's most beautiful sport-fishing fleets.

WATERFRONT MARINA, Manteo Historic District; (252) 473-3320; townofmanteo.com. The Waterfront Marina provides public docking facilities with water, cable TV, WiFi and power at each slip. Charges are on a per-foot basis for semiannual, annual, and transient boaters. Call ahead or radio the dockmaster on your approach to the marina. Laundry and shower facilities are available. The marina's boardwalk extends along the waterfront and is within walking distance of shops, restaurants, and other diversions. In Manteo you'll find friendly merchants and interesting sights, and several lovely inns offer a respite from your berth. A brief stroll across the bridge takes you to Roanoke Island Festival Park (see the **Attractions** chapter for more information).

Ferries

Landlubbers also can enjoy an Outer Banks arrival by boat thanks to the North Carolina Ferry System. One picturesque route is to follow US 70 east from New Bern to Havelock. Pick up NC 101, follow to NC 306, and then take the ferry to Bayview near historic Bath. Follow NC 99 to Belhaven, picking up US 264 to Swan Quarter. From here, you can take NC 94 across Lake Mattamuskeet, then US 64 to Manteo—or ride another ferry from Swan Quarter to Ocracoke Island. It sounds complicated, but signs will guide you.

An alternate route is to take US 70 through Havelock to Beaufort. US 70 continues from Beaufort to Harkers Island, following the Core Sound to NC 12, where the Cedar Island Ferry takes you to Ocracoke Island. The voyage across the Pamlico Sound is well worth the time it takes to arrive in Ocracoke. Cross Ocracoke Island from south to north via NC 12, and pick up the Hatteras Island Ferry to the upper Outer Banks.

Ferry passage is a good way to reduce your driving time if you're heading to the southern portion of the Outer Banks. It also gives you a chance to stretch and move around while still making progress. Unless you have your own boat or plane, ferry service is the only way to reach picturesque Ocracoke Island. The ferries transport cars to the island, although we suggest that you park your car after arriving on Ocracoke and get around on foot or by bike.

Following is information on the Outer Banks ferry services. Although it is rare to have a time change, you may wish to call ahead and verify departure times. You can get more information by writing to Director, 8550 Shipyard Road, Manns Harbor, NC 27953 or by calling (800) BY FERRY (294-3779). You can log on to ncferry.org and make your advance ferry reservations online. Truckers: For information about weight and size limitations, call the specific ferry location. The toll-free number is operable east of the Mississippi River only.

The Hatteras Inlet (Ocracoke) Ferry makes island-hopping easy.

HATTERAS INLET (OCRACOKE) FERRY. This state-run service links the islands of Hatteras and Ocracoke across the Pamlico Sound. The ferries accommodate 30 vehicles—including cars and large camping/recreational vehicles—and run frequently during the summer to avoid excessive delays. The Hatteras ferry does not require reservations, and the trip takes about 40 minutes. Public restrooms are at the Hatteras dock, and heads are onboard. At press time, the Hatteras Inlet ferry is free, however a fee structure is currently under consideration. For more information call (800) 368-8949 or (252) 986-2353.

HATTERAS OCRACOKE PASSENGER ONLY FERRY. A number of passenger questionnaires and studies over the years have have come to the same conclusion—Ocracoke is a very popular day trip destination. With that in mind, hoping to alleviate some of the congestion at the Hatteras Inlet Ferry, the Ferry Division of the North Carolina Division of Transportation (NCDOT) has introduced passenger only service to Ocracoke.

Unlike the car ferry which docks on the north end of Ocracoke Island 14 miles from the village, the passenger only ferry docks at Silver Lake in the heat of the town. With its compact, quaint business district, Ocracoke is a perfect day trip destination.

In its inaugural year—2019—NCDOT charged $4 for the round trip. There are provisions for bikes on the ship and no fee is charged for them. The passenger only schedule is seasonal. Check with the NCDOT Ferry Division on availability.

GETTING AROUND

By Auto

We've gotten you here; now we'll get you around.

Let's get the traffic report out of the way first. The number of travelers on our roads increases dramatically during the summer. Traffic more than triples from Memorial Day through Labor Day. We realize that visitors enrich our economy, and we welcome you—cars, trucks, SUVs, and all. If you're used to big-city driving, you'll find the summer traffic tolerable. Naturally roads get very congested during hurricane evacuations, despite the advance warnings county authorities give. If you bear in mind the following tips, your drive should be a smooth one.

The northern route up NC 12 through Duck and Corolla can get bogged down on summer weekends and during weekday lunch and dinner hours. If the weather's bad, many more people shop rather than go to the beach, so expect heavier traffic when skies are gray. Allow a minimum of an extra half hour when traveling to the northern Outer Banks on summer weekends. You may want to call the various municipalities or radio stations to see when traffic is heaviest during holidays. And if you must travel during peak traffic hours, try not to lose your cool. Relax—you're at the beach! There are plenty of places to stop for food, drinks, and shopping, though you may also want to pack some snacks, especially if you have young children.

While we do have congested areas to deal with from time to time, we have a simple road layout that makes getting lost almost impossible. These barrier islands, including Roanoke Island to the west, have only three major roadways. US 158 crosses the Wright Memorial Bridge into Kitty Hawk and winds through the center of the island to Whalebone Junction in Nags Head. This five-lane highway (the center lane is for turning vehicles only) is also called the Bypass, Croatan Highway, or the Big Road. In this book we will refer to it as the Bypass or US 158.

NC 12 runs along the beach, parallel to US 158 from Kitty Hawk to Nags Head. A two-lane road, it stretches from the southern border of the Currituck National Wildlife Refuge at the Villages at Ocean Hill development in Corolla to the ferry docks at Hatteras Island's southernmost tip. NC 12 picks up again on Ocracoke, spanning the length of the tiny island, ending in picturesque Ocracoke Village. NC 12 is also called Ocean Trail in Corolla, Duck Road in Duck and Southern Shores, Ocean Boulevard in part of Southern Shores, and either Virginia Dare Trail or the Beach Road from Kitty Hawk through Nags Head. In this book we refer to it as NC 12 (or occasionally as the Beach Road, when talking about that stretch from Kitty Hawk through Nags Head). On rainy days in summer, this road is extremely congested with visitors headed to shops and restaurants.

On Roanoke Island, US 64 is also called the Main Highway. This stoplight-filled road begins at the Nags Head–Manteo Causeway and runs across the Washington Baum Bridge through Manteo, across the William B. Umstead Bridge, and through Manns Harbor on the mainland. School traffic clogs US 64 on weekday mornings and afternoons. Some congestion has been alleviated by the Virginia Dare Memorial Bridge which bypasses Manteo.

US 158 and NC 12 run mainly north and south. Smaller connector streets link seaside rental cottages to year-round neighborhoods west of the Bypass.

If you truly want to relax and spend your vacation days island-style, kick off your shoes and travel on foot. You can walk for miles down the beaches, collecting shells and wading. In Kitty Hawk and Kill Devil Hills restaurants and fishing piers are usually close by, ensuring food and drink are near at hand. On Hatteras Island, Avon also features some piers and beachside dining. Most spots welcome casual diners.

By Bike

The Outer Banks boasts several paved bike paths. Running the length of Roanoke Island is a 7-mile asphalt path that has awakened the athlete in many locals, young and old, who are now regularly seen walking, riding bikes, and skating on the route. It's a wide, safe path that we are grateful to have.

An 11-mile bike path runs along NC 12 almost the entire length of the town of Nags Head. In South Nags Head the path is concrete, and in the rest of the town it is asphalt. The town of Kill Devil Hills sports a scenic asphalt route along Colington Road, running down the National Park Service property past the Wright Brothers National Memorial. That path connects to the multi-use path along Bay Shore Road.

The Kitty Hawk bike path connects to Bay Shore Road, parallels Kitty Hawk Bay on a beautiful little multi-use trail that leads to Moor Shore Road. At the end of Moor Shore Road, turn left onto Kitty Hawk Road. There is a wide shoulder along the road that is designed for bike riders. That path leads to the Woods Road multi-use path, giving riders a small glimpse of the majesty of Kitty Hawk Woods. The Woods Road connects with the Southern Shore trails.

Riders can take northern paths into Southern Shores on Dogwood Trail, Juniper Trail, or Ocean Boulevard. The Ocean Boulevard segment spans the 4-mile width of Southern Shores and continues through the quaint town of Duck.

While pedaling these paths or biking anywhere else on the Outer Banks, please wear a helmet. You can rent bikes at several rental services, and many accommodations offer bikes and helmets as a courtesy. Watch out—the sand that blows on the road can get in your eyes as you pass the dunes and can be slippery when you brake. Follow the normal rules of the road that apply to cars, stopping at lights and stop signs and yielding to pedestrians. There is a lot of activity near the beach, so whether you're on a bike or in a car, watch out for that rolling beach ball—it is usually followed by a child.

i **When biking any of the paths in the area, be sure to wear proper safety gear. Sand blown along the pavement can cause your wheels to catch or skid suddenly and unexpectedly. Also watch for vehicles pulling out of driveways onto the path before stopping. Full awareness is always recommended.**

Transportation for Hire

Even though you won't find any public transportation here, you do have a number of alternatives. Since demand for Uber, Lyft, taxicabs, and limousines can be great at times, make sure to call in advance.

A1 TAXICAB COMPANY, (252) 599-7777; a1taxiobx.com. Providing service to Kill Devil Hills, Kitty Hawk, Nags Head, Southern Shores, and Duck. Pick up is available from Corolla, Manteo, Mans Harbor, Rodanthe, Waves, Salvo, Buxton, Frisco, and Hatteras Village. Reservations can be made online or over the phone.

AIRPORT CONNECTION, (252) 305-1111; airportconnectionobx.com. Airport Connection's sedans deliver passengers from Raleigh, Richmond, Newport News, Norfolk, and Washington, DC, airports to any Outer Banks destination. Advance reservations are required for private cars, and a shared-ride service is available in season.

BEACH CAB, (252) 441-2500. The original cab company on the Outer Banks, this large operation picks up and delivers from Ocracoke to Corolla.

COASTAL CAB COMPANY, (252) 449-8787. Coastal Cab offers radio-dispatched 24-hour service on the Outer Banks. Service to airports in Norfolk and Raleigh is available with advance reservations. Credit cards are accepted for out-of-town trips.

THE CONNECTION, (252) 449-2777. This shuttle service operates daily between Norfolk and the Outer Banks, with door-to-door shared-ride and private service to Norfolk International Airport (other airports upon request) as well as Norfolk's bus and train stations. Full-size, air-conditioned passenger vans can accommodate groups, families, bicycles, surfboards, sailboards, etc. Drivers are fully licensed and insured. Private town cars are also available. Reservations are recommended.

COROLLA CAB, (252) 489-9408. Offering service in Corolla and Carova.

ISLAND HOPPER SHUTTLE, (252) 995-6771. Island Hopper Shuttle serves Hatteras Island with transportation to and from Norfolk International Airport, plus courier service on weekdays to Kitty Hawk and Manteo.

ISLAND LIMOUSINE, (252) 441-5466; islandlimo.com. The largest and oldest transportation company on the beach, Island Limo provides transportation to and from Norfolk International Airport via private sedan and limousine year-round. Taxi service is also available 24 hours a day (252) 480-8294. Ask about their minivan special for short taxi trips.

OUTER BANKS AIRPORT TRANSPORTATION AND SHUTTLE SERVICE, (252) 689-7433; obxshuttle.com. Transportation service providing ground transportation to and from all local and regional airports and train station. Serves all of Eastern North Carolina and Coastal Virginia.

Car Rentals
Whether you need something for getting around town or something more substantial, like a four-wheel-drive vehicle, to really explore the island, you have a number of rental options.

Cars Only

B&R RENT-A-CAR AT R. D. SAWYER MOTOR COMPANY, US 64 in Manteo; (252) 473-2141.

BUGGIN' OUT DUNE BUGGY/JEEP RENTALS, 2901 N. Croatan Hwy, Kill Devil Hills; (252) 261-0402.

DARE COUNTY REGIONAL AIRPORT, on Roanoke Island, off Airport Rd.; (252) 475-5570.

ENTERPRISE RENT-A-CAR, Kill Devil Hills and Manteo; (252) 480-1838, (800) 736-8222.

ISLAND CRUISERS, 26248 NC 12, Salvo; (252) 987-2097.

ISLAND JEEP & CAR RENTALS, 3000 N. Croatan Hwy, Kill Devil Hills; (252) 441-0771.

OUTER BANKS JEEP RENTALS, 2004 S. Croatan Hwy, Ste. 18, Kill Devil Hills; (252) 715-4400.

Beach Driving

Off-road access is possible on the Outer Banks but only in designated areas and at certain times of the year. Use of a four-wheel-drive (4WD) vehicle is mandatory. Check with each township for specific rules; some places even require a permit.

Generally, tagged, licensed, and insured 4WDs are allowed on the beach in Kill Devil Hills and Nags Head from October 1 through April 30. However, permits are required in Nags Head. Southern Shores and Kitty Hawk prohibit driving on the beach at all times. As far north as Corolla and Carova in Currituck County, there are specified areas where you can drive on the beach. Hatteras Island operates under the guidance of the National Park Service (252-473-2111); call with any questions you have concerning off-road driving.

 For beach access information for April through October, check online at nps.gov/caha/planyourvisit/off-road-vehicle-use.htm. Information is updated weekly. Some areas close for wildlife protection, however most beaches remain open for pedestrian and off-road vehicle use.

On Hatteras Island, driving is not allowed on the beach at Pea Island National Wildlife Refuge (the area from Rodanthe Pier north to Oregon Inlet), but farther south there are access areas marked by a sign featuring a symbol for off-road vehicles where you can travel on the beach.

Cape Hatteras National Seashore does require a permit to drive on the beach. A ten day permit is $50; annual permits are $120. Permits may be purchased either online at recreation.gov or at any of the three CHNS permit offices: **Bodie Island** at the north end of the Coquina Beach parking lot (8101 NC 12 Hwy, NagsHead, NC; **Hatteras Island** by the Cape Hatteras Lighthouse Visitor Center (46368 Lighthouse Rd., Buxton, NC); or **Ocracoke Island** by the NPS Visitor Center (40 Irvin Garrish Hwy, Ocracoke, NC).

Obviously, beach driving is not allowed at access areas that have signs with an X through the symbol. It's a good idea to stop at one of the National Park Service visitor centers or campgrounds to chat with a ranger before taking to the beach on wheels. Rangers supply up-to-date information on unusual conditions, such as eroded beach areas, that could prove hazardous to you and your vehicle.

Driving Rules & Safety Tips

The maximum speed for beach driving is 25 mph, but even that can be too fast on a crowded day. The speed limit is strictly enforced by park rangers and local law officials. Where the sand is soft, you may have to drive slower than 25 mph.

Beach drivers follow the same rules that apply when driving on asphalt: Keep to the right, pass on the left, etc. All vehicles must be street legal with valid plates, insurance, and inspection stickers, and driven by a licensed individual. Seat belts must be worn by anyone in the front seat. Standing is not allowed in any vehicle. If you are riding in the back of a pickup truck, you must sit on the bed, not on the side rail or wheel well. Jeep passengers must be seated and may not stand and hold onto the roll bar. No open containers of alcohol are allowed in vehicles.

Pedestrians have the right-of-way at all times on the beach, regardless of where they are in relation to your vehicle. Look out for children, pets, sunbathers, and anglers. Expect the unexpected. The wind often hampers hearing, so use caution when approaching pedestrians. If the wind is blowing away from them and toward you, they may not hear your approach.

When driving back to the road, keep your eye on pedestrian traffic. The edge of the Beach Road grabs the wheels a bit and can pull you to one side or another abruptly. Maintain a wide berth for anyone walking near you.

And a caution to pedestrians: Wear light clothing at night if you intend to walk near car traffic. While most drivers respect driving safety rules, some really let their hair down at the beach. Pedestrians need to be as conscientious as drivers on both sand and roadways.

Vehicle Preparation

Many, many drivers get stuck because they don't let air out of their tires before driving on the beaches. The National Park Service says its rangers generally drive with 20 pounds of pressure in their tires. This applies to vehicles of any size, from large trucks to smaller sedans. Lowering the pressure also helps prevent the engine from overheating when traveling through soft sand. Rangers advise reinflating tires when returning to the paved roads.

Don't block the beach ramps when you lock hubs or deflate tires. We suggest pulling well off to the side of the ramp or using the parking areas found at most vehicle accesses.

Driving on Sand

Once on the beach, try to drive on the firm, wet sand below the high-tide line. If there are previously made tracks, follow them. Areas may be untracked for good reason. Watch out for areas of the beach with shell-laden, reddish sand and depressions with a bit of standing water. These can be very soft.

Restricted Areas

You are prohibited from driving on, over, or in between the dunes for any reason at any time. The dunes and their fragile vegetation create our protective barrier and are extremely vital to the delicate ecology of animal and plant life.

Please obey all the area designations on the beaches. Many portions of the beach are roped off, allowing shorebirds and turtles to nest. These areas change throughout the seasons, so areas that were open in April could be closed in August. Through traffic can be curtailed by these closings, especially at high tide. Stay alert for changes, and respect the limitations. Violations can bring substantial fines.

When driving by the waterline, always drive behind surf anglers. You don't want to snap their nearly invisible monofilament fishing line or upset their fishing activity.

Accommodations

When it comes to accommodations, just like every other thing on the Outer Banks, you can have it as small and peaceful or big and busy as you choose. Visitors looking to stay a night, several days, or a week can choose from a range of family-owned seaside motels to multiple-story franchises of national lodging chains. The farther south you go, the fewer chain-owned accommodations you'll find; in fact, they almost disappear. North of Kitty Hawk, you'll find only two hotels and two bed and breakfasts. In recent years elegant inns and a variety of bed and breakfast establishments have opened their doors— offering a little more luxury and personal attention than the traditional barrier island hotels.

OVERVIEW

A few of these motels and hotels listed in this chapter require two-night minimums on the weekends, and many require at least three-day stays for Memorial Day weekend, July Fourth weekend, and Labor Day weekend, since those are, by far, the busiest times on these barrier islands. A lot of Outer Banks hotels also have suites, efficiency apartments, and cottage units that rent by the day or week. Of course, you can stay in any room in any of these accommodations for a week or longer if you wish.

More and more, however, the Outer Banks is a vacation rental destination, where there are an increasing number of private homes that rent by the week rather than hotel rooms renting by the night. In Dare County alone (excluding the Currituck beaches and Ocracoke), there are more than 15,000 rental cottages compared with only a couple of thousand rooms or apartment-style rooms in hotels, bed and breakfast inns, and cottage courts. Modest cottages that offer comfort and convenience line the ocean from Kitty Hawk through Hatteras Village. Many families and groups of friends choose to rent these cottages for a week's vacation or longer. Companies that lease these properties are included in the Weekly and Long-Term Cottage Rentals chapter.

Added to the mix are Airbnb and VRBO properties. Airbnb rentals especially are usually owned by Outer Banks residents and often offer more flexibility on length of a stay than traditional property management companies.

If you're planning a summer stay on the Outer Banks, call early for reservations. Most accommodations are filled to capacity from early June through the first week of September. Sometimes you can obtain walk-in rooms at hotels or motels during the week; however, if you know the exact week or weekend that you're planning to visit, your best bet is to book a room immediately.

Locations in Kitty Hawk, Kill Devil Hills and Nags Head are often indicated by milepost and town. Most of the hotels, motels, and inns are along NC 12. A few line US 158, which is also called the Bypass. Roanoke and Ocracoke Islands have several tucked beneath the trees off the beaten paths. Bed and breakfast inns are becoming more popular on the Outer Banks, with the largest numbers on Roanoke and Ocracoke Islands. There are now more than 180 bed and breakfast rooms on the Outer Banks.

Rates vary dramatically from one area of the Outer Banks to another, from oceanfront rooms to those across the highway, between in- and off-season times, and especially depending on the amenities offered with each unit. In general late fall, winter, and early spring prices are at least one-third lower than midsummer rates. The most expensive season, of course, is from mid-June to mid-August, when rates in general range from $150 a night for two people with two double beds to nearly $440 per night in some of the fancier establishments. Many hotels and motels honor AARP and other discounts and often allow children to stay free with paying adults.

More and more accommodations providers keep their doors open all year, catering to fall fishing parties, spring visitors, and people who like the Outer Banks best in winter when few others are around. If you prefer isolation at the beach and don't mind wind and temperatures in the 40s and 50s, November through February is a wonderful time to visit. September and October, however, are our favorite months. The ocean is still warm enough to swim in, the daytime temperature seldom drops below the mid-60s, most restaurants, attractions, and retail shops remain open, yet the prices are much lower and most of the bustle is gone once school starts up again.

> i Memorial Day through Labor Day is the peak season for Outer Banks vacations, but fall and spring are becoming increasingly popular times of year to visit. Rates are lower in the spring and fall than during the summer, and there are far fewer crowds. Both of these seasons can offer remarkably warm weather and almost all of the amenities of the summer vacation— except the warmest water temperatures.

How This Chapter Is Organized

Hotels in this chapter are arranged from north to south from Corolla through Ocracoke.

Price Code

The following price code is based on the average cost for a double-occupancy one-night stay in a room with two double beds during peak summer season. Extra charges may apply for holiday weekends, additional people in the room, efficiency apartments, or pets. These prices do not include local and state taxes. Unless otherwise indicated in the listing, all accommodations accept major credit cards.

$	Less than $100
$$	$100-$150
$$$	150-$225
$$$$	More than$225

HOTELS, MOTELS & INNS

Corolla

COROLLA VILLAGE INN, 1149 Persimmon St.; (252) 597-3422; corolla villageinn.com. Nestled in the heart of historic Corolla Village, the Corolla Village Inn offers luxury rooms in a newly constructed 12 room inn designed to fit in seamlessly with the architecture of the village. Surrounded by live oak, the inn's screened-in porches hearken back to a simpler time. Guest rooms are spacious suites with king beds, welcoming interiors, and local art.

HAMPTON INN AND SUITES OUTER BANKS COROLLA, NC 12, Pine Island; (252) 453-6565, (800) HAMPTON (426-7866); hamptoninn .com; $$$. Those looking for short-term lodgings on the northern Outer Banks have never had many options, but the oceanfront Hampton Inn helps fill the void. The inn has 123 sleeper rooms, a mix of guest rooms and studio suites. Room decor has a coastal theme with ceiling fans and private balconies. Each room has a television, microwave, refrigerator, hair dryer, ironing equipment, coffee maker, pay Nintendo, pay-per-view movies, and 2 two-line phones. Most rooms feature a pull-out sofa, and some have whirlpool tubs. Studio suites also feature a wet bar. The majority of rooms have an ocean view. Public areas include a heated indoor pool and whirlpool spa, an exercise room, a game room, four meeting rooms, coin-operated laundry facilities, and the Suite Shop with sundries, beach supplies, sodas, and snacks. Outdoors is a pool, kiddie pool, and a lazy river. Direct beach access is provided. Continental breakfast is served to guests each morning.

⭐ **THE INN AT COROLLA LIGHT,** 1066 Ocean Trl.; (252) 453-3340, (800) 215-0772; innatcorolla.com; $$$. Located within walking distance of the Currituck Beach Lighthouse, the Inn at Corolla Light, open year-round, is a luxurious place where guests can plan their days around an incredible array of recreational activities available nearly at their doorstep—or they may wish simply to relax in full view of the sparkling waters of Currituck Sound and bask in the serenity of this beautifully appointed facility. This upscale development offers wooded walking, biking trails, and every leisure amenity a vacationer could dream of: an indoor sports center with an Olympic-size pool, hot tub, saunas, clay tennis courts, racquetball courts, and fitness equipment; an oceanfront complex that boasts two outdoor pools, a video game room, a restaurant, and exclusive access to the beach; soundfront pools; play areas for basketball, shuffleboard, tennis, horseshoes, and more; and terrific shops and restaurants nearby (see the **Shopping** and **Dining** chapters). Guests of the inn have unlimited access to all of the resort's facilities. There is a nominal fee for use of the indoor tennis courts, but all other courts are free.

Guests may also use the inn's own waterfront swimming pool, hot tub, and private 400-foot pier on Currituck Sound. The inn furnishes bicycles to guests for leisurely tours of the resort's landscaped grounds. Guests are also invited to use the complimentary video library inside.

In season, parasailing, kayaking, ecotouring, and personal watercraft (Jet Skis, WaveRunners, and others) are available at a water sports-rental site on the resort. A championship golf course is nearby.

Some of the inn's 43 spacious guest rooms include kitchenettes, cable TVs, radios, DVD players, and private baths. Many have fireplaces and whirlpool tubs. The rooms are designed for single or double occupancy, and some are equipped with sleeper sofas, too. Guests can enjoy a free continental breakfast daily. Eight rooms are pet friendly (dogs only).

The Inn at Corolla Light has two- and three-night minimum stays on weekends. Special rate packages are offered throughout the year.

> **i** Stay off the beach dunes! The dunes are extremely fragile and a necessary barrier from erosion. Please use the walkways and accesses provided for you.

Duck

⭐ **SANDERLING INN RESORT**, 1461 NC 12; (252) 261-4111, (800) 701-4111; sanderlinginn.com; $$$$. The Sanderling Inn Resort is situated on 12 acres of oceanside wilderness about 5 miles north of the town of Duck. The Sanderling was built in the style of the old Nags Head beach homes, with wood siding, cedar-shake accents, dormer windows, and porches on each side.

Rocking chairs line the wide porches, providing a relaxing way to pass sultry afternoons while overlooking the ocean or sound.

All 87 rooms at the Sanderling are comfortable, lush, and accommodating. The inn provides guests with lounging robes, luxury soaps, toiletries, and a welcome gift.

Sanderling Inn is designed for the comfort and privacy of two guests per room, but sleeper sofas and cribs are available for an additional charge.

A separate building at the Sanderling houses conference and meeting facilities as well as the Presidential Suite, complete with whirlpool bath, steam shower, and two decks—one overlooks the ocean and the other overlooks the sound. For an additional charge, the inn's housekeeping staff provides laundry service with a 48-hour turnaround. Room service is provided by the Lifesaving Station restaurant (see the **Dining** chapter).

This is a complete resort with private beaches, a full-service spa, and state-of-the-art fitness center. The amenities, significantly updated and renovated in 2014, continue with an indoor pool, a separate whirlpool room, locker rooms, steam rooms, two outdoor pools, tennis courts, two fire pits lit each sundown, weather permitting and a natural walking or jogging trail. The Audubon Wildlife Sanctuary and the Pine Island Tennis and Racquet Club are nearby. An ecocenter offers kayaks for visitors to use. A seasonal outdoor pavilion and four three- and four-bedroom villas have been added to Sanderling's offerings. The villas are perfect for families.

The spa houses six treatment rooms and offers extended services, including manicures, pedicures, facials, massages, and more.

Wheelchair access is provided for all buildings on the property, and wheelchair-accessible rooms are available. The Sanderling Inn is open year-round. Four pet-friendly rooms are available.

Kitty Hawk

BAYMONT BY WYNDHAM KITTY HAWK, US 158, MP 4¼; (252) 261-4888; wyndhamhotels.com/baymont/kitty-hawk-north-carolina; $$$. Situated on the east side of US 158, Baymont by Wyndham has an outdoor swimming pool and is a short walk to lifeguarded Kitty Hawk Beach, where guests can use the motel's private access and oceanfront deck.

The inn provides a complimentary continental breakfast bar for guests each morning in the lobby. Non-smoking and wheelchair-accessible rooms are available. Year-round group rates are available. This motel is within walking distance of shopping and several restaurants and is open all year.

CYPRESS MOON INN, 1206 Harbor Ct.; (252) 202-2731, (800) 905-5060; $$$. You'll find Cypress Moon Inn nestled in the maritime forest with the sound just behind. Owners Linda and Greg Hamby have furnished their magical home with antiques throughout the residence.

Three soundfront rooms are available at the bed and breakfast. All rooms have a queen-size bed, entertainment centers, and refrigerators. Continental breakfast is served daily. You can choose to be served in the dining room, in your bedroom, or on your porch.

If you choose to spend a day away from the beach, guests are welcome to use the kayaks, stand up paddleboards, bikes or sailboards provided. A nice walkway leads to the water, and outdoor showers are available. The inn welcomes people age 18 and older and is smoke-free. Cypress Moon is closed for the month of December. Two homes offsite are also available for vacation stays.

HILTON GARDEN INN, NC 12, MP 1; (252) 261-1290, (877) 772-9444; hiltongardeninn.hilton.com; $$$$. The Hilton Garden Inn is conveniently located on the oceanfront across from the former Kitty Hawk Pier (once open to the public for fishing, but now the activity is only available to Hilton guests). The inn offers a choice of suites and rooms with a private balcony overlooking the ocean. All rooms are equipped with high-speed Internet access and a microwave, refrigerator, and coffeemaker. Indoor and outdoor pools and a fitness area are available. A guest laundry facility, business center, and restaurant are located here. The award-winning Great American Grill serves breakfast, lunch, and dinner on-site.

SEA KOVE MOTEL, NC 12, MP 3; (252) 261-4722; $$$. This family-owned and operated establishment rents 10 one-bedroom efficiency units, 10 two-bedroom units, and two cottages by the week only from April through November. It's across from the ocean and includes full-size kitchens and televisions in each apartment. A playground and outdoor pool also are available. No credit cards accepted.

Kill Devil Hills

BEST WESTERN OCEAN REEF SUITES, NC 12, MP 8½; (252) 441-1611, (800) 528-1234; bestwestern.com/oceanreefsuites; $$$$. All 71 one-bedroom suites in this oceanfront hotel are decorated and arranged like luxury apartments with a contemporary beach decor. The views are great, and you'll find everything you need for a truly luxurious beach vacation. Each room has a telephone, cable TV, free coffee, and a fully equipped galley-style kitchen. The bath area has a double vanity. Nonsmoking and wheelchair-accessible rooms are available. Upper-floor rooms have private balconies overlooking the ocean. Some first-floor units open onto the oceanfront pool and courtyard, while others offer a private patio. The Ocean Reef is one of the few facilities on the beach to have a penthouse suite; this one boasts a private Jacuzzi and rooftop deck.

A heated, seasonal outdoor pool and a whirlpool are available to guests in the courtyard, and the exercise room features a sauna. Other amenities include a laundry facility on the premises and year-round bar and food service. Children age 13 and younger stay free with adults. A two-day minimum stay is required on summer weekends. Ocean Reef is open all year.

CAVALIER BY THE SEA, NC 12, MP 8½; (252) 441-5585; thecavalier motel.com; $$$. The Cavalier has comfortable rooms with double and single beds and several one-room efficiency units with two double beds and kitchenettes right on the beach. Some rooms have full baths, while others have shower stalls. All are equipped with telephones, refrigerators, microwaves, cable TV, and free HBO. Three 1-story wings surround the adult swimming pool, the kiddie swimming pool, a volleyball court, a children's play area, and shuffleboard courts. The motel also has 13 cottages that rent by the week. Pets are allowed in the cottages only. There is some wheelchair access here, and ramps are on the premises. Parking is available outside each room, and the covered porch with outdoor furniture is just right for relaxing with a free cup of coffee while watching the sunrise. An observation deck sits atop the oceanfront section. Children age 12 and younger stay for free in their parents' rooms. The Cavalier Motel is open year-round.

COMFORT INN ON THE OCEAN, NC 12, MP 9½; (252) 441-6333; choicehotels.com/north-carolina/kill-devil-hills/comfort-inn-hotels/nc416; $$$$. This oceanfront hotel has 105 rooms, many with spectacular ocean views. Banquet and conference facilities accommodate 10 to 200 people. Amenities include an on-site restaurant and lounge, a coin-operated laundry, an outdoor pool, and a whirlpool. All rooms include telephone, cable TV with remote, free high-speed Internet access, microwave, and refrigerator. The Clarion has wheelchair-accessible rooms and is smoke free. Free breakfast is included. AARP and other discounts available. The Clarion is open all year. Pets are welcomed.

CYPRESS HOUSE BED AND BREAKFAST, NC 12, MP 8; (252) 441-6127, (800) 554-2764; cypresshouseinn.com; $$. This historic bed-and-breakfast inn was originally built as a private hunting and fishing lodge in the 1940s. Located 150 yards from the Atlantic Ocean, the inn, with its original tongue-and-groove cypress–paneled walls and ceilings, exudes a cozy, casual charm. Six guest rooms with queen-size beds and private shower baths are equipped with ceiling fans, cable TV, and central air. The wraparound porch is ideal for enjoying the ocean breezes. In cold weather relax with a good book in front of a blazing fire in the common room. Early risers awake to self-serve coffee and tea on the baker's rack outside the rooms; a full gourmet breakfast is served each morning. Afternoon refreshments are also served. Bikes, beach towels, and chairs, along with an outdoor shower and a courtyard with a pergola, are available. Cypress House is smoke-free. Children age 12 and older are welcome, and pets are not allowed.

DAYS INN MARINER MOTEL, NC 12, MP 7½; (252) 441-2021, (800) 325-2525; outer-banks.com/days-mariner; $$$. Rooms and apartments include a telephone, refrigerator, and cable TV. All the rooms have a fresh, contemporary beach look. There's easy access to the Atlantic, and the units are spacious enough to offer flexible living arrangements for families or groups. A recreation area has facilities for volleyball, and an outdoor swimming pool and showers are just off the ocean. All rooms are nonsmoking and wheelchair-accessible rooms are available. All Days Inn programs are honored, and AARP discounts are available with a card and member must be present. The Mariner is open year-round, except Christmas week, with rates discounted in the off-season.

DAYS INN WRIGHT BROTHERS, NC 12, MP 8½; (252) 441-7211, (800) 325-2525; obxlodging.com/day-inn-oceanfront; $$$–$$$$. An oceanfront property on a wide stretch of beach, this facility opened as an Outer Banks motel in 1948. It was built to resemble an old mountain lodge and offers an inviting lobby, decorated in the nostalgia of Old Nags Head, where guests can read the newspaper and sip a cup of free coffee. The room is further enhanced by Oriental rugs on polished hardwood floors and a fireplace large enough to take away the chill on cold beach evenings during the off-season.

Guests enjoy balconies with old-fashioned furniture and nice views. The 52 rooms include singles, doubles, kings, king suites, and efficiency units that sleep six and include a living room, adjoining bedroom, and complete kitchen. All rooms have telephones, cable TV, and refrigerators. Oceanfront rooms also have microwaves. Non-smoking and wheelchair-accessible rooms are available.

A complimentary continental breakfast is available throughout the year. Hot apple cider and popcorn are served around the fireplace during the winter, and lemonade and cookies are served in the summer. Leisure amenities include a large outdoor pool, sundeck, volleyball court, barbecue pit, and a boardwalk to the beach.

Children age 12 and younger stay for free, and AARP discounts are honored. There's a two-night minimum stay for summer holiday weekends, and Saturday check-ins are allowed only for weekly rentals. Daily and weeklong rentals are available throughout the year. This inn has won the prestigious Days Inn Chairmans award a number of times. Convenient to the Wright Brothers Monument.

DRIFTIN' SANDS, 1906 N. Virginia Dare Trl.; (252) 715-4100; driftin sandsmotel.com; $. A small family-run motel in the heart of Kill Devil Hills on the Beach Road. Rooms feature mini-fridges and microwaves. A small outdoor garden and picnic are with barbecue grills onsite. Smoke-free rooms are available.

JOHN YANCEY INN, NC 12, MP 10; (252) 441-7141, (800) 367-5941; outerbanksnchotel; $$$$. This family hotel is on a wide beach. Shuffleboard courts, an outdoor heated pool, and a playground are on the premises. The hotel has spacious rooms, with kings and doubles, housed in three buildings. The oceanfront units each have a balcony or patio so you can see and hear the waves from your room. Cable TV with optional in-room movies, a small refrigerator, and a telephone are in each room. Coffeemakers and coffee are provided in all rooms. Most of the rooms are nonsmoking, and this inn offers wheelchair-accessible units. WiFi is free on the premises. Other amenities include a coin-operated laundry, and pets are welcome in some rooms. Children age 18 and younger stay free, and rollaway beds are available for an extra fee to accommodate additional kids. A two-night minimum stay is required on holiday weekends. AARP and other discounts are honored. The John Yancey is open all year. Continental breakfast is served each day. YMCA passes available to the gym or pool.

THE OUTER BANKS INN, 1003 S. Croatan Hwy, MP 9; (252) 715-3500, (888) 322-9702; theouterbanksinn.com; $$. Centrally located at MP 9 on the Bypass, The Outer Banks Inn is a 40 room family-friendly motel. Amenities include free shuttle service to the beach, private pool, continental breakfast and complimentary YMCA passes complete with daycare.

OUTER BANKS MOTOR LODGE, NC 12, MP 9½; (252) 441-7404, (877) 625-6343; obxmotorlodge.com; $$$. An oceanfront motel with 30 efficiency units and 8 regular rooms. Each room has cable TV, a refrigerator, and a microwave. Wheelchair-accessible units are available. Amenities include an on-site washer and dryer, a playground, an outdoor swimming pool, and a restaurant. Outer Banks Motor Lodge is a smoke free motel. Open from March through November.

QUALITY INN CAROLINA OCEANFRONT, NC 12, MP 8; (252) 480-2600, (800) 954-5286; qualityinncarolinaoceanfront.com; $$$$. This 3-story property (central to Outer Banks attractions) includes 119 rooms that open along exterior corridors. They're filled with natural light and decorated tastefully. The building is T-shaped, so not all rooms have views of the

ACCOMMODATIONS

Atlantic; however, oceanfront units have private balconies. All rooms at this have refrigerators, microwaves, full baths, cable TV and Showtime, telephones, and coffeemakers. Non-smoking and wheelchair-accessible rooms are available. Amenities include an oceanfront pool and coin-operated laundry facilities. A complimentary breakfast is provided. Children age 18 and younger stay free with an adult. A two-night minimum stay is required on summer holiday weekends. Managers honor AARP discounts. The Inn is open all year. YMCA passes available for working out at the gym or using the outdoor or indoor pool.

RAMADA PLAZA RESORT AND CONFERENCE CENTER, NC 12, MP 9½; (252) 441-2151, (800) 635-1824; ramadainnnagshead.com; $$$– $$$$. This 5-story, 171-room oceanfront hotel was built in 1985. It's popular with tour groups and hosts many meetings throughout the year. All rooms have a balcony or patio, cable TV with pay-per-view movies, small refrigerator, and microwave. Bellhop and room service are available here. Nonsmoking, wheelchair-accessible, and pet rooms are offered, along with guest laundry facilities and an exercise room. Meeting facilities are on the fourth floor overlooking the ocean. Several suites are available to fit a variety of conference and workshop needs. An indoor swimming pool and Jacuzzi are off the second floor atop the dunes surrounded by a large sundeck. A flight of steps takes you onto the beach where volleyball is a popular pastime. Seasonal food and beverage services are available at the oceanfront bar adjacent to the pool. Peppercorns, the hotel's fine oceanview restaurant, serves breakfast and dinner year-round and offers lunch on the deck during the summer (see the **Dining** chapter). The Ramada Plaza Resort is open all year.

SEA RANCH HOTEL, NC 12, MP 7; (252) 441-7126, (800) 334-4737; searanchhotel.com; $$$$. Stay at the Sea Ranch for a classic Outer Banks vacation. It is locally owned and operated, with a 5-story oceanfront tower and a 2-story building that contains 50 motel-style rooms. Each unit has cable TV and free HBO, a refrigerator, microwave, coffeemaker, and telephone. About half of the hotel rooms have oceanfront views. Non-smoking rooms are available, and the hotel is wheelchair accessible. It has a heated indoor pool. The Sea Ranch is open year-round. A restaurant is located within the hotel.

SEE SEA MOTEL, NC 12, MP 9; (252) 441-7321, (800) 635-7007; cove realty.com; $$–$$$. A small, family-run motel across the street from the ocean, See Sea offers 21 rental units, including 11 motel rooms, 6 efficiencies, 3 two-bedroom apartments, and 1 three-bedroom cottage. The motel rooms and efficiencies rent by the day (the apartments and cottage require a one-week minimum stay in season). All units have a refrigerator, microwave, telephone, and cable TV. There's a pay phone on the premises. Laundry is on-site, and free coffee is provided. Amenities include an outdoor swimming pool and a picnic area. Non-smoking rooms are offered. See Sea Motel is open year-round.

SHUTTERS ON THE BANKS, NC 12, MP 8½; (252) 441-5581, (800) 949-3728; shuttersonthebanks.com; $$$. This modern family-owned and operated oceanfront motel is well-maintained and offers lots of amenities, including an outdoor heated pool with a whirlpool and patio, an indoor heated pool, a dune-top gazebo, and a private beach with lifeguard. A complimentary continental breakfast is served every morning. Laundry facilities are available on the premises. Free WiFi in all rooms.

The motel has 80 units, 8 of which are efficiencies. Most offer two double beds, but rooms with king-size beds are also available. Telephones, refrigerators, microwaves, TV with remote control and cable, and clock radios are provided in the units. Some rooms have direct access to the beach, while others have a small balcony overlooking the ocean. The efficiencies have an eating area and, when combined with adjoining rooms, create a good arrangement for family vacationers. Non-smoking units are available.

Children age 17 and younger stay for free. Discounts of 10 percent are provided for AARP and AAA members. The motel is also wheelchair accessible. A two-night minimum stay is required on summer weekends. Shutters by the Sea is open year-round.

TOWNEPLACE SUITES OUTER BANKS, 2028 Virginia Dare Trl.; (252) 457-2190, $$$. The Outer Banks' newest hotel, TownePlace offers Studio, and one-bedroom family suites with fully equipped kitchens, buffet breakfast and WiFi. Children welcome, pet friendly. The beach is just across the road from the hotel. Centrally located with a number of excellent restaurants close by.

TRAVELODGE NAGS HEAD BEACH HOTEL, NC 12, MP 8; (252) 441-0411, (888) 637-4859; nagsheadbeachhotel.com; $$$. This 97-room, 4-story hotel is across the highway from the ocean, so some guest rooms have views of the Atlantic, while others afford glimpses of the Wright Brothers National Memorial. Twelve of the first-floor guest rooms open directly onto the outdoor courtyard and pool. Each room has a microwave, refrigerator, color TV (with remote control, cable, and free HBO), telephone, and private balcony or patio, with non-smoking and wheelchair-accessible rooms available. A complimentary continental breakfast featuring cereals, pastries, juices, coffee, tea, and fresh fruits is served daily in the lobby from 7 to 9 a.m. Discounts are available to AARP members. Children age 18 and younger stay free in their parents' room, and pets are welcome for an additional charge. During summer holidays, three-night minimum stays are required. The hotel is open all year.

ACCOMMODATIONS

Nags Head

BLUE HERON MOTEL, NC 12, MP 16; (252) 441-7447; blueheronnc .com; $$$. The Blue Heron Motel is considered one of the Outer Banks' best-kept secrets among the small motels in the area. The family-owned facility provides a year-round indoor swimming pool, a spa, and outdoor pools. The Gladden family lives on the premises and pays careful attention to the management of the property. It's in the midst of fine Nags Head restaurants and offers plenty of beach for those who come to relax. All units have a full kitchen, cable TV, phones, and shower/tub combinations. A wheelchair-accessible room is available. Second- and third-floor rooms offer private balconies. The Blue Heron Motel is open all year and offers weekly rates.

CAHOON'S COTTAGE COURT, 7213 S. Virginia Dare Trl.; (252) 441-5358; cahoonscottages.com; $$–$$$. Located immediately adjacent to Jennette's Pier, Cahoon's Cottages are as old school as it gets. The beach is at your feet. This is a classic Cottage Court with efficiencies, two, three and four bedroom cottages. Cahoon's Market is next door.

COLONIAL INN MOTEL, NC 12, MP 11½; (252) 441-7392; colonial innmotel.com; $$$–$$$$. At the Colonial Inn Motel you can stay in an ocean-front room, standard room, efficiency unit, or apartment—some of which accommodate as many as 10 guests. Every unit has cable TV, air-conditioning, and fridge. All are wheelchair accessible. Enjoy the beach, swim in the pool, or fish off the adjacent Nags Head Fishing Pier. Pet-friendly rooms; open year-round.

COMFORT INN OCEANFRONT SOUTH, NC 12, MP 17; (252) 441-6315; choicehotels.com; $$$. The Comfort Inn Oceanfront South, a 7-story oceanfront hotel, is the tallest building on the Outer Banks. The light peach-and-teal exterior gives this hotel a clean, contemporary beach look. The 105-room hotel has deluxe oceanfront rooms with magnificent views from private balconies; oceanside and streetside rooms are available, too. Each room has a cable TV, phone, refrigerator, and microwave. Smoke free hotel. A honeymoon suite with a hot tub is popular, as are rooms with king-size beds. One wheelchair-accessible room is available. Corporate meeting rooms accommodate groups of 350 people. The oceanfront pool and deck are favorite places. Other amenities include a game room and a playground. A complimentary continental breakfast is offered in the lobby. The inn is open all year. Pets accepted in some rooms.

DOLPHIN OCEANFRONT MOTEL, NC 12, MP 16½; (252) 441-7488, (800) 699-1962; dolphinmotel.net; $$$. The Dolphin offers rooms and efficiencies. Some rooms have an ocean view. The breezeway to the beach and an outdoor pool add special touches. All rooms and efficiencies have fridges and cable TV. Nonsmoking rooms are available. The Dolphin opens the last Friday in March and closes the last Saturday in October. Pets are allowed. Families particularly enjoy the picnic area with charcoal grills, picnic tables, and playground. Free Wi-Fi.

FIN 'N FEATHER WATERSIDE INN, Nags Head–Manteo Causeway; (252) 441-5353, (866) 316-1843; obxwatersideinn.com; $$$. This charming motel along the water's edge is popular with anglers and hunters. If you're planning to come in the fall or spring, call well in advance for reservations. This motel's proximity to Pirate's Cove Yacht Club is convenient for anyone headed out for a day on the open seas. The motel also has its own boat ramp. Housekeeping units are available year-round at Fin 'N Feather and feature double-bed efficiencies. Each efficiency has a stove, a refrigerator, and cooking utensils. The rooms are clean and comfortable. Large windows open onto the water from either side and offer stunning views of the sound. All rooms are non-smoking, and dogs are welcome. Free Wi-Fi.

FIRST COLONY INN, US 158, MP 16; (252) 441-2343, (800) 368-9390; firstcolonyinn.com; $$$$. Back in 1932 this gracious old structure was known as Leroy's Seaside Inn. The landmark hotel was moved and refurbished, but it's still a favorite for those who like the ambience of a quiet inn. The old Nags Head-style architecture, resplendent under an overhanging roof and wide porches, has been preserved and is listed in the National Register of Historic Places.

In the sunny breakfast room, you can enjoy a complimentary continental breakfast and afternoon tea. Upstairs, an elegant but cozy library with books, games, and an old pump organ is a favorite place to read the paper or meet other guests. A great selection of jazz, as well as classical music, wafts throughout the reception area. Each room is appointed in English antique furniture. Special touches, such as tiled baths, heated towel bars, English toiletries, telephones, TVs, iron with ironing board, individual climate control, and refrigerators, are standard. Some rooms have a wet bar, kitchenette, Jacuzzi, DVD player, and private balcony; some rooms include an additional trundle bed or daybed for an extra person. The first floor is wheelchair accessible, and one room is designed for disabled guests. Smoking is not permitted in the inn.

Guests are invited to relax at the 55-foot swimming pool and sundeck behind the inn or to follow the private boardwalk across the street to the oceanfront gazebo. This magnificent year-round inn provides easy access to the ocean and is close to many shops and restaurants. The inn has a policy of Thursday night free for stays of five weeknights or longer (must include consecutive Sunday through Thursday stays).

HOLIDAY INN EXPRESS, 4701 S. Virginia Dare Trl.; (252) 441-0454, (888) 465-4329; ihg.com/holidayinnexpress/hotels/us/en/nags-head/nghob/hoteldetail; $$$. Centrally located on the Beach Road in Nags Head, is right on the beach. Guest rooms begin on the second floor of this 5-story building, and all oceanside rooms afford panoramic ocean views from private balconies. Continental breakfast is included. Discounts offered to US and Canadian active and retired service members.

THE ISLANDER MOTEL, NC 12, MP 16; (252) 441-6229; islandermotel. com; $$$. The Islander is a small, popular oceanfront property featuring an attractive landscape and well-maintained rooms. Most rooms have an ocean view, and all have either a balcony or patio, although some of the first-floor units tucked behind dunes do not offer ocean views. All have sitting areas, coffeemakers, and refrigerators. Some first-floor units offer kitchenettes. Guests enjoy the pool and private dune walk to the ocean. This property is convenient to Nags Head restaurants, shops, recreational outlets, and attractions. The Islander is open April through October. Free Wi-Fi.

OCEANSIDE COURT, NC 12, MP 15½; (252) 441-6167; keesouter banks.com/resort/oceanside-court; $$–$$$. There's nothing like an oceanside stay on the Outer Banks, and that's what you'll get here. So oceanside there's even a fish cleaning station onsite. Traditional cottage court with efficiencies, one-, two-, or three-bedroom cottages available.

OWENS' MOTEL, NC 12, MP 16; (252) 441-6361; owensmotel.com; $$$. The Owens family has owned and operated this attractive motel, one of the first on the beach, for 60 years. Adjacent to the family's famous restaurant (see the **Dining** chapter), this property across the highway from the ocean is well maintained. This 3-story oceanfront property includes efficiencies with large, private balconies. Each efficiency has a tile bath and shower, cable TV, and a full kitchen. Thirty-one additional rooms are located just across the street from the beach. Rooms are all tastefully furnished. Most have two double beds; four rooms have kings. All rooms include a refrigerator and a microwave. The motel swimming pool on the west side of the property provides an alternative to the ocean. There is easy access to Jennette's Pier, and a comfortable oceanfront pavilion with rocking chairs is enticing. Owens' Motel is open April through October.

SANDSPUR MOTEL AND COTTAGE COURT, NC 12, MP 15¾, (252) 441-6993; $–$$. On the beach, rooms have cable TV, mini fridges and microwaves. Some rooms have kitchenettes and decks. The motel's other amenities include an outdoor pool with a sundeck and lounge chairs, a playground, coin-operated laundry machines, and fish cleaning tables.

SEA FOAM MOTEL, NC 12, MP 16½; (252) 441-7320; seafoam.com; $$$. Historic Nags Head hotel included the National Register of Historic Places. This attractive oceanfront motel offers a choice of rooms, efficiencies, and cottages. Efficiencies accommodate two to four people, and cottages sleep up to six comfortably. The efficiencies and cottages rent weekly. Rooms are tastefully decorated, and some have washed-oak furniture. All rooms have cable TV with HBO, refrigerators, microwaves, and phones. Some have king-size beds, and each has a balcony or porch. Some units in the 1- and 2-story buildings have ocean and poolside views. Children are welcome, and they will enjoy the playground. Other features include a large heated outdoor pool, children's pool, sundeck, shuffleboard area, and a gazebo on the beach for guests' pleasure. Sea Foam Motel is within walking distance of several restaurants. Pets allowed in some rooms.

SURF SIDE HOTEL, NC 12, MP 15½; (252) 441-2105, (800) 552-7873; surfsideobx.com; $$$$. This attractive 5-story hotel is situated on the oceanfront; rooms facing north, south, and east have ocean views. Some rooms have views of Roanoke Sound as well. All rooms have private balconies and are decorated attractively in muted beach tones. Refrigerators, cable TV, hair dryers, coffeemakers, microwaves, irons and ironing boards, and phones are standard in all rooms. The honeymoon suites feature king-size beds and private Jacuzzis. An elevator provides easy access, and wheelchair-accessible rooms are available; so are nonsmoking rooms. An adjacent 3-story building offers rooms and efficiencies with either ocean or sound views. A continental breakfast is provided each morning, and the staff hosts an afternoon wine and snacks social hour for guests. You can choose between an indoor pool and hot tub that are open all year and an outdoor pool for swimming in warm weather. The Surf Side is open all year.

Roanoke Island

Manteo

BURRUS HOUSE INN, 509 Hwy 64; (252) 475-1636; burrushouse.com; $$–$$$. Newly-renovated, all-suite hotel with spectacular waterfront views of Shallowbag Bays. Suites include sitting room, kitchenette, luxurious bathroom, comfortable king or queen bedding and a private deck with hammocks and seating. Includes a welcome basket, continental breakfast, and afternoon tea or cocktail in the "Peacock Room." Complimentary use of kayaks, standup paddleboards and bikes included.

★ **THE CAMERON HOUSE INN,** 300 Budleigh St.; (252) 473-6596, (800) 279-8178; cameronhouseinn.com; $$$$. Comfort and elegance are the hallmarks at this well-appointed inn. Some rooms feature fireplaces, soaker tubs, or down-stuffed sofas, and all have luxurious tiled bathrooms. All rooms are nonsmoking and all have Internet access. A big breakfast is set out each morning, usually offering homemade muffins and breads, quiches, fresh fruit, granola, juices, coffee, and tea. Afternoon treats perk you up after a long day on the beach or visiting attractions, especially if you also take a moment to relax on the antique front porch swing or in the comfy wicker chairs. Small dogs allowed in one room. Children 12 years and older. The inn is in historic downtown Manteo, where restaurants, attractions, and shopping are all just a few minutes' walk away. The Cameron House is frequently the site for conferences, retreats, and small weddings.

DARE HAVEN MOTEL, US 64/264; (252) 473-2322; darehavenouter banks.com; $$–$$$. The Dare Haven, a family-run motel suited to the cost-conscious vacationer, is toward the north end of Roanoke Island and is a favorite place for families and fishing enthusiasts—there's enough room here to park your own boat and trailer. Visitors planning to attend *The Lost Colony* or visit any of the other Roanoke Island attractions and historic sites of Fort Raleigh find this location convenient. The motel-style rooms are basic, clean, and comfortable, and have cable TV and telephones. Most are decorated in traditional Outer Banks style, with paneled walls and wraparound porches. All are ground level. The motel is open all year, and some rooms are pet friendly. A large dog run is on-site.

THE ELIZABETHAN INN, US 64; (252) 473-2101, (800) 346-2466; elizabethaninn.com; $$$$. The Elizabethan Inn is a year-round resort facility with spacious shaded grounds, country-manor charm, and Tudor architecture reflecting the area's heritage. The hotel consists of three buildings providing more than 80 rooms, efficiencies, and apartments, plus a spa and an on-site restaurant. Non-smoking and wheelchair-accessible rooms are available. All rooms have cable TV with HBO, refrigerators, and direct-dial phones. Rooms are available with a king-size bed or two queen-size or double beds, and two rooms have whirlpool baths. All have coffeemakers. The inn's Nautics Hall Health & Fitness Complex is available for guests (see the **Recreation** chapter). Guests may also use the outdoor pool and a heated, competition-size indoor pool.

⭐ **ISLAND MOTEL & GUESTHOUSE,** US 64; (252) 473-2434; the islandmotel.com; $$–$$$. In the heart of Manteo, convenience is a hallmark at this neat little motel. Most of the 11 rooms have their own microwave or full kitchen, cable TV, air-conditioning, and two double beds. Foldaway beds are available for children. Daily, weekly, and monthly rates are offered. Amenities include courtesy bikes, fishing poles, other sports equipment, and surfing lessons. Non-smoking rooms are available, and smoking is not allowed in the main house. Dogs are allowed for a nominal fee. This motel is open all year.

The Island Motel also operates three adorable theme cottages located 1 block away. In-season rates start at $200 per night. These cottages are non-smoking and do not allow pets.

ROANOKE ISLAND INN, 305 Fernando St.; (252) 473-5511, (877) 473-5511; roanokeislandinn.com; $$$$. With the sparkling Roanoke Sound and quaint Manteo waterfront just a stroll away, you'll find yourself easing into the relaxed village pace the moment you step up to this attractive inn. The distinctive white clapboard with dark green shutters distinguishes a gracious, restored residence with the comforts of a small, well-designed bed and breakfast. The furnishings are handsome, reflecting the meticulous care of the owner, designer-architect John Wilson IV. Each of the inn's eight rooms features a private entrance, private bath, TV, and phone. Guests may choose to stay in the bungalow behind the inn, which is complete with antique tub and furnishings, wet bar, and refrigerator.

A light breakfast is offered in the butler's pantry. The private grounds are landscaped with gardenia, fig bushes, and native plants. Relax by the picturesque pond complete with koi and sweet-smelling lotus plants. Dip nets are provided so guests can net crabs along the bay's edge. Bicycles are furnished for touring the town and nearby historic attractions, including the *Elizabeth II* and the Outer Banks History Center. For a more adventuresome vacation, guests may rent a house on their own private island in the sound. Guests must provide their own boat to make the 10-minute journey to the home, available May through September. Roanoke Island Inn is open from April through October.

SCARBOROUGH HOUSE BED AND BREAKFAST, Fernando and Uppowac Sts.; (252) 473-3849; scarboroughhouseinn.com; $$$. The Scarborough House, owned by Phil and Sally Scarborough, opened in 1995. Each of the four guest rooms has its own refrigerator, microwave, and private bath. A romantic loft room has a king-size bed and a whirlpool bath. This inn is appointed with period antiques and other fine furnishings. A continental breakfast is served daily. Everything about these accommodations reflects the owners' care and personal touch. The Scarborough House is open year-round.

SCARBOROUGH INN, 524 US 64; (252) 473-3979; scarboroughinn manteo.com; $$–$$$. This small inn is a delightful and friendly place to stay. The 2-story structure was modeled after a turn-of-the-20th-century inn. Each of the 14 guest rooms is filled with authentic Victorian and pre-Victorian antiques and other interesting furnishings, mostly family heirlooms. The inn's main rooms are set away from the street and offer cable TV, phone, microwave, private bath, small refrigerator, and coffeemaker. Rooms in the 2-story inn have exterior entrances and open onto a covered porch. The annex has four units: two suites with queen bedrooms and sitting rooms and two regular queen rooms. The barn has two king rooms. All six units in the annex and barn are equipped with wet bars and small storage spaces for kitchen utensils and miscellaneous items. Scarborough Inn is open year-round.

⭐ **TRANQUIL HOUSE INN,** 405 Queen Elizabeth Ave.; (252) 473-1404, (800) 458-7069; tranquilhouseinn.com; $$$$. This lovely 25-room country inn on Shallowbag Bay was modeled after an old hotel that stood on this site. Richard Gere and Diane Lane stayed at the Tranquil House in 2007 while filming the movie *Nights in Rodanthe*. Although the inn looks authentically aged, it is enhanced by up-to-date conveniences: TVs, telephones, and private baths. Two of the 25 rooms are one-bedroom suites that feature a queen-size bed and a separate sitting room with sofa and two TVs. Large rooms on the third floor have high ceilings. The inn has one room equipped for disabled guests. A ramp to the first floor makes rooms on that level accessible to all. The spacious second-floor deck faces east toward the bay, where guests can view the *Elizabeth II*, the flagship attraction of Roanoke Island Festival Park is docked across the water. The inn's restaurant, 1587, specializes in gourmet cuisine and offers an extensive selection of wines. Guests have free use of bicycles. The inn is open all year.

> **i** Renaissance features abound within the Elizabethan Gardens on Roanoke Island. Several museum-quality Italian statues that adorn the site were imported from Pompeii in 1906. The Farnesi family crest is carved on the balustrade in the Sunken Garden. This family was patron to artists, including Michelangelo. It's a mystery—was the statuary carved by the Italian master?

THE WHITE DOE INN, Sir Walter Raleigh St.; (252) 473-9851, (800) 473-6091; whitedoeinn.com; $$$$. In a restored 1898 home, the White Doe Inn retains its turn-of-the-century charm and offers guests an elegant escape in its rooms and hideaways. It is one of the few Dare County houses listed on the National Register of Historic Places. The inn offers several guest rooms, each with a private bath and fireplace. Honeymoon suites are available. Lounge on the large wraparound porches; guests also have full use of the library, formal parlor, foyer, and dining room of this stately old home. Afternoon tea, coffee, and desserts are served, as is evening sherry. The inn serves a full Southern-style, four-course breakfast every morning. Bicycles and beach equipment are provided. Special events for up to 50 people, including weddings, reunions, or retreats, can be accommodated. The inn is open all year, and off-season rates are available. Spa and concierge service is available.

Wanchese

ISLAND HOUSE OF WANCHESE BED AND BREAKFAST, 104 Old Wharf Rd.; (252) 473-5619, (866) 473-5619; islandhouse-bb.com; $$$–$$$$. This old home, built in 1902, was converted into a bed and breakfast several years ago. Furnished in period antiques, with Oriental rugs and cabana fans, the small but cozy establishment offers many comforts, including private baths, cable TV, clock radios in every room, beach towels and chairs, and a hot tub for guests. Each of the four rooms and one suite has a double bed. Island House offers a breakfast buffet often including casseroles, grits, fresh fruit, sweets, and juice. Evening tea is served with snacks. A guest pantry is open 24 hours a day. This is a non-smoking establishment, but smoking is allowed on the porch. Kids 8 and up are welcome, as are small pets. Island House is open year-round.

WANCHESE INN BED AND BREAKFAST, 85 Jovers Ln.; (252) 475-1166, (252) 473-0602; wancheseinn.com; $$$. Dock your boat just behind this quaint bed and breakfast. Nestled in the heart of the fishing village of Wanchese, this delightful inn serves a full breakfast each day. Pets are not allowed. The inn is open all year.

Hatteras Island

Rodanthe

SEA SOUND MOTEL, Sea Sound Rd.; (252) 987-2224; seasoundmotel obx.com; $$–$$$. Family owned, the Sea Sound is between NC 12 and the ocean and offers efficiencies and regular motel-style rooms. The efficiencies have fully equipped kitchens including microwaves. Motel rooms feature either one double or two queen-size beds. All accommodations have heat and air conditioning, color TV, and phones, and coffeemakers. An outdoor pool is available. Sea Sound also features an outdoor grill, picnic area with table, and small basketball court. It's open March through November. This motel is non-smoking, and free WiFi is available.

Avon

AVON MOTEL, NC 12; (252) 995-5774; avonmotel.com; $$–$$$. This 45-unit establishment has been in business since 1954 and offers oceanside motel rooms and a handful of efficiency apartments. Motel rooms come with either two double beds or one queen-size or one king-size bed, and each has a microwave, compact refrigerator, and coffeemaker. The efficiencies have either two or three rooms with a variety of bed setups along with fully equipped kitchens. All rooms and efficiencies have air conditioning, cable TV with free HBO, and in-room phones. WiFi is free. Anglers will appreciate the lighted fish-cleaning station at the motel and the guest laundry. Pets are permitted. The motel is located near tackle shops, a fishing pier, four-wheel-drive beach accesses, windsurfing and beach shops, restaurants, and gift stores. The Cape Hatteras Lighthouse is 6 miles away. The Avon Motel is open March through December.

KORU VILLAGE, 40920 Hwy 12; (252) 995-3125; koruvillage.com; $$$$. Six luxurious one-and two-bedroom villas at one of the most inclusive spas on the Outer Banks. King or queen sized beds in all villas. Koru Village includes Pangea Restaurant, complete spa services, nightlife and the Avon Pier. Children and families welcome.

Buxton

⭐ **CAPE HATTERAS BED AND BREAKFAST,** 46223 Old Lighthouse Rd.; (252) 995-6005, (800) 252-3316; capehatterasbandb.com; $$$–$$$$. A short walk to the beach makes this bed and breakfast inn popular with sailboarders, as well as beach lovers, lighthouse enthusiasts, honeymooners, surfers, and couples who just want to get away. The 2-story inn offers several styles of accommodations. Each has its own entrance opening onto a covered porch running the length of the building. Rooms offer a wide variety of options. All units have cable TV and private baths. A large sundeck with comfortable chairs, a gas grill, and a table are available for guests' use. Complimentary breakfast changes daily and includes homemade goodies. Weekly rentals are available, with special accommodations available for honeymooners. The inn is open April through mid-December.

CAPE HATTERAS MOTEL, NC 12; (252) 995-5611, (800) 995-0711; capehatterasmotel.com; $$$$. Cape Hatteras Motel's efficiency units and motel rooms are popular with anglers, surfers, and folks who enjoy Hatteras Island's beaches. Sailboarders especially like this facility because it is near Canadian Hole, one of the best windsurfing and kiteboarding spots on the East Coast (see the **Attractions** chapter). Efficiencies sleep up to six comfortably, offer double beds as well as queen-size and king-size beds, and have full kitchens (they rent weekly, but nightly rentals also may be available). The newer, more modern town houses and apartments have a great view of the beach. The motel has an outdoor swimming pool and spa, and its position at the north end of Buxton is convenient not only to pristine, uncrowded beaches but also to restaurants and services. The Cape Hatteras Motel is open year-round.

CAPE PINES MOTEL, NC 12; (252) 995-5666, (866) 456-9983; capepinesmotel.com; $$$. Cape Pines Motel is a mile south of the Cape Hatteras Lighthouse. Each of the 26 rooms offers cable TV and a full bath. Furnishings have a contemporary beach look. Some rooms have queen-size beds. Cape Pines Motel has three apartments, each offering separate bedrooms, a living room, and a full kitchen. In the summer season the apartments rent on a weekly basis only. Deluxe rooms are available with microwaves, coffeemakers, and refrigerators. The owners like to say that the Cape Pines is so clean, you'd think your mother works here! Stretch out and relax around the pool and the lawn, which has picnic tables and charcoal grills. Fish-cleaning tables. WiFi is free. Cape Pines is close enough to walk or bike to shopping or attractions. The motel is open year-round and pet-friendly.

HATTERAS ISLAND INN, NC 12; (252) 995-6100, (800) 432-1441; hatterasislandinn.com; $$$$. The Hatteras Island Inn is in the heart of Buxton, close to the beach and shops. The 60 units and one suite with exterior access are standard motel-style rooms with king-size or double beds. Rooms are decorated in attractive, soft beach colors; all have cable TV with HBO, refrigerators, and microwaves. Some wheelchair-accessible rooms are available. Free ice and guest laundry are available. Guests have use of the outdoor swimming pool, gazebo, and 3-story watchtower, the latter two providing panoramic views of the ocean, the sound, and nearby Cape Hatteras Lighthouse (see the **Attractions** chapter). AARP and AAA discounts are honored. There is ample parking for boats and campers. The inn is open year-round.

★ **THE INN ON PAMLICO SOUND,** NC 12; (252) 995-7030, (866) 995-7030; innonpamlicosound.com; $$$$. This welcoming inn showcases the Pamlico Sound with awe-inspiring views from its numerous decks, porches, and docks, and from many of its rooms. No need to bring along beach towels or chairs; both are provided for guests. Kayaks and bicycles are also on-site for guest use. A swimming pool overlooks the sound. A 14-seat home theater room is a great spot to watch your favorite team or movie in high definition. All guest rooms have large televisions with DVD players. A movie library with over 2,200 titles gives viewers plenty to choose from, and a book lending library offers some great reading choices. No charges for guests to use any of these amenities. Free WiFi is offered as well. Rooms offer either king- or queen-size beds and are located with a sound view or a garden view. Fresh baked goodies and beverages are provided in the afternoons. Stocked guest beverage refrigerators, snack baskets, candy, and chocolate dishes are located throughout the inn. Cafe Pamlico is also located within this establishment. Well-behaved children over the age of 8 are welcomed. Pets are not allowed.

LIGHTHOUSE VIEW MOTEL, NC 12; (800) 225-7651; lighthouseview .com; $–$$$$. Lighthouse View is easy to find on the big curve in Buxton, where the Hooper family began serving vacationers in the 1950s. Located within a mile of the Hatteras Lighthouse, the motel has more than 85 units including motel rooms, efficiencies, duplexes, villa units, and cottages. Most units are oceanfront, and all are oceanside. The complex has an outdoor pool and hot tub. Surfers, sailboarders, and anglers enjoy the proximity to ocean and sound. Rooms have cable TV, phones, full baths, and daily maid service. Efficiencies accommodate two to six people and are equipped with complete kitchens. The oceanfront villas offer balconies on both the oceanside and soundside. The six duplexes offer two decks and sleep up to six people each. Efficiencies and villas usually rent on a weekly basis, and there is a three-night minimum stay, but they can be rented nightly when available. Note that there is no daily maid service for the villas, efficiencies, and duplexes, but linens can be exchanged. Wheelchair-accessible, one-room efficiencies are also available. Lighthouse View is open year-round.

OUTER BANKS MOTEL, NC 12; (252) 995-5601, (800) 995-1233; outer banksmotel.com; $$–$$$. Situated next to the Cape Hatteras Motel, this establishment offers beachfront motel-style rooms, efficiency units, and two- and three-bedroom cottages. Units accommodate up to eight people comfortably, and some of the units provide an ocean view. Rooms and the efficiency offer enclosed porches with sliding windows and screens for a relaxing evening listening to the ocean. The pine-paneled rooms have tiled baths, microwaves, toasters, and small refrigerators. All units have cable TV and telephones.

The owners also have additional cottages in Buxton Village, a mile from the ocean, near Connor's Market. Because these units are not oceanfront, rental rates are lower. If you rent one of these cottages, you are welcome to use the motel pool and beach facilities. The cottages are clean, simply furnished, and provide the basics for family vacationers, including cable TV. The motel has a coin-operated laundry, a fish-cleaning station, and a guest freezer to store your big catch. If you enjoy crabbing or you just want to paddle around on Pamlico Sound, the motel has several rowboats that guests may use free of charge. This motel is open year-round.

SWELL MOTEL, 46854 NC 12; (252) 489-4484; swellmotel.com; $$–$$$. Traditional family-owned motel. Reasonably priced. Amenities include free kayak rental, bikes, fish cleaning station, and grills to cook your catch. Pet-friendly rooms are available. Kids of all ages welcome. Open year-round.

TOWER CIRCLE MOTEL, 46239 Old Lighthouse Rd.; (252) 995-5353; $$–$$$. Small family-run motel featuring efficiencies rooms. Efficiencies have a small kitchen area with a small four burner range with an oven, sink, refrigerator, microwave and coffee maker. Single rooms have a small refrigerator, a counter area with a microwave and coffee maker. Some rooms are pet-friendly. Closed January and February.

Hatteras Village

BREAKWATER INN, NC 12; (252) 986-2565; harbormotel.com; $$–$$$$. This beautiful inn is in the heart of Hatteras Village. Convenient to restaurants, shops, and services, it's adjacent to the Hatteras charter boat fleet. Breakwater Inn has 21 rooms with 2 queen-size beds and a kitchenette and 2 oversize king suites with living area, full kitchen, a king-size bed, and a whirlpool tub. These rooms have a spectacular view of the Hatteras harbor. The 12 rooms in the Fisherman's Quarters are standard hotel rooms, and one large efficiency is located there also. All rooms have cable TV, microwaves, refrigerators, and telephones. Daily maid service and fresh linens are provided. Guests enjoy the in-ground pool and kiddie wading pool and the long, shaded porches. Pets are allowed in Fisherman's Quarters rooms for a one-time fee.

Ocracoke Island

THE ANCHORAGE INN & MARINA, NC 12; (252) 928-1101; the anchorageinn.com; $$$–$$$$. The Anchorage Inn overlooks Silver Lake and the village. Besides 35 motel-style rooms, the inn has a marina and fishing center, recreational amenities, an outdoor cafe, and gift shops nearby. The attractive 4-story redbrick building with white trim has elevator access to each floor. Accommodations offer some of the best bird's eye views available of the harbor and Ocracoke Village, especially from upper-floor rooms. Most of the rooms have some view of Silver Lake Harbor. Each of the rooms has a king- or queen-size bed or two double beds, full bath, and cable TV with Showtime and Cinemax. The fourth-floor units are nonsmoking rooms and have king-size beds. Wheelchair-accessible rooms are available. Pets are allowed in some rooms for a fee. This is also the only hotel in Ocracoke with an elevator. The Anchorage Inn offers its guests a complimentary continental breakfast, a private pool with a sundeck situated on the harbor, and an on-premise boat dock and ramp. The gazebo at Silver Lake is a perfect place to watch a sunset. Guests can walk to restaurants, shops, and the historic sites on Ocracoke Island. Bike rentals are available. Fishing charters, which depart from the dock across the street, can be booked with the marina's dockmaster. The inn is open March through November. Free WiFi.

BLACKBEARD'S LODGE, Back Rd.; (252) 928-3421, (800) 892-5314; blackbeardslodge.com; $$$$. Ocracoke's oldest hotel, Blackbeard's Lodge was built in 1936 by local entrepreneur, developer, and visionary Robert Stanley Wahab. The building's first floor originally housed Ocracoke's only movie theater on one side and skating rink on the other. "Rooms for hire" occupied the second floor and often accommodated visiting dignitaries, movie stars, and well-heeled types who flew their planes to the island, landed on the barren sand flats, and taxied right up to the front door. Blackbeard's units range from a room with one double bed to a room that sleeps eight with a full kitchen and dining area. All rooms have television. Some rooms feature whirlpool baths, while others may include a kitchenette, king-size bed, refrigerator, or wet bar. Several pet-friendly rooms are available; call ahead to reserve. A game room complete with pool table, foosball, and electronic games is available for inclement days or for nights when friendly competition is in order. A fleet of bicycles are for rent. The lodge has a heated swimming pool with sundeck, wraparound porch with rockers, fish-cleaning table, and free water access for rinsing the salt and sand off your vehicle if surf fishing or beach driving is your passion. Open all year. Free WiFi.

THE CAPTAIN'S LANDING, 324 NC 12; (252) 928-1999; thecaptains landing.com; $$$$. Breathe in the fresh sea air and feel the soft ocean breeze while you stay at the Captain's Landing on scenic Silver Lake in Ocracoke. Luxury suites and a penthouse apartment provide panoramic views of the lighthouse, the village, and harbor life. The first and second floors offer suites with queen-size beds, one-and-a-half baths, a sleeper sofa in the living area, a fully equipped kitchen, and a spacious private deck. The penthouse has a queen-size bed in the master suite and a guest room with two double beds. A sleeper sofa is located in the office. The penthouse has two full baths, a laundry room, expansive dining and living areas, and a well-stocked gourmet kitchen. Enjoy spectacular sunsets from the decks, which are accessible from most rooms. There's free WiFi, and bikes are available to take out for a spin.

⭐ **THE CASTLE BED & BREAKFAST ON SILVER LAKE**, 155 Silver Lake Rd.; (252) 928-3505, (800) 471-8848; thecastlebb.com; $$$–$$$$. Among the finest accommodations on Ocracoke Island, the Castle has been part of the local scenery and part of the island's rich history for more than 50 years. Each of the 11 bedrooms, are furnished with antiques and offer a private bath, television, small refrigerator, and phone. The house has a large living room with a surround-sound entertainment system, central air conditioning, and a custom 9-foot pool table. A full country breakfast is served from 8:30 to 9:30 a.m. (Breakfast is for bed and breakfast guests only.) The top of the Castle has a cupola, private to the Lighthouse Suite, which overlooks Silver Lake, with panoramic views from the sound to the ocean. A large deck extending from the cupola may be used for sunning, relaxing, or watching the sunset. The pier on Silver Lake offers large and small boat dockage in slips up to 50 feet. Dockage is available on a complimentary first-come basis for all guests. In addition to the Castle Bed and Breakfast, courtyard and villa suites are available. One-, two-, and three-bedroom suites are available, each with large whirlpool tubs, full kitchens, and spacious, comfortable living areas. Studio bedrooms are also available with kitchenettes. Everyone who stays at any of the Castle properties may use the heated pool, steam showers, sauna, bicycles, and the conference room.

THE COVE BED AND BREAKFAST, 21 Loop Rd.; (252) 928-4192, (877) 235-5121; thecovebb.com; $$$$. The Cove is a beautiful beach home located within walking distance of Ocracoke's many shops and restaurants. It is a large place—more than 5,000 square feet—and is within view of the sound and Ocracoke's lighthouse. Rooms come equipped with cable TVs and hair dryers. Each room has its own balcony and bath and free WiFi. Full breakfasts are served each day in the large common area. A large screened porch beckons you to sit a while and absorb the wonderful, clean Ocracoke air at the end of a beach day. The inn is a nonsmoking establishment; children age 15 and older are welcome, but pets are not. A public boat dock for launching a kayak or small craft is nearby. Complimentary bicycles are available for touring around town. Transportation is provided to and from the airstrip.

CREWS INN BED AND BREAKFAST, Back Rd.; (252) 928-7011; ocracokers.com; $–$$. The Crews Inn is a place to get away from it all in this vintage 1908 island home. Three rooms have private baths, and two share a bath. All have double beds. The wraparound porch is an especially nice spot for guests to gather, for the building is surrounded by large live oaks and is far enough away from traffic for easy chatting. This is a nonsmoking establishment. The inn serves mostly a continental but occasionally a full breakfast. Crews Inn is open year-round. No pets please.

EDWARDS OF OCRACOKE, Pony Island Rd.; (252) 928-4801, (800) 254-1359; edwardsofocracoke.com; $$. This charming motel, away from the center of Ocracoke and off the main route near the Back Porch Restaurant, consists of eight motel rooms, three efficiencies, six apartments, and two cottages. Most of the units have screened porches and phones. Some open onto a veranda. All have cable TV. Cottages rent weekly during the summer, and efficiencies require a three-day minimum stay. Some have refrigerators. The motel offers inexpensive accommodations in a family setting with a carefully landscaped green lawn, flower beds, and pine trees. The motel is open mid-March through Thanksgiving.

HARBORSIDE MOTEL, across from Silver Lake Harbor; (252) 928-3111; ocracokeharborside.com; $$. This Ocracoke island getaway offers 18 rooms and 4 efficiencies, all well-kept and comfortable with cable TV, phones, and refrigerators. Most rooms offer two double beds; one has three double beds, and two have one double bed. Guests can use the waterfront sundeck, docks, and boat ramp across the street. Harborside has its own gift shop offering clothing, books, gourmet foods, and small gifts. Other shops and restaurants of Ocracoke Village are within walking distance. The Swan Quarter and Cedar Island ferry docks are nearby. The same family has owned this property since 1965, and their hospitality and service are firmly established. A complimentary breakfast of homemade muffins, coffee, juice, and tea is provided. Children under 5 stay free. The motel is open Easter through mid-November. AAA members receive a discount.

THE OCRACOKE HARBOR INN, on Silver Lake Harbor, across from the Coast Guard Station; (252) 928-5731, (888) 456-1998; ocracoke harborinn.com; $$–$$$. This lovely 16-room, 7-suite inn overlooks picturesque Silver Lake Harbor. The inn's private decks with Adirondack chairs are a great place to kick back, relax, and enjoy the view. Each room features either two queen-size beds or one king-size bed and includes a mini fridge, cable TV, coffeepot, hair dryer, and climate control. The suites have two-person whirlpool tubs and kitchenettes. Suites are studio-style or one bedroom. Three 3-bedroom island homes and a two-bedroom apartment are also offered. Wheelchair-accessible rooms are available. A complimentary continental breakfast is served each morning. Also available are complimentary boat docking, outdoor showers, barbecue grills, bicycle rentals, and lots of outdoor decks. The Ocracoke Harbor Inn is open year-round. Pets are not allowed. Free WiFi.

OSCAR'S HOUSE, a block from Silver Lake Harbor; (252) 928-1311; oscarsbb.com; $$. Oscar's House was built in 1940 by the keeper of the Ocracoke Lighthouse and was first occupied by the World War II commander of the Ocracoke Naval Base. Stories abound about Oscar, who lived and worked on the island for many years as a fisherman and hunting guide. This guesthouse has operated as a bed and breakfast since 1984. The house retains the original beadboard walls, and all four guest rooms are delightfully furnished. One upstairs bedroom has a loft, creating a comfortable setting. Two baths, one upstairs and one down, accommodate guests, as does an outdoor shower (with dressing room). The large kitchen with a big table is available to guests; however, the stove is off-limits. Pets are not allowed. Oscar's House has a deck area complete with barbecue grills. Meals are eaten inside or outdoors. The house is within walking distance of all village shops and restaurants, and bicycles are free for guests. This bed and breakfast is open year-round.

PAM'S PELICAN BED AND BREAKFAST, across from fire station; (252) 928-1661, (888) 773-5422; pamspelican.com; $$–$$$. Built originally as a lodge, Pam's Pelican captures the feel of laid-back Ocracoke style that many vacationers seek while staying on the island. The four rooms are spacious, bright, and cheerful and have private baths. Amenities include cable TV, an in-room fridge, a small pool, and free use of bicycles (see the **Getting Here, Getting Around** chapter for more details). The lodge is open year-round. Pam's Pelican is pet-friendly.

PONY ISLAND MOTEL, NC 12; (252) 928-4411; ponyislandmotel.com; $$–$$$. At the edge of Ocracoke Village, a short distance from Silver Lake Harbor, Pony Island Motel offers 54 rooms, efficiencies, and suites and two cottages. The grounds are spacious and inviting. The inn hosts families and couples in search of peace and solitude on Ocracoke Island. Most of the units have either single or double occupancy, but the motel offers some rooms that accommodate up to five people. Each room has a telephone, refrigerator, cable TV, and wireless Internet. The efficiencies have fully equipped kitchens. Rooms are refurbished regularly but maintain a traditional decor. One wheelchair-accessible room is available. A 23-unit, 3-story addition overlooks the pool. Rooms have a kitchenette. Suites have a full kitchen and whirlpool tubs. The motel is within walking distance of the Ocracoke Lighthouse and other island attractions. Bike rentals and boat docking are available. The pool and spacious lawn with picnic tables and grills offer plenty of room for family activities. The Pony Island Restaurant, a local favorite, is next door (see the **Dining** chapter). Pony Island Motel is open year-round.

★ **SAND DOLLAR MOTEL, Sand Dollar Ln.; (866) 928-5571; sand dollarmotelofocracoke.com; $$–$$$.** This establishment is in the heart of Ocracoke Village behind the Back Porch Restaurant (there are no street signs). Fresh flowers welcome guests to the lobby. The Sand Dollar has 11 rooms and a 2-bedroom cottage. Two of the rooms are efficiencies with small microwaves and coffeemakers; all rooms have refrigerators and cable TV. Bedding options include queen- and double-size beds. One special room is connected to the pool and has a private deck and a king-size bed. Pets are not allowed. Guests enjoy a dip in the pool. Repeat visits are common at this neat little place, so book your stay early. Open year-round.

THURSTON HOUSE INN, NC 12; (252) 928-6037; thurstonhouseinn .com; $$$. The Thurston House Inn was built in the 1920s. The former home of Capt. Tony Thurston Gaskill is now on the Register of Historic Places in North Carolina and has been featured in *Our State Magazine*. The inn offers six rooms, each with a private bath. A phone is available in the hallway, and each room has cable TV and wireless high-speed Internet. All rooms are heated and air-conditioned and have private decks and porches with either king- or queen-size beds. Guests enjoy relaxing on the covered porches and deck, which connects the inn's two buildings. A continental breakfast is part of the package. Children older than age 16 are welcome, but require their own room. Smoking is allowed on the porches. The inn is within walking distance of Silver Lake, Ocracoke Lighthouse, and various stores, restaurants, and historic sites. Local airport pickup is available. Reservations are recommended. The inn is open March 1 through November.

WEEKLY & LONG-TERM COTTAGE RENTALS

If your idea of the perfect vacation is to settle down with all the comforts of a home away from home, the Outer Banks is a perfect choice. By far the most popular accommodations here are private beach cottages. More than 13,500 rental cottages are available in Dare County, and that's not including the thousands of cottages available in Corolla in Currituck County or on Ocracoke Island in Hyde County. From the unique off-road beaches of Carova just south of the Virginia line to the removed island of Ocracoke, accessible only by plane, boat, or ferry, you'll find a tremendous variety in price, location, and character. Although most vacationers stay for a week, longer- and shorter-term rentals are available throughout the year.

Most beach cottages are owned by individuals and are represented by a property management firm, although increasingly Airbnb is part of the mix. Usually these cottages reflect the individual tastes and preferences of their owners. Although property management firms or rental companies will set their own minimum standards for the homes they represent, beach homes vary widely in design, decor, and the amenities they offer. You can rent anything from a palatial nine-bedroom oceanfront mansion with a private pool, home office, and media room to a cozy little saltbox on the sound side.

Rental companies compete rigorously to secure the greatest possible number of bookings for their owners, and the trend is to add more amenities, thus encouraging guests to return again and again. In recent years many companies have encouraged their cottage owners to add greater value to a week's vacation

These brightly-colored, beachfront rental condos have all the luxuries of home—and then some! CATNAP72/GettyImages

by including, as standard, amenities that used to be luxuries. Whirlpool baths, hot tubs, appealing interior decorating, book and video libraries, fireplaces, baby cribs, and playpens are becoming increasingly common, particularly in the newer properties. Veteran visitors to the Outer Banks are accustomed to bringing their own linens and towels as only a few property management firms require their owners to provide linens.

Of course, you'll pay more for these luxuries. Rental prices are based primarily on the season, the cottage's proximity to the ocean, the number of occupants it "sleeps," and the amenities it offers. The peak, most expensive, season runs from mid-June through the end of August. Substantial discounts are offered in the fall and spring, considered "midseason" by most companies, and, of course, the best bargains are from late November to late March. More vacationers are discovering the joys of the Outer Banks during seasons other than summer: With its temperate climate, the Outer Banks offers a great variety of outdoor activities to enjoy, even if the weather is too cold for ocean swimming or lounging on the beach.

i Dr. Beach, also known as Dr. Stephen P. Leatherman, is known for annually publishing his list of "America's Best Beaches." Each year, it seems Ocracoke and Cape Hatteras make the top 10 ranking on his score sheet. Dr. Beach doesn't score just based upon personal preference; he actually develops his winning list from a score sheet of 50 standards, including quality of the water and accessibility. It's good to be on top!

LOCATION, LOCATION, LOCATION!

An "oceanfront" cottage is one that sits directly on the beach with no cottages or lots to the east facing the ocean. Some, but not all, have private walkways to the ocean, an especially convenient and important feature if the cottage sits behind a dune. (Dunes are fragile and need protection. It's against the law to climb them.) If your cottage doesn't have a private walkway, you'll have to use the community or public access; check on this when you make your reservation. Also, although most oceanfront cottages offer spectacular vistas, some have tall dunes obstructing the view from one or more levels. Oceanfront cottages without views are more the exception than the rule, but you won't encounter any disappointing surprises if you double-check at the time of rental.

There's no underestimating the convenience of an oceanfront cottage. You don't have to schlep the beach equipment very far, and when the little ones get cranky, you can sun yourself on your deck or patio and listen to the pounding surf while they nap inside.

The next best thing to oceanfront is "semi-oceanfront," which usually means one lot back from oceanfront. The distance to the ocean varies, but many semi-oceanfronts still offer good views of the water and reasonable beach-going convenience. In some areas, especially Kitty Hawk, Kill Devil Hills, and Nags Head, you'll have to cross the Beach Road (NC 12) to get to the surf.

When a cottage is described as "between the highways," it is located between the Beach Road and US 158. Actual distances from the beach vary, but you can expect a 5- to 15-minute walk. Cottages identified as "westside" are located west of US 158 in Kitty Hawk, Kill Devil Hills, and Nags Head. Those west of NC 12 in Corolla, Duck, and Southern Shores are referred to as "soundside." Of course, "soundfront" cottages are those with no houses or lots between them and the sound.

Westside or soundside cottages tend to be among the last to book and can offer a very affordable and pleasant alternative to costlier oceanside cottages. Many communities offer pools, tennis courts, hiking trails, and other amenities on the soundside to enhance rentals. Some vacationers have come to prefer the soundside areas for their tranquility and the convenience of certain water sports, such as windsurfing and canoeing. Finally, many soundfront cottages offer views as spectacular as those on the ocean. It's the place to be if you prefer the sunset to the sunrise. (See the **Real Estate** section for more information on individual communities.)

Most rental companies identify, either in terms of number of lots from the beach or distance measured in feet, how close (or far) cottages are to the ocean, so you should get an idea when you make your reservation how long a trek you can expect.

WHEN & HOW TO RESERVE YOUR COTTAGE

As you might imagine, properties closest to the ocean are snatched up quickly. Many rental companies offer returning guests the opportunity to make advance reservations for the next year as they check out, so cottages in prime locations will often have several weeks reserved even before the New Year. Expect to make your reservation in January or February if you have your heart set on a particular cottage on the ocean. Otherwise you'll still have a good variety from which to choose if you reserve by the end of March. Don't despair, however, if you can't make a decision until later. You might have to call around, but you can usually find something to rent, possibly even at the last minute. (One caveat: The pickings will be slim for spur-of-the-moment trips in summer months.)

Some rental companies still publish a color brochure or catalog describing their properties; the new editions typically are available after Thanksgiving. Increasingly, though, rental companies use the online services as their main tool to let the public know about their properties. You'll find photos and property descriptions not only in a company's brochure but on its website as well.

Online availability and reservation booking capabilities are often the easiest way to complete the process.

The rental company's catalog or website will almost certainly cover the essential elements of the lease. Make sure you read these thoroughly before making your reservation, and form a list of questions you want to ask the reservationist. You'd be surprised at how familiar many reservationists are with the properties they rent. This is also the right time to discuss any special needs anyone in your party may have. You'll typically be asked to secure your cottage with a deposit— usually 50 percent, with the balance due 30 days in advance of your visit.

> **i** "Cottage" is the traditional beach name for a vacation rental house on the Outer Banks. A "cottage" may be a tiny saltbox, of which there are only a few, or a mansion with numerous bedrooms, bathrooms, and Jacuzzis or hot tubs. Take your pick! Either way, it's a "cottage" to insiders

.AMENITIES

Rental companies list the amenities offered at each cottage on their websites and in their catalogs. In addition, most companies require their owners to supply certain amenities as standard. Typical standard items include air conditioning, telephone, television, DVD player, washer and dryer, barbecue, microwave— most appliances and items you'd expect to find in the typical home. Still, don't take anything for granted. Read the descriptions and your lease thoroughly to avoid misunderstanding.

Unless the lease stipulates that your rental is equipped with linens and towels, plan to bring your own. The cottage listing will tell you the sizes and number of beds in the home. You'll also need to supply your own toiletries, paper products, and cleaning supplies such as laundry and dishwashing detergents, sponges, and paper towels. It's a good idea to arrive with enough of the basics to get you through a half day so you won't need to visit the grocery store immediately.

If you don't feel like hauling a lot of extra stuff to the beach, you can rent just about anything you need, including linens, towels, beach equipment, bicycles, outdoor furniture, and recreational equipment. At the end of this chapter is a list of companies you can call in advance; many will deliver the items you request right to your cottage.

MINIMUM STAYS

During the mid- and off-seasons, you'll of course have more options than in peak season, when occupancy runs at close to 100 percent. During the summer it's very difficult to find a cottage to rent for less than a week. Most rent from Saturday to Saturday or Sunday to Sunday. Some families enjoy renting for two or even more consecutive weeks, but don't expect a price break.

You'll have better luck finding a shorter-term rental during slower seasons. Most companies offer what they call "partial" rentals from September through May or June. Some charge a flat fee for a three- or four-day period; others charge a nightly fee. Make sure you understand how the fee is determined. In the off-seasons many rental companies get creative to increase bookings. That's the time to look for special getaway packages. As you might expect, the mid- and off-seasons offer some excellent bargains and are especially popular with vacationers who don't have school age children in tow. If you have the option of enjoying the Outer Banks during the slower seasons, you'll be delighted with the meandering pace and quiet. Most restaurants and shops now stay open at least through Thanksgiving, and more and more are extending their operating times well beyond that. Visiting the Outer Banks during off-season holidays is becoming increasingly popular.

ACCOMMODATIONS

ADVANCE RENTS

Expect to pay an advance rent, typically 50 percent of the full lease amount, soon after you make your reservation. It's usually due within 10 days. Personal checks are commonly accepted if the reservation is made in plenty of time for the check to clear. Some companies allow credit card transactions, but be aware that some will charge an additional fee to cover the extra costs charged by the bank that handles the card. In most cases the balance of the lease amount is due 30 days prior to arrival. If payment is accepted at check-in, it's usually required in the form of a certified check or cash. Most rental companies will not accept a personal check upon arrival.

> **i** Before making your cottage reservation, check online to see if the homes you're interested in offer a virtual tour. If so, you'll be able to view several rooms within each home before making your choice.

SECURITY DEPOSITS

Besides advance rents, most rental companies also require their guests to pay a security deposit. This, of course, is for the owner's protection. The amounts required vary depending upon the company's policies. Cottages are typically inspected between check-ins to make sure everything is in order. If you notice any damage in a cottage just after arriving, inform your rental company immediately. A little extra caution on your part will help prevent any misunderstanding about who caused the damage. Remember that rental companies are anxious to please you, but they also answer to their owners.

If anything is damaged during your stay or is determined missing after you leave, expect to have an amount deducted from your security deposit. Cottages that allow pets usually require an extra deposit for possible pet damage and a standard fee for flea extermination after you and your pet depart.

HURRICANE EVACUATION REFUNDS

Most rental companies now offer insurance with each reservation made. In accordance with North Carolina's Vacation Rental Act, if a guest buys vacation insurance, or if a guest is offered insurance but declines the offer, the real estate company is not required to reimburse that guest for any rental days that he or she loses as a result of hurricane evacuation. Each rental company sets its own policy governing refunds in the event of a hurricane. The few remaining companies that do not offer insurance generally may issue a partial or full refund in the event of a mandatory evacuation. Each area's local government officials are ultimately responsible for issuing evacuation orders. The County of Currituck has jurisdiction over Corolla and the four-wheel-drive beach areas, Hyde County has jurisdiction over Ocracoke, and Dare County governs every place in between.

The island of Ocracoke is usually evacuated before all other areas because access and egress is only by ferry or boat, and the rough waters stirred up by a hurricane even hundreds of miles away will make passage difficult or impossible as the storm approaches. Hatteras Island also tends to evacuate early because sections of NC 12 quickly flood when waters rise. If a mandatory evacuation of your area is ordered, comply.

Most rental companies will not issue refunds for days you don't occupy the property once reentry is permitted. Most Ocracoke property managers make exceptions for refunds in case the ferries aren't operating. These policies do vary from business to business, so make inquiries along with your reservation.

Consider buying travel insurance, which will protect your vacation investment in a variety of unexpected scenarios.

HANDLING/INSPECTION FEES & TAXES

Some rental companies charge a handling fee for processing information and an inspection fee for cottage inspection following your checkout. This is a non-refundable fee assessed in addition to other charges.

In Dare County a combined 12.75 percent tax is added to all rents and fees. The taxes in Currituck County total 13.75 percent.

PET RULES & COSTS

Some cottage owners allow guests to bring pets, within certain limits, but you'll be assessed extra fees for the privilege. You can usually count on an extra cleaning and extermination fee and a higher security deposit. Rental companies will often restrict the size of the pets accepted (for example, dogs up to 75 pounds), but if your pet does not conform to the restrictions, ask the rental manager if it's possible to make an exception. Many companies will contact the cottage owner in an attempt to accommodate a reasonable request. Be aware, too, that some cottages will allow dogs but not cats and vice versa. Whatever you do, don't bring a pet "illegally"—this is almost always grounds for eviction without a refund.

CHECK-IN & CHECKOUT TIMES

Of course you're anxious to begin your vacation, but you'll save yourself (and others) aggravation if you respect check-in and checkout times. Rental companies need this time to clean and inspect cottages and perform minor maintenance.

Checkout is usually by 10 a.m.; check-in is usually at 4 p.m., give or take an hour. (These standard times account for the heavy traffic on Saturday and Sunday mornings and afternoons.) Most companies allow you to occupy your cottage earlier if it has been serviced properly, but don't arrive expecting this. If you want to travel during off-peak hours in the summer and plan to arrive several hours before check-in, head for one of the beach access areas that have showers and changing facilities, and just plan to spend the time relaxing. If you plan to check in after the rental company's office closes, most will make arrangements to leave your keys and cottage information in an outside box for pickup.

Be prompt when you check out. This is a courtesy to the rental company and the next guest. You might be assessed an extra fee if you overstay your welcome!

OCCUPANCY

The number of people your cottage can accommodate is listed in the description of the property in the rental brochure. This is determined by the number and type of beds and the septic and water capacity. Do not exceed the maximum occupancy or you could risk eviction. Most rental companies rent to family groups only and will not rent to minors. Any violation of this policy could result in a ruined vacation—and no refund.

MAIL, TELEPHONE, WIFI & FAX SERVICES

When you make a reservation, you can request the cottage's phone number to leave with those back home who may need to reach you. Often the cottage's physical address and telephone number are printed on your lease, which you'll receive after making your initial payment. Almost all cottages have telephones these days, although a few of the older ones do not (and with the proliferation of cell phones, this may not be a problem for you). At any rate, the caveat once again is to know exactly what you're renting. Of course, you'll be required to pay for long distance calls, and many home owners have a block on their lines to prevent direct dialed long distance calls. Either bring along a calling card or buy a prepaid phone card, but don't make calls from your cottage that will be charged to the homeowner.

If you expect to receive mail while on vacation, ask the reservationist for the proper mailing address and make sure you tell your correspondents to mark the envelope clearly with your name and cottage identification. The same common sense applies if you expect to receive faxes while you're on vacation. Most rental companies either have a fax machine set aside for guest use or will let you use theirs, but a fee is almost always charged. If you're expecting something important, it's a good idea to instruct the sender to call you when the fax has been sent to be sure it arrives. Rental companies are exceptionally busy during summer and peak holiday times, so your fax might be one of a few dozen that comes in over the course of a day.

If wireless Internet access is important to you while staying on the Outer Banks, be sure to check your rental cottage description. It will be listed, if the home offers this service. Most real estate companies offer this search option to help choose a home.

TRASH PICKUP & RECYCLING

Rental companies usually supply information on designated trash pickup days in the check-in packet. When you check out, bag your refuse securely and make sure the receptacle sits beside the road, ready for pickup.

Recycling is with few exceptions the renter's responsibility. Some communities provide recycling service and the proper bins, but in most areas you'll need to carry your recyclables to one of the collection points. Ask your rental company for the location nearest your cottage and for sorting instructions.

Many beach access areas now have recycling bins in addition to trash cans to keep the beach litter-free.

EQUIPMENT RENTALS & RELATED SERVICES

If you'd rather not take everything with you to the beach, Outer Banks equipment rental companies from north to south can provide almost anything you need or want, including baby furniture, beach chairs, umbrellas, bicycles, linens, fishing gear, grills, and more. You can also rent recreational equipment such as personal watercraft, boogie boards, surfboards, SUPs and kayaks. Check the **Water Sports** chapter for companies that specialize in these. The following listings cover companies that supply the widest variety of equipment and services.

AT YOUR SERVICE, (252) 261-5286; atyourserviceobx.com. Serving the needs of vacationers on the Outer Banks since 1988, At Your Service takes on such tiresome chores as running errands and buying groceries by acting as your personal concierge. The service has babysitters (it's the oldest babysitting and elder-care service on the Outer Banks). It can also help in stocking your vacation cottage with groceries and other necessities before you arrive, providing linens and cleaning service, arranging in-house personal chef service, and seeing to details to make a vacation run smoothly. At Your Service has a well-trained and competent staff.

BEACH OUTFITTERS, NC 12, Ocracoke; (252) 928-6261; ocracokeisland realty.com/beach-outfitters. Beach Outfitters, at Ocracoke Island Realty, is open all year and accepts reservations. Free delivery and pickup are available on Ocracoke Island with an order of more than $100. Available rental items include beach chairs and umbrellas, towels and linens, bikes, rollaway beds, baby equipment, TVs, DVD players, steamer pots, and kitchen appliances.

JUST FOR THE BEACH RENTALS, Corolla, Duck, and Kill Devil Hills; (866) 629-7368; justforthebeach.com. Delivery is available from Nags Head to Corolla, or you can stop in the store to browse through numerous items. Beach equipment, bikes, baby supplies, linens, fishing rods, and beach wheelchairs are among the items this company leases. See website for addresses.

METRO RENTALS, US 158 and Colington Rd., MP 8, Kill Devil Hills; (252) 480-3535, (866) 490-3535; weddingrentalsobx.com. This company specializes in wedding and catering needs, party supplies and tents, heavy equipment. Delivery to anywhere on the Outer Banks.

MONEYSWORTH BEACH HOME EQUIPMENT RENTALS, 947 West Kitty Hawk Rd., Kitty Hawk; (800) 833-5233; mworth.com. With Moneysworth, all items are delivered to your vacation home on your check-in day and picked up after you check out. This company has a wide assortment of beach and sports equipment, TVs, DVD players, grills, baby items, linens, and bicycles. And the best part is you do not have to be present for delivery or pickup service. They'll deliver whatever you need from Carova to Hatteras Village.

OCEAN ATLANTIC RENTALS, Corolla, Duck, Kill Devil Hills, and Avon; (800) 635-9559; oceanatlanticrentals.com. Ocean Atlantic combines quality equipment with reasonable rates and full service to give you the best values in rental ware on the beach. All baby items meet federal safety standards, and Ocean Atlantic uses well-known brand-name equipment. Beach umbrellas and chairs, bikes (including electric bikes), cribs, TVs, DVD players, kayaks, linens, grills, the latest videos and DVDs, and water sports equipment are among the items Ocean Atlantic offers. Surfing lessons for all skill levels are taught out of their four locations. Ocean Atlantic also has a full-service wedding rental package complete with dance floors and tents.

Candy-colored cabins are available as vacation rentals on Cape Hatteras.
THOSTEND/GETTYIMAGES

COTTAGE RENTAL COMPANIES

Many rental companies have more than one office, so check the listing to see which areas they serve. Listings proceed from north to south.

A company's inventory of cottages can change from year to year, but almost all companies offer some accommodations that allow pets, a few wheelchair—accessible cottages, and partial—week rentals in the mid- and off—seasons. In the following listings, we concentrate on which areas companies cover and approximately how many cottages they represent. We recommend that you contact companies directly for comprehensive information. Nearly all will supply you with a free brochure or catalog of their rental properties.

Multiple Locations

ATLANTIC REALTY, 1180 Duck Rd., Duck; 4729 N. Croatan Hwy, Kitty Hawk; (877) 858-4795; atlanticrealty-nc.com. This company manages rental homes and condominiums from Corolla to South Nags Head for year-round and seasonal rental. Pets are accepted in some units.

BEACH REALTY & CONSTRUCTION/KITTY HAWK RENTALS, Monteray Plz., Corolla; 1180 Duck Rd., Duck; US 158, MP 6, Kill Devil Hills; (800) 635-1559; beachrealtync.com. This company manages properties from Ocean Hill to South Nags Head. Year-round and weekly rentals available. Pets accepted in some units, some units are wheelchair accessible.

BRINDLEY BEACH VACATIONS, 1023 Ocean Trl., Corolla; 1213-C Duck Rd., Duck; 3719 North Croatan Hwy, Kitty Hawk; (877) 642-3224. Probably the largest property management company on the Outer Banks with more than 600 properties from Corolla to South Nags Head. Mostly weekly rentals.

HATTERAS REALTY, NC 12, 26006, Waves Plaza, Waves; 41156 Hwy 12, Avon; 57204 Atlantic View Dr., Hatteras; (800) 428-8372; hatterasrealty.com. Hatteras Realty manages properties on Hatteras Island for weekly rental only. Units may be rented by partial weeks during the offseason. Pets are accepted in some units. Wheelchair-accessible cottages are available. Every guest has free access to the pool and tennis courts at Club Hatteras. Vacationers have depended on Hatteras Realty for their accommodations since 1983. A fee-based kids' program for ages 4 to 12 both entertains and educates the little ones.

RESORT REALTY, TimBuck II Shopping Village, Corolla; 1248 Duck Road, Duck; MP 14½, Hwy 158, Nags Head; (252) 261-8282; 26200 W. Vista Dr., Waves; (252) 995-5891; resortrealty.com. Resort Realty manages weekly rental properties from Corolla to South Nags Head. Some three-night packages are available with a maximum of five days' notice. Some cottages allow pets. Renters leasing a special resort club home can check-in as early as 11 a.m.

SEASIDE VACATIONS, 1070D Ocean Trl., Corolla; 3620 N. Croatan Hwy, Kitty Hawk; (866) 884-0267; outerbanksvacations.com. Seaside Vacations offers the best service possible for every guest. The company represents a select group of vacation rental accommodations. Properties range from Corolla to South Nags Head and include condominiums, cottages, and palatial oceanfront estates. Staff members have personally visited every property and can make the best recommendations for a property based on a guest's needs. Check out their Club Seaside for fun fee-based activities.

SUN REALTY, 1500 S. Croatan Hwy, Kill Devil Hills, (252) 441-7033; 1135 Ocean Trl., Corolla,(252) 453-8822; 1316 Duck Rd., Duck, (252)-261-7911; 6385 N. Croatan Hwy, Ste. 101, Kitty Hawk, (252) 261-1152; 26148 Hwy 12, Salvo, (252) 987-2766; 41838 Hwy 12, Avon, (252) 995-5865; sunrealty nc.com. Sun Realty is one of the largest realty companies on the Outer Banks, with more than 30 years of making Outer Banks vacationers' dreams come true. Sun Realty prides itself on providing the highest level of customer service and lists the largest selection and variety of homes on the Outer Banks. A concierge is available within each Sun Realty location to help plan special events.

MIDGETT REALTY, 23198 Hwy 12, Rodanthe, (252) 987-2350; 39432 Hwy 12, Avon, (252) 995-5333; 57783 Hwy 12, Hatteras, (252) 986-2841; (866) 348-8819; midgettrealty.com. Midgett Realty manages properties from Rodanthe to Hatteras Village for weekly rentals. Three-night rentals are available during the off-season, and some units accept pets. Several wheelchair-accessible units are offered. Serving Hatteras Island has been a family tradition for more than 100 years.

STAN WHITE REALTY, 812 Ocean Trl., Corolla; US 158, MP 10½, 1232 NC 12, Duck; Nags Head; (800) 338-3233; outerbanksrentals.com. Stan White Realty rents properties from Corolla to Nags Head. Three-day golf packages available.

TWIDDY & COMPANY, 1127A Schoolhouse Ln., Corolla; 1181 NC 12, Duck; (800) 489-4339; twiddy.com. Twiddy & Company offers exceptional Outer Banks vacation rentals from Carova to Southern Shores. Special event and wheelchair-accessible homes are available, as are homes from the oceanfront to the sound. Weddings, corporate retreats, and other functions can be accommodated. Many of Twiddy's choice homes include private pools and spas; pets are allowed at some accommodations.

VILLAGE REALTY, 501B Hunt Club Dr., Corolla; US 158, MP 14½, Nags Head; (800) 548-9688; 1075 Irvin Garrish Hwy, Ocracoke, (252)-928-6261; villagerealtyobx.com. You are in good hands when you choose to rent from Village Realty. Village Realty represents oceanfront, soundfront, and in-between homes from Corolla through Nags Head, and includes the Currituck Club, the only golf community on the Currituck Outer Banks. Rentals at the Currituck Club include use of the pool, fitness center, and other amenities. Ask about golf packages. Some cottages allow pets. Linens and towels provided for every stay.

Currituck Mainland

KEES VACATIONS, 101 Pan Ridge Ct., Ste. A, Point Harbor; (866) 316-1843. One of the newest Outer Banks property management companies. Generally offers more flexibility in arrival and departure days and length of stay than traditional companies have done.

Corolla

COROLLA CLASSIC VACATIONS, 1196 Ocean Trl.; (866) 453-9660. Corolla Classic Vacations manages vacation homes in the Corolla area, including Pine Island, Ocean Sands, Ocean Lake, Crown Point, Ocean Hill, and Corolla Village. Many of the homes are equipped with elevators and are wheelchair accessible. Properties with access to golf, tennis, private pools, and hot tubs are available, and some units allow pets. Beds are made and bath towels are ready upon your arrival.

ÉLAN VACATIONS, Hunt Club Dr., Currituck Club Center; (866) 760-ELAN (3526); elanvacations.com. Élan Vacations is a full-service travel company representing luxurious vacation homes along the Outer Banks. Élan Vacations likes to provide a relaxing and fun-filled experience with highly personalized service to guests and owners. A concierge is available who can reserve anything from maid service to hang-gliding lessons to dinner reservations at your favorite restaurant. Élan guests are greeted with an assortment of gifts, including select North Carolina wine, coffee, and other Élan products.

KARICHELE REALTY, Timbuck II Shopping Village; (800) 453-2377; karichele.com. Karichele Realty manages properties in Corolla and the four-wheel-drive area. During the off-season, weekend packages are available. Pets allowed in some units. Wheelchair-accessible cottages also are available.

Duck

CAROLINA DESIGNS REALTY, 1197 NC 12; (800) 368-3825; carolina designs.com. Carolina Designs manages weekly rentals ranging from one-bedroom condos to eight-bedroom estates, with linens included. Properties are primarily from Corolla to Southern Shores and Nags Head. Many of the homes have pools and allow pets and most offer wireless Internet.

Southern Shores

SOUTHERN SHORES REALTY, 5 Ocean Blvd., Southern Shores; NC 12, Kitty Hawk; (800) 334-1000; southernshores.com. Southern Shores Realty manages year-round and weekly rentals throughout the Outer Banks. Weekend packages also are available year-round. Dogs are accepted in some units. Ramps and elevators are offered in some cottages.

Kitty Hawk

JOE LAMB JR. & ASSOCIATES, REALTORS, US 158, MP 2; (800) 552-6257; joelambjr.com. This company manages properties ranging from 2-bedroom cottages to 13-bedroom homes and year-round rentals from Corolla to South Nags Head. Three-night packages are offered during the off-season. Pets are accepted in some cottages. Wheelchair-accessible rentals are also available. Units in some developments include pool access. Many have private pools.

OUTER BANKS BLUE, 3732 N. Croatan Hwy; (252) 255-1220, (844) 557-3463; outerbanksblue.com. With properties from South Nags Head to

Corolla, Outer Banks Blue is noted as one of the most innovative property management companies on the Outer Banks. As an example, the company has gone to keyless entry for all their cottages, allowing guests to arrive on the Outer Banks on their schedule instead of at a specific check-in time.

Nags Head

COVE REALTY, between NC 12 and US 158, MP 13½; (800) 635-7007; coverealty.com. Cove Realty manages Dare County properties north of Oregon Inlet for year-round, weekly, and student rental. Pets are accepted in some units. Weekend packages are available during the off-season. Guests have access, for a small fee, to a swimming pool as well as to tennis courts in Old Nags Head Cove.

OUTER BANKS RESORT RENTALS, Croatan Centre, MP 13½; (252) 441-2134; outerbanksresorts.com. Outer Banks Resort Rentals manages sales and rentals of time-shares from Duck to South Nags as well as a few in Hatteras. Fifteen timeshare resorts are represented.

RENTALS ON THE OCEAN, 3022 S. Croatan Hwy, Pirates Quay; (252) 441-5005; rentalsontheocean.com. Do you want to reserve your spot on the beach and bring Fido, too? Rentals on the Ocean may have just what you're looking for. They offer cottages for families of all sizes from 2 to 26, and all

This modest beach house faces the ocean on a beach in Nags Head.
CATNAP72/GETTYIMAGES

their cottages accept pets. Every cottage is either oceanfront or oceanview. Rentals on the Ocean offers cottages year-round.

Roanoke Island

PIRATE'S COVE REALTY, Nags Head–Manteo Causeway, Manteo; (888) 314-5795; pirates-cove.com. Pirate's Cove Realty manages properties in the Pirate's Cove Resort for weekly rentals. Two-night weekends also are offered during the off-season. Some cottages accept pets. All units include access to an outdoor swimming pool, tennis courts, playground, and free boat slips. Pirate's Cove Realty also manages properties at the Shallowbag Bay Club, a nearby development on the water closer to downtown Manteo. These one- to three-bedroom luxury waterfront condominiums are in an upscale marina. Several secluded waterfront properties are also offered in downtown Manteo.

Hatteras Island

AVON COTTAGES, NC 12, Avon; (252) 995-4123; avoncottages.com. Each of Avon Cottages' rental homes has a magnificent view of the Atlantic Ocean. Eight are oceanfront, 7 are semi-oceanfront, and 11 are oceanside, ranging from 1 to 5 bedrooms. All cottages have a large combination living room/dining room/kitchen, plus central heat and air, a microwave oven, and remote color TV with HBO. Fully equipped kitchens include plates and utensils; you may bring your own sheets and towels or rent them on-site. Laundry facilities, outside showers, and fish-cleaning tables are provided. Parking is also available.

COLONY REALTY CORP., NC 12, Avon; (800) 962-5256; colonyrealty corp.com. Colony handles affordable long-term rentals in Avon, Buxton, Frisco, and Hatteras. Most of the units, which are single-family cottages or condos, will accept pets.

DOLPHIN REALTY, NC 12, Hatteras Village; (800) 338-4775; dolphin realtyhatteras.com. This company manages properties, including homes and one—room efficiencies, throughout Hatteras Island. Some are available for year-round rental. Pets are accepted in some units.

ACCOMMODATIONS

OUTER BEACHES REALTY, NC 12, Avon, Waves, and Rodanthe; (800) 627-1850; outerbeaches.com. Outer Beaches Realty manages a large selection of rental cottages from Rodanthe to Hatteras Village. Weekly and three-day rentals are available. A few allow pets. Some wheelchair-accessible properties also are offered. Dedicated exclusively to Hatteras Island, Outer Beaches Realty offers the island's largest selection of vacation rental cottages. Upon check-in you'll find a starter amenities bag inside your cottage. Concierge services are available, as well as luxurious signature Elite homes.

> **i** What's the weather like? During summer, of course, expect hot days and balmy nights. In spring and fall, temperatures can range from the 80s to the 40s. Winter weather fluctuates from warm (70s) and sunny to starkly cold (30s and 40s), with averages in the 50s. Bring a variety of clothing for maximum comfort.

SURF OR SOUND REALTY, NC 12, Avon; (800) 237-1138; surforsound .com. Surf or Sound Realty offers almost 500 cottages on Hatteras Island. Pets are accepted in some units. Wheelchair-accessible rentals also are available. You can make reservations on the website.

Ocracoke Island

OCRACOKE ISLAND REALTY, NC 12; (877) 646-2822; ocracokeisland realty.com. Ocracoke Island Realty manages weekly rental properties on Ocracoke. Three-night packages are available during the off-season. A few of these cottages allow pets.

YEAR-ROUND RENTALS

It can be quite a challenge to find a suitable property for long-term residential rental. However, it's not terribly difficult to find what most people on the Outer Banks call a "winter rental," a time period that usually refers to late fall through early spring, when the cottage is not usually booked for weekly rentals. If you're looking for year-round residential or seasonal accommodations during summer, you'll need to begin your search as soon as possible.

Some rental companies deal lightly in long-term rentals, but few make it a specialty. It's worth some phone calls to the companies that specialize in the areas in which you're interested, but a better bet is probably to check the classifieds in the local newspapers. If you plan to spend the summer working on the Outer Banks, ask your employer for suggestions. Some smart businesspeople are beginning to help their seasonal workers by offering housing.

Good places to look for long-term rentals are in Colington Harbour, on Roanoke Island, and between the highways in Nags Head, Kill Devil Hills, and Kitty Hawk. Southern Shores has a large year-round community. Currituck County, just north of the Wright Memorial Bridge, also offers some affordable options.

The following companies manage year-round rentals: Atlantic Realty, Colony Realty Corporation, Cove Realty, Dolphin Realty, Gateway Realty, Jim Perry & Company, Joe Lamb Jr. & Associates, Kitty Dunes Realty, Kitty Hawk Rentals/Beach Realty & Construction, Seaside Vacations, Southern Shores Realty, Stan White Realty & Construction, Sun Realty, and Wright Property Management. Most of these companies are listed in greater detail earlier in this chapter or in the **Real Estate** section.

CAMPING

Imagine drifting off to sleep on a bed of soft sand with the murmur of waves gently kissing the sandy shoreline. A whispering breeze ruffles your tent, ushering in the sounds of nocturnal creatures and the salt-laden air. Now imagine waking up to a spectacular sunrise over the ocean as gulls begin to wheel and turn above the waves and dolphins play just off the beach. Welcome to an experience you won't soon forget—camping on the Outer Banks. From spring through autumn, lovers of the outdoors make their way to the numerous campgrounds that line these barrier islands to experience nature. Whether choosing to bed down with nothing more than a tent and a sleeping bag or deciding to "camp" in a recreational vehicle, opportunities abound.

More than 100,000 people frequent the National Park Service campgrounds for their home away from home each year, while thousands of other nature lovers set up camp at privately owned campgrounds. Some private campgrounds only open during the summer season, offering few creature comforts besides cold showers, but others are year-round establishments providing electric and water hookups, sewage disposal, laundry facilities, swimming pools, game rooms, bathhouses, and cable television. Some campgrounds rent furnished RVs. All have well-maintained roads and drive-up sites that accommodate any type of vehicle. Note that taxes are not included in any of the prices quoted.

National Park Service campgrounds operate under the same rules and regulations and charge the same fees. NPS campgrounds do not take reservations (except the Ocracoke Campground between Memorial Day and Labor Day) and accept payment in cash or credit cards upon arrival. Sites operate on a first-come, first-served basis. The National Park Service provides lifeguards at Coquina Beach, Cape Hatteras Lighthouse, south of the Frisco Pier at Sandy Bay, and on Ocracoke Island. For more information on any of the local NPS campgrounds, call (252) 473-2111, and check the NPS website for the most up-to-date information on the opening and closing dates of each campground: nps.gov/caha.

Camping on the beach is prohibited, as is wilderness camping in open areas, including Nags Head Woods, Kitty Hawk Woods, and Buxton Woods. But there is one spot where wilderness camping is allowed—Portsmouth Island. This now-uninhabited island is accessible only by boat.

Remember, these islands are home to a variety of wildlife, locals included. Please respect their homes by not littering or disturbing the environment in any way. We want to keep it just the way it is so you can enjoy camping again next year.

Kill Devil Hills

JOE & KAY'S CAMPGROUND, 1193 Colington Rd.; (252) 441-5468. About a mile west on Colington Road, before you get to the first bridge, Joe & Kay's Campground has 70 full hookup sites rented on a yearly basis. An additional 15 tent sites are also available from April through November. Call for rates. Reservations aren't accepted, so sites are secured on a first-come, first-served basis. Credit cards and personal checks are not accepted.

Colington Island

OBX CAMPGROUND, 126 Marshy Ridge Rd.; (252) 564-4741; obxcamp ground.com. On Colington Island, close to the Wright Brothers Monument. RV sites only, no tent sites are available.

Nags Head

OREGON INLET CAMPGROUND (NPS), NC 12; (252) 473-2111; nps.gov/caha. The northernmost National Park Service campground on the Outer Banks, this facility offers 120 sites along the windswept dunes just north of Oregon Inlet. If you're arriving from the north, look for the campground entrance on the east side of NC 12 just before crossing the Marc Basnight Bridge. It is located on the ocean almost directly across from the Oregon Inlet Fishing Center. Water, cold showers, modern toilets, picnic tables, and charcoal grills are available here. There aren't any utility connections, but dumping stations are nearby. Most of these sites are in sunny, exposed areas on the sand. Park rangers suggest that campers bring awnings, umbrellas, or other sources of shade. You may need mosquito netting and long tent stakes. Oregon Inlet Campground is open April through October. Campers are limited to a two-week stay. Reservations are not accepted, and sites are assigned on a first-come, first-served basis. Golden Age Passport holders receive a 50 percent discount. This campground accepts cash, credit cards, and personal checks.

Roanoke Island

THE REFUGE ON ROANOKE SOUND, 2881 NC Hwy 345, Wanchese; (252) 473-1096; therefuge-roanokeisland.com. This reclaimed sand mine has become an environmental wonder. Convenient to fishing village of Wanchese and the small town beauty of Manteo. Limited sites for daily and weekly use available.

Hatteras Island

CAMP HATTERAS, NC 12, Rodanthe; (252) 987-2777; camphatteras.com. A 50-acre campground, Camp Hatteras is a complete facility open year-round, offering many amenities. The site includes 1,000 feet of ocean and sound frontage. Nightly and monthly reservations are accepted. All of Camp Hatteras's 400-plus sites have full hookups, concrete pads, and paved roads. Tent sites, laundry facilities, hot showers, full bathhouses, and picnic tables are also available. Camp Hatteras has expanded soundside with 92 paved full hookups.

For recreation this campground provides three swimming pools, a clubhouse, a pavilion, a marina, three stocked fishing ponds, two tennis courts, a nine-hole miniature golf course, volleyball, basketball, kayaks, sailboards, and shuffleboard. The jumping pillows, outdoor cinema theater, and an express train create more opportunities for all-ages fun. A free boat ramp for campers is available. Sports and camping areas are separate, so sleeping outdoors is still a quiet experience.

Personal checks and credit cards are accepted. Pets are allowed on leashes for an additional fee. WiFi is available.

CAPE HATTERAS KOA, NC 12, Rodanthe; (800) 562-5268; koa.com/campgrounds/cape-hatteras. A large campground approximately 14 miles south of the Marc Basnight Bridge across Oregon Inlet, Cape Hatteras KOA has about 300 sites, including one- and two-room "Kamping Kabins." These units feature locking doors, ceiling fans, electricity, and picnic tables, and each has a porch. Ask about wheelchair-accessible units. Friendly, attentive staff greet campers as they arrive at this well-equipped campground.

Besides hot showers, drinking water, and bathhouses, Cape Hatteras KOA offers campers a dump station, laundry facilities, two pools, a hot tub, a playground, a game room, a cafe serving breakfast and lunch, and a well-stocked general store. Campers can even take in a round or two of miniature golf or a whirl on the campground's "Fun Bike"—a low-slung three-wheeler ridden inside the park. The ocean is just beyond the dunes for fishing and swimming, and the sound is the perfect place to fish, crab, or watch spectacular sunsets. The campground's recreation program offers varied activities in the summer. Rates are extremely variable according to proximity to the beach, season, and accommodations. Call or check the website for details. Significant savings are available in the off-season, from December 1 through March 1.

CAPE POINT CAMPGROUND (NPS), Off NC 12, Buxton; (252) 473-2111; nps.gov/caha. The largest National Park Service campground on the Outer Banks, Cape Point is about 2 miles south of the Cape Hatteras Lighthouse, across the dunes from the Atlantic. This campground has 202 sites—none with utility connections. It's open from Memorial Day through September but does not accept reservations. Flush toilets, cold showers, drinking water, charcoal grills, and picnic tables are provided. Each site has paved access. A wheelchair-accessible area is available, and a dumping station is nearby.

The campground is a short walk from the ocean. Most of these sites sit in the open, exposed to the sun and wind. Bring some shade, long tent stakes, lots of bug spray, and batteries. Pets are allowed on leashes.

CAPE WOODS CAMPGROUND, Buxton Back Rd., Buxton; (252) 995-5850; capewoods.com. Clean, quiet, and green best describe this campground. Scattered throughout the pine, live oak, and ash trees are 125 sites, some for tents, some with water and electricity, and some with full hookups. Cape Woods is open year-round and gladly accepts reservations. This full-service campground provides fire pits, grills, and picnic tables, as well as hot showers in two bathhouses, one of which is wheelchair accessible and one of which is heated for winter campers. An outdoor swimming pool, a playground, a small game room, a volleyball court, and a horseshoe pit are also available. Children and grown-ups can freshwater fish in the surrounding canals. Laundry facilities are available, and ice and propane gas are for sale. Discounts are honored. It is open March through December.

FRISCO CAMPGROUND (NPS), NC 12, Frisco; (252) 473-2111; nps.gov/caha. Frisco Campground is operated by the National Park Service and sits about 4 miles southwest of Buxton. Just off the beach, next to ramp 49, this is the area's most isolated and elevated campground. Its undulating roads twist over dunes and around small hills, providing privacy at almost every site. Some tent areas are so secluded in stands of scrubby trees that you can't see them from where you park your car.

Frisco Campground has 127 no-frills sites, each with a charcoal grill and picnic table. Flush toilets, cold-water showers in bathhouses, and drinking water are available. There aren't any hookups here, but RVs are welcome. A wooden boardwalk crosses from the campground to the ocean.

Reservations aren't accepted; payment may be made with cash, credit cards, or personal checks. Call for rates. Pets are allowed on leashes. Frisco Campground is open April through October. Golden Age discounts are honored.

★ **FRISCO WOODS CAMPGROUND**, Frisco Woods, off NC 12, Frisco; (800) 948-3942; thefriscowoodscampground.com. This 30-acre sound-side campground boasts abundant forest and marshland beauty and at least 150 sites in a wooded wonderland. Electricity and water are available at 122 campsites. Full hookups are offered at 35 other sites, and there are 100 tent sites. Cabins have air conditioning and electricity. Amenities include an in-ground swimming pool, picnic tables, hot showers, free WiFi, coin laundry, a small country store, propane gas, and public phones. Kiteboarders like this campground because they can sail directly from the sites onto Pamlico Sound. Crabbing, fishing, kayaking, and wandering through the woods are also readily available to campers staying at Frisco Woods. Frisco Woods is open March 1 through December 1, and reservations are accepted. Pets are allowed on leashes. Weekly, monthly, and seasonal rates are available on request, and special event and group rates also are offered.

NORTH BEACH CAMPGROUND, NC 12, Rodanthe; (252) 987-2378; northbeachcampground.com. In the village of Rodanthe, North Beach Campground sits alongside the ocean south of the Chicamacomico Lifesaving Station. Here 110 sites, all with water and electric hookups, offer campers both tent and RV accommodations and a wide range of amenities. Bathhouse, hot showers, picnic tables, a laundry facility, an outdoor swimming pool, and a pump-out station are available. There aren't any grills here, and open fires aren't allowed, so bring your own grill or camp stove if you want to cook. North Beach Campground's grocery store sells fuel and convenience-store items. Pets are allowed on leashes. Reservations are accepted. The campground is open from March through November.

OCEAN WAVES CAMPGROUND, NC 12, Waves; (252) 987-2556; ocean wavescampground.com. Open March 15 through November 15, Ocean Waves Campground is a seaside resort with sites for RVs and tents. Of 68 spaces, most offer full hookups and concrete pads. Each has its own picnic table. Three bathhouses, hot showers, and laundry facilities are available. Campers enjoy the game room and outdoor pool. Asphalt roadways are well maintained. WiFi and a game room are available.

RODANTHE WATERSPORTS AND SHORELINE CAMPGROUND, NC 12, Rodanthe; (252) 987-1431; watersportsandcampground.com. This soundfront campground is open year-round for recreational vehicles and tents. Sailboarders and kiteboarders especially enjoy this campground because they can sail right to some of the campsites. Other campers enjoy swimming, boating, and fishing in the sound. The water sports business next door rents kayaks, sailboats, WaveRunners, surfboards, and bicycles (see the **Water Sports**

chapter). But what really keeps campers coming back are the spectacular, unobstructed sunset views.

Hot showers, picnic tables, and a few grills are on-site. If you'd rather not cook, you can grab a pizza from Lisa's Pizzeria right next door (see the **Dining** chapter). Pets are allowed. Reservations are recommended. Personal checks and credit cards are accepted. Call for nightly rates. When you pay for six nights, the seventh night is free.

SANDS OF TIME CAMPGROUND, North End Rd., Avon; (252) 995-5596; sandsoftimecampground.com. This year-round campground has 51 full hookup sites and 15 tent sites, some with full shade. Hot showers, flush toilets, laundry facilities, a dump site, picnic tables, and a pay telephone are offered to all Sands campers. Visitors enjoy swimming, fishing, and sunbathing at the nearby beach. The infamous Canadian Hole is just 2 1/2 miles away, making this a great spot to stay for your kiteboarding or windsurfing vacation. Grills aren't provided, and open fires are not allowed. Bring your camp stove to cook. Pets are allowed on leashes. Reservations are accepted and recommended for summer and fall. Credit cards are not accepted.

Ocracoke Island

BEACHCOMBER CAMPGROUND AND OCRACOKE STATION, NC 12, Ocracoke Village; (252) 928-4031; ocracokecamping.com. Less than a mile from Silver Lake and the nearest beach access, Beachcomber Campground has 29 sites with electricity and water and 7 tent sites. Hot showers and fully equipped bathrooms are available, as are picnic tables and grills. A deli on the premises offers fresh sandwiches. Gourmet groceries and a large wine selection are available, as well as beach supplies, souvenirs, and T-shirts. Leashed pets are allowed at Beachcomber. The campground is open year-round. Reservations are recommended for summer camping. Call for rates.

OCRACOKE CAMPGROUND (NPS), NC 12, Ocracoke Island; (800) 365-2267; nps.gov/caha. An oceanfront campground 3 miles east of Ocracoke Village just behind the dunes, this National Park Service campground maintains 136 campsites. No utility hookups or laundry facilities are available, but there are cold showers, a dumping station, drinking water, charcoal grills, and flush toilets. As at all NPS campgrounds, stays are limited to 14 days. The facility is open May through September. Since most of these sites sit directly in the sun, bring some sort of shade. Long tent stakes help to hold down tents against the often fierce winds that whip through this campground. The breeze, however, is a welcome relief from summer heat. Bug spray is a must in the summer. Ocracoke is the only campground on the island operated by the National Park Reservation Service. Call or visit the website from mid-May through mid-September to make reservations. Major credit cards are accepted. Sites are assigned on a first-come, first-served basis. Even though it looks like an inviting spot, camping on the beach is not permitted. Local officers and National Park Service personnel patrol the areas regularly and will ask you to leave.

TEETER'S CAMPGROUND, British Cemetery Rd., Ocracoke Village; (252) 588-2030; teeterscampground.com. Near the heart of Ocracoke Village, tucked in a shady grove of trees, Teeter's Campground offers 2 full-hookup sites, 12 sites with electricity and water, and 10 tent sites. Hot showers are available. Six charcoal grills are installed at tent sites, and each site has a picnic table. There aren't any public laundry facilities on Ocracoke, so don't plan to machine wash any of your clothes. Call for rates. Teeter's Campground is open March 1 through November. Reservations are recommended on holiday weekends. Credit cards are not accepted.

ACCOMMODATIONS

Dining

When you visit the Outer Banks, be sure to bring your appetite. In this seemingly remote area of the world, we have the basic ingredients from which world-class cuisine is created. We have bounty from the mainland, the sounds, and the ocean. We have innovative, educated, experienced chefs and restaurateurs. And we have an atmosphere that lends itself to an eclectic variety of hip, funky, chic, laid-back, comfortable, rustic, family-style places. In short we have cutting-edge cuisine and we know how to serve it.

OVERVIEW

Just across the Wright Memorial Bridge on the Currituck mainland grow the vegetables found on many Outer Banks menus: Silver Queen sweet corn, Red Bliss potatoes, sugar snap peas, luscious tomatoes, brightly colored bell peppers, slender green beans. And we can't forget about the fields of strawberries and melons or the orchards of trees laden with succulent peaches and figs. The source of smoke-cured country hams and the largest peanuts you've ever eaten lies farther inland. Wanchese Produce on Roanoke Island plays a starring role on a daily basis, supplying restaurants with herbs. Organic lettuce, mesclun mix, and bunches of fresh basil, thyme, rosemary, lemongrass, dill, and edible flowers are just a few of the fragrant wonders delivered to the back doors of kitchens all along this sandy bar.

And then there's the seafood. So much tuna is caught in the warm waters of the Gulf Stream that the tiny fishing village of Wanchese exports literally thousands of tons each year. In addition to tuna, local menus sport mahimahi, wahoo, and mako shark from the Gulf Stream. From inshore ocean waters and our sound waters come fresh flounder, Spanish and king mackerel, bluefish, black grouper, drum, striped bass (locally known as rockfish), speckled trout, gray trout, oysters, clams, mussels, shrimp, and crabs. Along Colington Road and the streets of Kitty Hawk Village, you can easily spot the long wooden shedder beds, brightly lighted all night long, where soft-shell crabs are gathered as soon as they molt.

Big-city purveyors supplement our local seafood and produce; while the grocery stores carry mainly the basics, our restaurants pride themselves on offering daring ingredients.

Wine has become one of our restaurants' biggest drawing cards. Wine dinners abound during the off-season, and many are attended by the vintners themselves. Wine-loving restaurateurs are happy to accommodate a variety of tastes, as evidenced by the increasing number of wines by the glass that we

Celebrating the role of the local men and women who gather the bounty of the sea to earn their living, the Outer Banks Seafood Festival features food prepared from fresh local seafood, music, and more.

see cropping up on lists. Lists of bottled wines lengthen each season, and restaurants along the northern beaches sometimes offer 100 or more varieties of the world's finest wines. A surprising number of Outer Banks restaurants have received coveted awards of excellence from *Wine Spectator* for their wine selections and for their pairing of wine with food.

Many area restaurants serve alcoholic beverages, at least for dinner; however, those in Southern Shores and those on Colington and Ocracoke Islands are forbidden to offer mixed drinks and serve only beer or wine. Some establishments allow brown bagging, which means you can bring in your own liquor.

Restaurants are opening earlier in the spring and staying open longer into the fall each year. The shoulder seasons have become popular times to dine out. Most eateries open by March and don't close their kitchens until after Thanksgiving. Some open briefly for the holidays. A few are busy enough to stay open year-round.

Dinner isn't the only meal to eat out, of course. Bakeries, diners, and even seafood restaurants serve big breakfasts, lunches, and weekend brunches. A few welcome bathing suit–clad customers just off the beach. The majority of restaurants, however, require you to wear shirts and shoes. Many cooks will package meals to go and some eateries deliver, with menus offering much more than just pizza.

If you're eating an evening meal out, feel free to dress as comfortably as you desire. Even most of the expensive, elite establishments welcome sundresses, sandals, and shorts. Restaurant managers say everything from evening gowns and suits to jeans and T-shirts is acceptable at their tables.

Reservations aren't taken at many restaurants. Others, however, suggest or even require them. The Blue Point and the Left Bank in Duck; Ocean Boulevard in Kitty Hawk; Colington Cafe on Colington Island; and 1587 in Manteo all get so booked up during summer that it's best to call at least three days ahead to secure a table. The fare at these fabulous places is well worth the advance planning.

If sticking to a budget is a concern, you can have homestyle meals from tuna steaks to North Carolina barbecue for less than $8 in many Outer Banks family-style restaurants. Sure, you'll find a few of the nationally popular fast-food chains, complete with drive-through windows, uniformed employees, and a known commodity, but if you want something ranging from a little bit different to extraordinary, read on. With our diversity of restaurants, you're bound to find something to suit any appetite.

Price Code

The following price code is based on the cost of main courses for one person and does not include appetizers, dessert, and alcoholic beverages. Many area eateries have senior-citizen discounts and children's menus. Most entrees include at least one vegetable or salad and some type of bread. Here's our breakdown: Prices do not include the 8.75 percent sales tax or the gratuity, which should be 15 to 20 percent, depending on the quality of service. Some restaurants offer early-evening dining discounts to encourage patrons to avoid peak dining hours. Most have at least two or three daily specials that change according to the availability of food and the whims of the chef.

$	Less than $12
$$	$12 to $22
$$$	$22 to $38
$$$$	More than $38

How This Chapter Is Organized

Restaurants in this chapter are arranged from north to south from Corolla through Ocracoke.

Seasons and days of the week each place is open are included with every profile. Unless otherwise noted, these eateries accept MasterCard and Visa, and many accept other major credit cards as well.

We've included some primarily carry-out and outdoor dining establishments that offer quick, cheap eats, cool ice cream concoctions, and perfect items to pack for a picnic or offshore fishing excursion.

AGAVE ROJA, 807 B Ocean Trl.; (252) 453-0446; agaveroja.com; Modern Mexican; $$. Agave Roja will burst your palate with exciting flavors when you try a meal at this relaxed, casually upscale restaurant. Mexican fare as well as new twists on Latino cooking are served here seven days a week for lunch and dinner. Full bar with an impressive selection of tequilas.

BACHUS WINE AND BEER BISTRO, Monterey Plaza, 891 Albacore St.; (252) 453-4333; bacchuswineandbeer.com; Classic deli; $$. A Corolla institution for 30 years. Amazing deli sandwiches, a very pleasant if small seating area, and the largest selection of wine in Corolla.

BUBBIE'S BURGERS, 788 Sunset Blvd., Timbuck II Shopping Village; (252) 453-4010; bubbiesburgersobx.com; Burgers and fries; $. Hand-formed burgers made fresh daily. Huge selection of toppings for their all beef Angus hotdogs. Sandwiches, fries, baskets and hand-dipped milkshakes—the real milkshakes.

COROLLA CANTINA, 1159 NC 12, Corolla Light Town Center; (252) 597-1730; obxcantina.com; Mexican cuisine with a coastal flair. Local seasonal seafood featured in many dishes, Vegetarian dishes available. Across from Whalehead Club. Full bar and pet friendly.

COROLLA PIZZA & DELI, Austin Complex, NC 12; (252) 453-8592; Pizza, deli, and sandwiches; corollapizza.com; $. This takeout-only deli serves hot and cold subs and sandwiches, Philly cheese steaks, and pizza by the pie or slice for lunch and dinner. Each pizza is made to order on hand-tossed dough. Regular red sauce and gourmet white pizzas, including the ever-popular chicken pesto pizza, are available. During the summer season Corolla Pizza offers free delivery after 5 p.m. You can walk in or call ahead to have your order waiting. Corolla Pizza is open seven days a week in summer. Call for off-season hours.

FAT CRABS RIB COMPANY, 1159 Austin St., Corolla Light Town Center; (252) 453-9931; fatcrabsobx.com; BBQ, chicken, and seafood; $$–$$$. Southern favorites are the specialty, from eastern North Carolina barbecue to the freshest seafood from local waters. Indoor and outdoor seating available. Nice kid's menu.

FIRST LIGHT BREAKFAST AND BURGERS, 790 Ocean Trl., Timbuck II Shopping Village; (252) 453-4664; firstlightcorolla.com; Breakfast, burgers, and more; $–$$. From breakfast to dinner this casual eatery has something for everyone. Restaurant offers full bar service and a kid's menu.

GIANT SLICE PIZZA, 785 Sunset Blvd; Timbuck II Shopping Village, (252) 453-3199; giantslicepizza.com; Pizza; $. An Outer Banks and Corolla favorite since 1994. Features hand-tossed, New York style pizza in their cast ovens with more than 18 toppings offered. Stromboli, calzones, baked wings and more.

ISLAND SMOOTHIE CAFÉ, 603 C Currituck Clubhouse Dr.; (252) 453-4545; islandsmoothiecafe.com; Smoothies and sandwiches; $. Fresh, healthy, made daily, and tasty. Smoothies use local fruit and produce when available. Great place for sandwiches. Cold brew coffee is a specialty.

LA DOLCE VITA, 798 C Sunset Blvd., Timbuck II Shopping Village; (252) 453-0069; ladolcevitacorolla.com; Classic Italian; $$–$$$. Wonderful classic Italian cuisine in a relaxed family friendly atmosphere. Small but nice wine list complements a full bar. Spectacular sunsets and homemade desserts.

LIGHTHOUSE BAGELS, 807 Ocean Trl.; (252) 453-9998; lighthouse bagels.com; Breakfast; $. Arguably the best bagels on the beach. Freshly made every day. Coffee and pastries also available.

LUCKY'S PIZZA AND SUBHOUSE, Monterey Plaza, 9610, 815 Ocean Trl.; (252) 597-3222; luckyspizzacorolla.com; Pizza; $$. The name says it all—they specialize in pizza and subs. Calzones, Stromboli and wings also available.

MAMA EASLEY'S GRUB HUT, 799 Sunset Blvd., Timbuck II Shopping Village; (252) 453-2398; mamaeasleys.com; Sandwiches; $–$$. Unpretentious casual lunch and dinner spot. Salads, sandwiches, baskets and a children's menu.

METROPOLIS, Ocean Club Centre, NC 12; (252) 453-6167; metropolis obx.com; Tapas; $–$$. Creativity reigns at this chic and urban tapas and martini restaurant. Diners return often to this contemporary and stylish dining experience. The menu at Metropolis is ever changing, using only the freshest ingredients available. Favorites include roasted red pepper and feta dip and tuna sashimi. Black and blue tenderloin medallions are served in the cooler months, along with the spicy shrimp taco. A full martini list includes 30-plus choices. Wine, liquor, and microbrew beers are served here as well. This Corolla hotspot is open until 2 a.m.

MEXIKIND TAQUERIA, 785 Sunset Blvd., Timbuck II Shopping Village; (252) 453-4380; mexikind.com; Mexican; $. Traditional Mexican recipes highlight fresh local ingredients. Huge burritos served. Gluten-free options available.

★ **MIKE DIANNA'S GRILL ROOM**, NC 12, Timbuck II Shopping Village; (252) 453-4336; grillroomobx.com; Seafood and steak; $$. Mike Dianna's Grill Room prides itself on creating an unforgettable dining experience and wants dining here to become a tradition in your family. Steaks, veal, lamb, ribs, chicken, and seafood are all cooked over a mesquite grill, bringing you aromatic wood cooking at its best. The homemade French bread that accompanies the meals is excellent. Four or five different fish specials are offered each night. The Grill Room is also known for its broad selection of international wines. The restaurant serves dinner nightly during the summer; call for off-season hours. A kids' menu is available. Live music is scheduled every Thursday evening in season. Private parties of up to 150 people may be held here.

NORTH BANKS RESTAURANT & RAW BAR, NC 12, Timbuck II Shopping Village; (252) 453-3344; northbanks.com; Seafood and steak; $$–$$$$. This 50-seat restaurant and raw bar serves lunch and dinner all year. Lobster, shrimp, oysters, clams, and mussels are available as well as filet mignon, fresh locally caught fish, grilled beef, chicken, and sandwiches. Diners enjoy the waterside view from this upscale but casual restaurant that boasts 28-foot vaulted ceilings. North Banks also offers desserts and appetizers as well as imported and domestic beers and wine. Order a flaming martini for an exciting start to your meal.

★ **NORTHERN LIGHTS BAKERY**, Corolla Light Town Center, NC 12; (252) 453-0201; Desserts; $. Got a sweet tooth that needs satisfying? Stop in at this adorable bakery and pick up delightful pastries, cupcakes, and sugary concoctions. Cakes are also available and can be made to order. Northern Lights also offers smoothies, coffees, and teas.

OFF THE WALL TAP HOUSE, 603 Currituck Clubhouse Dr.; (252) 489-5114; offthewalltaphouse.com; Beer and pub food; $$–$$$. More than twenty beers on tap, an outdoor seating area, innovative menu, and a great kids menu. Plenty of local beers, as well as hard to find European and domestic microbrews.

OH MY DOG, 1159 Austin St.; (252) 597-3294; obxohmydog.com; Hot dogs; $. Casual, inexpensive and family friendly, Oh My Dog, is perfect for the beach. Breakfast, baskets, and kid's menus are part of the fare.

OUTER BANKS BOIL COMPANY, 785 Sunset Blvd., Timbuck II Shopping Village; (252) 453-6578; outerbanksboilcompany.com; Seafood. Steamer pots to go. You steam or they'll steam it for you. Filled with fresh local ingredients as well as Andouille sausage shipped fresh from New Orleans. Second location in Kitty Hawk. Open mid-May through mid-September.

DINING

OUTER BANKS COFFEE COMPANY, 807 Ocean Trl.; (252) 453-0200; Coffee; $. A retail store and coffee bar located in the Monterey Shores Shopping Plaza (Food Lion). There's no indoor seating, although there are some tables along the sidewalk outside. What the Outer Banks Coffee Company does offer are fresh roasted beans—they roast their own—with a good selection of coffees as well as pastries and other items. Open seasonally, so check the hours.

PASQUALE PIZZA, 1210 Ocean Trl.; (252) 453-6111; pasqualepizza.com; Pizza; $–$$. As Italian as it gets. The owner is a native born Italian who came to the United State 40 years ago. Everything is scratch made on the premises. There is a small dining area for the dine-in crowd.

THE SHACK COFFEE & BEER GARDEN, 1148 Ocean Trl.; (252) 597-1500; corollacoffee.com; Coffee, beer, and sandwiches; $. Featuring an outdoor seating area that doubles as a beer garden at night, the Shack brings the Outer Banks experience outdoors. Excellent coffee, locally roasted beans, some innovative breakfast and lunch selections and smoothies. And yes, beer for the thirsty. Open seasonally, so check the hours.

PIZZAZZ PIZZA, 603 Currituck Clubhouse Dr.; (252) 453-8858; pizzazz pizza.net; Pizza $–$$. Great pizza at an affordable price. The baked subs are fantastic. Three locations on the Outer Banks: Corolla, Duck, and Nags Head.

PHILLY STEAK SUBS, 807 Ocean Trl., Monterey Plaza; (252) 453-4239; phillysteaksubscorolla.com; Sandwiches; $. The real deal Philly cheesesteak made on the classic Amoroso Italian rolls. Same for the subs. This is the way they're made in the City of Brotherly Love. A family-friendly restaurant.

SOOEY'S BBQ & RIB SHACK, 807 Ocean Trl.; Monterey Plaza; (252) 453-4423; sooeysbbq.com; BBQ; $$. Award-winning ribs and barbecue from an Outer Banks native. Pulled pork, beef brisket, and southern fried chicken are specialties, as well as their ribs. Four locations: Corolla, Duck, Kitty Hawk, and Wanchese.

SUNDOGS RAW BAR & GRILL, NC 12, Monterey Plaza; (252) 453-4263; sundogsrawbargrill.com; Traditional American; $–$$. Sundogs is the top sports-viewing facility in Corolla. It has the traditional decor of a sports bar and the features you

i Does a gourmet meal cooked in your rental cottage sound like a winning option? Call At Your Service at (252) 261-5286 or atyourserviceobx .com to arrange in-house personal chef service.

DINING

would expect—a long bar, a pool table, video games, and TVs. If there's a game on, customers like to sidle up to the bar, drink a few beers, and chow down on jumbo buffalo wings served with ranch or blue cheese dressing, beer-battered onion rings, mile-high nachos with tricolor tortillas, or personal flat-bread pizzas. A steam bar offers shrimp, crab legs, and more. For meals try hearty sandwiches like the Black Angus burger or the Carolina crab cake sandwich. Fish and chips are available along with a 12-inch Coney Island hot dog. There is a children's menu, a late-night menu, and a full bar. Sundogs is open year-round.

> **i** A great time to eat out on the Outer Banks is Sunday night. Many folks have just checked into their cottage and don't go out for dinner. Often you can get seated more quickly and have a wider choice of where to eat on Sunday evening.

UNCLE IKE'S BITS N' MORE, 814 Ocean Trl.; (252) 597-3305; ikesbites .com; Breakfast and lunch; $–$$. Serving up a hearty and innovative breakfast menu. Lunch and ice cream treats are part of the fare.

UNCLE IKE'S SANDBAR AND GRILL, 1159 Austin St., Corolla Light Town Center; (252) 597-1606; uncleikesobx.com; Sandwiches, salads, seafood; $–$$. Comfort food with a healthy beach flair is the specialty. Steam bar, vegetarian, a kid's menu, and gluten-free options are available. Everything is made to order. Late night menu is served until 1 a.m.

UPSIDE RESTAURANT, 797 Sunset Blvd., Timbuck II Shopping Village; (252) 597-3030; upsideobx.com; $$–$$$. Only upper deck with outdoor seating in Corolla. Overlooks Currituck Sound. Coastal cuisine with a gourmet twist keeps things interesting.

⭐ **URBAN KITCHEN,** 603-B Currituck Clubhouse Dr.; (252) 453-4453; urbankitchenobx.com; Regional, seafood, and steak; $$$. Foodie alert—this is the place to put at the top of your list for dinner. Simple seasonal fare is locally-sourced and the menu is changed every two weeks. This small upscale restaurant serves delectable fare. Located by Harris Teeter, insiders rave about the fried green tomatoes with crab, the delectable swordfish in chorizo broth, and the buttermilk tart. Eclectic comfortable décor makes diners feel comfy and welcome. Patrons are served on a first-come first-served basis—reservations are not accepted. Full bar.

AQUA RESTAURANT, NC 12; (252) 261-9700; aquaobx.com; Regional American; $$–$$$. Aqua is Duck's most sassy waterfront dining hotspot. Located on the sound, this restaurant serves lunch and dinner. Sophisticated regional cuisine is topped off by a glorious water view. Ingredients used here are organic and locally-grown whenever possible. An extensive wine list is offered. The staff is well-trained by one of the owners, who is a certified sommelier. Truly spoil yourself and complete your visit with a facial or massage at the Aqua Essence Day Spa located on the second level.

★ **THE BLUE POINT BAR & GRILL,** The Waterfront Shops, NC 12; (252) 261-8090; thebluepoint.com; Contemporary Southern; $$$. This insanely popular bistro with a million dollar view is one of our favorite places to dine on the Outer Banks. It's been open for dinner since 1989 and consistently receives rave reviews from magazines such as *Southern Living, Gourmet,* and *Wine Spectator.* The Blue Point's menu is contemporary Southern cuisine with cosmopolitan flair, and changes seasonally. Starters range from Hatteras tuna to fresh tomato-mozzarella stacks, each artistically arranged and flavored with a fresh combination of seasonings. Entrees include jumbo lump crab cakes served with Currituck corn on the cob, homemade soups, unusual seafood dishes, steaks, salads, and perfect pastas. Desserts, like warm Kentucky bourbon pecan tart with caramel ice cream or key lime pie, are divine. It's open for dinner, and reservations are highly recommended; in summer dinner reservations are required. The Blue Point is open for lunch Tuesday to Sunday from 11:30 a.m. to 2:30 p.m. and for dinner seven days a week in season; call for off-season hours.

★ **COASTAL CANTINA,** NC 12, Duck Waterfront Shops; (252) 480-0023; coastalprovisionmarket.com; Mexican; $. This inviting open-air eatery is a fun place to stop while shopping or for a dinner meal overlooking the Currituck Sound. The margarita machine provides fun, delicious treats. Quesadillas, tacos, burritos and salads are just a few of the offerings.

COASTAL CRAVINGS, NC 12; (252) 480-0035; cravingsobx.com; American, seafood; $–$$$. Sister restaurant to Coastal Cantina and Coastal Provisions in Southern Shores, this restaurant is super-popular with locals and visitors alike. Located in half of a convenience store, it surprises first-time diners with its elegant decor and delicious, award-winning food. Eat inside or on their inviting outdoor patio. Choose from prime steaks, crab cakes, or take-out seafood pots. Featured on *Diners, Drive-ins and Dives.* Full bar; live music on some nights.

DINING

DUCK DELI, 1223 Duck Rd.; (252) 261-3354; Deli and BBQ. $–$$. An iconic part of the Village of Duck life, Duck Deli has been a roadside eatery for over 30 years. Great breakfast and fantastic lunch. Don't look for fine china… just good food.

DUCK DONUTS, 1190 Duck Rd.; (252) 480-3304; duckdonuts.com; Donuts; $. Yes, this is the one that started it all. There are Duck Donuts in cities all over the eastern half of the country now, but it all started here. If you have never had a donut from Duck Donuts, there is a small bit of joy missing from your life.

⭐ **DUCK PIZZA,** NC 12, Scarborough Lane Shoppes; (252) 255-0099; duckpizza.com; Pizza; $$. Duck Pizza offers yummy specialty pizzas, subs, wraps, wings, stromboli, calzones, and more. Beer is served in the cafe. Free delivery is offered to Southern Shores, Duck, and Pine Island.

> ℹ️ It's not vacation if you spend the whole time in the kitchen. If you've got a houseful of people, consider hiring a personal chef. You can choose a chef who cooks all three meals in your house or one who just drops off dinner every evening. Ask your rental company for suggestions.

FISHBONES RAW BAR & RESTAURANT, NC 12, Scarborough Lane Shoppes; (252) 261-6991; fishbonessunsetgrille.com; Carribean, American, and seafood; $$. Specializing in locally caught seafood, this raw bar and grill has been a crowd pleaser since 1995. Fishbones won the Outer Banks chowder cook-off with an original recipe during its first year in business. Lunch items include sandwiches, crab cakes, fried seafood, and creamy soups such as tomato conch and, of course, chowder. Dinner entrees feature such Caribbean cuisine favorites as calypso eggplant and coconut shrimp, as well as pastas with fresh clam sauce, lobster tails, crab legs, and more than a dozen raw bar selections. The hot crab dip, barbecue shrimp, and conch fritters are outstanding appetizers. This is a casual place with a full bar, 5 types of beer on tap, 50 bottled beers from all over the world, a wine list, and several microbrews. Fishbones serves lunch and dinner seven days a week year-round, and specials change daily for both meals. Takeout is available for all menu items. Reservations are not accepted.

FISHBONES SUNSET GRILLE AND RAW BAR, NC 12; (252) 261-3901; fishbonessunsetgrille.com; Caribbean and seafood; $$. Sister restaurant

OBX Catch

Encompassing Currituck, Hyde, Tyrell, and Dare counties, OBX Catch is a branding campaign designed to help consumers identify which restaurants and seafood retailers are selling locally harvested seafood. Eighty percent of all seafood served nationally is imported and only 2 percent is FDA inspected. As part of a larger "local food" movement, OBX Catch is aimed at educating both locals and visitors about the benefits of requesting locally harvested, fresh seafood.

A diverse group of local fisherman, restaurants, seafood markets, grocers, and community members launched OBX Catch in 2010. The program uses a logo to identify which restaurants and retailers are providing local seafood—a Gold membership indicates more than 50 percent of seafood on the menu is locally provided, and a Silver membership indicates up to 50 percent. Individual dishes should bear the OBX Catch logo as well, assuring diners of the local origin of the catch.

The unique Atlantic coast ecosystem produces one of the most diverse year-round selections of fish and shellfish available, and it provides the greatest fishing revenue in North Carolina. But while our local seafood is plentiful, it is also highly seasonal. Summer is the time for soft-shell crabs and shrimp, flounder is best in the fall, and winter is better for oysters and sea trout, to name a few. Looking for the OBX logo at your seafood retailer will ensure that your meals are fresh, in season, and locally caught by our native watermen.

to the popular Fishbones Raw Bar & Restaurant, Fishbones Sunset Grille and Raw Bar has become another favorite Duck dining spot. The restaurant sits by the Currituck Sound and is the village's prime sunset-watching spot. It is patterned after the older Fishbones, with Caribbean-influenced entrees and appetizers, moderately priced food, a fun atmosphere, and good service for locals and visitors alike. Meals are served upstairs or down or outside on the deck. Dinners focus mostly on seafood, and the blackened fish and conch fritters are standouts. The raw bar serves all the freshest Outer Banks favorites. For lunch, seafood, sandwiches, and burgers are served. Lunch and dinner are served every day year-round. Breakfast in full season only.

KIMBALL'S KITCHEN, NC 12, Sanderling Resort; (855) 412-7866; sanderling-resort.com/dining-kimballs-kitchen.php; American and seafood;

$$$–$$$$. Enjoy panoramic vistas of the Currituck Sound and marsh grasses through a half moon–shaped window wall. Spotlighting grass-fed prime steaks and local fresh seafood, this upscale, coastally casual spot is popular with visitors to the inn and vacationers in the area. Offering pasta and risotto dishes in addition to the seafood tower and other offerings, this restaurant offers special children's pricing on entrees. Extensive wine and Champagne offerings. Serves Tuesday through Saturday in season.

THE LIFESAVING STATION AT THE SANDERLING, NC 12, Sanderling Resort; (252) 449-6654; sanderling-resort.com/dining-lifesaving-station .php; American; $$$. The Lifesaving Station, part of the Sanderling Resort north of Duck, is one of the Outer Banks' loveliest restaurants, housed in a restored 1899 lifesaving station that is a National Historic Landmark. The dining rooms reflect turn-of-the-20th-century coastal architecture and are enhanced with rich woods and brass, nautical antiques, and original artifacts of the lifesaving station. Contemporary American cuisine emphasizing local seafood is the specialty here. The restaurant serves breakfast, lunch, and dinner every day to everyone, not only guests of the resort, and has an award-winning wine list and a full bar. The upstairs Swan Bar and Lounge are good places to relax before or after you eat. A children's menu is available. Dinner reservations are highly recommended. All three meals are served seven days a week, year-round.

OUTER BEAN CAFÉ, 1245 Duck Rd.; (252) 715 5900; outerbean.com; Coffee, smoothies, and sandwiches; $. Much smaller version of the original Outer Bean in Kitty Hawk. Great sandwiches, wonderful coffee and smoothies. Limited seating outside.

THE PAPER CANOE, 1564 Duck Rd.; (252) 715-2220; papercanoeobx .com; American fusion; $$$. A rustic, yet beautiful setting on the Currituck Sound at north end of Duck. Cuisine is American fusion, meaning the tastes of the world seem to blend together in many of the dishes. Fresh seafood and "chef's whim" are always worth checking out.

PIZZAZZ PIZZA, 1187 Duck Rd.; (252) 261-8822; pizzazzpizza.net; Pizza; $–$$. Great pizza at an affordable price. The baked subs are fantastic. Three locations on the Outer Banks: Corolla, Duck, and Nags Head.

RED SKY CAFÉ, 1197 Duck Rd.; (252) 261-8646; redskycafe.com; Classic American; $$–$$$. Specializing in tasty yet healthy cuisine, Chef Wes Stepp has a well-deserved reputation for quality and flavor in his dishes. Lunchtime burgers are outstanding. Dinner standouts include shrimp and grits and the duck in Duck.

ROADSIDE RAW BAR & GRILL, NC 12; (252) 261-5729; obxroadside .com; $$. Occupying a renovated 1932 cottage, this restaurant is warm and homey, with hardwood floors inside and a patio with umbrella-shaded tables out front. Live jazz is performed here some evenings in season (see the **Entertainment** chapter).

A casual, fine-dining establishment, Roadside offers half-pound Angus burgers, fresh fish sandwiches, meat loaf, and a variety of salads, and sandwiches for lunch. Weather permitting, enjoy your meal on the patio while watching the summertime foot traffic in downtown Duck. The restaurant serves lunch and dinner year-round; call for off-season hours. Reservations are not accepted. There's live music nightly in season at the Backside Bar.

TREEHOUSE COFFEE, 177 Duck Rd.; (252) 722-3606; treehousecoffee nc.com; Breakfast; $. Marvelous little coffee shop with great pastries and very well-stocked wine and beer selection. Very pleasant seating area on the porch. Now serving a complete breakfast including homemade biscuits from the Rope Ladder Kitchen.

VILLAGE TAVERN, 1314 Duck Rd.; (252) 715-1414; villagetableand tavern.com; Classic American; $$–$$$. The newest restaurant in Duck offers spectacular views of Currituck Sound and sunsets. Local ingredients when available. Daily specials are innovative and worth checking out. Village Tavern features a very well-stocked bar with an excellent wine selections. Located at N'orBanks Sailing Center.

WAVE PIZZA, 1190 Duck Rd., Osprey Landing Sound Front Shops; (252) 255-0375; thewavepizza.com; Pizza; $$. Innovative pizzeria with an amazing view located on the town of Duck's Boardwalk. The specialty pizzas put some ingrates together in wonderful and different ways.

SOUTHERN SHORES

BARRIER ISLAND BAGELS, 5549 N. Croatan Hwy, The Marketplace; (252) 255-2888; barrierislandbagels.com; Bagels and sandwiches; $. Great bagels baked fresh daily. Fantastic sandwiches and good coffee. Everything needed for the perfect place for breakfast or lunch. Open year-round.

★ **COASTAL PROVISIONS WINE BAR AND CAFE**, NC 12, Southern Shores Crossing; (252) 480-0023; American and seafood; $$. At Coastal Provisions, it's about taste, service, and pleasure; food critics and diners always give high marks to this establishment. Diners are sure to be pleased with the combination of a chef's market, artisan cheese and deli, prepared meals to go, fresh and prepared local seafood, wine bar, and table service by candlelight. Famous for delicious lunch sandwiches, outstanding dinner cuisine and their upscale oyster bar, Coastal Provisions also caters and can accommodate small intimate celebrations as well as grand, upscale events.

COSMOS PIZZA, 5591 N. Croatan Hwy, The Marketplace; (252) 261-8388, cosmospizzaobx.com; Pizza; $–$$. An Outer Banks favorite for well over 20 years for good reason. The recipes are classic Italian and the ingredients are always fresh. There is a small seating area at the pizzeria. Pasta and salads are also available, as well as beer and wine.

OBX FROZEN YOGURT, 1 Ocean Blvd., Southern Shores Crossing; (252) 261-2697; Dessert; obxfroyo.com; $. Wonderful little family-owned self-serve frozen yogurt shop. Lots and lots of other sweet treats as well. Perfect for the whole family on a hot day or for an after dinner treat.

PIZZA STOP, 5385 N. Virginia Dare Trl.; (252) 261-7867; pizzastopobx. com; Pizza; $. Hand-tossed New York style pizza with homemade sauce and freshly grated cheese. Free delivery services to Southern Shores, Kitty Hawk, Martin's Point, and most of Duck and Kill Devil Hills.

SHUN XING CHINESE RESTAURANT, 5537 N. Croatan Hwy, The Marketplace; (252) 261-0202; shunxingobx.com; Chinese; $. Small restaurant serving well-made Szechuan-, Cantonese-, and Hunan-style dishes. Mostly takeout, but there is a small seating area.

SOUTHERN SHORES PIZZA AND DELI, 1 Ocean Blvd., Southern Shores Crossing; (252) 715-3940; southernshorespizza.com; Pizza; $–$$. Pizza the whole family will love with subs, calzones, and stromboli also on the menu. Classic Philadelphia Amoroso sub rolls used. Eat-in or take-out. Beer and wine available on premises.

STARBUCKS, 5597-A N. Croatan Hwy, The Marketplace; (252) 255-0790; Coffee; $. Yes, there is a Starbucks on the Outer Banks and to give them their due, they do a nice job. A classic small Starbucks coffee shop offering various pastries and other food items to go with your drink.

STEAMER'S RESTAURANT, 1 Ocean Blvd., Southern Shores Crossing; (252) 261-0224; steamersobx.com; Seafood; $$–$$$. Wonderful, comfortable restaurant specializing in seafood. However, the menu includes something for everyone, including the landlubber, and it's always well-prepared with fresh ingredients. Full bar service with a pleasant seating area around the bar.

ART'S PLACE, 4624 N. Virginia Dare Trl.; (252) 261-3233; artsplaceobx .com; Classic American; $–$$. An iconic Outer Banks burger haven on the Beach Road. And, yes, the burgers are that good. Sunday brunch is a belly-busting affair. It's a small place, but luckily there's some outside seating. Monday nights it's live jazz. Wednesday nights is open mic (see **Entertainment** chapter). Open year-round.

BAD BEAN BAJA GRILL, 3809 N. Croatan Hwy; (252) 449-2483; bad beanobx.com; Mexican; $$. Taking Mexican cuisine to the next level, Bad Bean shows how good the classic foods of Mexico can be when a skilled chef works the recipes. The burritos are huge. The fresh fish tacos and burritos change with availability. Full bar service.

BAREFOOT BERNIE'S, 3730 N. Croatan Hwy; (252) 261-1008; barefoot bernies.com; Caribbean American; $$. A local favorite serving great burgers, innovative Caribbean-inspired dishes and single-serve gourmet pizzas. Full bar with a very nice microbrew selection. First-come first-served seating and it gets very busy in the summer. The wait is worth it.

BLACK PELICAN OCEANFRONT CAFE, NC 12, MP 4; (252) 261-3171; blackpelican.com; American, Italian, and seafood; $$. This casual restaurant is in an old Coast Guard station and features an enclosed deck overlooking the Atlantic. It's roomy and wide, with three separate levels and a huge bar with several TVs. Hardwood floors, tongue-and-groove appointments, light gray accents, burgundy carpeting, and black bentwood chairs all add to the comfortable ambience of this moderately priced eatery. Gourmet pizzas are cooked in a wood-hearth oven. Try the steamed shellfish fresh from the sea. An extensive selection of appetizers are made from scratch. Dinner offerings include pasta and seafood specials, grilled or blackened to suit your taste. A children's menu is also available. Black Pelican serves lunch and dinner seven days a week, year-round.

CAPT'N FRANK'S, US 158, MP 4; (252) 261-9923; captnfranks.com; Hot dogs and shrimp; $. Capt'n Frank's is an institution on the Outer Banks, serving all-beef Oscar Mayer hot dogs with a variety of accompaniments. If "going to the dogs" doesn't appeal to you, Capt'n Frank's also offers barbecue sandwiches and addictive nacho fries—french fries with chili, cheese, hot peppers, and sour cream. Steamed shrimp is served nightly in season. Wash down the tasty morsels with a cold beer. Capt'n Frank's serves lunch and dinner daily Memorial Day through Labor Day. Off-season, the restaurant is open every day for lunch except Sunday.

DINING

HENRY'S RESTAURANT, US 158, MP 5; (252) 261-2025; henrysobx .com; American; $–$$. Everyone loves a trip to Henry's. Easy on the purse, this local favorite serves waffles, pancakes, sausages, and other hearty breakfast favorites until 1 p.m. each day. Lunch is also satisfying here with sandwiches and burgers among the most popular entrees. Dinner includes fresh fish, soups, and salads. A children's menu is available.

★ **HIGH COTTON BBQ,** NC 12 MP½; (252) 255-2275; highcotton bbq.com; BBQ; $$. For a flavorful taste of outstanding regional cooking, try High Cotton. These Tarheel natives prepare their barbecue by cooking it long hours over smoking hickory coals, producing Outer Banks barbecue at its very best. Ribs, beef brisket, and smoked or fried chicken are also available. Order with the traditional sides and some sweet tea, and you're in High Cotton. A kids' menu is available, and beer is served on premise. High Cotton is a popular choice to cater parties and weddings. Open March through December.

HURRICANE MO'S RESTAURANT & RAW BAR, NC 12 and East Kitty Hawk Rd., MP 4; (252) 261-0215; Seafood, vegetarian, and American; $$. This restaurant serves traditional fresh seafood, steaks, pasta, and many island-inspired creations in a cozy Tuscan-style dining room. Vegetarians have a wide selection, and there is a kids' menu. Seafood lovers enjoy the steamed and raw shellfish bar. This eatery has a full bar, including wine and beer. Nightly happy hour shrimp specials pack in fans of steamed shrimp! Check out the outdoor deck for wonderful place to enjoy a drink.

I GOT YOUR CRABS, 3809 N. Croatan Hwy; (252) 449-2483; igotyour crabs.com; Seafood; $$. The owner is a commercial fisherman, which pretty much tells the story of how fresh everything is. When crab is in season, it varies but mostly April through November, that's the dish to get. But the oysters are excellent as well. Serves wines from Sanctuary Vineyards, a local winery.

JIMMY'S SEAFOOD BUFFET, US 158, MP 4; (252) 261-4973; jimmys buffetobx.com; Seafood buffet and American; $$$. Jimmy's Seafood Buffet specializes in food and fun. Some say that the only thing more exciting than the food is the atmosphere. Start your evening off on the open-air thatched-roof porch, where the bar offers eight frozen drinks with a souvenir glass. "Kiddie cocktails" are available for the younger set. Inside this all-you-can-eat tropical paradise you'll find all of your favorite seafood and all you'll want of it! Choose from crab, shrimp, oysters, clams, and lobster. Landlubbers can opt for barbecued ribs, chicken, and prime rib, among more than 100 selections. There's also a soft-serve ice cream bar. Order from the menu as well. Jimmy's is open nightly for dinner starting at 2:30 p.m. in season; call for off-season hours.

JOHN'S DRIVE-IN, NC 12, MP 4¾, (252) 261-6227; johnsdrivein.com; Burgers and sandwiches; $. Home of the planet's best milk shakes, John's has been an Outer Banks institution for years. Folks have been known to drive 2 hours from Norfolk just to sip one of the fruit and ice cream concoctions, which are often so thick they won't flow through the straw. Sample a few and create some of your own combinations before deciding your favorite. The Mahi-mahi basket is amazing. Burgers are classic. Dogs get puppy cups of dog-friendly ice cream. Open May through September for lunch and early dinner. Closed Wednesday.

JOSEPHINE'S SICILIAN KITCHEN, NC 12, MP 4½, Dunes Shoppes; (252) 261-2669; obxitalianrestaurant.com; Italian, Mediterranean, and Greek; $$. From the moment you step into Josephine's, you'll feel transported to an authentic Italian restaurant. One of the newer hotspots in town, Chef Josephine Caggese reveals her passion for cooking in her delicious dishes. The menu changes weekly and be prepared for a small wait to get in during the season. Full bar.

LA FOGATA MEXICAN RESTAURANT, US 158, MP 4½; (252) 255-0934; Mexican; $. This traditional Mexican restaurant gets its name from the Spanish word for "campfire." For the price, La Fogata serves the best ethnic food on the beach. People wait in line to eat here on weekend nights. You'll see a lot of locals in this colorful spot year-round. Airy, bright, and decorated with Mexican art and photographs, the interior of this ultra-casual eatery usually hums with Latin tunes. The waiters bring baskets of crispy tortillas and bowls of homemade salsa as soon as they distribute the menus. All entree portions are generous, so save room for the main course. Recommended appetizers include the hot *queso* (cheese) dip and stuffed jalapeño peppers. Specialties include fajitas, enchiladas, and other traditional fare. Mixed drink and margarita prices among the lowest on the beach. Open for lunch and dinner year-round, seven days a week.

LONGBOARDS, 3833 N. Croatan Hwy; (252) 261-7377; longboardsobx.com; Classic American; $–$$. A great bar and gathering place in Kitty Hawk. Food goes well with the ambiance. Check out the handmade pizzas and wings.

OCEAN BOULEVARD, NC 12, MP 2; (252) 261-2546; obbistro.com; Fine dining; $$$. This cozy, upscale eatery gives you a great feeling from the moment you walk into the gold-walled dining room until you leave after a fabulous meal. It opened in 1995 and quickly became one of the most popular places on the Outer Banks. This elegant eatery will please even the most discriminating diners. The wine list has won the Wine Spectator Award of Excellence and contains more than 100 selections. Microbrewed beer is available and

DINING

the bar specializes in martinis. During summer, doors are open seven days a week. Reservations for dinner highly recommended. Music on the outside deck from 5 to 10 p.m. most days, weather permitting; later entertainment begins around 10:30 p.m. inside on Friday evening.

OUTER BANKS TACO BAR, US 158, MP 4½, Ocean Plaza; (252) 261-8226; obxtacobar.com; Mexican and seafood; $. Housemade corn tortillas and a free salsa bar are just two reasons to stop at Outer Banks Taco Bar. The quesadillas and burritos are delicious. Try a mojito or a margarita to round out your meal. Burgers are also served, and catering is available.

OUTER BEAN CAFÉ, US 158, MP 4½, Dunes Shoppes; (252) 261-6000; outerbean.com; Sandwiches, Middle Eastern, American, and vegetarian; $. With an almost European coffee bar feel to it, Outer Bean is a great place to meet a friend. There's a full breakfast and lunch menu offered, and whenever possible, food preparation is done with organic ingredients. Service can be a bit slow, but be patient—it's worth it. Seating is available at tables, the counter, and limited outdoor seating. Beer and wine on premise. Eat-in or take-out. Locals love it here and visitors will as well. Second smaller location in Duck.

POK'S ART, 3701 N. Croatan Hwy; (252) 715-4421; obxtogo.com; Asian; $$. Creative Asian-influenced dishes with an emphasis on Thai food. Chef Pok is one of the finest of the Outer Banks chefs and his touch is seen in the food. Take-out only.

⭐ **RUNDOWN CAFE**, NC 12, MP 1; (252) 255-0026; rundowncafe .com; Caribbean and American; $$. Open since 1993, this Caribbean-style cafe has been a big hit with locals, offering spicy, unusual alternatives to traditional Outer Banks seafood. Named for a Jamaican stew, Rundown serves island entrees flavored with African and Indian accents. There's a full bar, and the bartenders can come up with some pretty potent concoctions. Guinness stout, Bass, Pyramid, and Harp beers are on tap. The upstairs bar is a great place to soak in the sunset, catch a few rays, or linger over a cool cocktail after a hot day in the sun. The downstairs dining area is smoke-free. Lunch and dinner are served seven days a week. A kids' menu is available, and take-out orders are welcome. Rundown is closed in December and January.

RUSSO'S BISTRO AND BAR, 3712 N. Croatan Hwy; (252) 480-2855; russosbistro.com; $$–$$$$. Joey Russo is an amazingly creative chef so the menu tends to change with what is available and the season. Even his breakfast menu reflects his passion for food with a house-cured lox on bagel. Full bar service. Closed Monday and Tuesday; Dinner Thursday, Friday, and Saturday. Reservations strongly recommended.

DINING

SANYA ASIAN BISTRO, 3919 N. Croatan Hwy; (252) 261-1946; sanya obx.com; Asian; $$. Very well-prepared Asian dishes in a pleasant dining room. Excellent sushi preparations as well. Full bar service.

SHIPWRECK'S TAPHOUSE & GRILL, 4020 N. Croatan Hwy; (252) 261-7800; shipwrecksobx.com; Classic American; $$. Comfortable and roomy. Full bar service. The burgers are good and the seafood is done right. When the weather is right the wide doors are open and outdoor seating and a feeling of being outdoors is part of the experience. When the weather is right and the wide doors are open, eating a meal and sipping a beer outside is part of the experience.

STACK'EM HIGH PANCAKES, 3801 N. Croatan Hwy; (252) 261-8221; stackemhigh.com; Breakfast and lunch; $. For over 30 years, Stack'em High has been flipping pancakes, scrambling eggs, and being a part of Outer Banks life. Cafeteria-style ordering, but everything is cooked to order. It gets very busy in the summer on Saturday and Sunday mornings.

TRIO RESTAURANT & MARKET, 3708 N. Croatan Hwy.; (252) 261-0277; obxtrio.com; Soups, sandwiches, and cheese plates; $–$$. A favorite gathering place on the Outer Banks, TRiO has the largest wine by the glass and beer selection around. The sandwiches and cheese plates go perfectly with the wonderful wines and beers. Be sure to check out the wine and beer selections in the retail store. Live music most nights.

VILAI'S THAI KITCHEN, 5230 N. Virginia Dare Trl.; (252) 441-8424; vilaithai.com; Thai; $$. Small restaurant serving classic Thai dishes. Local ingredients used when available. Also serving sushi.

> ℹ Very few restaurants on the Outer Banks serve dinner past 8:30 or 9 p.m. During the lively summer season, however, you may be able to get a late dinner from one of the carry-out restaurants on the islands.

DINING

KILL DEVIL HILLS

AMERICAN PIE, NC 12, MP 9½; (252) 441-3332; americanpieobx.com; Pizza; $. For some mouthwatering fresh-baked pizza with a hand-tossed crust, step into American Pie. This restaurant serves only the freshest ingredients on their New York-style pizzas. Homemade stromboli, calzones, subs, and salads round out the menu. The homemade ice cream is a must to complete your meal. Patrons may dine indoors, outdoors, or order to take-out. Delivery is also available.

ASHLEY'S ESPRESSO PARLOUR, 100 E Helga St.; (252) 715-3430; alltimeroastingobx.com; Coffee; $. Ashley Linnekin has been roasting coffee on the Outer Banks for about 10 years, but she's out on her own now in this wonderful Latin America-inspired cafe she and her husband, Eric, created. It's all roasted in small batches and she is constantly looking for new coffees and improving what she has. Dog- and kid-friendly.

AWFUL ARTHUR'S OYSTER BAR & RESTAURANT, NC 12, MP 6; (252) 441-5955; awfularthursobx.com; Seafood; $$. Awful Arthur's is a comfortably casual place where you won't mind peeling seasoned shrimp or picking the meat from succulent crab legs with messy fingers. Seafood is the specialty. You'll find scallops, oysters, clams, mussels, homemade crab cakes, and daily entree specials. The bartenders are some of the fastest shuckers in town. Bass ale and several other varieties of beer are on tap, or order from a full line of liquor and specialty drinks. For landlubbers, several are available. At night Awful Arthur's is usually packed. A late night menu is available. Awful Arthur's T-shirts are seen all over the world and are local favorites. This popular eatery is open seven days a week year-round for lunch and dinner.

BEACHSIDE BISTRO, 1731 N. Virginia Dare Trl.; (252) 441-7126; obx beachsidebistro.com; American and seafood; $–$$$. Located in the Sea Ranch Resort Hotel, Beachside Bistro offers a marvelous oceanside breakfast, lunch, or dining experience. Freshly prepared dishes served in an intimate dining room make for a great experience. Weather permitting, the outside deck is the perfect place to enjoy a drink, an appetizer, and live music.

BOB'S GRILL, US 158, MP 9; (252) 441-0707; bobsgrillobx.com; American; $. Bob serves big, cheap breakfasts all year, seven days a week, until 2:30 p.m.—and that's hard to find around here. The blueberry pancakes are big enough to cover the entire plate. Eggs are made any way you want, and the hash browns flavored with onions and peppers are some of the best around. For lunch, have a hamburger, tuna steak, or another traditional hot or cold sandwich. Dinner is also served here; beer on premise.

BONZER SHACK, NC 12, MP 9; (252) 480-1010; bonzershack.com; Mexican, Southern, and American; $–$$. Bonzer Shack is a fun and delicious spot to eat and then hang out in the side yard and listen to live tunes while playing corn hole. The menu offers surprisingly great choices. Overstuffed fish burritos and mildly spicy chipotle chicken, both served with black beans and rice, are two of the delicious choices. A full bar specializes in beer and margaritas. This kid-friendly spot is open March through October.

BOOTY TREATS ICE CREAM AND SHAVED ICE, 1209 S. Croatan Hwy, (252) 722-5250; and 2600 S. Virginia Dare Trl., (252) 715-3385; bootytreats .com; Dessert; $. About as traditional as an ice cream shop gets. Hand-dipped ice cream and real deal milkshakes and malts. Shaved Hawaiian ice a specialty.

CAPTAIN GEORGE'S, 705 S. Croatan Hwy; (252) 480-6677; captain georges.com; American seafood; $$. Bring the family and a huge appetite. Captain George's buffet is sure to satisfy even the hungriest diner. Seafood is their specialty, but other items are on the buffet line. There is an a la carte menu and gluten-free selections.

CHILLI PEPPERS COASTAL GRILL, US 158, MP 5; (252) 441-8081; chilli-peppers.com; $$. World fusion with a southwestern twist describes the cooking at this fun, award-winning restaurant. Adventuresome diners are wowed by the chefs' wild concoctions. Many dishes have some type of chile in them. If you prefer a milder meal, they can do that and still tickle some untapped taste buds. The menu here changes frequently, with daily lunch and dinner specials sometimes stunning even the regulars. Weekly Tapas Nights, which feature little plates of dishes from a chosen cuisine, are held on Thursday nights in fall, winter, and spring. One week you might taste samples of German food, the next Italian, the next Moroccan, and so on and it's always a big hit with the locals. Sushi nights are also popular.

CHINA KING, Dare Center, 1728 N. Croatan Hwy; (252) 449-2198; china kingkdh.com; Chinese; $. Traditional Chinese food from a small restaurant next to the Food Lion. Mostly takeout, although there is limited seating available.

COUNTRY DELI, 1900 S. Croatan Hwy; (252) 441-5684; countrydeliobx .com; Sandwiches; $. Deli offers breakfast breads plus some of the biggest and best sandwiches on the beach. You can create your own sandwich or choose from several popular menu items. Side salads of macaroni, pasta, potato, and vegetables also are served. Pick from several types of chips; sour pickles come free with every option. Brownies and cheesecake are tempting dessert selections. Country Deli is open for lunch and dinner seven days a week during the summer and offers free delivery to Nags Head and parts of Kill Devil Hills. No credit cards accepted.

DARE DEVIL'S AUTHENTIC PIZZERIA, NC 12, MP 9; (252) 441-6330; daredevilspizzeria.com; Pizza; $. This pizza parlor has been in business for more than a decade and is known for its superb stromboli and hand-tossed pizzas. You can also order any item for takeout. Dare Devil's is open seven days a week for lunch and dinner from March through November.

FOOD DUDES, 1216 S. Virginia Dare Trl.; (252) 441-7994; fooddudes kitchen.com; Seafood, Southern, and Caribbean; $–$$. Seafood is where it's at with the fish of the day changing daily. There are burgers, veggie dishes, and a small kid's menu, but freshly prepared seafood is where Food Dudes made their reputation. There is a small but nice seating area.

FRONT PORCH CAFÉ, US 158 MP 6; (252) 449-6616; frontporchcafe .net; Coffee; $. The Front Porch Cafe sources top-quality coffee beans from all over the world, then roasts each batch by hand in their store. Freshly baked cinnamon rolls, scones, and muffins are available every day. Customers can also select from the wonderful varieties of teas on hand. Other locations are in Nags Head and Manteo.

FUJI JAPANESE STEAKHOUSE, 1201 S. Croatan Hwy; (252) 449-0628; fujiobx.com; Japanese, $$–$$$. Traditional Japanese steakhouse with all theatrics of a hibachi dinner prepared at the table. The menu also features very extensive sushi selections.

GOOMBAYS GRILLE & RAW BAR, NC 12, MP 7; (252) 441-6001; goombays.com; Caribbean seafood; $$. This island-style eatery is light and bright inside with lots of artwork, an outrageous fish tank, and a wall-size tropical mural in the dining room. The ambience is upbeat and casual, with wooden tables and chairs and a bare tile floor. The horseshoe-shaped bar, which is separate from the eating area, is a great place to try some of the delicious appetizers or drink specials. The kid's menu includes "Kiddy Cocktails" and advice: "Wash your hands, keep your elbows off the table. Don't feed the alligator under the table…" Key lime pie is always a smart choice for dessert. Goombays is open for lunch and dinner seven days a week in summer. Call for off-season hours. Goombays closes for December and January. The Sunday brunch is island-famous.

> **i** The soft-sculpture ceiling at Goombays Grille & Raw Bar is an amazing work of art. While sitting in the dining room, you can look up and imagine you're seeing what a fish sees when it glances up toward the ocean's surface.

JACK BROWN'S BEER & BURGER JOINT, 800 S. Virginia Dare Trl.; (252) 715-3328; jackbrownsjoint.com; Burgers; $. Jack Brown's keeps it simple—they serve freshly-made burgers with a wide array of toppings, and they serve beer. They do have a kid's menu so there are soft drinks. Service is quick and professional. The rustic throwback decor is worth a trip. Backyard has large seating area that features live music during the summer.

JK'S, US 158, MP 9; (252) 441-9555; jksrestaurant.com; Steak and seafood; $$$. Fine-dining insiders love JK's selection of mesquite-grilled meats. JK's serves Western beef shipped directly from Nebraska, lamb and veal from Summerfield Farms in Virginia, and ribs from the Midwest. A seasoned, professional staff fits right in with the classy, comfortable dining room and bar. Three to four varieties of fresh fish are offered nightly. The menu varies according to the best meats available, but generally it has prime rib, porterhouse steak, New York strip, Kansas City strip, top sirloin, veal rib chop, and lamb loin chops. Ribs and chicken are dry marinated with JK's special seasoning and are then mesquite grilled. JK's has a full bar and an excellent wine list with some really good values. Dinner is served from 5 p.m. year-round; takeout is available.

JOLLY ROGER RESTAURANT, NC 12, MP 6; (252) 441-6530; jolly rogerobx.com; Italian, seafood, and American; $$. Serving some of the locals' favorite breakfasts, this lively restaurant is open for three meals a day, 365 days a year. Besides the usual eggs, pancakes, sausage, bacon, and toast, Jolly Roger's bakery cooks up some of the biggest muffins and sticky buns you've ever seen. For lunch choose from sandwiches, local seafood, or daily specials. Dinner entrees include homestyle Italian dishes, steaks, broiled and fried fish, and a popular prime rib special each Friday. All the desserts are homemade, and special orders are accepted for items to go. The food isn't fancy, but the portions are enormous. You'll have no excuse if you leave here hungry. Jolly Roger also steams spiced shrimp in the separate bar area each afternoon and is the karaoke headquarters of the Outer Banks seven nights a week.

KILL DEVIL'S FROZEN CUSTARD & BEACH FRIES, 1002 S. Croatan Hwy; (252) 441-5900; killdevilsfrozencustard.com; Dessert and burgers; $. Classic frozen custard stand that also serves amazing burgers and fries. Should be on every family's Outer Banks to-do list. Picnic tables available.

THE KILL DEVIL GRILL, 2008 S. Virginia Dare Trl.; (252) 449-8181; thekilldevilgrill.com; Classic American; $$–$$$. Housed in a classic diner that has been listed in the National Register of Historic Places, this is a local and visitors' favorite. It can get really busy at time, but the wait is worth it. The front is the classic diner look with vinyl barstools and a couple of tables. The main dining area is large, but not large enough in the summer. Full bar service and a small but nice wine list.

LADLES SOUPS, 1901 S. Croatan Hwy; (252) 715-4800; ladlessoups.com/zuppa-toscana-2; Lunch; $. The concept is simple: homemade soup made fresh daily, all sandwiches and salads made to order and reasonable prices. A favorite lunchtime gathering place.

MAKO MIKE'S, US 158, MP 7; (252) 480-1919; makomikes.com; Seafood, Cajun, Mediterranean, and Asian; $$. This is the most outrageously decorated dining establishment on the Outer Banks. The fluorescent shark fins outside, decorated with swirls, stripes, and polka dots, don't give even a glimpse into what you'll see once you step inside. Some patrons compare it to an underwater experience. We think it's almost like visiting an octopus's garden complete with three separate levels of dining, fish mobiles dangling overhead, painted chairs, bright colors exploding everywhere, and murals along the deep blue walls. Can accommodate large groups. Live music during the summer.

> **i** If you're heading out for a day on the sand, Stop 'N' Shop Convenience and Deli on the Beach Road in Kill Devil Hills is a great place to stock up. It has one of the best delis on the beach, an excellent selection of wine and beer, everything you'll need for a successful day's fishing, and all the latest water toys, too.

MAMA KWAN'S GRILL AND TIKI BAR, US 158, MP 9½; (252) 441-7889; mamakwans.com; American, Asian fusion, and seafood; $$. Mama Kwan's is a favorite surf-style hangout in Kill Devil Hills, a haven of good food sandwiched between McDonald's and on French Fry Alley in a cedar-shake building. Mama's features local seafood, land food, and veggies with touches from around the world. Full bar, lunch and dinner daily. Late-night, Mama's becomes a popular hangout. Late night menu.

MAX'S ITALIAN RESTAURANT AND PIZZERIA, 1712 N. Croatan Hwy, Dare Center; (252) 261-3113; maxspizzaobx.com; Italian. $–$$. Don't let the pizzeria feel of the restaurant fool you—Chef Grant Sharp is a classically trained chef who turns out some of the best pizza and pasta dishes around. Everything is scratch made from fresh ingredients or when best imported. Hours vary in the offseason to accommodate family time.

MILLER'S SEAFOOD & STEAK HOUSE, 1520 S. Virginia Dare Trl.; (252) 441-7674; millersseafood.com; Steaks and seafood; $$–$$$$. A mainstay of the Outer Banks breakfast and dinner scene for well over 25 years. Millers does not serve lunch, closing at noon for four hours. Breakfast is huge. Dinner focuses on fresh local catch and steaks.

OUTER BANKS BREWING STATION, US 158, MP 8½; (252) 449-BREW (2739); obbrewing.com; Seafood, Asian Fusion, and Contemporary; $$. Everything about the Outer Banks Brewing Station is first class. Fine hand-crafted brews, inspired cuisine, and noble yet subtle decor all work together to provide a sublime culinary experience. Customers who expect standard brewhouse pub fare will be pleasantly surprised to find contemporary, cutting-edge cuisine prepared by trained chefs. The signature beers are always in demand. Ölsch is always on tap, and five other brews change according to the season, the brewer's whim, or the alignment of the stars. The food is billed as revolutionary, and it truly is outstanding. Specials are always appealing and diners are sure to leave hoping to return. Lunch and dinner served daily; kids menu available. Ask about the 93-foot wind turbine!

PLAZA AZTECA, 8714, 1502 S. Croatan Hwy; (252) 255-1062; plaza azteca.com; Mexican; $–$$. All the traditional Mexican dishes in a large yet welcoming dining area. Guacamole is made at your table side.

PEPPERCORNS, NC 12, MP 9½, Ramada Plaza Resort; (252) 441-2151; Seafood and American; $$. With a wide-open dining room overlooking the Atlantic Ocean, Peppercorns has a traditional family menu with something for everyone. Many Outer Banks favorites, including locally caught shrimp and crab cakes are served here. The soup du jour is always filling and delicious. Entrees include chicken stuffed with crabmeat, Andouille sausage, and smoked Gouda cheese, and jerk Mahi-mahi served with a mouthwatering pineapple sweet-and-sour sauce. Vegetarian entrees are always provided. There's a full bar and a children's menu. This restaurant is open daily year-round for breakfast, lunch, and dinner. There's nightly entertainment in season on the outdoor tiki deck and in the lounge. Peppercorns is a popular spot for banquets and wedding receptions.

PIGMAN'S BAR-B-QUE, US 158 MP 9½; (252) 441-6803; pigman.com; BBQ; $$. At this counter-service eatery you can get beef, pork, chicken, and barbecue. Try the low-fat creations: catfish, turkey, and tuna barbecue. The sweet potato fries here are spectacular. Catering is available. Pigman's is open for lunch and dinner seven days a week year-round. Piggy Lou's Little Squealers is a special menu for those younger than age 10 or older than age 65.

ROOSTERS SOUTHERN KITCHEN, 804 S. Croatan Hwy; (252) 441-4594; roosterssouthernkitchen.com; Southern American; $$–$$$. Innovative Southern cuisine in an open-style dining room. Try the bacon and eggs for an unexpected taste treat—house-smoked pork belly, house-made deviled eggs, Southern pepper jelly glaze. All of it created in the kitchen. Full bar with some a great selection of bourbons.

Farmers' Markets

Farmers' markets represent one of the oldest forms of taking merchandise directly to the consumer, and the Outer Banks offers several fine choices. All through Currituck, markets spot the highway and many offer delicious locally grown harvests, as well as shrimp, jams, and homemade breads. If driving in through Currituck, take a moment and stop at the Weeping Radish Brewery in Jarvisburg. Not only can you purchase fresh produce grown on the premises, hormone- and antibiotic-free meats and brats are also offered. Here are several fine farmers' market choices on the beach.

- **Dowdy Park**—3005 S. Croatan Hwy, Nags Head, Thursday 9–1 p.m.; Local farmers only; Mid-May to Columbus Day weekend.

- **Green Acres Farmers' Market**—NC 12, Wee Winks Plaza, Duck Island Farm, NC 12, Corolla; (252) 453-8285

- **Manteo Farmers' Market**—Downtown Manteo waterfront; (252) 305-4800; Open Saturday morning, 8–noon; May–sometime in fall; Also crafts, local art, and more.

- **Nags Head Produce**—US 158, MP 12½ beside Austin's Seafood; (252) 441-9154

- **Outer Banks Farmers' Market**—MP 10½, South Beach Plaza, Nags Head; (252) 480-5779

- **Sticky Bottom Produce Company**—NC 12, Hatteras; (252) 986-2381

- **Tomato Shack**—1195 Duck Rd., Duck

- **Tarheel Too**—Seagate North, Kill Devil Hills.

DINING

SAL'S NY PIZZA, 710 S. Virginia Dare Trl.; (252) 715-3145; salsnypizza obx.com; Italian, $–$$. Way more than just a pizza parlor, Sal's serves up some great sandwiches—try any of the paninis, and pasta dishes. Pool tables and games give it a one-of-a-kind feel.

SANDBARS RAW BAR & GRILL, 1716 N. Croatan Hwy; (252)-715-2882; sandbarsouterbanks.com; Seafood and pasta; $$. Specializing in serving the freshest seafood with the personal touch of either of the chef owners. Full bar and a late night menu.

SECRET ISLAND TAVERN, 504 S. Virginia Dare Trl.; (252) 441-7484; secretislandobx.com; Pub food; $. Taking over what was once Port o' Call Restaurant, Secret Island continues the tradition of live music. The menu is simple but the food is well-prepared. The drink menu, however, is extensive.

SLICE PIZZERIA, 710 S. Croatan Hwy, MP 8½; (252) 449-8888; slice pizzeriaobx.com; Italian; $. One of the most popular pizzerias on the northern Outer Banks, and for good reason. Thin crust or deep dish pizzas. A huge by the slice selection. The garlic knots and sausage rolls are amazing. Fantastic pasta dishes as well. Indoor and outdoor seating available.

TEN 0 SIX, 1006 S. Virginia Dare Trl.; (252) 441-9607; tenosixobx.com; American; $. Breakfast and lunch only, with breakfast prepared all day. And they prepare it as ordered. Check out the breakfast burritos especially. Burgers and baskets are excellent as well. A grab and go restaurant.

THE THAI ROOM, NC 12, MP 8½, Oceanside Plaza; (252) 441-1180; thairoomobx.com; Thai; $$. The Thai Room has been an insiders' favorite for years. Choose your own level of spice—from mild to gasping hot. If asked, "Very hot?"—think twice before you say yes. Besides the daily specials. Try the deep-fried soft-shell crabs when they're in season; they're perfectly crunchy and beyond description. The Thai Room is open for lunch and dinner year-round. All items are available for takeout. The restaurant also has a full bar where you can indulge in exotic drinks and Thai beer while you wait for a table or take-out order.

TWO ROADS TAVERN, 3105 N. Croatan Hwy, Seagate North; (252) 255-1980; tworoadstavern.com; Burgers and seafood; $–$$. Two Roads serves some of the best and most imaginative burgers on the beach. They do a great job with oysters as well. Full bar service and a very nice kids menu.

COLINGTON ISLAND

COLINGTON CAFE, 1029 Colington Rd.; (252) 480-1123; colingtoncafe .com; Seafood and American; $$$. Step back in time at this cozy Victorian cafe, nestled among live oaks on Colington Road. This popular restaurant is only a mile off the Bypass, but once you've arrived you'll feel worlds away from the busy beach. This restored old home set high on a hill is tranquil and absolutely lovely. Three small dining rooms are adorned in tasteful decor. Nightly specials may include wonderful pasta dishes, a mixed grill with hollandaise, game fish, and tender filet mignon. Seafood entrees depend upon what's just been caught. Only fresh herbs and vegetables are used in cooking and as side dishes. Beer and wine; open for dinner seven days a week, April through November.

DINING

COLINGTON PIZZA, 100 Colingwood Ln.; (252) 441-3339; colington pizza.com; Pizza; $. Very reasonably priced. Very local, but very good pizza. Free delivery to Colington Island.

THE SALTBOX CAFE, 1469 Colington Rd.; (252) 255-5594; thesaltbox cafe.com; Seafood and American; $$–$$$. Experienced chefs are the proprietors at this new restaurant in the heart of Colington. Enjoy an array of tasty eats in this charming cottage-style spot. Diners can choose from wide offerings on the menu, including soft-shell crab, leg of lamb, or a Cuban sandwich. Beer and wine available. Breakfast Thursday through Saturday with a wonderful Sunday brunch; lunch and dinner Monday through Saturday.

NAGS HEAD

BASNIGHT'S LONE CEDAR CAFE, Nags Head–Manteo Causeway; (252) 441-5405; lonecedarcafe.com; Seafood; $$–$$$. The Basnight family of Manteo operates this casual, upscale eatery where diners wearing everything from shorts to suits are welcome. This restaurant is one of very few in the state to be named a certified green restaurant. Shedders along the soundfront area of the restaurant provide a scenic spot for crabs to shed their shells and provide soft-shell crabs for diner. No chemicals are used at this toxin-free restaurant. Pretty much everything is delicious here, including the hot crab dip, sliced duck breast, and clam chowder. Vegetarian and children's offerings are available. Reservations not accepted.

BISCUITS N' PORN, 2112 S. Croatan Hwy; (252) 441-6446; Breakfast and lunch; $. It's cafeteria-style hot bar in a gas station convenience store, but there's a reason why there is always…always…a line. The absolute best (!) biscuits on the beach. Huge, fluffy, mouthwatering, amazing.

⭐ **BLUE MOON BEACH GRILL**, MP 13, Surfside Plaza; (252) 261-2583; bluemoonbeachgrill.com; Seafood and American; $$–$$$. This tucked—away restaurant is beyond worth seeking out . . . it's quickly risen to the top of the list as a favorite dining spot for locals and visitors alike. Food served here is always impeccably prepared and prices are reasonable. If you want to meet locals, have dinner at the bar and find out all the latest goings—on in town. Full bar, open year—round. Microbrews on tap. Be prepared for a brief wait . . . the Blue Moon is almost always packed. Lunch and dinner, year-round.

DARRELL'S 2 BBQ & SEAFOOD, 5000 S. Croatan Hwy, Outer Banks Mall; (252) 449-5400; darrells2obx.com; Seafood and BBQ; $–$$. The name says it all. The original Darrell's in Manteo has always been known for serving fresh fish, and that continues at Darrell's 2, but added to the mix is some great barbecue and craft beers and wine.

DIRTY DICK'S CRAB HOUSE, US 158, MP 10½; (252) 480-3425; dirtydickscrabs.com; Seafood; $$. The litany of crab choices at Dirty Dick's Crab House reminds us of Bubba's roster of shrimp in *Forrest Gump*. There are snow crab legs, soft-shell crab sandwiches, spiced crabs, crab cakes, and steamed crabs, plus steamed shrimp, clams, clam chowder, gumbo, jambalaya, and Cajun creole. The popular Dick Burger is a crab and shrimp patty with Cajun sauce. There are sandwich platter specials and offerings for the kids. You can purchase Dick's special spice and famous Dirty Dick's T-shirts. Crustaceans are cooked to order for takeout. Dirty Dick's has a sister Outer Banks location on NC 12 in Avon. Both locations are open seasonally; call for hours.

DUNE BURGER, 7304 S. Virginia Dare Trl.; (252) 441-2441; American; facebook.com/pg/duneburgerob; $. As old school Nags Head beach burger shack as it gets. Great burgers, killer hotdogs, and ice cream. Right across the street from Jennette's Pier.

THE DUNES, US 158, MP 16½; (252) 441-1600; thedunesrestaurant .com; Seafood and American; $–$$. When a large crowd or big family is gathering for a meal, this beautiful restaurant accommodates all in its three huge dining rooms. Breakfast at the Dunes is a Nags Head tradition—you can tell by the packed parking lot—where every early-morning entree in every imaginable combination is offered. A popular breakfast bar is available or order off the extensive menu. Lunches include great burgers and homemade crab cakes served with fries and coleslaw. Dinners feature local, well-prepared seafood moderately priced and a huge salad bar. All-you-can-eat specials are popular. There are also plenty of desserts to choose from if you're not already too full. The Dunes' R Bar is a full-service cocktail lounge. The Dunes serves every day except in late-December and most of January. A children's menu is offered.

FATBOYZ ICE CREAM & GRILL, 7208 S. Virginia Dare Trl.; (252) 441-6514; fatboyzobx.com; American; $. Classic burgers—the really tasty ones that are so good for the soul if not your health, killer crab cake and real milkshakes. It's what summer on the beach is all about. Outdoor seating available only.

FISH HEADS BAR & GRILL, 8901 S. Old Oregon Inlet Rd.; (252) 441-5740; fishheadsobx.com; American and seafood; $. Perched on top of a fishing pier, the ambiance is the Atlantic Ocean. Breakfast, lunch, and dinner are freshly prepared. Crabcakes are homemade. Live music in the summer. Open seasonally.

DINING

FRONT PORCH CAFÉ, 2515 S. Croatan Hwy; (252) 449-6616; frontporchcafe.net; Coffee; $. The Front Porch Cafe sources top-quality coffee beans from all over the world, then roasts each batch by hand in their store. Freshly baked cinnamon rolls, scones, and muffins are available every day. Customers can also select from the wonderful varieties of teas on hand. Other locations are in Nags Head and Manteo. Nags Head and Manteo serve beer and wine.

GRITS GRILL, US 158, MP 14; (252) 449-2888; gritsgrill.com; Breakfast; $. Just north of the Outer Banks Mall is Grits Grill, which has a strong local following. The restaurant offers a standard-fare breakfast and lunch menu plus fresh bakery items. This is the place to go to get real Southern grits with breakfast. Grits Grill specializes in take-out orders and is open all year from 6 a.m. to 3 p.m.

IT'S ALL GRAVY ITALIAN MARKET, 6705 S. Croatan Hwy; (252) 473-7326; Italian; itsallgravyobx.com. "Gravy" is Italian-American slang for any pasta sauce that has meat in it. For anyone from the Philadelphia area of Pennsylvania or New Jersey it's like a trip to South Philly. Subs, the real deal cheese steaks, and more. Closed Sundays and Tuesdays.

LA FOGATA MEXICAN RESTAURANT, US 158, MP 14; (252) 441-4179; lafogataobx.com; Mexican; $. Across from the Outer Banks Mall, La Fogata joins its original Kitty Hawk sister restaurant with the same name and some delicious Mexican food at affordable prices. These restaurants boast a strong Outer Banks following. The mall location has the same menu and similar decor as the Kitty Hawk restaurant (see the listing under Kitty Hawk for more information).

LUCKY 12, US 12, MP 12; (252) 255-5825; lucky12tavern.com; American and seafood; $–$$. Locals and visitors make Lucky 12 a frequent stop for great food with a fun atmosphere. Diners enjoy shrimp and oyster sandwiches, portobello mushroom sandwiches, and the Nags Mess burger is not to be missed. Finer dining options abound here as well. Open daily 11:30 a.m. until 2 a.m. Beer, wine, and full bar. Lots of TVs, both inside and out, carry a full sports package for sport enthusiasts' entertainment. Outdoor patio, pool, pinball, and more. Pizza served late night.

MILLER'S WATERFRONT RESTAURANT, 6916 S. Croatan Hwy; (252) 441-6151; millerswaterfront.com; Seafood and steaks; $$$–$$$$. Spectacular views across Roanoke sound enhance lunch and dinner featuring fresh seafood from local fishermen. Full bar service with a wonderful bar menu designed for sharing.

MULLIGAN'S, US 158, MP 13; (252) 480-2000; mulligansobx.com; American, Seafood; $$. Mulligan's can lay claim to serving some of the best burgers on the beach. The burgers are big, juicy, and tasty and come with a variety of toppings. Mulligan's also serves steak, seafood, and an array of pasta entrees for lunch and dinner. A new steam bar, upstairs and downstairs dining rooms, and two full bars make this hopping restaurant a great place to visit when you are hungry and don't want to wait forever on your food. Mulligan's is located in a bright yellow building across the street and just south of Jockey's Ridge. The interior is colorful and fun. A children's menu is available. The restaurant is open year-round and has gone green, recycling glass, oyster shells, and more. Evening entertainment includes poker on Tuesday night, and karaoke on Thursday and Friday.

NAGS HEAD PIZZA COMPANY, 7531 S. Virginia Dare Trl.; (252) 715-3455; nagsheadpizzaco.com; Pizza; $–$$. A build-your-own pizza company. Fresh ingredients and homemade sauce. Pickup and delivery only. Delivery from Kitty Hawk to Wanchese.

NEW CHINA BUFFET, 5000 S. Croatan Hwy, Outer Banks Mall; (252) 449-8000; Chinese; $. Chinese buffet with an extensive takeout menu. Very reasonable pricing.

NEW YORK PIZZA PUB, 2217 S. Croatan Hwy; (252) 441-2660; nypizza pub.com; Italian; $–$$. Family-friendly NY style pizza and pasta restaurant with a large seating area. There are some great steak and seafood items on the menu as well. Almost 30 big screen TVs make it a great sports bar and the late night entertainment is an Outer Banks favorite.

OLD NAGS HEAD CAFE, NC 12, MP 13; (252) 441-1141; nagsheadcafe .com; Southern and seafood; $$. For dining in or for take-out, Old Nags Head Cafe is sure to please. Entrees include favorites like shrimp and grits. A children's menu is available. Breakfast and lunch Tuesday through Sunday. Dinner Thursday through Sunday. Closed Mondays. Full bar. Call for off-season hours.

OWEN'S RESTAURANT, NC 12, MP 16½; (252) 441-7309; owens restaurant.com; Southern and seafood; $$$$. Clara and Bob Owens first owned a small food stand in Manteo. In 1946 they upgraded and opened a 24-seat cafe in Nags Head on the deserted strip of sand that's now filled with hotels, rental cottages, and thousands of vacationers who arrive each summer. This food-loving family now serves some of the best traditional Outer Banks-style seafood in the area. Dinner is the only meal served at Owens, and they do it right. Homey and upscale, the food is fresh and made from scratch. Locally caught seafood, often fresh off the boat, is broiled, fried, sautéed, or grilled each

DINING

evening. There is a mixed grill for patrons who prefer prime rib with their fish. The upstairs piano bar is marvelous.

PAMLICO JACK'S PIRATE HIDEAWAY, US 158, MP 16; (252) 441-2637; pamlicojacks.com; American and seafood; $$. This family-style restaurant has a killer deck and view of the Pamlico Sound. The food here is deliciously prepared and is island inspired. Legend has it that Pamlico Jack traveled from the Caribbean to the Keys, and then the Outer Banks and back again! And the menu offers the finest from each area. Open nightly.

PIER HOUSE RESTAURANT & CAPTAIN ANDY'S TIKI BAR, NC 12, MP 12, Nags Head Fishing Pier; (252) 441-5141; nagsheadpier.com; American; $. With an amazing ocean view on the beach, this family-style restaurant allows patrons to sit right above the ocean. You can feel the salt spray if you dine on the screened porch, and from inside the air conditioned building, you'll notice that waves sometimes crash beneath the wooden floor's slats. This is a great, easygoing place to enjoy a big breakfast before a day of fishing or to take a break from angling on a hot afternoon. The Em Special is an insiders' favorite for breakfast. Lunch includes sandwiches, soups, and seafood specials. Dinner entrees include local fresh seafood, steaks, and chicken. All-you-can-eat dinners are popular picks. Free sightseeing passes come with supper so you can stroll down the long pier after your meal and watch the anglers and surfers. Pier House Restaurant is open seven days a week from March through November. Breakfast, lunch, and dinner are served until mid-October, and the restaurant has all liquor permits.

> **i** Clean the fish you catch, and the Pier House Restaurant in Nags Head will broil or fry it right up for you.

PIZZAZZ PIZZA, 2515 S. Croatan Hwy; (252) 261-1111; pizzazzpizza.net; $–$$. Great pizza at an affordable price. The baked subs are fantastic. Three locations on the Outer Banks: Corolla, Duck, and Nags Head.

RED DRUM GRILLE AND TAPHOUSE, NC 12, MP 10; (252) 480-1095; Seafood and American; $$–$$$. Since opening in 1998, the Red Drum Grille and Taphouse has been carving out its niche on the Outer Banks. Glossy, deep rust-colored tables and cozy oak booths give the room a warm, inviting feel. The menu pleases just about everyone. Lunch can include something from the steamer or a large burger. Dinner items range from apple-glazed pork chops to a mixed grill of the day. Kids menu.

SAM & OMIES, NC 12, MP 16½; (252) 441-7366; samandomies.net; American and seafood; $$. Begun in 1937 as a place for early-morning anglers to indulge in a big breakfast before the Oregon Inlet charter fishing fleet took off, Sam & Omie's is one of the oldest family restaurants on the barrier islands. The restaurant, however, retains its old beach charm and continues to produce hearty, homestyle food based on traditional local recipes for breakfast, lunch, and dinner. Local fishermen congregate to contemplate the day's catch, and families flock to enjoy the low-priced, filling meals. For breakfast, omelets are a favorite. Insiders like to make a meal of the rich she crab soup and red chile poppers. Salads, sandwiches, hamburgers, fish fillets, turkey clubs, and more are also served. Open March through November, at least. Call for winter hours. Full bar.

SINGLE FIN BISTRO BAR & GRILL, 2424 S. Croatan Hwy; (252) 715-3983; singlefinobx.com; Thai and seafood; $$. Single Fin has quickly become a local favorite. Owner and Executive Chef Pok is one of the best of the Outer Banks chef's with an imaginative flair for food preparation. Great service, and a full sushi bar as well as a fully stocked bar.

SOOEY'S BBQ & RIB SHACK, 3919 S. Virginia Dare Trl.; (252) 449-6465; sooeysbbq.com; BBQ; $$. Award-winning ribs and barbecue from an Outer Banks native. Pulled pork, beef brisket, and southern fried chicken are specialties as well as their ribs. Four locations: Corolla, Duck, Kitty Hawk, and Wanchese. This one is located next to Kitty Hawk Kites.

SUGAR CREEK SOUNDFRONT SEAFOOD RESTAURANT, Nags Head–Manteo Causeway; (252) 441-4963; sugarcreekseafood.com; Seafood and American; $$–$$$. Sugar Creek is one of the most popular places on the beach for lunch and dinner. Eat at the full-service bar in this casual restaurant or sit at a table in one of the soundfront dining rooms. The seafood stew is extremely tasty and overflowing with shrimp and scallops. Marinated tuna is a must for fish lovers. The atmosphere is lively and fun. Sugar Creek is open from March through Thanksgiving, seven days a week. Next door at the Sugar Shack, you can eat at one of the tables or order great take-out food, including hamburgers and wraps.

SURFIN' SPOON, 2408 S. Virginia Dare Trl.; (252) 441-7873; surfin spoon.com; Dessert; $. The place to go for frozen yogurt on the Outer Banks. Opened by former pro surfer Jesse Hines and his wife, Whitney, in 2012, Surfin' Spoon was the first self-serve frozen yogurt on the beach. Great seating area inside, but crowd always spill over to outdoor deck. Summer hours noon to 11p.m. Closed Sundays.

DINING

TAIKO JAPANESE RESTAURANT, US 158, MP 14, Outer Banks Mall; (252) 449-8895; Japanese and sushi; taikosushiobx.com; $$. This Outer Banks restaurant serves sushi all day, for lunch and dinner. Taiko's sushi is top-notch, rolled tightly and cut into perfect, bite-size pieces. The miso and clear soups are refreshing, as are the udon and soba noodle dishes and the seaweed salad. Japanese-style entrees include steak teriyaki, shrimp tempura, and chicken sukiyaki. The dining room is peaceful and serene, with soft music and tasteful, understated Asian decor. Everything at Taiko is available for takeout. Taiko is open year-round, serving lunch and dinner daily in season. Call for off-season hours.

TALE OF THE WHALE, Nags Head–Manteo Causeway; (252) 441-7332; taleofthewhalenagshead.com; Seafood; $$–$$$. Family-operated and -owned for more than two decades, Tale of the Whale is situated on Roanoke Sound. You can enjoy the delightful views either looking through the expansive windows inside while savoring dinner or on the 75-foot deck and gazebo while sipping a refreshing cocktail. Tale of the Whale serves the freshest available food in generous portions. Seafood, pasta, steaks, and more are on the menu. Daily specials are offered and there is early bird pricing from 4 to 5 p.m. in season. Children's menu and full bar.

TORTUGAS' LIE SHELLFISH BAR AND GRILLE, NC 12, MP 11; (252) 441-RAWW (7299); tortugaslie.com; Seafood and American; $. A favorite on the Outer Banks, this upbeat eatery is housed in a turquoise cottage across from the ocean near a great surf break. Tortugas' features an enclosed porch furnished with handmade wooden booths, table seating, and an expanded bar that seats more than two dozen people. The creatively concocted food is good, and the atmosphere inside is fun and casual. The menu offers quick-fried fish bites, supersize fish and black bean burritos, sandwiches, seafood flavored with outrageous spices, and a full raw bar. Dinner entrees include pork medallions, steak stir fries, just-off-the-boat tuna steaks, succulent shrimp, and pasta plates. The daily specials are tempting; sushi is served on Wednesday night, and the place usually is packed with locals. The full bar offers loads of specialty drinks. This hip, laid-back eatery is open seven days a week for lunch and dinner from February through December. Call for winter hours. (See the **Entertainment** chapter.)

WAVERIDER'S COFFEE & DELI, 3022 S. Croatan Hwy; (252) 715-1880; waveridersobx.com; Breakfast; $. Waverider's is one of the places to be seen on the Outer Banks. Great coffee and wonderful smoothies, but the deli sandwiches are close to perfection and the breakfast sandwiches are guaranteed to start the day right. Beer and wine available. Occasional late night music.

WOO CASA KITCHEN, 4900 S. Croatan Hwy; (252) 715-0089, Spanish andAsian fusion; woocasakitchen.com; $. There's some real imagination that goes into the Woo Casa dishes. There's this, that and the other thing, which is how the menu puts it. In this there is the French Fry Taco with black beans, mixed greens, cabbage, cheddar cheese, pico de gallo. That includes their rice bowls that have a bit of everything in them. And The Other Thing are the brunch items and Hawaiian Style Poke tuna. Open Monday through Saturday. Closes at 6 p.m.

ROANOKE ISLAND

Manteo

1587, Tranquil House Inn, 405 Queen Elizabeth St.; (252) 473-1587; 1587 .com; Fine dining; $$$–$$$$. The offerings at this critically acclaimed restaurant are unusual, upscale, cosmopolitan, and some of the most ambitious on the Outer Banks. The ambience is elegant and romantic, and the constantly changing menu is always fresh and fabulous. Soups prepared each day might include Mediterranean mussels and crayfish with spring vegetables and feta cheese in a light tomato broth. Vegetarian requests are welcome. Full bar, extensive wine list.

⭐ **AVENUE GRILLE AND EVENTS**, The Waterfront Shops; (252) 473-4800; avenueeventsobx.com; Seafood and American; $$–$$$. Overlooking Shallowbag Bay and the state ship *Elizabeth II*, this is a favorite Manteo eatery for watching boats on the water or a romantic summer moon. It's a picturesque and relaxing restaurant with good service and equally admirable food. The owners have a passion for food, sustainability, and community. At this casual spot, diners will find local fresh seafood offerings, along with vegetarian and meat dishes. Locals and visitors reserve Avenue Grille for wedding receptions, family parties, or reunions, in addition to going in for a delicious lunch or dinner. Full bar with craft beers on tap and in bottle. Since this restaurant is less than a 10-minute drive from *The Lost Colony*, it's a good place to take in an early meal before the outdoor drama begins.

BIG AL'S SODA FOUNTAIN & GRILL, US 64/264; (252) 473-5570; bigalsobx.com; American; $. You can't miss Big Al's, on the main road in Manteo. Originally planned as an ice cream parlor, this spot has expanded into a full-blown soda fountain and family restaurant. It's definitely a place to take the kids. With '50s decor and memorabilia, Big Al's is a great place to kick back and enjoy some good ol' American food and fountain treats. Children's meals are reasonably priced. Kids can have fun in the game room, with a pinball machine, video games, and a jukebox. Big Al's serves lunch and dinner daily.

BLUEWATER, Pirates Cover Marina, Nags Head–Manteo Causeway; Seafood and American; $$–$$$. Diners will be tempted by the extensive oyster bar, where oysters are sourced from multiple waters. The post and beam architecture and hardwood floors make a beautiful setting, and the million dollar view of the sound spans 180 degrees. The rotisserie duck is incredible, and the aged beef equally amazing. Open year-round. Acoustic music on occasion. Full bar.

DARRELL'S RESTAURANT, US 64; (252) 473-5366; American and seafood; darrellsseafood.com; $$. This down-home restaurant started as an ice cream stand in 1960 and has been a favorite family-style eatery for the past two decades. It's common knowledge that the fried oysters at Darrell's are among the best in town. Menu items such as popcorn shrimp, crab cakes, grilled marinated tuna, and fried scallops are served and will provide more than enough to fuel you through the day. Meat eaters will be satiated by steaks, barbecued minced pork, and grilled marinated chicken. Daily specials, children's menu. Beer and wine served; open lunch and dinner year-round every day but Sunday.

FRONT PORCH CAFÉ, 300 US 64; (252) 473-3160; frontporchcafe.net; Coffee; $. The Front Porch Cafe sources top-quality coffee beans from all over the world, then roasts each batch by hand in their store. Freshly baked cinnamon rolls, scones, and muffins are available every day. Customers can also select from the wonderful varieties of teas on hand. There is a second location in Nags Head. Both locations serve beer and wine.

GARDEN DELI & PIZZERIA, US 64; (252) 473-6888; gardendelipizza .com; Pizza and sandwiches; $. Shaded by pine trees, this tiny restaurant has a breezy outdoor deck perfect for summer dining. Here New York–style stone-oven pizzas are cooked to order and packaged to go, if you wish. The Philly cheesesteaks, paninis, burgers, gyros, and a wide assortment of deli sandwiches, homemade salads, and antipasto salads are wonderful. Lunch and dinner are served Monday through Saturday, year-round. Delivery available.

HUNGRY PELICAN, The Waterfront Shops; (252) 473-9441; thehungry pelican.com; Sandwiches; $. Deli sandwiches are the house specialty at the Hungry Pelican. Sandwiches are piled high and your bill won't break the bank. Soups, salads, and several side dishes are also offered. The homemade desserts are delicious and the aroma of their fresh-baked bread fills the air. Seating can be found outdoors or inside with a gorgeous Manteo waterfront view.

THE LOST COLONY BREWERY, 208 Queen Elizabeth Ave.; (252) 473-6666; lostcolonybrewery.com; Seafood and American; $$. This eclectic eatery consistently overflows with local and visiting patrons. The innovative cuisine has a nouveau American flair. Most of the entrees and specials are so unusual we haven't seen them anywhere else on the Outer Banks. The beer comes from the onsite microbrewery and a good selection of wine is also available. You can eat inside the dining room or dine outdoors along the sidewalk. Reservations are accepted for parties of six or more. The Lost Colony Brewery is open for lunch and dinner seven days a week in summer. Hours are reduced off-season, so call for specific schedules.

OLD TOWNE CREAMERY, 500 N. Main Hwy, Corner of Ananias and Hwy 64/264; (252) 305-8060; Dessert; oldetownecreamery.com; $. Sundaes, milkshakes, hand-dipped ice cream—that's as classic as it gets. For the hungry there are hot dogs and hamburgers.

THE ORTEGA'Z GRILL, Sir Walter Raleigh St.; (252) 473-5911; ortegaz .com; Mexican and Latin; $–$$. Bring some spice to your life at the Ortega'z Grill. Ortega'z serves delicious southwestern cuisine. Everything here is prepared fresh in-house; even the tortillas are homemade. Three main choices for the Latin entrees are delicately roasted chicken, tender beef, and pulled pork. Sandwiches are also served, and dinner entrees are available in the evenings. Open 11 a.m. to 9 p.m. Monday through Saturday. Ortega'z serves beer and wine, takeout is available, and there is a menu just for the smaller tykes in your party.

POOR RICHARD'S SANDWICH SHOP, The Waterfront; (252) 473-3333; poorrichardsmanteo.com; Sandwiches; $. With half the workforce in Manteo making a beeline to Poor Richard's every day, this casual eatery is a local gathering spot for reasonably priced food with fast counter service and interesting offerings. Try the cucumber sandwich with cream cheese—a cool meal that surprises your palate. Cold and grilled sandwiches are made to order, and specials are offered daily. Homemade soups, meatless chili, hot dogs, and salad plates, are also available. Breakfast includes scrambled egg and bacon sandwiches, bagels and cream cheese, and fresh fruit. Steamed shrimp is available for lunch and dinner. You can eat inside at a roomy booth or take your meal out on the back porch and enjoy the waterfront view. Poor Richard's is open daily in the summer for breakfast, lunch, and dinner. Occasionally the restaurant hosts live music in the evening. Open year-round. **Poor Richard's After Hours** is located in front of the restaurant, serving wine and beer. Live music is offered in season Thursday through Saturday. Vegetarian requests are welcome. Full bar, extensive wine list.

SHADDAI PERUVIAN RESTAURANT, 112 Hwy 64; (252) 423-3013; facebook.com/shaddairestaurant; Peruvian; $$. It's not at all like Mexican cuisine, with a heavier emphasis on the spices and herbs of the Andes mountains. The ceviche is outstanding, but the Peruvian chicken keeps them coming back.

T.L.'S FAMILY RESTAURANT, 812 US 64; (252) 473-3489; American; $–$$. If this was a diner, it would be diner food. Great service, very good basic food, and lots of it. Hush puppies come with every meal.

UNCLE BUCK'S HOMEMADE ICE CREAM, 207 Queen Elizabeth Ave.; (252) 423-3118; bigbucksicecream.com; Ice Cream and espresso; $. They make their own ice cream and it's very rich. Wonderful selection of chocolates created by the chocolatier owners and espresso. A great place to relax on a hot day.

Wanchese

GREAT GUT DELI, 219 Thicket Lump Dr.; (252) 473-2479; Deli; $. The only thing better that can compete with the sandwiches are the prices and the view. Definitely check out the tuna salad.

JOHANNA'S—CAFÉ LACHINE, 1064 Old Wharf Rd.; (252) 305-9690; cafelachine.com; American; $–$$. Fresh, usually local, ingredients are highlighted by a chef who knows how to use them. Relaxed atmosphere in a pleasant setting. The pastries and desserts are amazing.

O'NEAL'S SEA HARVEST, 618 Harbor Rd.; (252) 473-4535; Seafood. Iconic restaurant from the family of one of the original Outer Banks boat captains. Fresh fish is a given. Open for lunch only. Closed Sundays.

WANCHESE MARINA, 4457 Mill Landing Rd.; (252) 473-3247; wanchese marina.com/the-landing-grill; Breakfast, deli, and seafood; $. Heading out on a charter for the day? Wanchese Marina serves up big breakfasts. Lunch menu includes deli sandwiches, pizza, and the freshest fish around.

HATTERAS ISLAND

Rodanthe

THE DOUGH SHACK, 24782 NC 12, Rodanthe; (252) 987-5104; Pizza and doughnuts; thedoughshackobx.com; $. A breakfast pizza…now that's different. It's an egg-based NY pizza dough with breakfast toppings. Or freshly made doughnuts. Of course, there's pizza later in the day, as well as wings, subs and sandwiches.

LISA'S PIZZERIA, NC 12, Rodanthe; (252) 987-2525; lisaspizzeria.net; Italian; $. Specialty pizzas, deli sandwiches, subs, calzones, chicken parmigiana, and salads are among the most popular items at this restaurant. Lisa's also serves breadsticks, hot wings, and garlic and cheese bread. Beer and wine are available, and there's a separate children's menu. Lisa's serves lunch and dinner seven days a week beginning at 11 a.m. from early April through November. All items can be eaten inside the restaurant, carried out, or delivered. Serving the Tri-Villages for over 30 years. Call for off-season hours.

SHEILA'S CAROLINA KITCHEN, 25099 NC 12, Rodanthe; (252) 987-2629; American; $. Huge breakfasts and open for lunch. Noted for its fast and friendly service. Located in the KOA campground.

Waves

ATLANTIC COAST CAFE, NC 12, Waves; (252) 987-1200; atlanticcoastcafe.com; American and seafood; $–$$. For breakfast, lunch, or dinner, stop into Atlantic Coast Cafe—your taste buds will be glad you did! This spot, across from the KOA campground, serves breakfast starting at 7 a.m. Lunch and dinner include choices like the shrimp Reuben, fish wrap, burgers, and seafood. Crab cakes and other choices are available for dinner. Sides include potato salad and mac 'n cheese, a surefire kid pleaser. Frozen coffee, chai teas, and smoothies are available all day. Eat inside or outdoors on their cool soundside deck. Free Wi-Fi.

BOARDWOK SOUTH, 26006 NC 12, St. Waves Plaza, Waves; (252) 987-1080; boardwoksouth.com; Asian and seafood; $$–$$$. There's the classic Chinese dishes—Lo Mein, fried rice and General Tso's Chicken. Then there's the tuna with a choice of an Asian vinaigrette, sesame, or Cajun. There's crab cakes and egg rolls, too. Just a great combination of tastes and styles.

GOOD WINDS SEAFOOD & WINE, NC 12, Waves Village Kiteboarding Resort; (252) 987-1100; goodwindsrestaurant.com; Seafood, American, and Asian; $$–$$$. Overlooking the Pamlico Sound from its second-floor location in the Kitty Hawk Kites Kiteboarding resort, Good Winds offers a variety of yummy choices. Excellent local seafood is featured along with specialties like Asian noodle bowls and conch fritters. Breakfast, lunch, and dinner are served here, alongside an incredible view of the sound and kiteboarders riding the wind and waves.

TOP DOG CAFE, NC 12, Waves; (252) 987-1272; American and seafood; $. Specializing in burgers that weigh up to one-and-a-half pounds, Top Dog Cafe also serves steamed seafood, Philly-style steak subs, shrimp and oyster baskets, all-beef hot dogs, salads, and appetizers. The owners Joe and Pat offer a casual Florida Keys atmosphere, and diners can choose to eat on the shady screened porch or on the sundeck. This establishment has a kids' menu and sometimes live music. Beer and wine are served. Open for lunch and dinner; call for hours and days.

UNCLE FRANK'S OBX, 25972 NC 12, Waves; (252) 715-5200; uncle franksobx.com; Hot dogs and BBQ; $. The dogs are all beef Kosher hot dogs loaded up with everything from French fries and coleslaw to sauerkraut and mustard. Pulled pork barbecue sandwiches for some variety. Open 11:30 a.m. to 5:30 p.m. Closed Sunday and Monday.

WATERMAN'S BAR & GRILL, 25706 NC 12, Waves; (252) 987-2000; American, seafood, and steaks; watermensbarandgrill.com; $$–$$$. The view is sublime, the seafood always fresh, and the steaks are grilled to perfection. Lunch features wraps and quesadillas. Live music during the summer. Open March 1 through December 1.

WAVES MARKET, 26006 NC 12, St. Waves Plaza, Waves; (252) 987-2352; facebook.com/wavesmarket; Deli; $. A deli counter in a small market turning out some of the best sandwiches anywhere. Breakfast is served all day.

Avon

BROS SANDWICH SHOP, 41934 NC 12; (252) 995-9595; brossandwich shack.com; Burgers and sandwiches; $. What happens when two brothers with classical culinary training open a sandwich shop? You get amazing burgers, great sandwiches, and more.

BURGER, BURGER, 40618 NC 12; (252) 995-0311; facebook.com/obx burgerburger; Burgers, sandwiches, and wraps; $. Huge selection of burgers and toppings, but that's not all they have. Great fried chicken sandwiches and fresh fish sandwiches and wraps.

DIRTY DICK'S CRAB HOUSE, 1934 NC 12; (252) 995-3425; dirtydicks crabs.com; Seafood; $$. The litany of crab choices at Dirty Dick's Crab House reminds us of Bubba's roster of shrimp in *Forrest Gump*. There are snow crab legs, soft-shell crab sandwiches, spiced crabs, crab cakes, and steamed crabs, plus steamed shrimp, clams, clam chowder, gumbo, jambalaya, and Cajun creole. The popular Dick Burger is a crab and shrimp patty with Cajun sauce. There are sandwich platter specials and offerings for the kids. You can purchase Dick's special spice and famous Dirty Dick's T-shirts. Crustaceans are cooked to order for takeout. Dirty Dick's has a sister Outer Banks location in Nags Head. Both locations are open seasonally; call for hours.

GIDGET'S PIZZA PASTA, NC 12, Hatteras Island Plaza; (252) 995-3109; pizzagidget.com; Pizza, pasta, and sandwiches; $. Gidget's is a popular comfy spot to have lunch or dinner. Pizza, pasta, subs, salads, and more are offered here. Service is quick and friendly. Beer, microbrews, and wine; kids' menu.

KETCH 55 SEAFOOD GRILL, 40396 NC 12; (252) 995-5060; ketch55 .com; Seafood and breakfast; $–$$$. Includes Stu's Donuts & Breakfast. Ketch 55 is all about seafood. Yes, they have some great comfort foods like meatloaf and pork chops, but this is the place to go for fresh seafood prepared in the traditions of the Outer Banks. Stu's Donuts has a wonderful breakfast menu, including their Dirt and Worms donut—Chocolate frosting, Oreo crumbles, and gummy worms. Not everyone's taste, unless you're 10.

THE FROGGY DOG RESTAURANT & PUB, 40050 NC 12; (252) 995-5550; froggydog.com; Seafood, steaks, and pasta; $$–$$$. For over 30 years the Froggy Dog has stood the test of time. Open for breakfast, lunch, or dinner and with late night entertainment, there is something for everyone. Combine the best of two worlds with the Pesto Mere Bulles, a pesto pasta with scallops and shrimp.

LA FOGATA MEXICAN RESTAURANT, 41934 NC 12; (252) 986-1118; Mexican; $. A traditional Mexican restaurant, La Fogata gets its name from the Spanish word for "campfire." For the price, La Fogata serves the best ethnic food on the beach. People wait in line to eat here on weekend nights. You'll see a lot of locals in this colorful spot year-round. Airy, bright, and decorated with Mexican art and photographs, the interior of this ultra-casual eatery usually hums with Latin tunes. The waiters bring baskets of crispy tortillas and bowls of homemade salsa as soon as they distribute the menus. All entree portions are generous, so save room for the main course. Recommended appetizers include the hot queso (cheese) dip and stuffed jalapeño peppers. Specialties include fajitas, enchiladas, and other traditional fare. Mixed drink and margarita prices among the lowest on the beach. Open for lunch and dinner year-round, seven days a week.

MAD CRABBER, 40606 NC 12; (252) 995-5959; themadcrabber.com; Seafood; $–$$. Family-owned for over 25 years, Mad Crabber serves up some of the best seafood dishes on the Outer Banks. They don't do anything fancy. They just make sure it's fresh. Steaks and burgers, too, but go for the seafood.

NINO'S PIZZA, 41188 Palazzolo Rd.; (252) 995-5358; Italian; $–$$. The pizza is amazing, but the pasta dishes are worth checking out as well. Free delivery to Avon.

OCEANA'S BISTRO, NC 12; (252) 995-4991; oceanasbistro.com; Seafood and American; $–$$. Oceana's Bistro, located across from the Avon Pier, is the place to be with a menu that will please any palate. Appetizers range from bruschetta with mozzarella to sesame seared tuna. Quesadillas, sandwiches, and overstuffed potatoes are offered, too. For a fuller meal the menu has offerings like prime rib and seafood specialties. Homemade soups and desserts are served daily. Breakfast, lunch, and dinner are all available here. Small but very nice wine list. Open year-round.

PANGEA TAVERN, 41001 NC 12; (252) 995-3800; pangeatavern.com; American; $$-$$$. Spacious tavern across the street from Koru Village and at the foot of Avon Pier. Very good seafood plates. Excellent beer selection and the kids menu is one of the best around. Dinner only.

POHOUSE GOOD EATS & LIBATIONS, 39450A NC 12; (252) 995-3353; pohouseobx.com; Seafood; $$–$$$. Fresh seafood prepared from scratch. On Pamlico Sound and the view is sublime. Check out the po' boy for a real treat.

TURNER'S HIGH MOON & GRILL, 40618 NC 12; (252) 995-6666; turnershighmoon.com; $$. A musical theme weaves through the menu, which makes sense since there's nightly entertainment in the summer. There's some good Greek, Italian, and American choices singing their songs.

UGLIE MUGS COFFEE SHOP, 40534 NC 12; (252) 995-5590; Coffee; $. With lots of ugly mugs lining the walls, Uglie Mugs is aptly named. Good espresso drinks and a nice pastry selection.

Buxton

ANGELO'S PIZZA, 46903 NC 12; (252) 995-6364; facebook.com/Angelos PizzaBuxtonNC; Pizza; $. Great pizza, subs, burgers—this is the place where people go when they're hungry at night. They make the dough every day, some innovative toppings. That's what has kept them in business since 1994.

BEACH HOUSE GRILL, 47048 NC 12; (252) 995-3117; facebook.com/ TheBeachHouseGrill; Seafood; $$–$$$. The newest casual restaurant in Buxton is earning rave reviews for service, seafood, and burgers.

BUXTON MUNCH COMPANY, 47359 NC 12, Osprey Shopping Center; (252) 995-5502; buxtonmunch.com; Seafood and sandwiches; $. Be patient. It's worth the wait. Buxton Munch is a small place where everything—the Crabby Patties, the fish tacos, and the burgers—are prepared to order. And it's been that way since 1999.

CAFÉ PAMLICO, 49684 NC 12; (252) 995-4500; innonpamlicosound
.com/dining; Fine dining; $$$$. One of the finest restaurants on the Outer
Banks. Outstanding food preparation and presentation. Part of the Inn on
Pamlico Sound overlooking the water. This is the perfect place for a romantic
dinner for two. Reservations highly recommended.

DIAMOND SHOALS RESTAURANT, NC 12; (252) 995-5217; diamond
shoals.net; Seafood, Asian, and American; $$–$$$. The parking lot at this
eatery, which is within walking distance of several Buxton motels, always seems
to be crowded around breakfast time. Here you'll find one of the best breakfasts
on Hatteras Island, featuring all your early-morning favorites. Diamond Shoals
is also open for lunch and dinner, with plenty of local seafood choices, a salad
bar, and some good nightly specials. Steaks and other landlubber specials are
available. Mixed drinks, wine, and beer served. Separate sushi bar and seafood
markets.

ORANGE BLOSSOM CAFE AND BAKERY, NC 12; (252) 995-4109;
orangeblossombakery.com; Breakfast; $. The Orange Blossom starts the day
with delicious baked goods for breakfast. The famous Apple Uglies—huge
apple fritter-style pastries piled high with fruit—are favorite early morning
treats. This restaurant is open year-round, except for a spell during the winter,
for takeout or eat in. Open Wednesday through Sunday for breakfast, 6:30 to
11 a.m. An array of organic coffees are also available here.

POP'S RAW BAR, 48967 NC 12; (252) 995-7734; Seafood; $$. Seafood,
beer, bar. That sums it up. But the seafood is always fresh, the beer is cold, and
the bar is friendly. Can't miss the place. It's right across from Cape Hatteras
Secondary School.

RUSTY'S SURF & TURF, NC 12; (252) 995-4184; rustyssurfnturf.com;
Steaks, seafood, and salads; $$$–$$$$. Chef-Owner Rusty Midgett brings
global styles of preparation to local seafood. This fun and cheerful restaurant
has local artwork adorning the vibrant walls. Colorful and flavorful dishes
include Rusty's shrimp and grits and Asian-style steak kebab. Beer and wine
served on premise.

SANDBAR & GRILL, 49252 NC 12; (252) 995-3413; sandbarandgrille
.com; Seafood; $$–$$$. Perched at the end of a spit of land, Sandbar & Grill
set the standards over 20 years ago for fresh seafood and evening entertainment.
There's a full arcade room as well. But it's the fresh seafood that keeps people
coming back. That and the view.

Frisco

GINGERBREAD HOUSE BAKERY, NC 12; (252) 995-5204; Breakfast and pizza; $. From this tiny cottage flanked by gingerbread-style fencing, breakfast and dinner are served Monday through Saturday in season. To start the day, sample egg biscuits, French toast, omelets, or waffles. The fresh-sqeezed orange juice is a real treat. By early evening you can order a gourmet pizza made on the bakery's own dough. Crusts range in thickness from hand-tossed to pan-depth and are offered in white and whole wheat varieties with 30 toppings to choose from. Ice cream, brownies, and sweet breads all are great dessert options. During the summer the Gingerbread House also delivers from Buxton to Hatteras Village, and its bakers make super specialty cakes on a day's notice for any occasion. No credit cards accepted.

QUARTERDECK RESTAURANT, 54214 NC 12; (252) 986-2425; quarter deckhi.com; Seafood; $$. When you've been in business for over 40 years you must be doing something right. The Quarterdeck does great seafood; This is where you go to get flounder or oysters done right.

Hatteras Village

BREAKWATER RESTAURANT, NC 12, Oden's Dock; (252) 986-2733; breakwaterhatteras.com; Seafood and steak; $–$$$$. If dining in a comfortable atmosphere with a stunning view of Pamlico Sound or relaxing on a deck at sunset sounds good, then this restaurant is the place for you. The dinner menu features fresh, innovative seafood dishes, prime rib, veal, and pasta, all served in generous portions. Insiders rave about the blackened scallops and the tuna tortilla. A good selection of beer and wine is available. Children's menu items are also offered. Check for winter hours.

DINKY'S WATERFRONT RESTAURANT, NC 12, Village Marina; (252) 986-2020; villagemarinahatteras.com; American and seafood; $–$$. A fabulous view of the sound accompanies each meal at Dinky's, which is located on the second floor of Village Marina. Diners can choose from the delicious daily specials or order fresh seafood, hand-cut steaks, chicken, or pasta. Excellent desserts and good beer and wine lists complete the offerings at Dinky's, where families are welcome. Wednesday is sushi night; Friday is prime rib night. Open for dinner from 5 to 8:30 p.m. year-round.

HARBOR DELI, 58058 Hatteras Ct.; (252) 986-2500; hatterasdeli.com; $. Get your breakfast or lunch sandwich right in the heart of the Hatteras docks.

HATTERAS SOL WATERSIDE RESTAURANT, 58646 NC 12; (252) 986-1414; hatterassol.com; International; $$$. Chef Chris Setzer seems to have taken a piece of every culinary experience he's had and applied it to this eclectic menu. It works spectacularly well. For desert be sure to try the Blood Orange-Lemon Curd Creme Brulee.

KAT'S DELI, 56193 Tracy Ct.; (252) 986-2000; facebook.com/delibythe beach; Deli; $. Freshly made sandwiches, subs, paninis, and bagels. Open 11 a.m. to 5 p.m. daily.

SONNY'S WATERFRONT RESTAURANT, 57878 NC 12; (252) 986-2733; sonnyshatteras.com; Seafood and breakfast; $–$$$. Sonny's is the place people go to meet for breakfast or lunch in Hatteras Village. Dinner is when the foods really shine. Everything if fresh, it's well made and the service is very good.

ROCCO'S ITALIAN RESTAURANT, 57331 NC 12; (252) 986-2150; Italian; $. Rocco's is about as Italian as it gets. Pizzas, thin crust or Sicilian, pasta dishes, and subs. Open March 1 through October.

THE WRECK TIKI BAR, 58848 Marina Way A-4; (252) 996-0162; thewreckobx.com; Pub food; $$. Mostly a lunch spot with late night music on Thursdays. But the paninis are awesome, and the quesadillas excellent. Very nice kids' menu as well. Located at Hatteras Landing so the water views are amazing. Closed Mondays.

OCRACOKE ISLAND

1718 BREWING OCRACOKE, 1129 Irvin Garrish Hwy; (252) 928-2337; facebook.com/pg/1718BrewingOcracoke; Brew Pub; $$. Ocracoke's own microbrewery. The beer is excellent and they brew their own birch beer and ginger soda. The food stands out as well. Check out the crab stuffed pretzel.

⭐ **THE BACK PORCH RESTAURANT,** 110 Back Rd.; (252) 928-6401; backporchocracoke.com; Seafood and American; $$$. Whether you dine on the wide screened-in porch or eat in the small nooks or open dining room of this well-respected restaurant, you'll find that dinners at the Back Porch are some of the most pleasant experiences on the Outer Banks. This older building was renovated and refurbished to blend with the many trees on the property. It's a quiet place to enjoy appealing entrees and comfortable conversation. Overall it's one of our favorite restaurants on the 120-mile stretch of barrier islands and well worth the two-hour trip from Nags Head. Advertising "original dishes with a personal touch," the menu is loaded with fresh vegetables and local seafood and changes seasonally to offer the freshest ingredients. All sauces, dressings, breads, and desserts are made in the restaurant's huge kitchen and each

DINING

piece of meat is hand cut. All the desserts are divine. Freshly ground coffee is served here, and the wine selections and imported beer are as ambitious as the menu. If you get hooked—as we are—you can try your hand at some of the restaurant's recipes at home by buying a copy of Back Porch Cookbook. Dinner is offered nightly in season. Call for off-season hours. **The Back Porch Lunchbox**, next to the Pony Island Motel, offers homemade bag lunches or picnics for the beach or ferry. Sandwiches, cold steamed shrimp, baked goods, drinks, and fruit are available.

DAJIO, NC 12; (252) 928-7119; dajiorestaurant.com; Seafood and American; $$–$$$$. In the heart of Ocracoke Village, Dario serves only the finest local ingredients whenever possible. Breakfast, brunch, lunch, and dinner are served here. There is an all-day menu that is geared toward sandwiches and more quickly prepared food. Menu is contemporary. Live music is often enjoyed by patrons in the bar area.

EDUARDO'S TACO STAND, 950 Irvin Garrish Hwy; (252) 928-0234; eduardosocracoke.com; Mexican; $. Real deal Mexican cuisine with fresh local ingredients. Breakfast items include chorizo and egg tacos and burritos. Open year-round. Closed on Monday.

FLYING MELON, 181 Back Rd.; (252) 928-2433; Seafood, Creole, Southern; $$. The Flying Melon has unique decor and yummy food to tempt any palate. The dinner entrees are often Louisiana-inspired dishes made with fresh ingredients and local seafood. Kids' menu, beer, and wine available. Dinner only. Open year-round Tuesday through Sunday; call for off season hours.

GAFFER'S, 1050 Irvin Garrish Hwy; (252) 928-3456; gaffersocracoke.com; $$. There's something for everyone at Gaffer's. Burgers, steamed shrimp, fresh seafood; and a full bar. A great kids' menu as well. Full bar service.

GRACEFUL BAKERY, 294 Irvin Garrish Hwy; facebook.com/graceful bakery; $. Maybe the best bakery on Ocracoke. Coffee is good, too. Opens at 7 a.m. for the early birds.

HELIO'S HIDEAWAY, 589 Irvin Garrish Hwy; (252) 928-3354; facebook .com/HeliosHideaway; Mediterranean and Greek; $$. Helio's is a takeout stand with a real Mediterranean flair. Lamb meatballs, stuffed pita sandwiches, and falafel.

HOWARD'S PUB & RAW BAR RESTAURANT, NC 12; (252) 928-4441; howardspub.com; Seafood and American; $–$$. Fun-loving and casual, Howard's Pub has an expansive menu. Don't be overwhelmed by the selection of more than 200 imported, domestic, and microbrewed beers. The crew at Howard's Pub has established its "little corner of paradise" as the choice hangout for families, couples, and singles alike. The restaurant's various areas—including the long wraparound bar, the main floor and game area, the large screened porch, and the ocean-to-sound-view deck—provide plenty of room for your group. The upstairs deck affords breathtaking views of the ocean, sound, salt marshes, and sand dunes. There are big screen TVs, darts, and board games for entertainment, and live entertainment many nights. Raw bar, pizza, seafood, and more are served at this must-stop for everyone visiting Ocracoke. Most visitors pick up a souvenir T-shirt.

JASON'S RESTAURANT, NC 12; (252) 928-3434; jasonsocracoke.com; Seafood, pizza, and sandwiches; $–$$. On the north end of the village, Jason's has a casual, come-as-you-are atmosphere that welcomes islanders and vacationers alike. You can sit outside on the spacious screened porch or hang at the bar and watch the chefs at work. Standouts on the menu are pizzas and Italian specialties, including lasagna and vegetarian lasagna, spaghetti with meatballs, chicken parmigiana, and fettuccine Alfredo. Dinner menu includes New York strip steak, Jamaican jerk chicken, and seafood. Jason's also includes a complete gluten-free menu. Sushi night every Wednesday. Beer and wine are offered. Lunch and dinner are served daily year-round, 11 a.m. until 9 p.m.

★ **JOLLY ROGER PUB & MARINA**, NC 12; (252) 928-3703; jolly rogerocracoke.com; American, and seafood; $$–$$$. Jolly Roger is the perfect place to kick back and relax on Ocracoke Island. Although a roof, canopy, and umbrellas cover many of the dining tables, the entire restaurant is open, with tables on large decks overlooking the harbor. There's nothing fancy here— wooden tables, paper plates, and plastic cutlery—but the service is good, the beer is cold, and the food is wonderful. The menu features homemade soups, sandwiches, salad plates, local seafood, and daily specials. Stop in for live entertainment at sunset; you'll hear the music wafting down the street as you stroll through the village. Beer and wine are served, and there's a good-size bar on premise. Jolly Roger serves lunch and dinner daily in season.

OCRACOKE COFFEE CO. & ISLAND SMOOTHIE, 226 Back Rd.; (252) 928-7473; ocracokecoffee.com; Coffee; $. Ocracoke Coffee is the neatest place on the island to take care of caffeine and sugar cravings. The aromatic eatery offers bagels, pastries, desserts, brewed coffee drinks, espresso, shakes, whole-bean and ground coffees, and loose tea. The shop is nestled under tall pines on Back Road, within an easy walk of almost anything in the village. We know you'll find your way here in the morning (everyone does), but why not walk in after dinner for something sweet as well? The shop's feel is way hip, but it's also cozy and inviting, and the folks frothing your concoctions are friendly as can be. Look for more than 10 varieties of smoothies for a cool respite from the summer heat. Ocracoke Coffee is open daily from 7 a.m. to 9:30 p.m., and live music plays during summer evenings on the deck. The shop closes December through March.

OCRACOKE OYSTER COMPANY, 875 Irvin Garrish Hwy, (252) 928-0200; ocracokeoystercompany.com; Seafood; $$–$$$. This is the place to get oysters. Raw oysters, oysters ceviche, oysters sushi, and BBQ oysters. They're local—Ocracoke has become an important oyster farming location, so what could be better? There are other items on the menu, and they're good, but it is the Ocracoke Oyster Company, after all.

PONY ISLAND RESTAURANT, NC 12; (252) 928-5701; Breakfast, American, and seafood; $$. A casual, homey place that people have come back to time and again since 1960, this restaurant features big breakfasts of biscuits, hotcakes, omelets, and the famous Pony Potatoes—hash browns covered with cheese, sour cream, and salsa. Dinner entrees include interesting fresh local seafood creations, pastas, steaks, and salads. Beer and wine are served, and homemade desserts finish the tasty meal. If you clean your catch, the restaurant will cook it for you. Children's menu.

SMACNALLY'S RAW BAR AND GRILL, NC 12, on Silver Lake; (252) 928-9999; smacnallys.com; Seafood and burgers; $–$$. sMacNally's is smack in the middle of the village action, at the Anchorage Inn Marina, and is a popular gathering spot on the island. It's an outdoor establishment, on the docks, with the smell of salt and fresh-caught fish coming off the water and charter boats tied up practically to the bar. Fishermen walk off the boats and have a beer in their hand before they can say "Budwei . . ." sMacNally's claims to serve the coldest beer on the island. Patrons hang around the raw bar and at tables on the dock. The raw bar serves fresh local seafood, including oysters, clams, and shrimp. A grill cooks burgers and the like. Lunch and dinner; open in season; children's menu. It's closed in the colder months. Steamed seafood buckets and boxed lunches are sold to go.

SWEET TOOTH & GIG BAKERY AND DELI, 1015 Irvin Garrish Hwy; (252) 928-3481; Deli. Classic deli sandwiches and a full breakfast sandwich menu including bagels and lox. Fresh baked goods daily.

SORELLA'S PIZZA & PASTA, 59 Irvin Garrish Hwy; (252) 928-7777; Italian; $–$$. From Italy straight to the heart of Ocracoke, these are classic pasta dishes: Gnocchi Carbonara, Linguine Bolognese, and more. The pizza is classic as well.

THAI MOON, NC 12, Spencer's Market; (252) 928-5100; facebook.com/ ThaiMoonOcracoke; Asian; $–$$. Here's something different on Ocracoke Island: ethnic food, which is a refreshing change of pace on the Outer Banks. Thai Moon offers authentic Thai specialties for take-out only. Chicken, pork, beef, and vegetarian options are available. Pad thai and fried rice with shrimp, chicken, or bean curd are specialties. Sushi is a popular item here as well. Thai Moon is open for lunch and dinner Tuesday through Saturday, and for dinner only on Sunday and Monday. Call for off-season hours. Cash only.

TAQUERO 504SUAZO'S, 58 Creek Rd.; (252) 588-2139; Tex-Mex; $. Not on the main drag so it definitely qualifies as a hidden gem, but check it out. Great burgers and the Mexican influenced dishes are outstanding.

DINING

Attractions

The Outer Banks' biggest attraction is, of course, the water. Nine hundred square miles of water surround these islands, providing a huge, liquid playground for swimmers, boaters, sailors, surfers, anglers, waders, and divers. For those who don't want to get wet, just being on these narrow islands with 175 miles of Atlantic Ocean beaches and views of sparkling blue from every angle is enough.

Nature is so stark and apparent on the Outer Banks that no man-made attraction could ever compare with its glory. But we also have an abundance of stellar man-made attractions, many the sole reason people travel to the Outer Banks. These attractions satisfy history buffs, nature lovers, arts aficionados, and thrill seekers.

OVERVIEW

Some of the Outer Banks attractions were created by men and women out of pride for the significant historic events that took place here, such as the Wright brothers' first flight and the first attempted English settlement in the New World. Others, like *The Lost Colony* outdoor drama, are themselves as much a part of history as the events they portray.

If you're accustomed to metropolitan-area prices, you're in for a real treat. Local attractions are affordable, with most costing less than $15 and many open for free. The priciest attractions are worth every penny and still affordable compared with city prices. Most places offer special family, child, or senior discounts. While some of the attractions stay open year-round, many close in the winter months or strictly curtail their hours. Call ahead.

The Outer Banks is not just the home of two of the most significant events in the nation's history—the first English-speaking colony and the first powered flight—it's also gifted with an extraordinary coastline.

Between lighthouses, lifesaving stations, wild horses, and shipwrecks, visitors can get lost in our long, lively history.

Wide-open wildlife refuges spread across the islands, and fluorescent-lighted fish tanks glow at the state aquarium. You can dive into history by boarding a reproduction 16th-century sailing ship or scuba dive into the Atlantic to explore a Civil War shipwreck. There's never enough time to see everything the Outer Banks has to offer.

In this chapter we highlight our favorite attractions. Many others are there to be discovered; insiders often share their own secret spots. Many of these places have free admission or request nominal donations. We begin with the northernmost communities and work southward. Each area has its own section, so pick your pleasure.

Also, read the **Recreation**, **Shopping**, **Arts & Culture**, **Kidstuff**, and **Entertainment** chapters for more exciting, educational, and unusual things to do and places to play on the Outer Banks.

COROLLA

COROLLA CHAPEL, Old Corolla Village Rd.; (252) 453-4224. The Corolla Chapel, built in 1885, is one of Corolla's most-treasured historic structures. Snuggled into the soundside village, 2½ blocks behind the lighthouse, the chapel served generations of native Corollans in its small sanctuary. In its early years the church was used primarily by Missionary Baptists, although originally it was supposed to be interdenominational. Catholic Masses were first said at the church in 1917 and continued on a sporadic basis through the world wars for Coast Guard personnel stationed nearby. In 1938 the Baptists dropped Corolla from their circuit, saying it was too remote, and the church became interdenominational. In the 1960s Corolla's population reached its all-time low, and the church was no longer used. It lay idle for 25 years.

The last living trustee of the chapel was John Austin, and when he died, the church passed to the hands of his son, who died in 2017. In 1987, as Corolla began to grow again, Austin invited Pastor John Strauss to be the minister of the chapel. Strauss led a restoration, adding a vestibule, bathroom, and storage area in 1992. With regular interdenominational services, he also began to develop a following. The church outgrew its small chapel. In the summer months the village chapel that seats only 100 would have that many (or more) people standing outside. On Easter 2001 Pastor Strauss offered communion to 2,000 people during four services. This led to construction of a new church building across the road from the original chapel. The old Corolla Chapel was then moved across the street and melded into the new sanctuary to form the shape of a cross. The new sanctuary has the same tongue-and-groove beaded-board paneling and details as the old one, so that the two blend seamlessly together, inside and out. The new facility was designed to hold 200 to 250 worshipers.

Today, Pastor Jim Southern leads services at the Corolla Chapel. The best way to see the Corolla Chapel is to attend a service. Interdenominational services are held year-round on Sunday at 10 a.m. From Memorial Day through October, an additional Sunday service is held at 8:30 a.m. Four interdenominational services are held on Easter; one is a sunrise service on the beach.

The church is also available for weddings.

CURRITUCK BANKS NATIONAL ESTUARINE RESEARCH RESERVE, off NC 12. A few miles north of the Currituck Beach Lighthouse,

The Currituck Beach Lighthouse (in background) and the pink boathouse are both listed on the National Register of Historic Places. SGOODWIN4813/GETTYIMAGES

the multistory mansions become sparser and the paved two-lane highway dead-ends at a sand hill. Here a wildlife sanctuary provides a safe haven for endangered piping plover, wild boar, and other wildlife. The reserve itself is about 965 acres (approximately 1 1/2 square miles), most of it in the wetland and shallow waters of Currituck Sound. However, the Nature Conservancy owns a tract north of the Reserve and Currituck County has an easement with US Fish and Wildlife that prohibits development. In combination the feeling is the Reserve is larger than its listed 965 acres.

There are two trails that lead into the reserve and the trailhead is easily accessed. Heading north from Corolla, about a mile past the Currituck Beach Lighthouse there will be a very sharp bend to the right with a small parking lot immediately on the left. That is the trailhead for this beautiful stroll through a maritime forest.

There is a boardwalk that is 2/3 of a mile leading to the Currituck Sound. For the more adventurous, look for the Maritime Forest Hiking Trail sign on the right side with step coming off the boardwalk. The Maritime Forest Trail is 1 1/2 miles there and back following easily seen blue blazons marking the path. The trail is suitable for anyone over the age of eight.

Please, close the gate! The Corolla herd does wander through the Currituck Reserve. Their lives are endangered if they wander through the paved road area of Corolla.

Late spring, summer and early fall, bug repellant is a necessity.

⭐ **CURRITUCK BEACH LIGHTHOUSE, off NC 12; (252) 453-4939;** currituckbeachlight.com. Visitors can climb the 214 steps to the top of the lighthouse, coming eye to eye with the 50,000-candlepower lamp that still flashes every 20 seconds and can be seen for 18 nautical miles. The climb up the narrow, winding staircase is not for the faint of heart, but a panoramic view of the Currituck Outer Banks is your reward.

The Lightkeepers' Residence, a beautiful Victorian dwelling, was constructed of precut, labeled materials and was shipped for assembly on-site by the US Lighthouse Board. The residence was abandoned when the lighthouse was automated in 1939 and keepers were no longer needed on-site (though they still visited once a week to change batteries and perform maintenance). The residence, on the National Register of Historic Places, fell into serious disrepair but was restored by a group known as Outer Banks Conservationists, starting in 1980. The residence is not open for tours, except by appointment during the first two weeks in Nov. Today the keeper's main duties, among many others, are keeping the lighthouse open for tourists, overseeing preservation work, and hiring volunteers and staff.

In 2015 the Currituck Beach Lighthouse celebrated its 140th anniversary as a working lighthouse. Be sure to visit the on-site museum shop. Visitors climb the lighthouse for a fee of $10, cash or check only. Children younger than age 8 climb for free. School groups and other large groups are offered a discounted rate. The lighthouse is open daily from Easter through Thanksgiving. Climbing hours are 10 a.m. to 6 p.m. during Eastern Standard Time and to 5 p.m. during daylight saving time. If you're climbing, you must go up at least 15 minutes before closing time. During periods of lightning or high winds, the lighthouse tower may be closed to climbers.

HISTORIC COROLLA VILLAGE SCHOOLHOUSE AND COROLLA VILLAGE LANES, (252) 453-3341. Though everyone refers to the whole Currituck Outer Banks as "Corolla," technically Corolla is the small village center on the unpaved road behind the lighthouse. Few people realize that Corolla was a thriving community that began to grow in 1875 after the lighthouse was built. In 1890, at the peak of the area's waterfowl-hunting market, 200 residents lived in the village. The village population declined during World War II and the following years. Only a few residents lived in Corolla well into the 1980s, when a paved public road was opened to the area and development of the Currituck Outer Banks began. The faces of the Currituck Outer Banks and Corolla Village have changed dramatically, but you can still get a sense of the old village by walking on the dirt road on the west side of NC 12 behind the lighthouse. In the shade of the oaks and pines, it is easy to imagine the life of the early residents. A few of the historic buildings from the old village remain and have been restored to look as they did when

The Wild Horses of Corolla

Corolla's wild horses are part of the mystique of the Outer Banks: a symbol of the roots, endurance, and resilience of an isolated land and its tough inhabitants. They are also the symbol of the toll taken by breathtaking growth in Corolla.

Visitors to the northernmost stretches of barrier beach no longer see pastoral views of horses grazing on golf courses or newly planted lawns. They no longer see the majestic beasts loping on oceanside sands. They won't even see close-ups of the few that were once corralled at the Currituck Beach Lighthouse.

There are no horses left in Corolla. They now roam exclusively north of Corolla in the 4WD area of Carova where a fence that runs from sound to sea keeps them safe from the summer traffic of Corolla.

Genetic testing has established a direct link between the Corolla Wild horses and the Spanish mustangs of the Conquistadores. The horses have the compact, stocky conformation and, according to one scientist, the genetic markers of the barb horses that were brought to the Outer Banks as early as 1523 by Spanish explorers. One native Outer Banker who has studied the "Banker ponies" said they may be the oldest breed of horse in North America. Though the horses have Spanish origins, they are a breed all their own, due to nearly 400 years as an isolated species. The horses are recognized as a significant cultural and historical resource by the state of North Carolina.

Before development in Corolla intensified in the mid- and late 1980s, wild horses ranged freely among the sea grasses and dunes of the northern barrier islands. A late discovery for developers, the area didn't have electricity until 1968, telephone service until 1974, or a public paved road until 1984. Tourists driving on the new road were charmed that undomesticated horses milled freely in plain view. Less than 10 years later, horses were lounging in shade under rental cottage decks, nosing through garbage cans, and strolling nonchalantly through the grocery store's automatic door.

Tourists took to feeding and petting them—or attempting to. Close calls with horse bites and kicks became part of the local lore. But as the area grew, the interaction between horses and humans became more dangerous. After the road between Duck and Corolla was made public in 1984, 17 horses were killed in vehicle accidents in just four years. A group of local citizens established the Corolla Wild Horse Fund in 1989 to protect the animals after three pregnant mares were killed. The group rallied public support, managing to have the county pass an ordinance to help protect the horses from harm. The wild horses, in fact, became the area's most popular attraction.

Still, horse fund volunteers and staffers were unable to protect their charges. After a poll revealed that most people wanted to preserve the horses in their own environment instead of relocating them, the fund erected a mile-and-a-half-long fence, stretching from sound to sea near where the pavement ends in Corolla. The idea was not to enclose the wild animals but to allow them to roam freely—but safely—in the 11 miles of sand, beach grass and public and private land north of the fence. On March 24, 1995, the horses were herded behind the fence. But the Corolla wild horse story was not yet over.

Like clever children, some of the herd, which numbered 100 by then, strayed around the fence up to Virginia, where they were not welcome. Other horses, led by a particularly stubborn stallion, began sneaking back into Corolla Village. They were always herded back home, but the few recalcitrant horses always found a way out. In 1999 the Corolla Wild Horse Fund took

Direct descendants of the mustangs of the Spanish Conquistadores, the Corolla Wild Mustangs have been a part of the Outer Banks for 400 years.

the wandering horses to the private Dews Island in Currituck Sound, where they had 400 acres to graze. Today the herd numbers between 100 to 110 living north of the fence and roaming the vast area between the off-road ramp and Carova on the Virginia state line.

There are a number of companies specializing in Wild Horse tours in Corolla, including the Corolla Wild Horse Fund. The tour guides are informative and offer the best chance of seeing the horses—they can be very elusive at times. Currituck County law requires people to be no closer than 50 feet from the horses. The law is for the protection of humans and horse. These are not domesticated animals.

Please do not feed them. One of the distinguishing characteristics of the Corolla Wild Horses is their adaptation to a diet of sea oats and dune grasses. A number of horses of the herd have required medical care and some have died after eating food given to them by people.

A horse that has visited a vet is removed from the herd.

The horses are better protected than ever. The staff at the Corolla Wild Horse Fund is responsible for overseeing the health and safety of the herd. Volunteers are needed to help with activities such as a census, marking the horses, and taking health samples. The Corolla Wild Horse Fund Office is on Corolla Village Road. The office phone number is (252) 453-8002. The mailing address is PO Box 361, Corolla, NC 27927, or you can visit corollawildhorses.com.

they were built. Waters Edge Charter School opened in 2012 and brought the old schoolhouse back to life, offering instruction to kindergartners through eighth graders in this idyllic spot. A walking-tour map is available at many of the shops in the area or at Twiddy & Company Realtors, whose owners took charge of restoring the buildings.

⭐ **OUTER BANKS CENTER FOR WILDLIFE EDUCATION**, NC 12, Currituck Heritage Park; (252) 453-0221; ncwildlife.org. Located between the historic Whalehead Club and the Currituck Lighthouse, the 22,000-square-foot center is devoted to teaching the history of the culture and wildlife of North Carolina's northeastern coastal region. A self-guided tour through the diorama of the marsh educates visitors about the regional ecology. Regional history is explored through the boating, hunting, and fishing heritage. Salt marsh ecology can be experienced firsthand. A wonderful film, Currituck, Life by Water's Rhythms, shows regularly in the theater. The Center has one of the largest decoy collections in the world. Special events for adults and children are regularly scheduled; call or check the website for dates and times. Admission is free for most programs. A gift shop is on the premises.

PINE ISLAND AUDUBON SANCTUARY, NC 12, between Duck and Corolla. Set between remote villages of sprawling vacation rental cottages, Pine Island Audubon Sanctuary is a secluded, outdoor enthusiast's paradise and a major resting area for birds along the great Atlantic flyway. Ducks, geese, rabbits, deer, fox, and dozens of other animals make their home in this 2,600-acre wildlife refuge on the northern Outer Banks. Hundreds of other species fly through during spring and fall migrations.

Live oaks, bayberry, inkberry, pine, yaupon, holly, and several species of marsh grass grow naturally in this wild, remote wetland habitat. The Pine Island Clubhouse and grounds are privately owned, but if you're a member of the Audubon Society, tours are available.

Hikers, bikers, and strollers can park at Sanderling Inn to access a 2.5-mile clay trail through a portion of the sanctuary. The maintained path is open year-round.

WHALEHEAD CLUB, NC 12, Currituck Heritage Park, (252) 453-9040; visitwhalehead.com. Overlooking the windswept wetlands of Currituck Sound, this grand dame of days gone by was once the Outer Banks' biggest, most modern structure. Today the Whalehead Club is one of the area's most magnificent attractions and affords a romantic trip back in time to an era of lavish accommodations and elaborate ornamentation. The house was built as

A rare view of an iconic 1920s art nouveau building, The Whalehead Club in Corolla anchors Currituck County Heritage Park.

ATTRACTIONS

a private residence between 1922 and 1925, when the Currituck Outer Banks was in its heyday as a waterfowl-hunting paradise. The owners, a wealthy northerner named Edward Collins Knight and his wife, Marie Louise LeBel Knight, originally called their home Corolla Island because the house was situated on an island-like mound that was created when a circular canal was dug around the lot. The Knights spent their winters and hunted at Corolla Island from 1925 to 1934. The 21,000-square-foot house has seen many uses since then. It sat empty for years, as relatives of the Knights were not interested in the remote location. In 1940 the house was sold to Ray Adams of Washington, DC, for a reported $25,000. It was Adams who named the home the Whalehead Club.

Ray Adams died at the Whalehead Club on New Year's Eve 1957 and the property was sold to an educational foundation that created the Corolla Academy, an all-boys school. Three years later, the school closed and one of the most bizarre pieces of the Whalehead Club's history followed.

At the time there was no development around Corolla and a rocket research company, ARC, needed a place to test Beryllium as a fuel for space exploration. Very powerful and stable, the element had a lot to recommend it as a fuel. Unfortunately it's also very toxic. In 1969 ARC realized they could not overcome the toxicity of the fuel and they closed their operation down and sold the property.

The surrounding 2,200 acres were subdivided for development, but the building itself was largely unoccupied and for the next 30 years when Currituck County stepped in and began its restoration.

The house, on the National Register of Historic Places, is now owned by Currituck County and has been restored to the way it looked in 1925. The multimillion-dollar restoration project began in 1999 with the replacement of the copper roof. The exterior was painted its original canary yellow. The interior has been completely restored, down to the paint, cork floors, Tiffany glass, and art nouveau details. A team of researchers and restoration specialists has tracked down as much information as possible to make the restoration as accurate as possible.

Visitors are welcome and can take a guided tour of the house. Tours begin on the half hour and include a self-guided exhibition on display in the basement gallery. A special "behind the scenes" tour is offered daily (by reservation only). Guides are very knowledgeable about the home as well as the history of the area. The museum shop stocks tasteful merchandise that is unique to the Whalehead Club, including handcrafted jewelry, picture frames, ornaments, and birdhouses made from the original copper roof shingles. The Whalehead Club is situated on 39 acres known as Currituck Heritage Park. It offers an ideal location for picnics, leisurely walks, fishing, or enjoying a beautiful Outer Banks sunset.

The Whalehead Club is open from May 1 through October 31 and during the weeks of the Easter, Thanksgiving, and Christmas holidays (but not on the actual holidays themselves). House tours take place daily in season beginning at 9 a.m. The last tour begins at 4 p.m. The tours last 45 minutes. Admission cost ranges from $5 to $7 for adults and $5 for school-age children. A variety of themed tours are offered, most geared toward specific interests and age groups. Call or check the website for details.

DUCK

DUCK BOARDWALK, Soundside. The Duck Boardwalk is a mile-long pedestrian only boardwalk spanning the shallow waters of the Currituck Sound along the town's shoreline. Offering some of the most spectacular sunsets on the Outer Banks, the boardwalk includes two kayak ramps and a number of shops and restaurants.

DUCK TOWN PARK, NC 12; (252) 255-1286; townofduck.com. Native soundside plants provide the backdrop for the grassy gathering space. A playground and parking lot are on the premises, and the gazebo and amphitheater house performing acts. Cultural and community events are held throughout the summer and fall. Regularly scheduled events include a children's story hour, a summer evening music series, and *The Lost Colony* show highlights. The popular annual Duck Jazz Festival is held in mid-October. Check the website for details, or call the events hotline at the number listed above. A soundside boardwalk, nature trails, a public kayak and canoe launch, a picnic pavilion, and a gazebo are also open to the public.

US ARMY CORPS OF ENGINEERS FIELD RESEARCH FACILITY, NC 12; (252) 261-6840; frf.usace.army.mil. Set on a former navy weapons test site, the Waterways Experiment Station of the US Army Corps of Engineers has helped scientists study ocean processes since 1977. This 173-acre federally owned scientific mecca has gained a reputation as one of the premier coastal field research facilities in the world. Just north of Duck Village, the site includes state-of-the-art equipment to monitor sand movement, wave forces, water currents, temperatures, and sedimentation. Its 12 full-time employees regularly host dozens of scientists from around the globe to conduct experiments on sand movement, beach erosion, and coastal dynamics. In 1997, during the world's largest near-shore research experiment, 250 coastal engineers gathered at the research facility to study the near-shore zone of breaking waves to determine the dynamics of beach erosion.

Besides the 1,840-foot pier, the US Army Corps of Engineers' experiment station owns a 125-foot observation tower and a 35-foot-tall Coastal Research Amphibious Buggy, the CRAB, which carries people and equipment from the shore into the sea. The Corps works in cooperation with the US Army and Navy and the National Oceanic and Atmospheric Administration, using the latest technologically advanced equipment to improve the design of coastal navigation projects. Research conducted at the station could eventually alter the way engineers design bridges, help people pick sites for beach nourishment projects, improve projections about where the shoreline might erode, determine how and why sandbars move, and predict what effect rock jetties might have on Oregon Inlet. Surfers are cautioned to avoid surfing immediately north of the pier. Instruments are attached to poles throughout the surf creating hazardous conditions for anyone in that area of the water. Tours of the facility are no longer available due to security concerns.

> **i** Scotch bonnets, the North Carolina state shell, are rarely found on the Cape Hatteras National Seashore beaches but are often found on the remote beaches of Portsmouth Island. Whole sand dollars can be found there, too.

KITTY HAWK

KITTY HAWK WOODS RESERVE, 983 West Kitty Hawk Rd.; (252) 261-8891; nccoastalreserve.net. A 1,900 acre protected maritime forest of remarkable beauty and diversity, Kitty Hawk Woods calls out to be explored. From 1910 to 1920 there was a logging operation in Kitty Hawk Woods run by the Tunis Lumber Company of Elizabeth City. To move the felled trees to Albemarle Sound where they were rafted together for their journey to Elizabeth City mills, a train track was built and then loaded onto rail cars.

The Ridge Trail is the remnants of that time. The path is flat, compact and seems to be raised above the surrounding terrain. The Ridge Trail is by far the best for bikes. There are some challenges, some hills and features that will give a bike rider a bit of a test, making it a fun trail to ride. We do not recommend taking the trail to the Albemarle Sound on a bike.

Creeks and canals intersperse the Reserve and are easily paddled by kayak. Experienced kayakers can certainly handle this on their own, but a number of outfitters take tours out onto creeks.

The other way is to explore the trails either on foot or bike. There are three trailheads, but unfortunately no convenient trailhead parking available. Insiders know the reward is truly worth the effort. Ridge Road trailhead and Birch Lane are the easiest to locate. One trailhead is at the end of Birch Lane on the east side of the Reserve. The Birch Trail is about a mile and a half long. It is not a loop trail, so you will return on the same path. Birch Lane is off US 158 about a half mile past the end of the Wright Memorial Bridge.

Ridge Road is off Tillett Street which connects with the Woods Road. Go to the end of Tillett and turn right at the Austin Cemetery. Turn Right again onto Ridge Road. Go to the end of Ridge where there is a cleared patch of dirt leading up to a wooden barrier. There will be a playground on the left. The wooden barrier is the entrance to Kitty Hawk Woods. The Ridge Road Trail is a loop trail that connects with the Barlowe Trail. This third trailhead option begins at the intersection of Amadas Lane and Colleton Avenue.

All of the paths are an easy walk. There may be some dead fall requiring a little bit of a scramble, but there are no real barriers to stop anyone.

MONUMENT TO A CENTURY OF FLIGHT, off US 158 Bypass, behind the Aycock Brown Welcome Center; (252) 441-6584; monumenttoacentury offlight.org. This sculpture garden was conceived by local artist Glenn Eure and brought to fruition by the nonprofit group Icarus International. It features stainless steel pylons placed in ascending order by height, symbolizing the steps humans have taken to reach the heavens. Adorning the pylons are black granite slabs that name 100 of the most important moments in the history of flight. The courtyard contains 5,000 bricks, each engraved with a personal message.

KILL DEVIL HILLS

NAGS HEAD WOODS ECOLOGICAL PRESERVE, Ocean Acres Dr.; (252) 441-2525; nature.org. If you've had a little too much sun, or if you'd like to spend time in a secluded forest on a part of the Outer Banks few people get to see, allocate an afternoon for the Nature Conservancy's Nags Head Woods Ecological Preserve, west of US 158. The maritime forest itself is well hidden, and many rare plant and animal species live within this protected landscape. It's one of the most tranquil settings on the Outer Banks.

The Nature Conservancy, an international, nonprofit conservation organization, oversees this maritime forest. Nags Head Woods is not a park—it is an example of a successful private-public partnership between the Nature Conservancy, the towns of Nags Head and Kill Devil Hills, and private landowners. More than 5 miles of trails and footbridges wind through forest, dune, swamp, and pond habitats, as well as graveyards and farm sites from the 19th and early 20th centuries. No camping, firearms, picnicking, or alcoholic beverages are allowed in the preserve. Bicycling, pets on leashes, and other activities that might damage the trails are restricted to the Old Nags Head Woods Road, which winds from north to south through the woods. For more information, write to the Nature Conservancy at 701 West Ocean Acres Dr., Kill Devil Hills, NC 27948. All donations are welcome, and memberships start at $50. Monies support the preserve's environmental education and research programs.

ATTRACTIONS

⭐ **WRIGHT BROTHERS NATIONAL MEMORIAL, US 158, MP 8;** (252) 441-7430; nps.gov/wrbr. Set atop a steep, grassy sand hill in the center of Kill Devil Hills, the trapezoidal granite monument to Orville and Wilbur Wright is within easy walking distance of the site of the world's first powered airplane flight. Below where this lighthouse-style tower now stands, on the blustery afternoon of December 17, 1903, the two bicycle-building brothers from Dayton, Ohio, soared over a distance of more than 852 feet, staying airborne for an unheard of 59 seconds in their homemade flying machine. The monument was erected to honor Orville and Wilbur Wright in 1932.

In the low, domed building on the right side of the main drive off US 158, the National Park Service operates a visitor center, gift shop, and museum. Here you can view interpretive exhibits of humankind's first flight and see displays on later aviation advancements. Exhibits about the Wright brothers' struggles to fly include parts of their planes, engines, and research notes. Reproductions of their gliders are displayed in the flight room, and rangers offer free guided historical tours year-round. The visitor center is itself an attraction. Opened in the early 1960s, it is recognized as a significant example of modernist architecture. It's one of only a handful of examples of modernist architecture built in eastern North Carolina during the 20th century, mainly because the National Park Service was one of a few groups in the region that had the financial resources to hire architects from outside the region. The Philadelphia architectural firm of Ehrman Mitchell and Romaldo Giurgola designed the building to reflect the natural environment of the Outer Banks and symbolically portray flight in static form. The horizontal roof with a shallow concrete dome reflects the surrounding landscape of beach and dunes, while the overhang of the dome represents the soaring possibilities of flight. The National Historic Register-listed structure is considered a key work in the Philadelphia school of expressive modernist architects.

The 100th anniversary celebration of the first flight was held in December 2003. An olive-shaped, domed Centennial Pavilion was added for the celebration. The Centennial Pavilion houses a US Air Force exhibit, NASA exhibit, and exhibits from the Cirrus Corporation and the Wright Experience. The Wright Experience details the story of replicating the original Wright *Flyer*. Harry Combs, the deceased Wright brothers' historian and aviator, donated more than $1 million to build and replicate the *Flyer* housed here.

Outside the exhibit center four markers set along a sandy runway commemorate the takeoff and landing sites of each of Orville and Wilbur's December 17 flights. Reconstructed wooden sheds replicating those used at the Wrights' 1903 camp and hangar also are on the grounds and open to visitors. These sheds are furnished with tools, equipment, and food canisters similar to those the brothers used. A short hike takes you from the visitor center to the monument hill, but if you'd rather drive or ride, parking is available closer to

The iconic testament to Wright Brothers at the National Park Service Wright Brothers Monument in Kill Devil Hills is not the only tribute to the Wilbur and Orville Wright. This monument, paid for and erected by the citizens of Kitty Hawk in 1928, commemorates the site of Bill and Addie Tate's home where the brothers stayed in 1900.

the base of the hill. Paved walkways make access easy. The grass is filled with cacti and sandspurs, so you're advised to stay on the paths. Also, be aware that the walk up the monument hill is longer and more strenuous than it looks. On a hot summer day, consider visiting the site in the morning or late afternoon, when the sun is not as strong.

Besides tours, the exhibit center at the Wright Brothers National Memorial offers a variety of summer programs. Grounds and buildings are open to vehicles from 9 a.m. until 5 p.m. Labor Day through Memorial Day. Hours are from 9 a.m. to 6 p.m. in the summer. Thirty-minute flight-room talks are given by rangers every hour on the hour, year-round. Expect the entire tour to take about one to two hours. Add an additional 30 minutes if you'd like to attend a program.

Cost for entry at the guard gate is $10 for adults ages 16 and older, and admission is good for seven days. Persons age 15 and younger get in free, as do seniors with Golden Age Passports and other passports, which are available at the gate.

NAGS HEAD

⭐ **JOCKEY'S RIDGE STATE PARK,** US 158, MP 12; (252) 441-7132; jockeysridgestatepark.com. The East Coast's tallest sand dune and one of the Outer Banks' most phenomenal natural attractions, Jockey's Ridge has long been a favorite stop for tourists. In the early 1970s bulldozers began flattening the surrounding dunes to make way for a housing subdivision. A Nags Head woman, Carolista Baum, singlehandedly stopped the destruction and formed a committee that saved Jockey's Ridge. State officials made the sand hill a protected park in 1975, but the dunes are unruly. Since then the steepest side of the hill has shifted more than 1,500 feet to the southwest. Jockey's Ridge is also getting shorter. At the turn of the 20th century, the highest mound was estimated at 140 feet. In 1971 it was about 110 feet tall. Today the 1.5-mile-long, 420-acre-plus dune—which varies from 90 feet to 110 feet in height—is open to the public year-round until sunset. It's a popular spot for hang gliders, summer hikers, small children who like to roll down the steep slopes, and teenagers who delight in sandboarding or flinging and flipping themselves down the sandy hills. Sandboarding is allowed only from October 1 through March 31. More than one million people visit Jockey's Ridge each year. Park headquarters are near the northern end of a parking lot off the west side of US 158. You'll notice an entrance sign at MP 12, Carolista Drive, in Nags Head.

A visitor center, museum, and gift shop are near park headquarters. The free museum features photo displays of the history and recreation at the dune and a diorama of the animals that inhabit the area. Information panels of plants and animals and an auditorium where slide shows and videos are shown are also at the facility. Maps available from the park ranger indicate walking areas. Two trails—the Soundside Nature Trail, a very easy 45-minute walk, and Tracks in the Sand, a 1.5-mile trek—are open to hikers looking for a change of scenery. Jockey's Ridge State Park offers natural history programs throughout the summer, including stargazing and wildlife discovery evening hikes and early-morning bird watching and natural history discovery adventures. Fantastic educational programs for kids are also offered, but rangers warn that they fill up fast, and many require advance registration. Call for program schedules. Sheltered picnic areas are available for lunches.

It's a long hike to the top of the ridge. Bring sandals, shoes or boots. Don't try it barefoot in summer; you'll burn your feet. Also, some lower areas adjacent to US 158 are covered with broken glass. At the top of Jockey's Ridge, you can see both ocean and sound. Cottages along the beach look like tiny huts from a miniature train set. Kite-flying and hang-gliding enthusiasts catch the breezes that flow around the steep summit, shifting the sand in all directions. (See the **Recreation** chapter for information on hang gliding.) There is also a fascinating soundside trail that leads to a small maritime forest by Roanoke Sound.

If your mobility is impaired, a 360-foot boardwalk affords wheelchairs and baby strollers a slightly sloping incline onto a wooden platform overlooking the center of the dune. For the visually impaired, audio guides are available at the park office. Park rangers can also provide a ride on a four-wheeler to the top of the dune if you call 24 hours in advance. The park opens at 8 a.m. every day except Christmas. Closing time depends on the season: November through February, 6 p.m.; March and October, 7 p.m.; April, May, and September, 8 p.m.; and June through August, 9 p.m.

NAGS HEAD BEACH COTTAGE ROW, Historic District, NC 12, MP 12–13. The long row of rustic, weatherworn cottages on the ocean in Nags Head around mileposts 12 and 13 is famously known as the "Unpainted Aristocracy." The homes have been on the National Register of Historic Places since 1977. They feature the Nags Head-style cedar siding grayed in the wind and salt, wraparound porches, propped-open shutters, dormers, and gabled roofs. Although Nags Head was a vacation destination earlier, it wasn't until 1855 that an Elizabeth City doctor built the first house on the oceanfront. He was lonely, so he sold the land around him to other people who vacationed in the wooded area by the sound. By 1885, 13 homes sat at the ocean's edge. Many of the cottages are still in the original families. Nine of the original 13 are still standing. Two were replaced with similar structures, one was destroyed by fire, and one was razed. Several other cottages scattered between mileposts 12 and 13 have interesting histories, although they are not considered part of the Unpainted Aristocracy. The land around these homes is private, and the homes are occupied. Feel free to drive by or walk by and admire, but please respect the owners' privacy and don't trespass on their property.

BODIE ISLAND

BODIE ISLAND LIGHTHOUSE AND KEEPERS' QUARTERS, west of NC 12; (252) 441-5711. This black-and-white beacon with horizontal bands

Patterned after the Cape Hatteras Lighthouse, Bodie Island Lighthouse opened in 1872 and stands guard over Oregon Inlet.

is one of four lighthouses standing along the Outer Banks. It sits more than a half mile from the sea, in a field of green grass, closer to the sound than the ocean. The lighthouse itself is not open for climbing, but the setting is worth the trip. The keepers' quarters have exhibits about the lighthouse and a small bookshop. The grounds are perfect for a picnic, and nature trails lead into the wide expanses of marshland behind the tower, through cattails, yaupon, and wax myrtle. The trails end up at Roanoke Sound, offering a view of the private camp on Off Island. The slough that rushes through the water between Bodie and Off Islands is a popular fishing hole, and anglers often line the banks.

The current Bodie Island Lighthouse is the third to stand near Oregon Inlet, which opened during a hurricane in 1846. The first lighthouse was built south of Oregon Inlet in 1847 and 1848 and was the only one in the 140 miles between Cape Hatteras and Cape Henry, Virginia. The lighthouse developed cracks and structural damage within 10 years and had to be removed and rebuilt. The second light was also built south of Oregon Inlet. It was complete and lighted in 1859. Confederate forces destroyed the second tower during the Civil War so that it wouldn't fall into Union hands. The 170-foot lighthouse that stands today was built in 1872, this time north of Oregon Inlet because the inlet was moving south at a steady pace. Wanchese resident Vernon Gaskill served as the last civilian lightkeeper of the Bodie Island Lighthouse. The US Coast Guard operated the light for many years, and it was transferred to the National Park Service in 2000. The visitor center is open from 9 a.m. until 5 p.m. every day except Christmas. The grounds are always open.

Bodie Island Lighthouse can be climbed and the view from the top is worth the effort. South and a little to the east, the spectacular Marc Basnight Bridge arcs over Oregon Inlet. Looking west the marsh, wetlands and islands that dot Pamlico and Roanoke Sounds spread out at the base. Roanoke Island can be seen, as well as the town of Nags Head and the bridges that connect the Outer Banks with Roanoke Island.

Tickets for the climb are $10 for adults and $5 for senior citizens (62 or older), children 11 years of age and under, and the disabled. Tickets are sold on a first come first serve basis beginning at 9 a.m. Climbs are 20 minutes with a limit of eight climbers per climb. Ticket holders are given a climb time at purchase and should be at the site five minutes before their climb. The Bodie Island Lighthouse is open from the third Friday in April through Columbus Day.

CAPE HATTERAS NATIONAL SEASHORE, Bodie, Hatteras, and Ocracoke Islands; (252) 473-3111; nps.gov/caha. Cape Hatteras National Seashore is a tremendous treasure for the residents and visitors of the Outer Banks. Here you will find the Outer Banks' most captivating open spaces, where long reaches of rugged dunes, windblown brush, wide beaches, and soundside wetlands are protected from development. Established in 1953 by the National Park Service and dedicated in 1958, the Cape Hatteras National Seashore includes part of Bodie Island and most of Hatteras and Ocracoke Islands, except for the village centers and Pea Island National Wildlife Refuge. The northern boundary begins south of Whalebone Junction in Nags Head, and the southern boundary is on Ocracoke Island. This was the very first national seashore in the nation. It consists of some of the narrowest land inhabitable by humans—skinny stretches of sand often less than a half mile wide. The national seashore provides miles-long stretches where there is not one single structure obscuring the view. Designated shorebird and sea-turtle sanctuaries are well marked for protection on the beaches.

The Cape Hatteras National Seashore beaches are some of the cleanest and least crowded on the East Coast. If you're looking for solitary recreational space or simple peace and quiet, you'll find it here. Most of the beaches do not have life guards, however, so make sure you know swimming safety precautions before going in. Lifeguards are stationed in summer at Coquina Beach on Bodie Island, at the beach near the Cape Hatteras Lighthouse, and at the Ocracoke Guarded Beach. Numerous access points are offered all along NC 12, the highway that threads through the seashore. Three of the Outer Banks' four lighthouses are located within this national seashore, and there are four campgrounds in the Cape Hatteras National Seashore (see the **Accommodations** chapter). Camping is prohibited on the beach.

The Cape Hatteras National Seashore is dedicated to community outreach and has summer programs to help visitors learn more about the natural surroundings. The National Park Service provides guided beach walks, bird walks, campfires, fishing trips, history tours, dozens of kids' programs, snorkeling trips, turtle talks, and much more. The schedules are lengthy, so the best way to find out about programs is to pick up the information at one of the visitor centers or download it online. Driving on the beach is allowed in the Cape

The Historic Keepers Quarters at Bodie Island Lighthouse, a part of Cape Hatteras National Seashore. WILSILVER77/GETTYIMAGES

Hatteras National Seashore at certain access points only. A permit is required to drive on the beach. Permits can be purchased at any of the Park's offices. Four-wheel-drive vehicles may enter only at designated ramps. Soundside off-road travel is permitted on established roads or trails. Off-road access ramps are available at the visitor centers. Beach bonfires require a permit. Several day-use areas are available throughout the area, and nature trails provide visitors with an up-close look at the seashore environments. Personal watercraft like Jet Skis and WaveRunners are prohibited in Cape Hatteras National Seashore.

Three visitor centers are established in the national seashore. The Bodie Island Visitor Center (252-441-5711) is on NC 12, in Nags Head heading south. The Cape Hatteras Visitor Center (252-995-4474) is in Buxton next to the Cape Hatteras Lighthouse. The Ocracoke Island Visitor Center (252-928-4531) is near the Cedar Island ferry dock. All provide extensive information on camping and activities in the national seashore.

COQUINA BEACH, NC 12. Though not as broad as it once was due to storms, Coquina Beach is still one of the widest beaches on the Outer Banks and a favorite getaway. Just 6 miles south of Whalebone Junction, this beach has half the crowd but all the amenities you need: a lifeguard in the summer, a bathhouse, restrooms, outdoor showers, and lots of parking. Part of the allure of this remote area is that it's miles away from any business or rental cottage, making it a superb spot to sunbathe, swim, fish, and surf. The sand is almost white, and the beach is relatively flat. Drawing its name from the tiny butterfly-shaped coquina clams that burrow into the beach, at times almost every inch of this portion of the federally protected Cape Hatteras National Seashore harbors hundreds of recently washed-up shells and several species of rare shorebirds. Coquinas are edible and can be collected and cleaned from their shells to make a chowder. Local brick makers also have used the shells as temper in buildings.

LAURA A. BARNES, Coquina Beach, NC 12. One of the last coastal schooners built in America, the *Laura A. Barnes* was completed in Camden, Maine, in 1918. This 120-foot ship was under sail on the Atlantic during a trip from New York to South Carolina when a nor'easter drove it onto the Outer Banks in 1921. The *Laura A. Barnes* ran aground just north of where it now rests at Coquina Beach. The entire crew survived. In 1973 the National Park Service moved the shipwreck to its present location, where visitors view the remains of the ship behind a roped-off area that includes placards with information about the *Laura A. Barnes* and the history of lifesaving.

OREGON INLET AND THE MARC BASNIGHT BRIDGE, NC 12, Oregon Inlet. The view from the crest of the Marc Basnight Bridge has to be the most beautiful vista on the Outer Banks. If only there was a place to pull over and enjoy it more fully! As you drive over you get a sweeping glimpse of this infamous inlet and all its surrounding shoals, sandbars, and spoil islands. Sea captains call this the most dangerous inlet on the East Coast—and with good reason. Since 1960 at least 30 lives and an equal number of boats have been lost at Oregon Inlet. The current through the inlet i dangerously swift and reckless, and shoals form alarmingly fast, causing boats to run aground. The only outlet to the sea in the 140 miles between Cape Henry, in Virginia Beach, and Hatteras Inlet south of Hatteras Island, Oregon Inlet lies between Bodie Island and Pea Island National Wildlife Refuge. It is the primary passage for commercial and recreational fishing boats based along the northern Outer Banks. Even though it's often dredged, the inlet is sometimes impassable by deep-draft vessels.

Oregon Inlet was created during a hurricane in September 1846, the same storm that opened Hatteras Inlet between Hatteras Village and Ocracoke Island. It was named for the side-wheeler *Oregon*, the first ship to pass through the inlet. In 1964 the Herbert C. Bonner Bridge was built across the inlet, and was replaced by the Marc Basnight Bridge in 2019. Before the bridge was built, travelers relied on ferry boats to carry them across Oregon Inlet. Four-wheel-drive vehicles can exit NC 12 on the northeast side of the inlet and drive along the beach around the inlet. Fishing is permitted along the catwalks of the bridge and on the beach. Free parking and restrooms are available at the Oregon Inlet Fishing Center. There are also parking and portable toilets on the southern end of the bridge. This trip is especially beautiful at sunset or sunrise.

The restored Oregon Inlet Life Saving Station stands on the coast at Pea Island National Wildlife Refuge in Cape Hatteras National Seashore.
KENNETH_KEIFER/GETTYIMAGES

OREGON INLET COAST GUARD STATION, NC 12. In the 19th and early 20th centuries, the federal government operated two lifesaving stations at Oregon Inlet. The Bodie Island station was on the north side of the inlet. The Oregon Inlet station was on the south. Both of these original facilities are now closed. The Oregon Inlet station is a picturesque reminder of the history of the Outer Banks and how quickly changes occur. Some restoration work has been done on the station, but it is still not considered safe for the public. There is plenty of parking next to the station, and you can walk around the grounds and out to the jetties, but you can't go inside the building. This is also a popular and lucrative fishing spot. You can fish from the rock jetties, wade out into the deep cove, or walk the catwalk on the south end of the bridge.

The Bodie Island station has been replaced by the Oregon Inlet Coast Guard station, which includes a 10,000-square-foot building, a state-of-the-art communications center, maintenance shops, an administrative center, and accommodations for the staff. Coast Guard crews have rescued dozens of watermen off the Outer Banks. They also aid sea turtles and stranded seals by helping the animals get back safely to warmer parts of the ocean.

OREGON INLET FISHING CENTER, NC 12; (252) 441-6301; oregon-inlet.com. Sportfishing enthusiasts, or anyone remotely interested in offshore angling, must stop by this bustling charter-boat harbor on the north shore of Oregon Inlet. All vessels charge the same rate. A day on the Atlantic with one of these captains may give rise to a marlin, sailfish, wahoo, tuna, or dolphin on the end of the line. (See the **Recreation** chapter for details.) An exciting afternoon activity is to head to the boat docks at Oregon Inlet Fishing Center between 4 and 5 p.m. When the charter boats return to the docks, you'll have an opportunity to see a variety of Gulf Stream creatures as the mates unload the boats and hurl the huge fish on the docks. In summer the docks are crowded with spectators. Next to the fishing center store is a display case housing a 1,152-pound blue marlin, caught in 1973 and brought back to this fishing center. The store stocks bait and tackle, supplies, hot dogs and snacks, T-shirts and hats galore, and more. The fishing center has an air-fill tank for putting air back into your tires after driving on the beach (there's a four-wheel-drive access across the street). The boat ramp at the fishing center provides easy access to some of the best fishing grounds on the East Coast. There is plenty of parking, and restrooms are on-site.

ROANOKE ISLAND

Roanoke Island brims with attractions. Anyone visiting the Outer Banks should definitely come over for the day, although with many new bed and breakfasts, restaurants, and shops in town, it's becoming more of an overnight destination in its own right.

If you're planning to visit many of the attractions on Roanoke Island, a Roanoke Island Attractions Pass or Queen's Pass will save you up to 25 percent of the admission fees. The Attractions Pass combines admission to the North Carolina Aquarium, the Elizabethan Gardens, and Roanoke Island Festival Park. The Queen's Pass allows admission to the same three attractions, plus *The Lost Colony*. Children younger than age 5 can visit all of these attractions except *The Lost Colony* for free. The passes are good for one calendar year and are available at the local attractions and the Outer Banks Visitors Bureau.

> **i** Virginia Dare, the first child born to the colonists on Roanoke Island, was born on August 18, 1587. Each year on that day a wonderful celebration is held at the Elizabethan Gardens. Madrigal singers fill the air with their beautiful songs, and a 45-minute play is performed at this free event. The play changes each year.

Manteo

⭐ DOWNTOWN MANTEO, Off US 64; Queen Elizabeth Ave and Budleigh and Sir Walter Raleigh Sts. Named for a Roanoke Island Native American who accompanied English explorers back to England in the 16th

The Manteo waterfront has a wonderful small town feel in a picturesque setting.

century, Manteo is one of the oldest Outer Banks communities and has long been a commercial and governmental hub for the area. When Dare County was formed in 1870, this area along Shallowbag Bay became the county seat. Roanoke Island provided a central location that everyone could reach by boat. It wasn't until 1873, when a post office was established here, that the county seat became known as Manteo. In 1899 Manteo incorporated and became the Town of Manteo. Today hundreds of permanent residents make this Roanoke Island town their home, and many more county residents commute from other towns to work. On Budleigh Street, many of the county and town offices are scattered in older office buildings. Manteo's bed and breakfast inns, restaurants, and shops beckon tourists, and thousands of visitors arrive each summer to explore this historic waterfront village. (See the Roanoke Island section of the **Area Overview** chapter.) On the docks of Manteo's waterfront, 53 modern dockside slips offer boaters overnight or long-term anchorage. A comfort station with restrooms, showers, washers, and dryers also serves vessel crews and captains. Shop and dine within walking distance in Manteo—or better yet, bike. This is a town to enjoy on two wheels.

Across the street from the waterfront, in the center of the downtown area, independently owned shops, eateries, and businesses offer everything from handmade pottery to books to clothing, all in a 4-square-block area. Picnic benches afford a comfortable place to rest and enjoy the view across the bay to Roanoke Island Festival Park, where the state's replica 16th-century sailing ship Elizabeth II rocks gently on small sound waves. A wood-plank boardwalk leads along the town's waterfront. One end bustles with kayak and boat tours coming and going, boaters docking in the harbor, and tourists strolling along the docks or exploring shops and restaurants. Around the corner is a gazebo for resting and a long pier for fishing or crabbing. A children's playground with equipment is on the corner, as are picnic tables. At the far end of the docks, you'll find a bit of serenity, where the activity diminishes and the only company you'll have is a few cattails. If, as most visitors do, you reach the Banks via US 158, you can get to Manteo by traveling south until you reach Whalebone Junction. Bear right onto US 64 at the traffic light near Sugar Shack Restaurant. Continue across the causeway and high-rise bridge past Pirate's Cove, then bear right at the intersection, turning onto US 264 Business. Turn right at either of the town's first two stoplights to go downtown.

★ **THE ELIZABETHAN GARDENS,** Off US 64; (252) 473-3234; elizabethangardens.org. Created by the Garden Club of North Carolina Inc. in 1960 to commemorate the efforts of Sir Walter Raleigh's colonists at establishing an English settlement, these magnificent botanical gardens offer an exquisite, aromatic environment year-round. They include 10.5 acres of the state's most colorful, dazzling flora. The flower-filled walkways contrast with the windblown, barren Outer Banks beaches. The tree-lined landscape is divided into a dozen gardens, where translucent emerald grass fringes marble fountains, and beauty blooms from every crevice. Although this botanical refuge is

This 10-acre formal garden adjacent to The Lost Colony *is filled with historic statuary, fountains, and paths that wind through native trees.*

breathtakingly beautiful all year, vibrant with seasonal colors and fragrances, it is perhaps the most striking in spring. Azaleas, dogwood, pansies, wisteria, and tulips bloom around every bend. Rhododendron, roses, and lace-cap and other hydrangea appear in May. Summer brings fragrant gardenias, colorful annuals and perennials, magnolia, crape myrtle, Oriental lilies, and herbs. Chrysanthemums and the changing colors of leaves signal the beginning of fall, and camellias bloom from fall through the winter. In the center of the paths, six marble steps down from the rest of the greenery, sits the crown jewel of the Elizabethan Gardens: a sunken garden, complete with Roman statuary, tiered fountains, and low shrubs pruned into geometric flower frames. The famous Virginia Dare statue nearby is based on an Indian legend that says Virginia, the first English child born in America, grew up among Native Americans (see the Roanoke Island section of the **Area Overview** chapter).

Special events include the spectacular WinterLights holiday display. The entire gardens are illuminated and the glow is bound to put any Scrooge into the spirit of the season. Other events include: Easter Eggstravaganza, gardening classes, kids' summer camps, cooking classes, art classes, and more. The gardens are closed Thanksgiving Day, Christmas Eve, Christmas Day, and New Year's Day. From March through November the gardens open at 9 a.m., and closing time varies depending on the season (between 5 and 7 p.m.). When *The Lost Colony* is running, the gardens stay open until 8 p.m. so that visitors can tour the gardens then head next door to see the outdoor drama. Season and daily passes are available.

FORT RALEIGH NATIONAL HISTORIC SITE, off US 64; (252) 473-5772; nps.gov/fora. When you visit Fort Raleigh, don't expect to see a fort. What exists on the site is a small earthworks fortification. It is not a daunting barricade but a lovely spot drenched in American history. On the north end of Roanoke Island, near the Roanoke Sound's shores, Fort Raleigh marks the beginning of English settlement in North America. Since this attraction is next to the Elizabethan Gardens and *The Lost Colony*'s Waterside Theatre, many people combine a trip to all three. Designated as a National Historic Site in 1941, this more than 500-acre expanse of woods includes the "outerwork"—an area built intentionally away from living space—along with a soundside beach, the National Park Service's Cape Hatteras National Seashore headquarters, the Fort Raleigh Visitor Center, and nature trails. The Fort Raleigh Visitor Center offers interpretive exhibits in a small museum. The museum is not particularly interesting to children, though adults will be fascinated by the story of the colonists who attempted the first English settlements in the New World. A 17-minute video provides an introduction to the historic site. Also, a 400-year-old Elizabethan room from Heronden Hall in Kent, England, is on display. It was removed from an authentic 16th-century home. The room gives visitors a feel for the type of accommodations the aristocratic English were used to at the time of the attempted settlements. A gallery inside displays artifacts excavated from the site and copies of watercolors by John White, governor of the Roanoke colony.

Outside, Fort Raleigh has a variety of options for experiencing the history of Roanoke Island. Behind the visitor center is the earthworks, which is not very impressive but gives you an idea of the original. The Thomas Hariot Nature Trail, named for the scientist who accompanied one of the voyages, winds through the woods behind the visitor center. Hariot's descriptions of the New World are quoted on interpretive signs along the trail. The pine-needle path leads to the sandy shores of Roanoke Sound. Self-guided tours and tours led by park service personnel are available at this archaeologically significant site. Interpretive programs on African-American history, European colonial history, Native American history, and Civil War history are offered in the summer. Fort Raleigh National Historic Site is open year-round from 9 a.m. to 5 p.m. seven days a week. Hours are extended in the summer. The grounds of Fort Raleigh provide a place for a picnic, especially under the huge live oaks on the grass median of the parking lot. Restrooms are on-site.

> **i** Keeping the tradition of pirates and rum alive on the coast, the Outer Banks first craft distillery has opened in downtown Manteo. Outer Banks Distilling produces Kill Devil Rum, sold in local restaurants, bars and the NC ABC store. Visitors can visit stop by 510 Budleigh and learn the secrets of creating small batch rum. Kill Devil Rum merchandise, tours, and samples are available. Visit outerbanksdistilling.com for specific tour details.

FREEDMEN'S COLONY SITE, WEIRS POINT, AND FORT HUGER, (252) 473-5772. At the northernmost end of Roanoke Island, on the east side of the Manns Harbor bridge, are several historic landmarks that are part of the Fort Raleigh National Historic Site. You can access these sites by the Freedmen's Trail, a 2-mile, self-guided trail that starts near the Elizabethan Gardens entrance. You can get there by car and park in the sizable lot or ride a bike along the Manteo Bike Path, which ends at this site. Weirs Point is an attractive, wide public beach on Croatan Sound, where the water is warm and shallow. Picnic benches, a Dare County information kiosk, and restrooms are provided at Weirs Point. Watch for stumps and broken stakes in the water. The tide creeps up quickly, so keep blankets out of its encroaching flow. Next to the beach is an exhibit about the Freedmen's Colony, a community for runaway slaves between 1862 and 1867. During the Civil War Roanoke Island was seized by Union soldiers in 1862. After that, runaway slaves were welcomed on the island, given food, and allowed to settle in the Union camp. Slaves from all over northeastern North Carolina flocked to the safe haven. Male freed slaves worked for the Union forces for $10 a month plus rations and clothing. Women and children were paid $4 a month. In 1863 the colony was officially established, and the freed slaves were given land and agricultural tools. Many of the freed slaves joined the Union effort, but the ones who remained behind were given health and education services. By 1866, however, most of the freedmen were forced to leave. Exhibits at the site explain the story.

In 1901, from a hut on Weirs Point beach, one of the unsung geniuses of the electronic age began investigating what was then called "wireless telegraphy." Reginald Fessenden held hundreds of patents on radiotelepathy and electronics, but he died without any credit for many of them. In a letter dated "April 3, 1902, Manteo," Fessenden tells his patent attorney that "I can now telephone as far as I can telegraph. . . . I have sent varying musical notes from Hatteras and received them here with but 3 watts of energy." Thus, the world's first musical radio broadcasts were completed on this soundside sand of the Outer Banks.

About 300 yards north of Weirs Point, under 6 feet of water, lay the remains of Fort Huger. This was the largest Confederate fort on the island when Union troops advanced in 1862. The island migrated quite a bit in the past 145 years; the fort formerly sat securely on solid land.

THE LOST COLONY, Off US 64, Waterside Theatre; (252) 473-3414; thelostcolony.org. The nation's longest-running outdoor drama has been running for over 80 years. This historical account of the first English settlement in North America is a must-see for Outer Banks visitors. It's almost as legendary as the story it depicts. Pulitzer Prize-winning author Paul Green brought the history of English colonization to life through an impressive combination of Elizabethan music, Native American dances, colorful costumes, and vivid drama on a soundside stage in 1937. His play continues to enchant audiences today at Waterside Theatre, near Fort Raleigh, on Roanoke Island. *The Lost Colony* is a theatrical account of Sir Walter Raleigh's early explorers, who first settled on the shores near the present-day theater in 1585. (Andy Griffith got his start playing Sir Walter Raleigh for several seasons.) Children and adults are equally captivated by the performers, staging, and music; many locals see the show every year and always find it spellbinding. If you have youngsters, come early and have them sit in the front row by the stage. The closer you sit to the stage, the more you'll enjoy the award-winning show.

There have been a number of famous names associated with the show, including set designer William Ivey Long, who won a second Tony Award in 2001 for his costume design work on *The Producers*. Long also created costumes for *Cinderella*, *Hair Spray*, *Young Frankenstein*, *Bullets over Broadway*, and more. Long has been the costume designer for *The Lost Colony* for more than 20 years

First produced in 1937, Paul Green's historic drama tells the story of the first attempt by the English to colonize the new world. The play is the longest-running outdoor drama in North America.

and has been associated with the show since he was a young boy, when his parents worked on *The Lost Colony*.

The Waterside Theatre is well designed, and all of the seats are pretty good. Adult tickets begin at $35. Seats in the Producer's Circle offer the most panoramic view of the show and cost slightly more. Group discounts are available for 20 or more people. Group reservations must be made in advance. It can get chilly in the evenings when the wind blows off the sound, so we recommend sweaters, even in July and August. Mosquitoes at this outdoor drama can be vicious, especially after a rain, so bring plenty of bug repellent. The theater is wheelchair accessible and the staff is glad to accommodate special customers. The show begins at 8:30 p.m. and runs six nights a week (closed Sunday) from the end of May through late August. This is probably the most popular summertime event on the Outer Banks, so we recommend that you make reservations, though you can try your luck at the door if you wish. Make paid mail reservations by writing *The Lost Colony*, 1409 US 64/264, Manteo, NC 27954; or reserve tickets by phone. Tickets are available online, by phone, or at several Outer Banks businesses. If a production is rained out, ticket holders can exchange their passes for another night or get a refund.

Children's shows are also a tradition at Waterside Theatre. Past shows have brought *Pirates! A Boy at Sea* and *How I Became a Pirate*, and the energetic cast

ATTRACTIONS

Backstage tours at *The Lost Colony* are offered within the season for only $8 per person. Get an up-close look at the theater, costume shop, and prop rooms. The tours are held Monday through Saturday at 6:30 p.m. and take a maximum of 50 people. Call (252) 473-3414, ext. 225, to reserve a spot.

is sure to please kids of all ages. Tickets are $10. Check the website for more detailed information.

THE MOTHER VINE, off Mother Vineyard Rd. The oldest known grapevine in the United States grows on Roanoke Island. When the first settlers arrived here, the Outer Banks were covered with a variety of wild grapes. The Mother Vine is one of those grapevines, so old that it may have been planted even before Europeans arrived in the New World. Certainly it was already old in the 1750s, as records attest, and scuppernong grapevines do not grow swiftly. Another story is that this vine was transplanted to Roanoke Island by some of the Fort Raleigh settlers. Whichever story is true, the Mother Vine is more than 400 years old, and it's still producing fine, fat, tasty grapes. In fact, for many years a small winery owned by the Etheridge family cultivated the vine on Baum's Point, making the original Mother Vineyard wine until the late 1950s. The Mother Vine is on private property and a bit out of the way. To find it, drive north from Manteo on US 64. About 0.75 mile past the city limits, turn right onto Mother Vineyard Road. Go less than a half mile, where the road makes a sharp turn to the right at the sound. About 300 feet past the turn, on the left, the patient old vine endures beneath a canopy of leaves, twisted and gnarled, ancient and enduring. Please stay on the road if you're sneaking a peek.

Insiders call the box office before attending a show at Waterside Theatre and reserve a backstage tour and a Waterside sunset picnic to create a memorable experience.

⭐ **THE NORTH CAROLINA AQUARIUM AT ROANOKE ISLAND,** 374 Airport Rd.; (252) 473-3494; ncaquariums.com. The North Carolina Aquarium on Roanoke Island is an outstanding facility. The theme of the aquarium is Waters of the Outer Banks, and visitors get to see a variety of marine communities: coastal freshwaters, wetlands, estuaries, roadside ditches, the Gulf Stream, and the Graveyard of the Atlantic on the ocean floor. A major attraction is the Graveyard of the Atlantic tank, holding about 2.35 million pounds of salt water. The tank's highlight is a 53-foot-long replica of a Civil War ironclad, the USS *Monitor*. Expert scuba divers who have seen the real *Monitor* wreck say the replica is extremely accurate. Scuba divers give educational presentations from the tank and answer spectators' questions while inside. Also in the tank are sea turtles and nearly 1,000 other sea creatures, including sharks, cobia, tarpon, jack crevalle, bluefish, and black and red drum. Wetlands on the Edge is another favorite exhibit. In this tree-filled atrium, river otters swim and play in a clear pool of river water, while visitors watch through a glass screen. Also here are several American alligators that bask in the sunlight near their pond. The Coastal Freshwaters exhibit explores freshwater marine animals and habitats. From ponds and lakes to the Albemarle Sound, this exhibit displays turtles, sunfish, gars, and bowfins. The Croatan Sound tank showcases the fish that local anglers catch. Marine Communities features nine tanks representing environments from grass flats to the Gulf Stream, displaying blue crabs, summer flounder, puppy drum, lobster, a porcupine puffer, and much more. Close Encounters is the touch tank area, where kids can touch horseshoe crabs and other creatures. The **Sea Turtle Assistance and Rehabilitation (STAR) Center** offers a fascinating look into sea turtle care and rehabilitation. Staff members are on hand to answer questions. Open year-round from 9 a.m. to 5 p.m. daily, except Christmas and New Year's Days. Prices range from $10.95 to $12.95.

OBX AERO TOURS, Main Terminal, Airport Rd., Manteo Airport; (252) 441-TOUR (8687). For a bird's-eye view of the Outer Banks and a shocking perspective on how fragile the barrier islands really are, take a 30-minute air tour over the land and ocean in a small plane. Pilots will gear tours to passengers' wishes but usually head south to Bodie Island Lighthouse and back. Bring your camera for this high-flying cruise. Rates begin at $80 per flight. Biplane flights in an open-air-cockpit authentic 1941 Waco are also available from the same site. These five- to seven-minute trips take you back in time, complete with goggled leather helmets. Longer trips are also offered. Air tours are offered year-round, weather permitting. Advance reservations are accepted.

i First Friday on Roanoke Island is held from 6 to 8 p.m. on the first Friday of each month, beginning in April. Discover the magic of historic downtown Manteo. Locals and visitors mingle at this special night, which offers music, shopping, and dining. For more information call (252) 473-5121.

OLD SWIMMING HOLE, Airport Rd.; (252) 473-1101, ext. 313. Go for a swim after a visit to the aquarium. Right next door, the county facility maintains a beach, picnic tables, grills, picnic shelter, kids' playground, sand volleyball court, and restrooms. The beach is lifeguarded from 10 a.m. to 6 p.m. from Memorial Day to Labor Day. Families with small kids love the sound waters.

OUTER BANKS HISTORY CENTER, 1 Festival Park; (252) 473-2655. Adjacent to the visitor center at Roanoke Island Festival Park, the Outer Banks History Center is a remarkable repository of North Carolina state and regional history. The North Carolina State Archives, Division of Archives and History, Department of Cultural Resources, administers this Outer Banks treasure. Opened in 1988, the history center collection includes 100,000 manuscript items, 35,000 books, 35,000 photographs, 1,500 periodical titles, a large collection of important maps, hundreds of audio and video recordings, microfilm, and ephemera. Some of the more than 700 maps in the collection are more than 400 years old. The collection also includes items relating to lighthouses and other Outer Banks architecture, local history about towns, shipwrecks, the US Lifesaving Service, Civil War artwork, and *The Lost Colony* outdoor drama records and memorabilia. Materials are housed in closed stacks to ensure security and the climate control needed for preservation. However, staffers at the history center are knowledgeable and happy to help anyone access the facility's vast resources. Journalists, authors, history buffs, students, scientists, genealogists, and casual tourists find the stop worthwhile. A special gallery features archived materials and photographs, and traveling exhibits are displayed from time to time. The reading room and gallery are open year-round from 9 a.m. to 5 p.m. Monday through Friday. The Outer Banks History Center is a public facility and is free of charge.

PIONEER THEATRE, 113 Budleigh St.; (252) 473-2216. This nostalgic movie house is the best place to see movies on the Outer Banks and the oldest theater continuously operated by one family in the United States. The original Pioneer Theatre, opened in 1918 by George Washington Creef, was located a block over and showed silent films accompanied by a local pianist. The current Pioneer Theatre opened in 1934 and is now run by Creef's great-grandson, Buddy Creef. This movie house is a family gathering place for Manteo locals. All of the movies are first run (G, PG, or PG-13), and people come regardless of whether they're interested in the show. Friday night the place is overrun with school kids, so it's best to avoid that night unless you're one of them. This theater is definitely old-fashioned in its prices and you won't get gouged at the candy counter either. Perhaps most importantly, the popcorn is popped on premises. One movie is shown every night at 8 p.m., as long as there are at least three people in the theater. Listings change weekly, without fail, on Friday.

Check the billboard on the highway in Manteo, or call the theater for the current listing and a brief synopsis of the movie.

PIRATE'S COVE YACHT CLUB, Nags Head–Manteo Causeway; (252) 473-3906; fishpiratescove.com. If you're interested in what the boats are catching in the Gulf Stream, head over to Pirate's Cove Yacht Club between 4 and 5 p.m. When the charter boats return to their slips, the catches of the day are thrown out on the docks to be picked up by the fish cleaners. Visitors are welcome to stroll along the boardwalk and watch. You might see tuna, wahoo, dolphin (the fish, not the mammal), cobia, or any of a number of fish. This is especially exciting for kids, who may not have seen such big fish before. If you would rather see the fish on the end of your own line, charter opportunities are available at Pirate's Cove. See the **Recreation** chapter for more information.

ROANOKE ISLAND FESTIVAL PARK AND *ELIZABETH II*, 1 Festival Park; (252) 475-1500; roanokeisland.com. An expansion of the Elizabeth II Historic Site, Roanoke Island Festival Park is one of the largest attractions on the Outer Banks. This vibrant history, educational, and cultural arts complex offers top-quality facilities that add a tremendous variety to the year-round interests on Roanoke Island. Visitors explore the evolution of Roanoke Island and the Outer Banks from the late 16th century to the early 1900s through living-history interpretation, exhibits, film, and visual and performing arts programs.

The site includes the 8,500-square-foot **Roanoke Adventure Museum**, where interactive displays allow you to touch, see, and hear the history of the Outer Banks. In the Film Theater, *The Legend of Two Path* and *The Birth of a Colony* are shown regularly. There's an outdoor performance pavilion that offers concerts on lush pastoral lawns; a gallery, with art shows that change monthly; a small theater where special films and plays are held in an intimate setting; and a museum store bursting with treasures.

Porches, lawns, and boardwalks add charm, and you're just as likely to encounter an Elizabethan settler there as you are inside. The Children's Performances, held in the summer months in the Film Theater, are excellent. Special music festivals are held at Festival Park occasionally. See the website or call for details, and also see the **Annual Events** chapter.

The *Elizabeth II*, designed in 1983 as the centerpiece for the 400th anniversary of the first English settlement in America, is a representative sailing ship similar to the one that carried Sir Walter Raleigh's colonists across the Atlantic in 1585. Interpreters clad in Elizabethan costumes conduct tours of the colorful 69-foot ship. The original Elizabeth was constructed when Thomas Cavendish mortgaged his estates to build the ship for England's second expedition to Roanoke Island. With six other vessels, the Elizabeth made the first colonization voyage to the New World in 1585 and landed on the Outer Banks. There wasn't enough information available about the original vessels to reconstruct an exact replica, so shipbuilders used the designs of vessels from 1585 to build the *Elizabeth II*.

Constructed entirely from wood on the Manteo waterfront, every baulk, spar, block, and lift of the ship is as close to authentic as possible, with only three exceptions: a wider upper-deck hatch for easier visitor access; a vertical hatch in the afterdeck to make steering easier for the helmsman; and a controversial pair of diesel engines that were installed in the *Elizabeth II* in 1993. The 115-horsepower motors help the grand sailing ship move under its own power, instead of relying on expensive tugboats. The state ship stays on the Outer Banks most of the year, but during the off-seasons it sometimes travels to other North Carolina ports, serving as the state's only moving historic site.

Explore the Roanoke Island Festival Park grounds and you'll discover the Settlement Site, a recreation of the first English military establishment on North American soil. Try on armor, learn how nails were made, and more at this staffed camp.

Visitors will also want to check out American Indian Town. Explore coastal Algonquian culture and history. This exhibit takes visitors on a journey to a native community as it would have been in the 1500s, when the English first stepped foot onto this faire soil.

Roanoke Island Festival Park is open year-round. A coastal Algonquian home is recreated, along with work areas, and a ceremonial dance circle. Hours vary according to season. Admission is $10 for adults, $7 for students, and free for children younger than 5. Group rates are available. Call ahead for a schedule of events. Check the website listed above for a discount coupon.

Wanchese

MILL LANDING, NC 345, Wanchese. Near the end of a winding 5-mile road, past a long expanse of wide, waving marshlands overflowing with waterfowl, Wanchese is well off the beaten path of most visitors (see the section on Roanoke Island in the **Area Overview** chapter) and remains one of the most unspoiled areas on the barrier islands. At the very end of NC 345, one of the most picturesque and unchanged areas of the Outer Banks is often overlooked: Mill Landing, which embodies the heritage of the Outer Banks. Here active fishing trawlers anchor at the docks, their mesh still dripping seaweed from the wide roller wheels. Watermen in yellow chest waders and white rubber boots (known locally as Wanchese wingtips) sling shark, tuna, and dolphin onto cutting-room carts. Pieces of the island's past float silently in the harbor, mingling with remade boats that are still afloat and sunken ships that have long since disappeared.

WANCHESE SEAFOOD INDUSTRIAL PARK, 615 Harbor Rd.; (252) 473-5867. A 69-acre industrial park on a deep harbor at Wanchese, this

Howl with Red Wolves

Visit the Alligator River National Wildlife Refuge in Dare County mainland to hear the red wolves howl. One of the most threatened species in the country, red wolves have made a comeback in northeastern North Carolina due to careful management since the early 1980s. Unfortunately, some wolves continue to be illegally shot, so hearing these special animals is a rare gift to be cherished.

After sunset you meet a refuge staff person at Creef Cut Wildlife Trail at the intersection of US 64 and Milltail Road. After a brief talk about the red wolves, you are led (in vehicles) about 6 miles back into the dark refuge. On the way you might even see some bears. In the dark woods, you get out of your car and listen as the staff person howls to elicit howls from the wolves. The wolves' response will give you goosebumps. You can't see the wolves, which makes them even more mysterious and adds to the allure of this experience.

The two-hour howl tours are held every Wednesday at 7:30 p.m., June through August. This experience costs $10, and preregistration is required. Call (252) 796-5600 to register.

Free Howls are also held on Saturday near Earth Day, April 22, at 7 p.m., and again Memorial Day weekend. Additional free dates are in October for National Wolf Awareness Week, in November for a Full Moon Howl, and the Holiday Howl in December. Call to obtain the starting times and alternate dates.

state-supported facility was built in 1980 with $8.1 million in state and federal funds. It was designed to attract large-scale seafood-processing companies to set up shop on the secluded Roanoke Island waterfront. After federal promises about stabilizing Oregon Inlet failed to materialize, few deep-draw fishing trawlers could keep risking the trip through the East Coast's most dangerous inlet. Oregon Inlet continued to shoal terribly through the 1980s, and the seafood park remained largely vacant until 1994, when some smaller area businesses and fish-processing plants began establishing themselves there. Unpredictable weather patterns still affect the channel's navigability. The industrial park is an educational attraction for anyone interested in the maritime world of boatbuilding and sea harvesting. Visitors are welcome to drive or walk through and visit the boat docks. Stop by the office if you have questions.

NORTH POND TRAIL, NC 12. A birder's favorite, this wheelchair-accessible nature trail begins at the visitor center parking area and is about a mile long. The trail runs along the top of a dike between two man-made ponds that were begun in the late 19th century and completed by the Civilian Conservation Corps in the 1930s. The walkway includes three viewing platforms, marshland overlooks, and mounted binoculars. Wax myrtles and live oaks stabilize the dike and provide shelter for scores of songbirds. Warblers, yellowthroats, cardinals, and seaside sparrows land during biannual migrations. The quarter-mile Salt Flats Trail starts at the north end of the North Pond Trail. The US Fish & Wildlife Service manages Pea Island refuge's ecosystem. Workers plant fields with fescue and rye grass to keep the waterfowl coming back. Pheasants, muskrats, and nutria live along these ponds year-round.

PEA ISLAND NATIONAL WILDLIFE REFUGE, NC 12; (252) 987-2394. Pea Island National Wildlife Refuge begins at the southern base of the Marc Basnight Bridge and is the first place you come to when entering Hatteras Island from the north. The beach along this undeveloped stretch of sand is popular with anglers, surfers, sunbathers, and shell seekers. On the right side of the road, heading south, salt marshes surround Pamlico Sound, and birds seem to flutter from every grove of cattails.

The small Pea Island Wildlife Refuge visitors center includes a mile and a half trail that leads to the heart of impoundments where heron and other waterfowl abound.

Founded on April 12, 1938, the Pea Island refuge was federally funded as a winter preserve for snow geese. President Franklin D. Roosevelt put his Civilian Conservation Corps to work stabilizing the slightly sloping dunes, building them up with bulldozers, erecting long expanses of sand fencing, and securing the sand with sea oats and grasses. Workers built dikes near the sound to form ponds and freshwater marshes. They planted fields to provide food for the waterfowl. With 5,915 acres that attract nearly 400 observed species of birds, Pea Island is an outdoor aviary. Few tourists visited this refuge when Hatteras Island was accessible only by ferry. After the Bonner Bridge opened in 1964, motorists began driving through this once isolated outpost. Today Pea Island is one of the barrier islands' most popular havens for birders, naturalists, and sea-turtle savers. Endangered species, from the loggerhead sea turtle to the tiny piping plover shorebirds, inhabit this area. Pea Island's name comes from the "dune peas" that grow all along the now grassy sand dunes. The tiny plant with pink and lavender flowers is a favorite food of migrating geese.

Four miles south of the Marc Basnight's southern base, the Pea Island Visitor Center offers free parking and easy access to the beach. If you walk directly across the highway to the top of the dunes, you'll see the remains of the federal transport Oriental. Its steel boiler is all that remains of the ship, which sank in May 1862. On the sound side of the highway, in the marshes, ponds, and endless wetlands, whistling swans, snow geese, Canada geese, and 25 species of ducks make winter sojourns in the refuge. Savannah sparrows, migrant warblers, gulls, terns, herons, and egrets also alight in this area from fall through early spring. In summer American avocets, willets, black-necked stilts, and several species of ducks nest here. Bug repellent is a must on Pea Island from March through October. Ticks also cause problems. Check your clothing before getting in the car, and shower as soon as possible if you hike through any underbrush.

> **i** The shipwreck site of the USS *Monitor* was the first site in the United States to be designated a National Underwater Marine Sanctuary. The *Monitor*, a Civil War ironclad, sank in 240 feet of water about 16 miles off Cape Hatteras in a storm on New Year's Eve of 1862. The sanctuary is federally protected, and divers can visit only if they have a federal permit.

PEA ISLAND VISITOR CENTER, NC 12; (252) 987-2394. A paved parking area, public restrooms, and the Pea Island Refuge Headquarters are 4 miles south of the Oregon Inlet bridge on the sound side of NC 12. Refuge volunteers staff this small welcome station year-round and are available to answer questions. Visitors see exhibits on wildlife, waterfowl, and bird life and browse the small gift shop. In summer the facility is open seven days a week from 9 a.m. to 4 p.m. In the off-season the center is open Thursday through Sunday from 9 a.m. to 4 p.m. It's closed Christmas Day. Free nature trail maps are available, and in summer months special nature programs are offered, such as bird walks, turtle talks, and guided canoe tours.

Hunting, camping, and driving are not allowed in the refuge. Open fires are also prohibited. Dogs must be kept on leashes on the east side of the highway. Firearms are not allowed in the refuge; shotguns and rifles must be stowed out of sight even if you're just driving straight through Hatteras Island. Fishing, crabbing, boating, and other activities are allowed in the ocean and sound but are prohibited in refuge ponds.

About 3 miles farther south on NC 12, a kiosk just beyond the refuge headquarters marks the site of the remains of the nation's only African-American lifesaving station.

HATTERAS ISLAND

Avon

CANADIAN HOLE, NC 12, Avon. If a breeze is blowing, pull off the west side of the road between Avon and Buxton (1.5 miles south of Avon) into the big parking lot on the sound. Known as Canadian Hole, this is one of America's hottest windsport spots—and a magnet for visitors from Canada. Whether you ride a sailboard or not, this sight is not to be missed. On windy afternoons more than 100 sailboarders and kiteboarders spread out along the shallow sound, their brightly colored butterfly sails gently skimming into the sunset. There's a nice bathing beach here, so bring chairs and coolers and plan to watch the silent wave riders, some of whom are famous in windsurfing circles. The state recently expanded the parking area here. See the **Recreation** chapter for more details.

Buxton

THE *ALTOONA* WRECK, Cape Point. Four-wheel-drive motorists may enter the beach at the end of Cape Point Way on ramp 44. Here the Outer Banks juts out into the Atlantic in a wide elbow-shaped curve near the Cape Hatteras Lighthouse. The beaches in this area offer some of the barrier islands' best surf fishing. Three rules of the beach: have your National Park Service off-road permit with you at all times; do not try to drive on the beach in anything but a four-wheel-drive vehicle; and be sure to let the proper amount of air out of your tires before traversing sand (see the **Getting Here, Getting Around** chapter for more information). For those not driving on the beach, park on solid ground near the road and walk over the ramp to a foot trail. The path begins at the base of the dune.

At the edge of a seawater pond, you'll catch a glimpse of the remains of the shipwreck *Altoona*. Built in Maine in 1869, the *Altoona* was a two-masted, 100-foot-long cargo schooner based in Boston. It left Haiti in 1878 with a load of dyewood bound for New York. On October 22, a storm drove it ashore near Cape Point. Lifesavers rescued its seven crew members and salvaged some of the cargo, but the ship was buried beneath the sand until uncovered by a storm in 1962. The sea has broken the big boat apart since then, but you can still see part of the bow and hull beneath the waves.

BUXTON WOODS NATURE TRAIL, Cape Point. Leading from the Cape Point Campground road about 0.75 mile through the woods, the Buxton nature trail takes walkers through thick vine jungles, across tall sand dunes, and into freshwater marshes. Small plaques along the fairly level walkway describe the area's fragile ecosystems. People who hike this trail learn about the Outer Banks' water table, the role of beach grass and sea oats in stabilizing sand dunes, and the effects salt, storms, and visitors have on the ever-changing environment. Cottonmouths seem to like this trail, too, so beware of these unmistakable snakes. They are fat, rough-scaled, and stubby looking in brown, yellow, gray, or almost black. If you see a cottonmouth, let it get away—don't chase it. If it stands its ground, retreat. This hike is not recommended for all, but picnic tables and charcoal grills just south of the nature trail provide a welcome respite for everyone. The walk is fine for hardy nature lovers who don't mind mingling with the outdoor elements. In other words, bring your bug repellent!

A rare maritime forest at the confluence of temperate and sub-tropical zones, Buxton Woods is a 1,000 acre preserve that calls out to be explored.

★ **CAPE HATTERAS LIGHTHOUSE, off NC 12; (252) 995-4474; nps .gov/caha.** The Cape Hatteras Lighthouse is one of the most beloved and famous lighthouses in the nation, especially after it survived a move of more than 1,600 feet in 1999. The nation's tallest brick lighthouse at 208 feet, this black-and-white striped beacon was shown the world over as it was precariously jacked up and moved along roll beams to its new location away from the encroaching sea. The monumental relocation project was named the 2000 Outstanding Civil Engineering Achievement by the American Society of Civil Engineers. The lighthouse now stands the same distance from the Atlantic Ocean as it did when it was first built in 1870.

The original Cape Hatteras Lighthouse was built in 1803. The tower sat near Cape Point and was only 90 feet tall. Lit with whale oil, it was barely bright enough to be seen offshore. Erosion weakened the structure, and in 1861 Confederate soldiers removed the light's lens. The current Cape Hatteras Lighthouse was erected in 1870 with more than one million bricks and 257 steps. A special Fresnel lens that refracts light increased its visibility. The lighthouse was 1,600 feet from the ocean when it was built, but by 1987 it was only 120 feet from the crashing waves. After years of study, the National Park Service came to the conclusion that it had to "move it or lose it." The lighthouse was moved 1,600 feet back from the shore in just a few weeks, from June 17 to July 9, 1999. About 20,000 visitors a day watched. It reopened to the public on May 26, 2000. Its 800,000-candlepower beacon, rotating every seven and a half seconds, can be seen 18 miles out to sea. The view from the top of the Cape Hatteras Lighthouse is surreal and unforgettable. Try to make the climb while visiting the historical site.

The visitor center, called the **Museum of the Sea**, and the bookstore, both housed in the historic former keepers' quarters, were moved to this location before the lighthouse was moved. Restrooms are located here. If you continue past the parking area, you'll pass the picnic area and the Buxton Woods Nature Trail. If you continue on, you'll come to the Cape Point Campground and off-road vehicle ramps. The beach here is famous for swimming, sunbathing, surfing, and fishing, and you can take four-wheel-drive vehicles along many sections of the beach year-round. Park rangers and volunteers willingly answer questions and can be found in the visitor center and on the historic district grounds. Visitor center and bookstore hours are 9 a.m. to 6 p.m. daily in season, 9 a.m. until 5 p.m. off season, closed only Christmas Day.

In Buxton, signs along NC 12 lead you to the lighthouse. To the left you can visit the original lighthouse location, marked by a circle of granite stones that are etched with the names of 83 former lighthouse keepers. To the right are a parking area and the lighthouse's new location.

DIAMOND SHOALS LIGHT, off Cape Point, Buxton. You can only visit this attraction in private boats, but you can see this unusual light tower from the eastern shore of Cape Point and from the top of the Cape Hatteras Lighthouse. Its bright beacon blinks every two seconds from a steel structure set 12 miles out in the sea. Diamond Shoals once held a lighthouse, but waves beat the offshore rocks that held the structure so badly that federal officials gave up the project. Three lightships have been stationed on the shoals since 1824. The first sank in an 1827 gale. The second held its ground from 1897 until German submarines sank it in 1918. The third beamed until 1967, when it was replaced by the current light tower. Diamond Shoals, the rocks around the tower, are the southern end of the treacherous near-shore sandbars off Hatteras Island.

Rodanthe

CHICAMACOMICO LIFESAVING STATION, NC 12; (252) 987-1552; chicamacomico.net. With volunteer labor and long years of dedication, this once-decrepit lifesaving station is beautifully restored and open for tours. Its weathered, silvery-shingled buildings sparkle on the sandy lawn, surrounded by a perfect picket fence. Even the outbuildings have been brought back to their former uses. Today, the nonprofit Chicamacomico Historical Association oversees and operates the lifesaving station. Volunteers set up a museum of area lifesaving awards and artifacts in the main building and have recovered some of the lifesaving equipment for the boathouse. Volunteers take school groups on tours of the station, showing how the britches buoy helped rescue shipwreck victims and explaining the precise maneuvers surfmen had to follow on shore.

The station is open from Easter weekend through the Saturday after Thanksgiving, Tuesday through Saturday from 9 a.m. to 5 p.m. Various programs have been added to the roster and are offered every open day in the summer and on Wednesday, Thursday, and Friday in the off-season. At 2 p.m. programs might include a guided tour, a knot-tying class, or a storytelling hour. All programs are suitable for all ages. The guided tour gives more details on the site, the lifesaving service, and the equipment used. Group tours can be accommodated with advance notice. Admission is free, although donations are welcome and are greatly needed to further the restoration and expand the programs at this site. Call for additional program information.

Frisco

FRISCO NATIVE AMERICAN MUSEUM, NC 12; (252) 995-4440; nativeamericanmuseum.org. This enchanting museum on the sound side of NC 12 in Frisco is stocked with unusual collections of Native American artifacts gathered since the 1930s, plus numerous other fascinating collections. The museum boasts one of the most significant collections of artifacts from the Chiricahua Apache people and has displays of other Native American tribes' works from across the country, ranging from the days of early humans to modern time. Hopi drums, pottery, kachina dolls, baskets, weapons, and jewelry are displayed in homemade cases. The museum property includes outdoor nature trails through 3 acres of woods, with a screened-in pavilion, a large pond, and three bridges on the land. Hours are 11 a.m. to 5 p.m. Tuesday through Sunday, year-round. Admission is $5 per person or $15 per family. Seniors are charged $3. Group rates are available. The museum and trails are also designed to accommodate the vision impaired.

Hatteras Village

GRAVEYARD OF THE ATLANTIC MUSEUM, NC 12; (252) 986-2996; graveyardoftheatlantic.com. The Graveyard of the Atlantic Museum showcases the maritime history and heritage of the Outer Banks and its people, from the earliest exploration and colonization to the present day. Particularly emphasized are the years from 1524 to 1945. Exhibits include artifacts from historic shipwrecks, unique "beach finds," and locally carved ships' models; there is a special exhibit on Billy Mitchell in Hatteras. Admission is free, and donations are gratefully accepted. Expect to spend about 30 minutes to tour the museum.

HATTERAS-OCRACOKE CAR FERRY, NC 12, north end of Ocracoke Island; (252) 986-2353, (800) BY FERRY (293-3779). The only vehicle link between Hatteras and Ocracoke Islands, this free, state-run ferry carries passengers and vehicles across Hatteras Inlet daily, year-round, with trips from 5 a.m. to midnight. You can get out of your vehicle and walk around the open decks or stay inside the car. A passenger lounge a short flight of steps above the deck offers cushioned seats and wide windows. Free restrooms also are on the deck; however, there's no food or drink to be found on this 6-mile crossing, so pack your own picnic. Beware if you decide to break bread with the dozens of birds that fly overhead; after they eat they, too, look for free bathrooms. And they'll follow—overhead—all the way to Ocracoke. The experience is exciting but can be messy.

A day trip to Ocracoke is a must for every Outer Banks visitor, whether you're staying in Corolla or on Hatteras Island. (See the Ocracoke section of the **Area Overview** chapter for more about Ocracoke.) The free ferry is the only way to get there besides by private boat or airplane. On summer days more than 1,000 passengers ride the flat ferries. A 12-mile stretch through open marshlands and pine forests lies between the ferry and Ocracoke Village. NC 12 picks up at the ferry docks and continues to the southern end of the island. On the left, wide-open beaches await avid four-wheelers and those who like to have a piece of the seaside to themselves.

HATTERAS-OCRACOKE PASSENGER ONLY FERRY, NC 12, Hatteras Village and NC 12, Silver Lake, Ocracoke Island; (252) 986-2353, (800) BY FERRY (293-3779); ferry.ncdot.gov/#. New in 2019, the North Carolina Ferry

System has introduced a high speed passenger only ferry between Ocracoke and Hatteras. Bikes and strollers can be accommodated. There is a free tram service in Ocracoke, although the Silver Lake docks are a very easy walk to Ocracoke's business district. During its introductory year, a round-trip fare is $6 per person. Children 3 and under ride free. There is also a $1 charge for a bicycle. That is less than the original proposal so the fare may change. Reservations are recommended.

OCRACOKE ISLAND

BRITISH CEMETERY, British Cemetery Rd. Beneath a stand of trees, on the edge of a community cemetery, four granite gravestones commemorate the crew of the British vessel HMS *Bedfordshire*. This 170-foot trawler was one of a fleet of 24 antisubmarine ships that British Prime Minister Winston Churchill loaned the United States in April 1942 to stave off German U-boats. On May 11 of that year, a German submarine torpedoed and sank the British ship about 40 miles south of Ocracoke. All four officers and 33 enlisted men aboard the *Bedfordshire* drowned. US Coast Guard officers stationed on Ocracoke found four of the bodies washed ashore three days later. They were able to identify two of the sailors. Townspeople gave Britain a 12-by-14-foot plot of land and buried the seamen in a site adjacent to the island's cemetery. The British and Canadian navies hold an annual ceremony at the sight.

DEEPWATER THEATER, School Rd.; (252) 928-4280; molassescreek .com. Deepwater Theater is the home of Ocracoke's most famous band, Molasses Creek. This high-energy acoustic folk-fusion band plays bluegrass and ballads and rolls everything together with a wacky sense of humor. Gary Mitchell, Marcy Brenner, Lou Castro, Gerald Hampton, and fiddler Dave Tweedie compose the band, which has a loyal following in the United States and abroad. Based on the island, they play here all summer and at other times of the year. Molasses Creek performs all over the nation, and it was featured on National Public Radio's *A Prairie Home Companion* with Garrison Keillor. Each Wednesday, Ocrafolk Opry picks and grins and warms your soul. On Thursday, Molasses Creek performs in a show also appropriate for the whole family. Tickets go on sale 30 minutes before each show, shows begin at 8 p.m. Pricing varies with shows; details are listed on the website.

HAMMOCK HILLS NATURE TRAIL, NC 12. A 0.75-mile nature trail north of Ocracoke Village, Hammock Hills covers a cross-section of the island. The 30-minute walk begins near the sand dunes, traverses a maritime forest, and winds through a salt marsh. Hikers learn how plants adapt to Ocracoke's unusual elements and the harsh barrier island weather. Bring your camera on this scenic stroll. We highly recommend bug repellent in spring and summer months. Watch out for snakes in the underbrush. The well-marked trailhead is on NC 12 just across the road from the National Park Service campground.

OCRACOKE ISLAND MUSEUM AND PRESERVATION SOCIETY, Silver Lake; (252) 928-7375. A visit to the Ocracoke Island Museum provides a wonderful peek into Ocracoke as it once was. The home of Coast Guard Capt. David Williams, the historic, 2-story house was moved to this location in 1989 and restored to its former early-19th-century glory by the Ocracoke Preservation Society. The original wainscoting, floors, staircases, and wood-burning stove are still intact. Inside, a bedroom, living room, and kitchen are set up with period furnishings donated by local families. Original photographs of island natives are throughout. Exhibits about fishing and seafaring are especially interesting, as is the exhibit on the island's traditional brogue. Upstairs, the museum has a small research library that the public can use with the museum personnel's permission. Admission is free, and the museum is open from Easter through the end of November. In summer hours are 10 a.m. to 5 p.m. Monday through Friday, and 11 a.m. to 4 p.m. on Saturday. Off-season hours are 10 a.m. to 4 p.m. Monday through Friday, and 11 a.m. to 4 p.m. on Saturday.

OCRACOKE ISLAND VISITOR CENTER, NC 12; (252) 928-4531. The National Park Service's Ocracoke Island Visitor Center, at the southern end of NC 12, is full of information about the island. It's in a small building with a large lawn next to the Cedar Island ferry docks. If you're arriving on the island from the Hatteras ferry, stay on the main road, turn right at Silver Lake, and continue around the lake counterclockwise until you see the low brown building on your right. Free parking is available at the visitor center. The visitor center is open March through December from 9 a.m. to 5 p.m. Hours are extended in the summer. Rangers offer free summer programs, including a beach walk, a walk through the village, turtle talks, a pirate play, snorkeling, an evening campfire, kids programs, and more. Programs last from 30 to 90 minutes and offer a fun way to learn more about the history and ecology of the island. Check at the front desk for changing weekly schedules. Restrooms are open to the public in season.

OCRACOKE LIGHTHOUSE, southwest corner of Ocracoke Village. The southernmost of the Outer Banks' four lighthouses, this whitewashed tower is the oldest and shortest. It is the second-oldest lighthouse in the nation. It stands 77.5 feet tall and has an askew iron-railed tower set on the top. The lighthouse is not open for tours or climbing, but volunteers occasionally staff its broad base, offering historical talks and answering visitors' questions. Inquire about possible staffing times at the visitor center or National Park Service offices.

Ocracoke's lighthouse still operates, emitting one long flash every few seconds from a half hour before sunset to a half hour after sunrise. It was built in

1823 to replace Shell Castle Rock Lighthouse, which was set offshore closer to the dangerous shoals in Ocracoke Inlet. Shell Castle Light was abandoned in 1798 when the inlet shifted south. On the right side of the wooden boardwalk leading to the lighthouse, a 2-story white cottage once served as quarters for the tower's keeper. The National Park Service renovated this structure in the 1980s. It now serves as the home of Ocracoke's rangers and the structure's maintenance supervisor.

On the right side of the wooden boardwalk leading to the lighthouse, a 2-story white cottage once served as quarters for the tower's keeper. The National Park Service renovated this structure in the 1980s. It now serves as the home of Ocracoke's rangers and the structure's maintenance supervisor. To reach the light, turn left off NC 12 at the Island Inn and go about 800 yards down the two-lane street. You can park near a white picketed turnoff on the right. Visitors must walk the last few yards down the boardwalk to the lighthouse.

OCRACOKE PONY PENS, NC 12. The Ocracoke Pony Pens are one of the most popular attractions on Ocracoke Island. The National Park Service maintains a herd of about 30 horses in a 180-acre pasture located off NC 12, about 6 miles south of the Hatteras–Ocracoke ferry docks. Visitors can walk up to the pens to view these once-wild horses. An observation platform allows a good view of the ponies.

A little boy fishes off a pier in Ocracoke Island while the ferry passes by.
THEHUHMAN/GETTYIMAGES

Ocracoke ponies have played a large role in the history of the island. At times the herd's population ranged from 200 to 500, all of the animals roaming free on the island. No one is really certain how the horses arrived at the island, but legend says they swam ashore from Spanish shipwrecks off the coast. The horses adapted well to a diet of marsh grasses and rainwater. The locals used this natural resource for work and recreation, and even the Coast Guard and US Lifesaving Service employed the ponies. The pen is free to visit and donations are certainly welcome.

PORTSMOUTH VILLAGE, by private boat access, Portsmouth Island; (252) 728-2250; nps.gov/calo. The only ghost town on the Eastern Seaboard, Portsmouth Village is about a 20-minute boat ride south of Ocracoke Island and was once the biggest town on the Outer Banks. Today the 23-mile-long, 1.5-mile-wide island is owned and managed by the National Park Service as part of Cape Lookout National Seashore. Wilderness camping, hiking, shelling, fishing, and other activities are available on the wide beach. Free, self-guided walking tours of the village are a fascinating way to see how islanders lived in the 19th century.

There is a visitor center on-site, staffed by volunteers who commit to living on the island for extended periods of time. You can see the old post office, the church, the old Coast Guard station, and other buildings. Some of the homes are private, their owners granted extended leases in exchange for restoration work. Portsmouth Island is a rugged adventure, and there are few conveniences. Restrooms are provided in the visitor center, and there's a comfort station (toilets only) on the other side of the village. You must bring your own water, food, insect repellent, and sunscreen. Mosquitoes are notorious in the summer and fall.

You can get to the island by private boat or with a charter service. Capts. Rudy and Donald Austin runs round-trip boat trips to the island, daily in summer and by appointment in the off-season. Call at least one day in advance for reservations, (252) 928-4361 or (252) 928-5431. Portsmouth Island ATV Excursions, (252) 928-4484, leads guided tours of the village and island on ATVs from April through November. Call for reservations and information.

Entertainment

For many of us who live here—and for many visitors as well—the best evening entertainment is watching the sun set over the sound waters. Soundfront decks, piers, gazebos, and public beaches are perfect spots to toast your friends and the setting sun. It's not uncommon for us to rush home in the evening, call our friends, and arrange for a rendezvous spot at which to watch the sunset. Many locals sail or motor their boats out into the sound in anticipation of our favorite entertainment, provided free each day. Moonrise over the ocean is pretty spectacular, too, and under a Carolina moon, just about anything is possible.

OVERVIEW

The Outer Banks after hours isn't like other resort areas. So many families—and early-rising anglers—come here that many people bed down for the evening early. We don't have the huge strips of late-night entertainment joints that you find in many other vacation destinations, but a number of bars and dance floors are scattered across the barrier islands.

Families enjoy a variety of early-evening entertainment options here. Miniature golf, go-kart tracks, movie theaters, bumper boats, and a bowling alley are listed in the **Recreation** chapter. And don't forget *The Lost Colony* outdoor drama; that's detailed in the **Attractions** chapter.

There are plenty of places to shoot pool, catch sporting events on big-screen TVs, play interactive trivia, throw darts, listen to some quiet music, or boogie the night away to a live band.

Outer Banks musicians play everything from blues to jazz to rock to alternative and country tunes. Both local and out-of-town bands take the stage often during the summer season. Several area nightclubs assess nominal cover charges at the door, usually ranging from $1 for dueling acoustic guitar duos to $20 or more for the national acts that grace these sands between mid-May and Labor Day. Many acoustic acts, however, are heard for free.

If live music is what you're listening for, the *Virginian-Pilot*'s weekly *Coast* supplement—available free at area grocery and convenience stores and motels—has up-to-date listings plus music scene information in the "After Dark" column. (See the **Annual Events** and **Arts & Culture** chapters for more nighttime possibilities.)

Alcoholic beverages are available at most Outer Banks lounges until around 2 a.m. Beer and wine are offered throughout the barrier islands. In Southern Shores and on Colington, Roanoke, Hatteras, and Ocracoke Islands, it is illegal to serve mixed drinks. However, with the exception of Colington Island, state-run ("ABC") stores sell liquor in each of these areas. Most nightclubs in areas that serve only wine and beer allow brown bagging, which means customers may bring in their own alcohol for the evening. Call ahead to make sure that brown bagging is allowed where you're going.

Several restaurants on the Outer Banks offer late-night menus or at least raw and steamed bar food until closing. Every nightclub operator will be glad to call a cab to take you home or to your hotel or rental cottage after an evening of imbibing. Beware: The legal drinking age in North Carolina is 21, and the blood-alcohol content level for a drunken-driving arrest is only 0.08. Law enforcement is strict.

Check the **Dining** chapter for sunset entertainment options. Several spots also feature outdoor acoustic music until dark—but this section is for those who like to stay out late.

COROLLA

MIKE DIANNA'S GRILL ROOM, NC 12, Timbuck II Shopping Village; (252) 453-4336; grillroomobx.com; Seafood and steak; $$. Live music on the deck nightly. Also the location of the Mustang Rock and Roast in October and Mustang Spring Jam in May.

SUNDOGS RAW BAR & GRILL, NC 12, Monterey Plaza; (252) 453-4263. Sundogs is a sports bar, so expect a lot of people hanging out watching Monday Night Football and the like. But it's also a gathering spot, where people linger at the bar until the late hours. A pool table and video games provide other entertainment. Sundogs also has a comedy night each week in the summer.

DUCK

CRAVINGS, NC 12; (252) 480-0035; cravingsobx.com. Featured on *Diners, Drive-ins and Dives,* Cravings offers dynamite food and occasional live music. Full bar. Check the website for updates on specials and music offerings.

ROADSIDE RAW BAR & GRILL, NC 12; (252) 261-5729. Low-key, casual, and serving great food, Roadside is a favorite early-evening hangout for locals and tourists alike. This 1932 restored cottage with hardwood floors exudes a cozy, homey feeling. The Backside, aptly named because it's on the back side of the restaurant, brings live outdoor music to the stage as long as the weather is good. Full bar service is offered at the Backside. Roadside is open year-round, but call for off-season hours.

KITTY HAWK

LONGBOARD'S ISLAND GRILL, US 158, MP 4; (252) 261-7833. A popular nightspot for locals year-round, this restaurant features a large, three-sided bar and beautiful terrariums and aquariums throughout the dining area. It's open seven days a week and has karaoke on Wednesday through Saturday nights year-round. Once a month or so, a live band appears on Saturday nights. Longboard's is popular all year with the 30-plus crowd. It's open until 2 a.m. in season and has a late-night munchies menu.

OCEAN BOULEVARD, NC 12; (252) 261-2456; obbistro.com. Friday and Saturday nights are hopping at Ocean Boulevard with acoustic performers on the outdoor patio. On Friday evenings around 10 p.m. or so, the restaurant hosts a band indoors. Many locals swing by on Friday night to catch up at the end of the week. This is a popular spot, and the music is always good.

PAPARAZZI OBX, 3848 N. Croatan Hwy; (252) 715-1673; paparazziobx .com. Located in what was once a movie theater, Paparazzi offers year-round entertainment on its stage. They regularly book national touring acts. There is a bar service on premises.

RUNDOWN CAFE, NC 12, MP 1; (252) 255-0026; rundowncafe.com. Live music on the deck, and it's a beautiful setting. Generally on Friday, but other days as well.

TRIO RESTAURANT & MARKET, US 158, MP 4½; (252) 261-0277; obxtrio.com. Kitty Hawk's top place to see and be seen is at TRiO. Patrons at this hotspot come to taste the world at this wine, beer, and cheese shop/restaurant/nightspot. In the retail portion, visitors can purchase wines and beers from all over the world. In the bistro section, enjoy feeding your passion for wine or beer or order from the cheese-centric menu, featuring casually inventive food. Self-serve tasting machines allow patrons to sample wines from any price range—if you haven't experienced a taste of wine that retails for $100 a bottle, now you can afford to do so! Other food offerings include dips, hummus, sandwiches, salads, and more. It's all delicious here. Live music upstairs most evenings. Check the website for schedules.

> **i** For up-to-date nightlife listings, the *Coast*, a free tabloid published by the *Virginian-Pilot*, is one of the most comprehensive place to get the scoop. You'll find it in racks everywhere.

KILL DEVIL HILLS

JOLLY ROGER RESTAURANT, NC 12, MP 6; (252) 441-6530; jolly rogerobx.com. Adorned with hanging plants and colorful lights, the lounge is separate from the dining area at this mainstay restaurant. The bar is open seven nights a week. Every night Jolly Roger hosts karaoke or offers interactive TV with games covering sports, movie trivia, and more. Both draw a regular audience, and prizes are even awarded to some of the big winners. Locals love this place. People from their early 20s to late 60s enjoy relaxing and dancing in this lounge.

> i A good source for entertainment schedules on the Outer Banks and in nearby cities is 99.1 the Sound radio station, which airs daily updates on who's performing where and when. This information is also on the web at 991thesound.com.

⭐ OUTER BANKS BREWING STATION, US 158, MP 8½; (252) 449-BREW (2739); obbrewing.com. Outer Banks Brewing Station is one of the hottest restaurants and nightspots on the beach. Outside, it looks like a big white barn with silos at either end (the silos are for making beer). Inside, it's absolutely inviting and city chic, with a stretch-length bar, high ceilings, warm wood tones, an open kitchen, innovative house-made beer, well-chosen wines, and sublime food. The brew is a big draw, with selections like a Hefeweizen wheat beer, Lemon Wheatgrass Ale, and Kölsch summer brew. After dinner hours, the Brewing Station stays open late, treating a crowd of lingerers to "righteous music"; blues, jazz, and funk bands and sometimes acoustic acts play all year. Both regional bands and national acts are booked here. Outtdoor back picnic and bar area is ideal for families. Afternoon acoustic music is featured in the summer. Also a very popular location for fundraisers with the owner donating the space. Expect large crowds on band nights. Live entertainment is held Friday and Saturday in season. You can also expect music most every night in the summer. The Brewing Station is open until 2 a.m. seven nights a week. Call or check the website for entertainment schedules.

PEPPERCORNS, NC 12, MP 9½, Ramada Plaza Resort; (252) 441-2151. Enjoy a breathtaking ocean view from the plate-glass window wall while visiting with friends and listening to acoustic soloists or duos in the Ramada's intimate lounge area. Live music is performed daily throughout summer and often starts earlier here than elsewhere on the Outer Banks—sometimes they get started at 8 p.m. This is an open, laid-back place with booths, tables, and a full bar. The music is never too loud to talk over. But if you'd rather listen, some of the best guitar talent on the beach shows up here in season.

ROOSTERS SOUTHERN KITCHEN, 804 S. Croatan Hwy; (252) 441-4594; roosterssouthernkitchen.com. A great bar with great music nightly during the summer. Twice a week in the off-season. Some of the best of the Outer Banks musicians play here.

SECRET ISLAND TAVERN, 504 S. Virginia Dare Trl.; (252) 441-7484; secretislandobx.com; Pub food; $. Taking over what was once Port o' Call Restaurant, Secret Island continues the tradition of live music. Live music and entertainment year-round nightly during the summer.

NAGS HEAD

BASNIGHT'S LONE CEDAR CAFE, Nags Head–Manteo Causeway; (252) 441-5405; lonecedarcafe.com. Spring, summer and well into the fall, look for live acoustic or jazz music in the lounge. Summer almost every night.

MULLIGAN'S, US 158, MP 13; (252) 480-2000; mulligansobx.com. Mulligan's is heralded as a popular evening hot spot and maintains its image as the Outer Banks' own version of TV's *Cheers*. Mulligan's serves microbrewed beer on tap or in iced-down bottles. Wine and liquor are available. Acoustic music plays on weekends in the off-season and on Wednesday, Friday, and Saturday in summer.

> **i** Parents looking for some alone time without the children should ask their vacation rental company about babysitting services and children's programs in the area. These types of services are growing in popularity on the Outer Banks.

PAMLICO JACK'S PIRATE HIDEAWAY, US 158, MP 16; (252) 441-2637; pamlicojacks.com. Amazing sunset vistas create the perfect setting for outdoor music in season.

⭐ **TORTUGAS' LIE SHELLFISH BAR AND GRILLE, NC 12, MP 11;** (252) 441-7299; tortugaslie.com. Our favorite place to meet friends for a laid-back evening—or to hang out with long-lost local pals—Tortugas' offers probably the most comfortable atmosphere you'll find on the Outer Banks most of the year. The bar winds around a corner to allow at least a half dozen more stools to slide under the refurbished countertop. Old license plates are perched on the low, wooden ceiling beams, and the sand volleyball court remains ready for pickup games out back all summer. Bartenders serve black and tans in pint glasses—that's right, Tortugas' has Guinness and Bass ale on tap. Beer is served by the longneck bottle or by the iced-down bucket. Shooters, mixed drinks, and tropical frozen concoctions are sure to please any palate. The steamer is open until closing, so you can satisfy late-night appetites with shellfish or fresh vegetables. Whether you're visiting or here to stay, Tortugas' is one place you won't want to miss. Most nights it remains open until 2 a.m. Tortugas' closes for a brief spell in December and January.

HATTERAS ISLAND

AVON CAFE, NC 12, Avon; (252) 995-7866; avoncafe.com. Avon Cafe offers occasional late-night bands. Check the website for details.

THE FROGGY DOG RESTAURANT & PUB, NC 12, Avon; (252) 995-5550; froggydog.com. Late-night acoustic music plus karaoke singers take the stage at this casual Hatteras Island nightspot. The Froggy Dog is open nightly in season, serving beer and wine and entertainment on most Sundays; call for schedule.

SANDBAR & GRILL, 49252 NC 12, Buxton; (252) 995-3413; sandbarandgrille.com; Seafood. Perched at the end of a spit of land, Sandbar & Grill offers beautiful views and nightly entertainment on Thursdays and Fridays during the peak season.

WATERMAN'S BAR & GRILL, 25706 NC 12, Waves; (252) 987-2000; watermensbarandgrill.com. The view is sublime, and the music outstanding. Features a wide variety of sounds, from blues, electric to acoustic. Live music during the summer. Open March 1 through December 1.

OCRACOKE ISLAND

COYOTE MUSIC DEN, 284 Irvin Garrish Hwy; (252) 256-2081; coyotemusic.net. Home of national recording artist Coyote. All members of the band make their home on Ocracoke. Other artists also perform at the Den.

HOWARD'S PUB & RAW BAR RESTAURANT, NC 12; (252) 928-4441; howardspub.com. This is our absolute favorite place to hear live bands. Featuring the friendliest crowd of locals and visitors around, Howard's Pub has an atmosphere and feeling all its own. Once you've visited you'll plan to stop at this upbeat and casual place at least once during every visit to Ocracoke. Howard's is open late nights—and is a great spot to mingle with locals. The pub serves more types of beer than any place we know—more than 200 varieties are available. There's a second-floor outdoor deck with breathtaking, ocean-to-sound views, perfect for catching sunsets or falling stars. A huge, screened porch—with booths and table seating for relaxing in the evening breezes—borders an entire side of the spacious wooden building. The dance floor has more than doubled in recent years. Two big-screen TVs and numerous smaller ones offer sports fans constant entertainment. Howard's has a dartboard, a pool table in the off-season, board games, and card games available free for playful patrons. The full menu, including pizza, sandwiches, hamburgers, and raw bar items, is offered until closing time. Bands play most nights during summer season and on weekends during winter. Music covers rhythm and blues, bluegrass, jazz, rock, and originals. The occasional open-mike and karaoke nights are favorites for locals and visitors alike. Howard's Pub never charges a cover, and even when electricity fails the rest of the island, this place is equipped with a generator so the crew keeps cooking—and the beer stays cold.

JOLLY ROGER PUB & MARINA, NC 12; (252) 928-3703. A waterfront eatery with an open bar overlooking Silver Lake, this pub has a huge outdoor deck that's covered in case of thunderstorms. Local acoustic guitarists perform Caribbean and country music with no cover charge Thursday and Friday nights. Jolly Roger serves beer, wine, and great food throughout the warm summer months.

Shopping

Shopping on the Outer Banks is a unique pursuit—and a busy one on rainy days when attention shifts from the beach to the stores. Still, rain or shine, there's so much to explore and to be found on side streets in quiet villages or between the Beach Road (NC 12) and the Bypass (US 158), not necessarily visible from the road. So take your time. Consider it a treasure hunt.

OVERVIEW

Many shops have seasonal hours, and most close from December to March. During the height of the summer season, the majority are open seven days a week (some with extended evening hours). A good many shops in Southern Shores, Kitty Hawk, Kill Devil Hills, and Nags Head are open year-round, though not every day. Corolla and Hatteras shopping tends to be more seasonal, but some businesses keep their doors open through the fall and winter.

This chapter lists of some of our favorite shopping spots on the Outer Banks, organized by community, beginning at the northern reaches of Corolla and Duck and running south through Ocracoke Island. Outer Banks retailers offer service, goods, variety, and a hometown greeting that's second to none. And just to show how much Bankers appreciate your business, we'll share an insiders' secret: There are unbeatable sales on the Outer Banks during our shoulder seasons.

SHOPPING VILLAGES

Corolla

COROLLA LIGHT TOWN CENTER, NC 12. The shops of Corolla Light Town Center are clustered outside the entrance to the Corolla Light development. Several choices in dining, shopping, and convenience items are available. Among others, you'll find Ocean Threads, Corolla Bait and Tackle, Island Revolution, and more.

MONTEREY PLAZA, NC 12. The plaza is anchored by a chain grocery store and is speckled with locations to purchase ice cream and other goodies. There is plenty of parking here and lots of great shopping opportunities. TW's Bait and Tackle, Gray's Department Store, Birthday Suits/OBX Gear, Dockside Seafood, and Corolla Surf Shop are among the stores located here.

TIMBUCK II SHOPPING VILLAGE, NC 12; timbuckii.com. More than 60 shops and restaurants can keep the entire family entertained for the day. Visitors will want to stop at places like Corolla Raceway, Kitty Hawk Kites, Tar Heel Trading, Michael's Gems and Glass, Coastal Karma, Eclectic Treasures, 158 Surf and Skate, DogNutz, Dophin Watch Gallery, and much more.

Duck

DUCK WATERFRONT SHOPS, NC 12. These shops provide all kinds of shopping opportunities. Entertainment is provided by dozens of mallards and other web-footed friends paddling around the Currituck Sound shallows just below the railings. Shoppers delights in places like Life's a Beach, a Lilly Pulitzer Shop, Barr-ee Station, Barr-ee Station Swimwear Outlet, Duck's General Store, and Islands by Amity.

SCARBOROUGH FAIRE, NC 12. Scarborough Faire features a series of boutiques in a garden setting. Walking through this shopping village is quite peaceful, as the shops are connected by a walkway through the woods. Located here are Island Bookstore, Urban Cottage, Gray's Department Store, Ocean Annies, Luxury, and more.

SCARBOROUGH LANE, NC 12. Scarborough Lane features amenities you won't find elsewhere in Duck Village, including covered parking and public restrooms. Among shops here are Outer Barks, Birthday Suits, Tar Heel Trading, The Wooden Feather, Diane's Lavish Linens, and Duck Pizza.

Kitty Hawk

BUCCANEER'S WALK, US 158, MP 4. Next to Capt'n Frank's well-known hot dog restaurant is Buccaneer's Walk complex. Here, shoppers enjoy B&B Antiques, Puzzles, Pranks and Games, and the versatile clothes at Kena Active Wear.

THE DUNE'S SHOPS, US 158, MP 4½. Three great places to eat anchor the oldest shopping plaza on the Outer Banks—Josephine's, Pok's Art and Outer Bean Café.

Kill Devil Hills

DARE CENTRE, US 158, MP 7. Belk is the anchor store at this mall and shoppers will also find a beach goods store, Atlantic Dance boutique, and more.

SEAGATE NORTH, 3105 N. Croatan Hwy. Eclectic blend of locally owned shops and businesses. Tar Heel Two Produce, the oldest produce stand on the Outer Banks is on the south end.

Nags Head

CENTRAL SQUARE, US 158, MP 11. Antiques stores are located here, as well as a musical instrument store.

CROATAN CENTRE, US 158, MP 14. This fun group of shops features gifts and more. Soundfeet Shoes carries a great selection of hard-to-find brands, many are European. Also located here are Ocean Threads, Island Tobacco, and Rock-a-Bye Baby gently used children's wares.

JOCKEY'S RIDGE CROSSING, US 158, MP 13½. At this complex, Kitty Hawk Kites and Kitty Hawk Sports anchor the spot. Visitors also find Miss Kitty's Old Time Photos, Life on a Sandbar, Salty Paws pet shop, and more.

OUTER BANKS MALL, US 158, MP 15. Stores like Outer Banks Furniture, West Marine, the Cottage shop and more are fun for an afternoon of shopping.

TANGER OUTLET, US 158, MP 16½. Tanger is a discount outlet shopping center brimming with great buys. Stores like Rack Room Shoes, J. Crew, Aeropostale, Nine West, Gap, and other familiar brands can be found here.

Roanoke Island

PHOENIX SHOPS, Downtown Manteo. Several independent retailers are located here, among them: YOUnique Boutique, offering wearable art; Roanoke Island Running Company, outfitting athletes; and Washed Ashore fine art store, among others.

WATERFRONT SHOPS, Downtown Manteo. Fun stores like Sisters Boutique, offering generational goods for women of every age, Acre Lane Home Decor, Andrus Gallery, and more are found here.

Hatteras Island

HATTERAS LANDING, NC 12, Hatteras Village. Insiders enjoy shopping at Kitty Hawk Kites, Forbes Candy, Carolina Outdoors, and the Farmer's Daughter at this spot.

HATTERAS PLAZA, NC 12, Avon. Shop at Ocean Threads for clothing, Jewels by the Sea for some sparkly jewelry, and enjoy a Wonderberry Yogurt.

REGIONAL STORES WITH MULTIPLE LOCATIONS

THE COTTON GIN, Timbuck II, Corolla; Duck Road, Duck; 5151 S. Croatan Hwy., Nags Head; cottongin.com. An iconic Outer Banks store carrying clothing, gifts and something for everything. Original Cotton Gin Store in Jarvisburg on Mainland is under construction following 2019 fire.

★ **GRAY'S DEPARTMENT STORE,** Little Timbuck II, Corolla; Big Timbuck II, Corolla; Waterfront Shops, Duck; US 158, MP 4, Kitty Hawk; (252) 261-1776; grays-sportswear.com. Gray's Department Store is an Outer Banks clothing tradition for men and women. Celebrating more than 50 years of business, Gray's offers top brand swimwear, sportswear, and more.

★ **KITTY HAWK KITES/KITTY HAWK SPORTS,** Timbuck II, Corolla; Monterey Plaza, Corolla; NC 12, Duck; US 158, MP 12½, Jockey's Ridge Crossing, Nags Head (main store); Whalebone, 7517 S. Virginia Dare Trl., Nags Head; Manteo Waterfront, Manteo; Waves Village, Rodanthe; Island Shops, NC 12, Avon; Hatteras Landing, Hatteras; Community Square, Ocracoke; (877) 359-8447; Wee Winks Square, Duck; US 158, MP 12½, Jockey's Ridge Crossing, Nags Head (main store); kittyhawk.com. This Outer Banks institution is visited by most vacationers and locals alike, because creating adventure seems to be one of the missions of the company. The stores carry stunt and recreational kites, toys, OBX gear, high-end footwear, and also book adventures from hang gliding to dolphin tours. The sister store, Kitty Hawk Sports, offers surfwear, surf gear, kayaks, stand-up paddleboards, and more. Kids from 8 to 80 are certain to find something entertaining within these stores.

NAGS HEAD HAMMOCKS, TimBuck II, Corolla; (252) 453-4611; NC 12, Duck; (252) 261-1062; US 158, MP 9½, Kill Devil Hills; (252) 441-6115; nagsheadhammocks.com. Over four decades of relaxing their clients have made this hammock store a huge success. Purchase a hammock, a rope chair, or a porch swing to while away the hours; it'll be a souvenir you won't regret!

ANTIQUES AND VINTAGE

B&B ANTIQUES, US 158, MP 4, Buccaneer's Walk, Kitty Hawk; (252) 715-1050. You'll never know what you'll stumble across in this delightful store, and you'll want to make it a must-see on your list of fun places to stop on your travels.

CENTRAL SQUARE MALL, US 158, MP 11, Nags Head. Several antiques stores are located in this small mall.

DOWNPOINT DECOYS, NC 12, Captain's Landing, Ocracoke; (252) 928-3269. This small, rustic shop sells decoys both old and new. Also lures, painted oars, and wildlife art.

HOTLINE, US 158, MP 3½, Kitty Hawk; US 158, MP 10, Nags Head; US 64/264, Manteo. This community thrift shop benefits the local women's shelter and other important community needs. You'll discover some great finds in shoes, clothes, furniture, and more.

OUTER BANKS QUILTS & ANTIQUES, 108 Sir Walter Raleigh St., Manteo; (252) 473-4183. This shop is filled to the brim with quilt pieces, antiques, and collectibles.

SOMETHING OLD SOMETHING NEW, US 158, MP 9½, Kill Devil Hills; (252) 480-3030. Vintage dresses and jewelry to fit any occasion can be found here. Rent or own.

SHOPPING

BOOKS

BOOKS TO BE RED, School Rd. and NC 12; Ocracoke; (252) 928-3936. A lovely historic home under a canopy of trees houses this shop. A wonderful selection of new-age journals, best sellers, fiction and nonfiction, and children's books can be purchased here. **Deepwater Pottery** is housed here as well.

BUXTON VILLAGE BOOKS, NC 12, Buxton; (252) 995-4240, buxton villagebooks.com. This independent bookseller stocks best sellers and local lore.

DOWNTOWN BOOKS, 105 Sir Walter Raleigh St., Manteo; (252) 473-1056; duckscottage.com. Best sellers, children's books, a great atmosphere and a killer selection of local titles.

DUCK'S COTTAGE BOOKSTORE, Waterfront Shops, Duck; (252) 261-5510; 105 Sir Walter Raleigh St., Manteo; (252) 473-1056; duckscottage .com. This gem of a store offers a wide variety of books and toys. Author signings are frequently held here as well.

ISLAND BOOKSTORE, Corolla Village, Corolla; (252) 453-2292; Scarborough Faire, Duck; (252) 261-8981; US 158, MP 4½, Kitty Hawk; (252) 255-5590; islandbooksobx.com. Cookbooks, best sellers, business books, and magazines are the big draw here.

CLOTHING

CHARLOTTE'S, Queen Elizabeth St., Manteo; (252) 473-3078; shop charlottes.com. This quality women's boutique features traditional and contemporary fine and casual clothing.

★ **THE FRENCH DOOR**, US 158, MP 11, Nags Head; (252) 441-4042; thefrenchdoorobx.com. Let your personality shine in a new outfit from The French Door. Clothing found here is colorful, unique, and comfortable. Other offerings include jewelry, home decor, and accessories. This shop is an Insiders' favorite.

IZABELLE'S CLOSET, Beacon Shops, Hatteras Village; (252) 986-6575. Find just what you need for the beach or beyond at Izabelle's Closet. Stylish hats, accessories, and clothing are found here.

MERMAID'S FOLLY, Irvin Garrish Hwy, Ocracoke; (252) 928-RAGS (7247); mermaidsfolly.com. Sea-spirited clothing and T-shirts can be found at this casually diverse store.

PLUM CRAZY, NC 12, Duck Soundside Shops, Duck; (252) 261-1125. Bubbling over with unique and unusual clothing choices, this shop offers jeans and more to the discriminating shopper.

SLEEPING IN, 101 Fernando St., Manteo; (252) 475-1971; sleepinginobx .com. Surround yourself in luxury with high-quality linens and fine lounge-wear from this well-appointed store.

CRAFTS, ART & JEWELRY

BELLA FIORE POTTERY, 109 Lighthouse Rd., Ocracoke; (252) 928-2826. Handmade pottery is offered in this working artist studio and gallery. Also featured are natural body products and other art pieces.

CLOUD NINE, Pirate's Quay, 3022 S. Croatan Hwy, Nags Head; (252) 441-2992. Jewelry, fine art, and Ginny. A great place to take kids to make their own beaded jewelry.

DARE COUNTY ARTS COUNCIL GALLERY, 300 Queen Elizabeth Ave, Manteo; (252) 473-5558; darearts.org. Artistic cultural center of the Outer Banks. Paintings, jewelry, pottery, and more.

ISLAND ARTWORKS, British Cemetery Rd., Ocracoke; (252) 928-3892. It's fun to browse this brightly colored shop. Fused glass and mosaics, jewelry, and photography are just a few of the items offered here.

LEE ROBINSON GENERAL STORE, NC 12, Hatteras; (252) 986-2381. Downstairs, it's an upscale convenience store, upstairs a delightful gift shop. Check out the jewelry and the home decor for a fun stop.

MY SECRET GARDEN, 101 Sir Walter Raleigh St., Manteo; (252) 473-6880. Unique garden accessories, custom wreaths, hand-painted furniture, and more delights await you in this charming shop.

OCRACOKE RESTORATION, NC 12, Ocracoke; (252) 928-2669. Eclectic and whimsical, Ocracoke Restoration has vintage jewelry, yard art, stained glass, and more.

HOME DECOR

COTTAGE CHIC, 3834 N. Croatan Hwy, Kitty Hawk; (252) 489-7543; cottagechicobx.com. Repurposing vintage doors, shutters, and broken down furniture into a new look and feel.

SPRY CREEK DRY GOODS, Corolla Village, Corolla; (252) 453-0199. Finds from all over the globe will tempt any shopper. Portuguese pottery, glass items, and local art can all be found here.

SURF SHOPS

Surf shops abound on the Outer Banks and the list is extensive. We've listed a few of the favorites and many of these shops offer surf gear, surf lessons, and rentals.

BIRTHDAY SUITS, Monteray Plaza, Corolla; (252) 453-4862; Scarbourgh Lane, Duck; (252) 261-7297; MP 9¾, Nags Head; (252) 441-5338. Find the perfect suit for all shapes and sizes at this store.

CAVALIER SURF SHOP, NC 12, MP 13½, Nags Head; (252) 441-7349. Clothes, skimboards, shoes, and rentals are packed into this friendly surf shop.

DUCK VILLAGE OUTFITTERS (DVO), NC 12, Duck; (252) 261-7222; NC 12, Salvo; (252) 987-1222. Popular surf brands are carried for men, women, and kids. Rental and surf equipment for sale as well.

ISLAND REVOLUTION, NC 12, Corolla Light Town Center; (252) 453-9484. Stylish surf brands carried here as well as jewelry and accessories.

NATURAL ART SURF SHOP, NC 12, Buxton; (252) 995-5682; naturalart. com. This is a true "surfer's surf shop" and boards are made, sold, and repaired here. Clothing for all ages is available and the shop rents gear as well.

RIDE THE WIND SURF SHOP, NC 12, Ocracoke; (252) 928-6311. Board rentals, sales, and surf clothes are all available at this spacious shop.

WAVE RIDING VEHICLES, US 158, MP 2, Kitty Hawk; (252) 261-7952. Get the hottest fashion for men, women, and groms at WRV. Rentals and more. The logo stickers are very popular items, too.

WHALEBONE SURF SHOP, US 158, MP 10, Nags Head; (252) 441-6747; whalebonesurfshop.com. Friendly and knowledgeable, the staff here will help you find the right swimsuit or surfboard.

Kidstuff

The beach is always a popular lure for children. They can play tag with the waves, build whimsical sandcastles, fly a kite, play volleyball, or dig for treasure they just know has been left. The Outer Banks is a large sandy playground, with opportunities for exploration that are only limited by your imagination. For kids this means the possibilities are infinite, especially on sunny days at the beach. If the skies are overcast or the temperature too cold to play by the shore, they'll need a little more help from you (and us!) to entertain themselves.

Read the chapters on **Recreation**, **Attractions**, and **Water Sports** for a more complete listing of activities children will enjoy. **Kidstuff** takes a look at the not-so-obvious, as well as some favorites.

CHILDREN'S THEATER AND STORYTELLING

DUCK TOWN PARK, downtown Duck. Duck Town Park hosts Story Time on Thursday from 10 to 11 a.m. Also catch the educational moment on Tuesday at 10 a.m. hosted by the North Carolina Aquarium. Wednesday at 10 a.m. brings a magic show for family enjoyment. Each Thursday night brings an outdoor concert from 6:30 to 8 p.m. Performances change weekly; check the website townofduck.com.

THE LOST COLONY CHILDREN'S THEATRE, Waterside Theatre, Manteo; (252) 473-2127; thelostcolony.org/childrens-programs. Performers and technicians with *The Lost Colony* stage imaginative selections for kids. The shows play each Tuesday and Wednesday June through August at 2 p.m. at Roanoke Island Festival Park. The cost is around $10 per ticket.

STORYTIME AT THE DARE COUNTY LIBRARY, Manteo, (252) 473-2372; Kill Devil Hills, (252) 441-4331; Hatteras, (252) 986-2395. Preschool

---

Family Fun on the Run

Family-friendly 5K running and fitness events are held all over the Outer Banks beginning in April and held throughout December, hosted by Outer Banks RunCations. Events include runners of all levels, including families, children, and fitness walkers. For the schedule or registration, visit runcations .com or call (252) 489-8239.

Two young boys head out to fish on the beach. FERTNIG/GETTYIMAGES

Close-up

More Family-Friendly Fun

While every effort is made within these pages to reveal the many opportunities to explore the Outer Banks, occasionally new opportunities will come along after the book has gone to press. Following are some favorite Internet sites that Insiders check out to keep up with the latest!

Facebook Sites

Oregon Inlet Idiots—local happenings.

Outer Banks Voice—reliable news source.

Hidden Outer Banks—local happenings.

North Beach Sun—news and local happenings.

Outer Banks Vintage Scrapbook—historical.

Island Free Press—Hatteras/Ocracoke-focused news.

Ocracoke Observer—news of Ocracoke.

Websites

outerbanksvoice.com—local news.

outerbankschild.com—youth information.

hiddenouterbanks.com—local happenings.

outerbanksthisweek.com—weekly updates for entertainment, festivals, art shows, and more.

islandfreepress.org—Hatteras and Ocracoke news.

ocracokeobserver.com—local news

story hours are held at the libraries to acquaint young kids with the library and help them enjoy books at an early age. Story hours include games, songs, puppets, stories, and plays, sometimes with guest storytellers. Programs last 30 to 45 minutes and are held once a week at each of the library locations: Tuesday in Hatteras, Wednesday in Manteo, and Thursday in Kill Devil Hills. Separate programs are held for 2-year-olds, 3- to 5-year-olds, kindergarten to first graders, and second graders to fifth graders.

SUMMER CHILDREN'S SERIES, Roanoke Island Festival Park, Manteo; (252) 475-1506; roanokeisland.com. Roanoke Island Festival Park offers excellent children's programming with its Summer Children's Series. In June and early July, programs are held Wednesday and Thursday at 10:30 a.m. and change weekly. Past performances have included puppet and marionette shows, storytellers, and plays. The usual fee is waived if you have paid for park admission. Programs are held in the Film Theater, which seats about 200 people. Tickets are $5.

KIDS' CAMPS

COASTAL STUDIES INSTITUTE SUMMER DAY CAMPS, CSI, Roanoke Island; coastalstudiesinstitute.org. From learning about the science of estuaries to exploring Outer Banks shipwrecks, the CSI camps are some of the most educational and fun on the Outer Banks. Registration begins in March.

THE ELIZABETHAN GARDENS, off US 64, Roanoke Island; (252) 473-3234; elizabethangardens.org. Families savor this oasis of serenity and fun. Special children's events are held throughout the summer on Tuesday through Thursday at 10 a.m. Check the website or call for details. Any visit to the Gardens is time well spent.

JOCKEY'S RIDGE STATE PARK, US 158, MP 12, Nags Head; (252) 441-2588; jockeysridgestatepark.com. A wide range of educational nature programs are offered for kids. Take a dune hike and learn about the animals and plants in the area. Choose from a soundside hike, sunset on the ridge, crabby clinic, birding on the sound, and lots more. All programs are free and open to the public.

JUNIOR LIFEGAURD CAMPS, Kill Devil Hills; kdhnc.com/257/Ocean -Rescue-Division. Taught by the Kill Devil Hills lifeguards, the five day camp emphasizes education, first aid, and ocean safety. Activities include physical training, marine environment education, and board sports. June and July.

THE NORTH CAROLINA AQUARIUM AT ROANOKE ISLAND, Airport Rd., Manteo; (252) 473-3493; aquariums.state.nc.us/ri. The aquarium leads the Aquatic Adventures Summer Camp for students ages 6 to 7, 7 to 9, and 10 to 12. The camps last for five half-days, with children learning about the Outer Banks waters and habitats through many hands-on activities and field trips. Each weeklong camp for the 10- to 12-year-olds concludes with a sleepover at the aquarium. Also, the aquarium can be rented for sleepover parties among the fishes and sharks.

OCEAN ATLANTIC RENTALS SURF SCHOOL, Corolla Light Town Center, Corolla; (252) 453-2440; oceanatlanticrentals.com. Kids and adults can learn to catch waves in the Ocean Atlantic Rentals Surf School. Classes are taught by a professional out of each of the four Ocean Atlantic locations, and the instructors will teach students of all skill levels. Other locations are at: Duck Road, Soundfront, Duck; (252) 261-4346; NC 12, MP 10, Nags Head, (252) 441-7823; and NC 12, Avon, (252) 995-5868.

> **i** Learning to surf while staying on the Outer Banks is a popular and exciting pastime. When choosing a surf school, ask if the instructor is first-aid certified and confirm that only beginner boards are used (soft or soft-top boards).

OUTER BANKS FAMILY YMCA, US 158, MP 11, Nags Head; (252) 449-8897; ymcashr.org/outer-banks. The YMCA has weeklong day camps for all ages. Full-day camps are for ages 5 to 12. Each week has a special theme, and kids do activities related to the theme in addition to going to the pool and ocean and on field trips. The YMCA also hosts several sports camps in beach volleyball, girls' field hockey, soccer, basketball, and junior ocean rescue. Day passes are available for the superb skate park. Call for information.

Arts & Culture

The Outer Banks is the kind of place where many artists envision spending their days painting the beauty that surrounds them or sculpting forms wrought by visions brought forth by the ocean. For many this dream has come to fruition, and the beach has become a haven for artists of all kinds. The powerful influence of the ocean and wetlands appears in many works of art, as do the abundant wildlife and spirit of the residents as they work and play. Our historic landmarks provide inspiration for an artistic appetite. The relative isolation of our barrier islands, though seen by some as a drawback to year-round living, is a real plus to the artist, especially in the off-season. This is the time to contemplate and study, then commune with the muse and put insights into a tangible piece of art. When a nor'easter blows on a gray February day, the muse may be an artist's only visitor! Take the time to visit our many galleries and talk with some of our local artists and writers. Through their eyes you are sure to gain more appreciation of this special area.

OVERVIEW

You can get a feel for this fascinating visual arts arena, which runs the gamut from conceptual art to classical painting, by attending several annual events. One of the longest running of these is the Dare County Arts Council's **Frank Stick Memorial Art Show**, which was started back in 1978. The show is held at the Ghost Fleet Gallery in Nags Head every February and features more than 150 artworks (see the **Annual Events** chapter for more information).

For some family fun of the artistic kind, set aside the first weekend in October for the Arts Council's annual **Artrageous Art Extravaganza**, which features hands-on creative booths with cookie decorating, hat creations, weaving, face painting, and much more. Fashion shows, food, live music, art collaborations, and local art and craft booths highlight the event.

Many new and one-time-only art events and cultural opportunities occur on the Outer Banks. Visitors who would like to catch up on the latest events should consult the following event calendars: OBX Entertainment, obxentertainment.com; Outer Banks Visitors Bureau, outerbanks.org; Town of Manteo, townofmanteo.com; and the Town of Duck, townofduck.com.

Private visual art studios are scattered from Corolla to Ocracoke for art seekers. Many local artists offer lessons, mostly in watercolor and other painting techniques. We do have many landscape painters here, but our 50 or more commercial art/craft galleries are packed with expressions as individual as grains of sand.

The Outer Banks has become a bona fide art community. Artists living here and in the surrounding areas are a close-knit group, sharing tips and encouraging each other in their endeavors. Perhaps because of the lifestyle here, our artists are eager to meet visitors.

Local theater groups present plays, comedies, and dramas both seasonally and year-round. Music streams from some night clubs, and standup comics perform summer stints. Symphonies, vocal groups, and individual classical, folk, and pop artists enliven our local auditoriums throughout the year.

We begin with a description of major arts organizations and follow with a north-to-south excursion through the Outer Banks' eclectic galleries and other creative venues. Please see the **Annual Events** chapter for arts events.

ORGANIZATIONS

DARE COUNTY ARTS COUNCIL, Old Courthouse, Manteo; (252) 473-5558; darearts.org. The Dare County Arts Council supplies the Outer Banks with a wide variety of creative opportunities with the help of countless volunteers, generous patrons and members, and some state and county support. This nonprofit group has a permanent office/gallery in downtown Manteo at the address above. The gallery hosts visual arts shows, and visitors are encouraged to stop by to view these shows or to gather information on arts and cultural events in the area. Office hours are 10 a.m. to 5 p.m. Monday through Friday and occasional weekends when volunteer staff is available.

The council is affiliated with the North Carolina Arts Council as the local distributing agency of the state's Grassroots funds. The DCAC also partners with other area arts organizations, such as Theater of Dare and the Writers' Group.

DCAC operates on funds from grants, fundraisers, and annual memberships. Memberships generally range from $40 and up. This is a great way to support the arts in the community.

ICARUS INTERNATIONAL, (252) 441-6584; monumenttoacenturyof flight.org. Icarus International was founded in 1993, purposely a decade before the centennial of flight in 2003, with the goal of celebrating flight through the arts. The organization has been widely successful in its efforts to raise the awareness of the history of flight. Each year Icarus International holds an international visual arts competition and a literary competition based on a flight-related theme. Literary entries are published annually. Icarus International also sponsors an annual portrait commission for inductees into the First Flight Shrine at the Wright Brothers National Memorial. In 2003 the group completed the $1 million Icarus Monument, celebrating 100 years of flight. The monument is located at MP 1 in Kitty Hawk, behind the Aycock Brown

Welcome Center. Icarus International has created a book called Pioneer Aviators of the World. It tells the story of the first pilots from 100 countries.

ROANOKE ISLAND FESTIVAL PARK, 1 Festival Park, Manteo; (252) 475-1500, (252) 475-1506 (24-hour events line); roanokeisland.com. Roanoke Island Festival Park blends art, history, and education in celebration of Roanoke Island's role as birthplace of English-speaking America. The state park is on its own small island across from the Manteo waterfront, also the home berth of the *Elizabeth II*. Completed in 1998, the park features a variety of cultural opportunities year-round. The park's art gallery is a beautiful space that holds month-long art shows. At receptions for these shows on Sunday afternoon, arts-minded folk meet. The Film Theater shows *The Legend of Two Path*, a 45-minute film depicting the English landing on Roanoke Island from the Native Americans' point of view, and the new film *The Birth of a Colony*; other top-notch cultural arts performances and films are also staged in the theater. The outdoor pavilion seats up to 3,500 people on the lawn and is a marvelous place to watch cultural arts performances. On-site are an adventure museum, a museum store, and the Outer Banks History Center. The museum has been completely renovated and visitors begin the journey in England and follow the colonists over to the New World on the Outer Banks, with the journey ending around the 1960s.

ROANOKE ISLAND HISTORICAL ASSOCIATION, 1409 US 64/264, Manteo; (252) 473-2127; thelostcolony.org. *The Lost Colony*, a unique outdoor drama, is staged throughout the summer in a waterside theater on Roanoke Island (see the **Attractions** chapter). Each year *The Lost Colony* entices 125 actors and crew from across the nation to answer the casting call for the symphonic drama that chronicles the fate of the first English settlement in America. Many of *The Lost Colony* thespians try out for the Lost Colony's Children's Theater that wows junior audiences during the summer months with classics such as *Sleeping Beauty* and *Pirates! A Boy at Sea*. Others take on roles as time-warped sailors for hilarious and educational interpretive tours of the *Elizabeth II*.

GALLERIES

Corolla

DOLPHIN WATCH GALLERY, 793 Sunset Blvd.; (252) 453-2592; dolphinwatchgallery.com. Dolphin Watch Gallery features the works of owner/artist Mary Kaye Umberger. This artist creates hand-colored etchings on handmade paper drawn from scenes indigenous to the Corolla area, including wildlife, ducks and other waterfowl, seascapes, and lighthouses. Other art pieces here include pottery, stoneware, carvings of marine life, and wax sculptures (candles shaped by hand, with flower petals molded by the artist's fingertips). The gallery is open year-round; call for off-season hours.

Duck

DUCK POTTERY, 102 Flight Dr.; (252) 261-6697; duckpottery.info. Visit award-winning artist Fred Vallade at his studio/gallery, where his one-of-a-kind ceramic art is created and is on display. Vallade attempts to "embrace the unpredictable" in this working studio gallery. Open 10 a.m. to 4 p.m. daily in season.

SEADRAGON & YELLOWHOUSE GALLERY, 1240 Duck Rd., The Waterfront Shops; (252) 441-6928, (252) 261-4224; seadragonyellow housegallery.com. Highlighting the photography of international award-winning photographer Eve Turek, the Yellowhouse Gallery has combined with Seadragon to offer even more fine art, jewelry, and creative pottery.

THE WOODEN FEATHER, NC 12, Scarborough Lane; (252) 261-2808; woodenfeather.com. The Wooden Feather proudly showcases the best of American ingenuity and creativity with award-winning hand-carved decoys and shorebirds as well as driftwood sculptures. The gallery features an outstanding collection of antique decoys. Garden accessories, jewelry, and gifts are sold here as well. The store is open seven days a week from March through December, with longer hours during the summer season.

Kill Devil Hills

THE BIRD STORE, 807 S. Croatan Hwy, MP 8½; (252) 480-295; the birdstoreobx.com. The shelves of The Bird Store are stocked full with hand-carved birds from local artists as well as antique decoys. There are also print, fish carvings, and more.

KDH COOPERATIVE GALLERY AND STUDIOS, US 158, MP 8½; (252) 441-9888; kdhcooperative.com. This is an artist-operated cooperative, the dream and reality of artist and owner Julie Moye. It's a centralized place to see the work of local artists. The juried members of this cooperative show their work and assist in running the gallery. Oil, acrylic, watercolor, pastels, pen and ink, ceramics, jewelry, fiber, furniture, candles, pottery, glass, and metal are featured. Each member serves on panels to hang and display art, jury, organize shows, and assist customers during daily business hours.

Upstairs is the Artists' Attic, a lively studio space and classrooms. Several artists have set up studios upstairs and often work during business hours. Visitors are welcome upstairs to talk with the artists and watch them work.

The other half of the upstairs is classroom space, where classes are held year-round for children and adults. Pottery, drawing, photography, stained glass, mosaic, candle making, blacksmithing, and basket-making are some of the classes offered, or you can design your own class and pitch it to the staff. KDH Cooperative offers art classes for kids, including creative writing, drawing, and comic-strip drawing, as well as summer art camps and classes on school holidays.

Nags Head

GLENN EURE'S GHOST FLEET GALLERY, 210 E. Driftwood St., Gallery Row; (252) 441-6584. Glenn Eure, sometimes referred to as the "grandfather of Outer Banks art," was a printmaker and visual artist, whose work took a variety of forms including etching, wood cutting, calligraphy, serigraphy, and relief carving in addition to drawing, wood carving, and oil, acrylic, and watercolor painting. Eure passed away in 2018 just weeks before his 87th birthday, but his wife Pat Eure continues to run the Ghost Fleet Gallery, an original art establishment that primarily features Glenn's work. His oeuvre includes a series of collagraphs (thin collages run through a printing press) honoring Wilbur and Orville Wright's first flight. The fine-art prints, each hand-pulled by the artist, contain flight imagery from da Vinci's time to the present. Glenn specialized in large canvases that bulged out from their frames—irregular shapes that were painted in a nonobjective style. He also produced lighthearted watercolors that featured boat scenes. Other artists' work is rotated throughout the West Wind and Second Dimension galleries. Off-season, the Gallery hosts several community shows. Open year-round.

JEWELRY BY GAIL, 207 East Driftwood St., Gallery Row; (252) 441-5387; jewelrybygail.com. Gail Kowalski is a designer-goldsmith who has won national recognition for her creations in precious metals and stones. Her pieces have been regularly spotted on Hollywood's elite on the red carpet. Most of the jewelry designed and made here falls into the "wearable art" category. Check out Selections by Gail, a department of very high-quality but moderately priced handmade jewelry from all over the world. Kowalski personally selects each piece exhibited here. The Charming Lights sterling and gold lighthouse jewelry collection is a favorite. Images of the four local lighthouses are fashioned into earrings, pendants, and charms. The gallery is open Monday through Saturday, and is closed in January.

SEA GREEN GALLERY, 2404 Virginia Dare Trl.; (252) 715-2426; seagreengallery.com. Sea Green Gallery celebrates the fine art of re-use. Here Insider's will find tumbled antique glass mirrors, repurposed African glass jewelry, broken china jewelry, sea glass jewelry, soy candles in vintage vessels, and more. Open year-round.

ARTS & CULTURE

SEASIDE ART GALLERY, NC 12, MP 11; (252) 441-5418; seasideart.com. Original etchings and lithographs by Picasso, Whistler, Rembrandt, and Renoir are among the thousands of original works of art on display at Seaside Art Gallery. Sculptures, paintings, drawings, Indian pottery, fine porcelains, Mexican silver jewelry (including the work of William Spratling), seascapes, and animation art from Disney and Warner Bros. are spread throughout numerous rooms in this sprawling gallery. Seaside is a Gold Circle dealer for Disney Classic Figurines. Prints by David Hunter are meticulously rendered and range from biblical portraiture to peaceful coastal scenes. The gallery hosts several competitions annually, including an International Miniature Art Show (see the May listings in the **Annual Events** chapter) and the Icarus International Art Show. Printmaking workshops are held here each year by David Hunter. The gallery is open year-round.

Roanoke Island

HUBBY BLIVEN WILDLIFE ART, 543 Ananias Dare St., Roanoke Island; (252) 473-2632. Bliven runs a full-service frame shop and wildlife art gallery featuring his own work. He also operates a museum on the premises that includes Civil War, World War I, World War II, and Native American artifacts. Bliven's shop is the place to go if you're looking for lighthouse photos that include all eight North Carolina sentinels framed together or as individual prints. This group includes the Prices's Creek lighthouse in Southport, a rare find. Bliven is very fortunate to have been given access to photograph this structure on private property. His shop is open year-round.

ROANOKE ISLAND FESTIVAL PARK ART GALLERY, Manteo; (252) 475-1506; roanokeisland.com. Gallery shows change monthly, featuring the works of an individual artist or sometimes groups of artists. The Priceless Pieces Past & Present Quilt Extravaganza is a popular show, held every year in March, with dozens of quilts made or owned by locals. Each monthly show has an opening reception on a Sunday afternoon. Roanoke Island Festival Park is closed in January and part of February.

SILVER BONSAI GALLERY, 905 US 64/264, Manteo; (252) 475-1413; silverbonsai.com. Silver Bonsai Gallery, nestled in one of the island's original homes, is a distinctive art gallery. Owners Ben and Kathryn Stewart, both metalsmiths and bonsai artists, sell their own creations here, as well as the works of other artists, and can often be seen at work in the studio at the back of the gallery. The Stewarts create simple yet elegant silver and gold jewelry and sculpture and design special pieces upon request. The gallery sells a broad range of fine art by local artists, including paintings, wood, glass, sculpture, quilts, and more. Silver Bonsai is open seven days a week, but closes for the month of January.

WANCHESE POTTERY, 107 Fernando St., Manteo; (252) 473-2099. Customers can watch local potters Bonnie and Bob Morrill at work in their studio in downtown Manteo. This shop is known for its beautiful, useful art graced with delicate, lead-free glazes. One savvy insider bought a handsome mug here that holds a generous amount of coffee, sits easily without wobbling, and has an exquisite glaze that turns a morning routine into an artistic awakening. Choose dinnerware, oil lamps, hummingbird feeders, mugs, bowls, and pitchers among other items. The shop also features some handmade baskets and fresh cooking herbs. Wanchese Pottery is open all year. Winter hours are 1 to 5 p.m. Thursday, Friday, and Saturday.

Hatteras Island

GASKINS GALLERY, NC 12, Avon; (252) 995-6617. The Gaskins Gallery focuses on original local art and custom framing. Artists and owners Denise and Elizabeth Gaskins feature exclusively original family art, including their own watercolors and those of their grandmother. The paintings generally are coastal scenes or florals. You'll also find pottery, decorator prints, and posters. The Gaskins Gallery is open year-round.

> **i** Early Christmas shoppers love a summer outdoor art show. The **New World Festival of the Arts** in Manteo in August welcomes 80 artists from the Outer Banks and all along the East Coast. You'll find pottery, paintings, metalwork, photography, basketry, painted tiles, and so much more. This show is held midweek. For more information, see the **Annual Events** chapter.

MICHAEL HALMINSKI PHOTOGRAPHY, NC 12, Waves; (252) 987-2401; michaelhalminski.com. Michael Halminski began photographing the coastal environment when he moved to Hatteras Isalnd in 1973. His work is marked by his skill as an artist and by his intimate knowledge of the people, wildlife, and landscapes of the Outer Banks. Gallery hours are Monday through Saturday 10 a.m. to 6 p.m.

PEA ISLAND ART GALLERY, Salvo; (252) 987-2879; peaislandartgallery .com. Owner/Artist in Residence Kim Robertson presents the work of over 100 local and regional artists in a historic replica of the 1874 Chicamacamico Life-Saving Station. Works on display include glass, handmade jewelry, photography, mixed media, and more.

RED DRUM POTTERY, NC 12, Frisco; (252) 995-5757; reddrumpottery .com. Accomplished potters Rhonda Bates and Wes Lassiter work in this studio, and you can watch them as they turn their wonderful creations at the wheel. These are well-crafted pieces, whether they are intended for functional or decorative use. It's definitely worth a stop to see their bowls, pitchers, vases, vessels, platters, teakettles, miniatures, and fabulous fish- and crab-imprinted hanging wall tiles. Do you raku? Come try it in the early evening—call for an updated schedule. The gallery is open seven days a week year-round.

SANDY BAY GALLERY, NC 12, Hatteras Village; (252) 986-1338; facebook.com/sandybaygallery. This gallery features original fine art and crafts with an emphasis on Outer Banks artists. Sandy Bay is filled with original watercolor and acrylic paintings and photography, as well as crafts by potters, jewelers, glass artisans, and paper, wood, stained-glass, and fiber artists. The hand-carved decorative waterfowl, including egrets, blue herons, sandpipers, and dowitchers, have grace and personality. Glass boxes with silver trim by Mary Anne feature a geometric collage of colored and clear glass reminiscent of Mondrian's paintings. You also can choose from a selection of prints. The gallery is open March through Christmas Eve.

SEAWORTHY GALLERY, NC 12, Hatteras; (252) 986-6510. Fine art, glazed potter, exquisite jewelry, and more. The Seaworthy Gallery houses an extraordinary diversity of fine art. Worth a special visit while in Hatteras Village.

STUDIO 12, 41008 NC 12, Avon; (252) 995-7899; studio12hatteras.com. A hands-on art gallery that also features the fusion glassware and art of Carolyn Schena and her husband Gary's pottery. A great place to take kids on a rainy day so they can create their own art.

Ocracoke Island

ISLAND ARTWORKS, British Cemetery Rd.; (252) 928-3892; island artworks.com. Owner-artist Kathleen O'Neal has lived on Ocracoke for more than 25 years. "Art jewelry" aptly describes most of the finds here. O'Neal does all the copper enameling and silver- and goldsmithing work herself. The gallery also features local and North Carolina artwork such as large, contemporary-style watercolors of island scenes by Debbie Wells and the fused-glass work of Libby Hicks. Local photography, sculptural assemblages created by O'Neal, glass art, hand-carved wooden boxes, and mixed-media art are just some of the exciting discoveries at Island Artworks. It's a real fine art experience. This colorful shop is open from mid-March until Christmas.

OVER THE MOON, British Cemetery Rd.; (252) 928-3555; overthemoon giftshop.com. Over the Moon will make you feel just so when you see all of the divine art pieces they have available for any budget. Jewelry, porcelain pieces, hammock chairs, and more are available in this shop. Open Easter through Thanksgiving.

VILLAGE CRAFTSMEN, Howard St.; (252) 928-5541; villagecraftsmen .com. The artwork in this well-known gallery includes North Carolina pottery, handmade wooden boxes, jewelry, and other original items. The focus is on excellent craftsmanship and variety. Owner Philip Howard also sells his pen-and-ink and watercolor prints here. See the **Shopping** chapter for more about this local landmark, open year-round except the month of January.

JURIED ART EXHIBITIONS

The Outer Banks offers several juried art exhibitions each year. While the traditional definition of "juried" implies that work is selected for showing by judges, most shows here have an open-entry policy, and the work is judged for excellence and originality. Entry fees generally average $10 to $15.

Here we've listed the major shows in the area; for detailed information, call either the galleries mentioned or the Dare County Arts Council (252-473-5558). New shows are always cropping up, so keep in touch with the arts council. See the **Annual Events** chapter for more art activities.

Nags Head

INTERNATIONAL MINIATURE ART SHOW, Seaside Art Gallery, NC 12, MP 11, Nags Head; (252) 441-5418; seasideart.com. Any artist may enter this May show held at Seaside Art Gallery. Work entered cannot exceed 40 inches. The show features mini paintings, drawings, sculpture, wood-turned bowls, collages, and more.

Roanoke Island

FRANK STICK MEMORIAL ART SHOW, Old Courthouse, Manteo; (252) 473-5558; darearts.org. This mid-winter show is open to Dare County residents and Dare County Arts Council members. All genres of art are welcome; some restrictions (including the size of the work) apply.

MOLLIE FEARING MEMORIAL ART SHOW, Old Courthouse, Manteo; (252) 473-5558; darearts.org. The Dare County Arts Council puts on this annual art show, held at the beautiful Festival Park Art Gallery. Dare County Arts Council members and Dare County residents are invited to enter this show, which is held in May. Call DCAC at the number above for information.

Recreation

From early on these barrier islands have lured sunbathers, swimmers, surfers, and outdoor enthusiasts in search of excellent sportfishing and waterfowl hunting. The appeal has since widened to include more outdoor activities: windsurfing, hang gliding, parasailing, scuba diving, biking, golf, tennis, and in-line skating, just to name a few. And for a respite from these more strenuous workouts, you can choose among sightseeing cruises, ATV excursions, and beachcombing.

OVERVIEW

Not all activities involve a fee. You can spend an afternoon walking the wide beaches searching for shells, fly a kite or take a hike through Nags Head Woods, one of the most marvelous preserved maritime forests on the Atlantic Seaboard. Bike paths line roads along the sounds and the sea, through towns, and along the Wright Brothers National Memorial. If you need to get to sea for a while and enjoy the Outer Banks from a different vantage point, ride the free, state ferry to Ocracoke Island.

When you've had a little too much fun in the sun, there are indoor activities such as bowling alleys, movie theaters, a laser tag arena, and noisy, state-of-the-art video arcades. Don't forget to check out the **Kidstuff** chapter for additional activities geared toward children.

If you're looking for parks, the Dare County Parks and Recreation Department has several throughout the county, some with playgrounds, tennis courts, picnicking sites, and ball fields. Call (252) 473-1101, ext. 313, to find the one nearest you.

AIRPLANE TOURS

Even people who have lived on the Outer Banks for years are awestruck when they first view this stretch of islands from the air. Small planes offer tours daily most of the year from Corolla through Ocracoke. Bring your camera—these adventures provide great photo opportunities of both sea and sound shores and otherwise inaccessible wetlands.

Reservations are strongly recommended at least a day in advance of takeoff. All flights depend on the wind and weather. For information on charter flights to Norfolk and other destinations off the Outer Banks, refer to the air service section in the **Getting Here, Getting Around** chapter.

RECREATION

Hatteras Island

BURRUS FLYING SERVICE, NC 12, Frisco Shopping Center, Frisco; (252) 986-2679. Burris Flying Service offers sightseeing tours of Hatteras Island and the surrounding areas. The short tour, about 30 minutes, takes you around Cape Hatteras and the lighthouse, while the longer tour, about an hour, can go either north to Rodanthe or south to Ocracoke Island. Both short and long tours fly two or three passengers. Additional trips are available, including a summer sunset tour. This is unparalleled opportunity for aerial photography. Tours are offered daily from May 1 through October 31. Advance reservations are recommended.

Roanoke Island

COASTAL HELICOPTERS, 410 Airport Rd., Dare County Regional Airport, Manteo; (252) 475-4354; obxairtouradventures.com. A great way to see the Outer Banks from the air. Bring a camera. A helicopter makes an amazing platform for photography.

KITTY HAWK AERO TOURS, Main Terminal Airport Rd.; (877) 359-8447; kittyhawk.com. Based at the Manteo Airport, these air tours fly 10- to 30-minute trips in Cessna aircraft year-round. Flights take you soaring south over Oregon Inlet, flying above the waves to see shipwrecks, over Jockey's Ridge and Roanoke Island, and back to circle the Wright brothers monument. Prices begin at $80. Tours are offered from 10 a.m. to 5 p.m. in the off-season, and from 9 a.m. to sunset during summer. If you're up for more high-flying excitement, try a trip in a 1941 Waco biplane, with its open cockpit. The 28-, 20- and 35-minute trips take two passengers around the central Outer Banks. Leather helmets and old-fashioned Red Baron–style goggles are included in the price. Biplane tours are offered May through September from 9 a.m. until sunset. Reservations are preferred for both types of flights.

OBX BIPLANES & WARBIRDS, 410 Airport Rd., Dare County Regional Airport, Manteo; (252) 475-4354; obxairtouradventures.com. Book an air tour in an open cockpit biplane or a 1943 T-6 trainer that was used to train airmen in WWII.

ALL-TERRAIN VEHICLE, 4WD & HORSE TOURS

Whether you're cruising along the beach or chasing a sunset up the marshy sounds on an all-terrain vehicle (ATV), you're limited to 15 mph, and you can't ride on the dunes. These tours are available only on the northern Outer Banks north of Corolla.

RECREATION

Corolla

BACK BEACH WILD HORSE TOURS, 1159 Austin St.; (252) 453-6141; seewildhorses.com. Back Beach Wild Horse Tours include some tales of pirates and the history of the area.

BACKCOUNTRY OUTFITTERS AND GUIDES, Corolla Light Town Center; (252) 453-0877; outerbankstours.com. Backcountry Outfitters and Guides offers Wild Horse Safari Tours that head to Carova, near the North Carolina border, looking for the famous wild horses—and they find them. Two-hour tours are led in Chevy Suburbans that hold up to 10 people. After the 15-mile drive up the beach to the horses' stomping grounds, passengers unload from the vehicle and take a few photos, while the guide educates everyone about the horses. Along the tour you'll see other wildlife, plus the elements of the Outer Banks ecosystem. These tours take place year-round. Corolla Outback Adventures also offers four-wheel-drive/kayak expeditions. All tours and rentals are weather dependent. Backcountry fans can also choose Segway Safari Tours or Kayak Adventures.

BOB'S WILD HORSE TOURS, 817 B Ocean Trl., Monterey Plaza; (252) 453-8602; corollawildhorsetours.com. With over 20 years of experience taking tours out to see the wild horses, Bob's Wild Horse Tours is one of the most experienced of the outfitters.

Several local companies conduct tours specifically to catch a glimpse of the wild horses that make their home along the shore. McIninch/GettyImages

RECREATION

COROLLA JEEP ADVENTURES, 9606, 1070 Ocean Trl.; (252) 453-6899; corollajeepadventures.com. Offering a wide variety of ways to experience the Carova area of the Outer Banks, Corolla Jeep Adventures offers kayak tours, ATV tours and more in addition to guided tours seeking the Corolla Wild Mustangs.

COROLLA OUTBACK ADVENTURES, NC 12, Wee Winks Shopping Center; (252) 453-4484; corollaoutback.com. This outpost on the northernmost area of the Outer Banks was the first outfitter to take visitors on Wild Horse tours and conducts guided tours in specially designed Land Cruisers. Even though the area is becoming more populated, you can still catch a glimpse of wild horses, rare waterfowl, wild boars, and feral hogs. Tours are two hours.

COROLLA WILD HORSE TOURS, 1210 Ocean Trl.; (252) 207-0511; seecorollawildhorses.com. Large open seating vehicles make these tours ideal for large groups of families.

> **i** Beach glass is anything but trash on the Outer Banks. Beachcombers compete to find it. One of the best spots to find these colorful tumbled treasures is on the beaches in the town of Nags Head.

Ocracoke Island

PORTSMOUTH ISLAND ATV EXCURSIONS, NC 12; (252) 928-4484; portsmouthislandatv.com. A Portsmouth Island ATV Excursion allows you to ride the shoreline of one of the most beautiful and remote beaches in the world on an island famous for its shorebirds, sea turtles, and seashells. Excursions begin with a 20-minute boat ride from Silver Lake Harbor in Ocracoke Village. Once on the island, you will discover the historic deserted village of Portsmouth, a settlement that in 1860 was a thriving port town with more than 685 residents. Now owned by the National Park Service, Portsmouth Island is home to the only ghost town on the East Coast (see the **Attractions** chapter for more details). As part of the tour, you will be guided through the village's US Lifesaving Station, the Methodist church, the post office and general store, and the village visitor center.

ATHLETIC CLUBS

Despite all the outdoor activities the Outer Banks has to offer, many locals and visitors still crave vigorous indoor workouts at traditional gyms and health

RECREATION

clubs. These fitness centers are open year-round and include locker room and shower facilities. They are open to the public for annual, monthly, weekly, and walk-in daily membership rates.

Corolla

PINE ISLAND RACQUET CLUB, 290 Audobon Dr.; (252) 453-8525; pineislandrc.com. Pine Island Racquet Club is an integral part of the Sanderling Inn Resort and Conference Center, a 12-acre luxury resort located

Traveling on two wheels? Pick up a Dare County bicycle trails map published by the North Carolina Department of Transportation. It's free at the Outer Banks Visitors Bureau.

5 miles north of Duck. The fitness center is located 3 miles north of the conference center and is a fully equipped facility. State-of-the-art exercise equipment and the latest in cardio machines are available for use, along with three tennis courts and a pro shop. Walk-in charges are $20 and weekly charges are $60.

Kill Devil Hills

CROSSFIT OUTER BANKS, 504 W. Lake Dr., Unit W; (252) 441-7400; crossfitouterbanks.com. Large gym specializing in crossfit fitness programs that utilize all muscle groups.

Nags Head

MOMENTUM FITNESS, 2500 S. Virginia Dare Trl., Ste. B; (252) 202-2917; momentumobx.com. Indoor and outdoor fitness programs that include boot camp fitness. Some instructors are former professional athletes. Geared toward family involvement and personal service.

OBX SPORTS CLUB, US 158, MP 10½; (252) 441-8361; obxsportsclub .com. Come spin, pilox, chisel, weight lift, and more in this upscale fitness environment. Certified instructors and a knowledgable staff make this sports club a popular choice. Daily, weekly, and monthly passes available.

OUTER BANKS FAMILY YMCA, US 158, MP 11; (252) 449-8897; obxymca.org. This facility includes a fitness room with weight and cardiovascular equipment. A wood-floored exercise room is available for activities like aerobics, yoga, Pilates, and karate. The 7,000-square-foot gymnasium is marked for both basketball and volleyball and can be used for indoor soccer. An 8,000-square-foot indoor pool, 25 meters long with 6 lanes, is one highlight of the YMCA. Swim lessons, water aerobics, and lap times are available. A hot tub can accommodate up to 10 people. Another highlight is the outdoor skate park: With more than 14,000 square feet of quarter pipes, bank ramps, pyramids, and a "tot lot" for little tykes, this is a challenging, state-of-the-art skate park. A concrete bowl section with a snake run completes the park. Day passes and week passes are available for the skate park.

The Y also has an outdoor water park that features two swimming pools. The upper pool is known as the deep well pool, with a depth of 12 feet and a 1-meter platform diving board. An area in this 150-gallon pool is designated for water sports like water polo and volleyball. The lower pool is known as the family pool and has a zero-grade entry. Two 25-yard lap lanes are available for recreational swimming. There's also a hydrotherapy area, as well as a very fun 20-foot waterslide.

Wellness programs and family programs, such as Parents Night Out, are available, as is a nursery where children are actively stimulated while parents work out. Children and youth sports leagues include soccer, hockey, basketball, volleyball, and wrestling, and there are adult basketball and volleyball leagues. Call for membership rates. Day passes are issued for most of the facility, except to the outdoor pool which is restricted during mid-March to October 1 to members of other YMCAs who have a membership card with them. Other YMCA members are charged a fee, and access is limited in summer.

Roanoke Island

NAUTICS HALL HEALTH & FITNESS COMPLEX, US 64, Manteo; (252) 473-2101. A competition-size, indoor heated pool is the centerpiece of this health club at the Elizabethan Inn, where water aerobics, swimming lessons, and lap times are offered throughout the year. There's a workout room with Nautilus and Paramount equipment, free weights, Stairmasters, treadmills, and an aerobicycle. Low-impact and step aerobics instruction is available daily. Other amenities include an outdoor pool, a hot tub, a racquetball court, sundecks, a sauna, and massage therapy on the premises. Nautics Hall is open from 6 a.m. to 9 p.m., Monday through Friday, and from 9 a.m. to 9 p.m. on summer weekends. On Sunday during the off-season, hours are 9 a.m. to 5 p.m. Monthly memberships cost $50 per person.

Hatteras Island

THE FORTS STRENGTH & FITNESS, 50448 NC 12, Frisco, (252) 305-9899; thefortstrengthandfitness.com. Small fitness center offering personal service and expert fitness advice.

RAISE THE BAR GYM & FITNESS, 40618 NC 12, Avon; (252) 986-5047; raisethebaravon.com. The only fitness center on the Outer Banks open 24 hours.

Ocracoke Island

ANGIE'S GYM, 141 Sand Dollar Rd.; (252) 928-2496; angies-gym.com. Ocracoke's only fitness center, Angie's Gym is a self-service gym. Membership is required to use the facilities.

BIKING

The Outer Banks is a bike rider's paradise, a place where there is something for everyone. Multi-use paths are ideal for families. Wide shoulders specifically designed for bike riders line many of the roads making longer rides safer and much easier. Looking to go off-road or a good place for fat tires with gears? Check out Kitty Hawk Woods or the dirt roads running through Nags Head Woods. Buxton Woods on Hatteras Island also allows bikes on its paths, but the paths are often very sandy. Looking for a real challenge? It is possible to ride all the way from the Currituck Beach Lighthouse in Corolla to the Hatteras Ferry Dock on multi-use paths and wide shoulder along the highways designed for bike riders. The new Marc Basnight Bridge has bike lanes on both sides of the road. The view from the top in a car is amazing. The view from the top on a bike would be absolutely breathtaking.

A couple of tips when riding a bike on the Outer Banks: Remember that thing about the Wright Brothers coming to the Outer Banks to learn about flight because of the constant winds? It wasn't hyperbole. The wind here is a constant. Try to go out, if at all possible, riding into the wind on any trip longer than five miles. You'll thank us for that advice on the return leg of your ride.

Although the Outer Banks is mostly flat, there are some hills—actually dunes and relict dunes left over from a few thousand years ago. The beach cruisers with the fat tires and big seat is great for just pedaling along the beach road or short trips. For longer rides a bike with gearing to help get up some of those hills is preferred.

Finally…wear a helmet and put your cell phones away.

While there is little crime on the Outer Banks, bicycles do disappear. Lock up carefully, and never leave your bike parked overnight in a front yard or in an easily accessed spot. If your bike is stolen, call the local police. Sometimes bikes are taken on nocturnal joy rides and later found by police, so call them before you panic. It's also a good idea to record your bike's serial number for identification purposes.

Popular Bike Rides

Corolla. Currituck County has invested heavily in creating multi-use paths that parallel NC12. Any of the paths are suitable for all ages. There are some break in the paths that put riders on the shoulder of NC12. Any experienced rider should have no trouble navigating the shoulders. However, the shoulders are not recommended for younger riders.

Duck. Almost anywhere in the town. The Town of Duck has built bike paths that parallel NC12. There also a multi-use path. The bike path is ideal for older riders who have good control of their bikes because it is right next to the road. For those riders it's wonderful because you're not constantly asking people to get out of your way. The mule-use path is better for younger riders. Duck has plans to extend the bike path to the north end of the town at the Currituck County line.

Kill Devil Hills, Bay Drive multi-use path. One of the most popular family paths. The path parallels Kitty Hawk Bay from the town line on the north to Canal Street. The path does continue to the Wright Brothers Monument, and bike riders can enter the park for free next to the airport.

Kitty Hawk, Woods Road multi-use path off US 158. Turn onto the Woods Road. Park at the David Pruitt Park just past the Dominion Power offices. Shaded by the canopy of Kitty Hawk Woods, this is one of the most beautiful rides of any of the multi-use paths. There are a couple of very small hills, but this is suitable for almost all riders. Bear right at Tillett, connect with W. Kitty Hawk Road and head back to the Austin Cemetery.

Kitty Hawk Woods, Ridge Road Trail. Follow direction for the Woods Road Multi-use path, but when you get to the Austin Cemetery, turn right and then right again onto Ridge Road. The end of Ridge Road is the trailhead. This is a moderately challenging mountain bike ride. There will be some carries over deadfall. Absolutely beautiful.

Pine Island, Pine Island Trail. This ride is suitable for any fat tired bike, including beach cruisers. The Pine Island Trail is a 21/2 mile packed earth path. At one time it was the road to Corolla before NC 12 was built. Park behind the Pine Island Raquet Club and head south to the trail. Any bike rider age 12 and up should be able to manage the trail.

Nags Head, Beach Road multi-use path. The Nags Head Multi-use path parallels the Beach Road for its entire length, extending all the way into South Nags Head and ending on NC 12 as it heads to the Marc Basnight Bridge. Crossing NC 12, the ride can be extended to the Bodie Island Lighthhouse. This is a pretty long ride. No hills, but it's a long ride as a round trip.

Nags Head Woods. Park at the visitor's center. Turn left out of the parking lot and have fun. These are all dirt roads suitable for off road bikes.

Roanoke Island, Manteo multi-use path. Park at the parking lot on either side of the William Umstead Bridge, old US 64. The multi-use path extends all the way into Manteo and is shaded for much of it.

Hatteras Island, Tri-Villages multi-use path. There is a multi-use path that Dare County has constructed that runs the length of Rodanthe, Waves, and Salvo to the Cape Hatteras National Park Service day use parking lot just south of Salvo. It's a pleasant ride suitable for all ages.

Bike Rentals

Beach Outfitters, NC 12, Ocracoke; (252) 928-6261

Bike Barn, Wrightsville Ave., Kill Devil Hills; (252) 441-3786

KDH Cycle, NC 12, MP 8½; (252) 480-3399

Kitty Hawk Cycle Co., NC 12, MP 2½, Kitty Hawk; (252) 261-2060

Lee Robinson General Store, Hatteras Village; (252) 986-2381

Ocean Atlantic Rentals, NC 12, Avon; (252) 995-5868

Ocean Atlantic Rentals, NC 12, Corolla Light Town Center, Corolla; (252) 453-2440

Ocean Atlantic Rentals, NC 12, Duck; (252) 261-4346

Ocean Atlantic Rentals, US 158, MP 9¾; (252) 441-7823

Slushie Stand, NC 12, Ocracoke; (252) 928-1878

BOWLING

Even the most dedicated sun—worshippers need an occasional afternoon or evening in air conditioned comfort.

NAGS HEAD BOWLING CENTER, US 158, MP 10, Nags Head; (252) 441-7077; obxbowlingcenter.com. Open for year-round league and recreational play, this is the Outer Banks' only bowling center. Twenty-four lanes are available for unlimited members of a party as well as a billiards room, pro shop, video arcade, and a cafe serving light meals, sandwiches, wine, beer, and hamburgers. Laser light and glow-in-the-dark bowling are offered at 10 p.m.

RECREATION

on Friday and Saturday nights. Nags Head Bowling is open from 10 a.m. to midnight Monday through Thursday; and 10 a.m. to 1 a.m. Friday through Sunday. Call for league information.

CLIMBING

KITTY HAWK KITES, NC 12, Monterey Plaza, Corolla; (252) 453-3685; Jockey's Ridge Crossing, US 158, MP 12½, Nags Head; (252) 449-2210; Hatteras Landing, NC 12, Hatteras; (252) 986-1446; kittyhawk.com. If you're itching to climb, try one of Kitty Hawk Kites/Carolina Outdoors's climbing walls. Two climbs and basic instruction cost around $7 per person. Rappelling equipment, climbing shoes, and ropes are all part of the package. In the Nags Head store, scale the 22-foot-high wall with four main routes and an overhang for extra challenges. At Monterey Plaza, there's a 25-foot climbing wall with four main routes and an overhang. The Nags Head location is open year-round, but only on weekends in winter. The climbing wall in the Nags Head location is indoors, while the walls at Corolla and Hatteras are outside.

The Casey R. Logan Disc Golf Course in Kill Devil Hills is a beautiful but challenging course.

DISC GOLF

CASEY R. LOGAN DISC GOLF COURSE, 120 Veterans Dr., Kill Devil Hills; (252) 449-5300; kdhnc.com/833/Disc-Golf-Course. A beautiful, challenging 18-hole disc golf course laid out beneath the towering trees of a maritime forest. Novices play the yellow tees; more experienced try the red tees. The course is at the end of a gravel road. Go to First Flight Middle School and look for the road to the right of the football field. Late spring, summer and early fall—insect repellant is recommended.

DOLPHIN TOURS, BOAT RIDES & PIRATE TRIPS

Most Outer Banks boat cruises are included in the **Recreation** chapter. However, a few unusual ventures are mentioned here. These trips, of course, are weather dependent and available only during warmer spring and summer months. Reservations are recommended for each of these tours. Unlike sailing and more participatory water adventures, you don't have to be able to swim to enjoy these activities, and you probably won't even get wet on board these boats as they ply the shallow sounds.

Nags Head

NAGS HEAD DOLPHIN WATCH, US 64, Nags Head–Manteo Causeway; (252) 449-8999; nagsheaddolphinwatch.com. If you're interested in bottlenose dolphins, this is the best way to get to know more about them. Nags Head Dolphin Watch is run by a team of independent dolphin researchers who conduct the trips to pay for their ongoing research. The team of expert naturalists leads dolphin watches through Roanoke Sound three times a day, six days a week, beginning the week before Memorial Day through the end of September. Two-hour tours are given on a speedy covered pontoon boat holding 36 people. Along the way you'll see bottlenose dolphins and learn about their fascinating feeding and social behavior and also about local ecology, history, and wildlife. The trained naturalists take photos of the dolphins' dorsal fins on every trip, and they call dolphins they see by name.

Roanoke Island

CRYSTAL DAWN, US 64, Nags Head–Manteo Causeway, Pirate's Cove Marina, Manteo; (252) 473-5577; crystaldawnheadboat.com. Sunset cruises around Roanoke Island take place every evening except Sunday throughout the summer on this sturdy, 2-story 65-foot vessel that accommodates 100 passengers. Trips include commentary about the Outer Banks, while the boat cruises past Andy Griffith's house, Roanoke Island Festival Park, and Jockey's Ridge. The boat departs at 6:30 p.m., returning about 90 minutes later. This is also a fishing headboat.

DOWNEAST ROVER, Manteo Waterfront Marina, Manteo; (252) 473-4866; downeastrover.com. A 55-foot topsail schooner, the Downeast Rover tall ship is a modern reproduction of a 19th-century sailing vessel. Two-hour cruises onto the placid waters of Roanoke Sound delight passengers with views of dolphin, osprey, heron, and seabirds. A hands-on adventure is also possible on this lovely boat: Passengers may help trim the sails and take a turn at the wheel. Tickets can be purchased on the *Downeast Rover,* which also has a ship's store and restroom on board. Deck seating and a below deck lounge are available. Reservations are recommended, but not required. Private charters for weddings, parties, and other special occasions are available. The *Downeast Rover* sails from early spring to late fall.

OUTER BANKS CRUISES, Queen Elizabeth Ave., Manteo; (252) 473-1475; outerbankscruises.com. Outer Banks Cruises offers dolphin tours, sightseeing tours, and evening cruises aboard the 53-foot covered pontoon boat *Capt. Johnny,* which can accommodate 49 passengers. The dolphin-watch tours are offered in Roanoke Sound from June through October, and ninth-generation native Capt. Stuart Wescott has a knack for finding the playful mammals. He even recognizes many of them by their fins and knows the names given them by local researchers. Dolphin sightings are guaranteed: If you don't see any on your trip, you are given a rain check for a free ride another time. The shrimp and crab cruise is educational, fun, and very popular. Evening cruises are available by charter; call for schedules and rates. The *Capt. Johnny* is docked on the Manteo waterfront next to the little bridge that heads to Roanoke Island Festival Park.

Hatteras Island

MISS HATTERAS AND *CAP 'N CLAM,* NC 12, Oden's Dock; (252) 986-2365; hatterasfishingcaptain.com. The *Cap N Clam* is a fishing headboat that also offers family-style pirate cruises that are a hit with the kids. The pirate cruise is Wednesday, Thursday, and Friday in summer from 6 to 7 p.m. The crew dresses as pirates and tells tales about Blackbeard and the area's pirate history as you cruise around Pamlico Sound. Complimentary swords and eye patches are given to every passenger. Cruises are available June through September. The boat can hold 40 people.

RECREATION

Ocracoke

THE WINDFALL II, NC 12, The Community Store Docks; (252) 928-7245; schoonerwindfall.com. Sail around Blackbeard's former haunts aboard this gaff-rigged schooner that seats up to 30 passengers. One-hour cruises depart from the Community Store docks several times daily during summer months. Call for the schedule.

GO-KARTS

If you're looking for a way to race around without getting a speeding ticket, several go-kart rental outlets offer riders a thrill a minute on exciting, curving tracks. Drivers have to be at least 12 years old to take the wheel at most of these places, but younger children are often allowed to strap themselves in beside adults to experience the fast-paced action.

COROLLA RACEWAY, NC 12, Timbuck II Shopping Village, Corolla; (252) 453-9100; corollaraceway.com. Corolla Raceway is the sister track of Nags Head Raceway. In Timbuck II Shopping Village, it features one large track with 16 cars. The go-kart raceway is open Easter through November. Corolla Raceway also has freestanding, gas-powered bumper cars. For more entertainment a family arcade is on-site. Summer hours are 10 a.m. until 11 p.m. daily.

HANG-GLIDING

The closest any human being will ever get to feeling like a bird is by flying beneath the brightly colored wings of a hang glider, with arms outstretched and only the wind all around. Lessons are available for fliers of all ages. Just watching these winged creatures soaring atop Jockey's Ridge or catching air lifts above breakers along the Atlantic is enough to make bystanders want to test their wings.

KITTY HAWK KITES, US 158, MP 13, Nags Head; (252) 441-4124; kittyhawk.com. Kitty Hawk Kites, the country's most popular hang-gliding school, offers various ways to learn how to fly. The company's headquarters, in Nags Head across from Jockey's Ridge State Park, face the main training site on the largest sand dune in the East. Here learn to fly solo 5 to 15 feet over the soft, forgiving sand, or soar through the clouds at altitudes up to 2,000 feet with an instructor. Either method, offered at various locations along the Outer Banks, is an exhilarating experience you'll never forget and undoubtedly will return home to brag about. If hang-gliding has kindled your desire to fly, Kitty Hawk Kites can also help you train to become a certified pilot. A number of packages are designed to help you achieve your goal. This school, the world's largest, has taught more than 250,000 students to fly since 1974. No experience is

Learning to Hang-glide on Jockey's Ridge State Park in the Outer Banks.
JillLang/GettyImages

necessary, and there are no age limitations. As long as you weigh within the parameters, you can fly! Tandem hang-gliding instruction is offered at the Currituck Airport. There are no age restrictions and no minimum weight requirement for tandem instruction, which is also accessible to the disabled. Kitty Hawk Kites offers two methods of instruction—by plane or boat. Reservations are required for most recreation, so be sure to call ahead. Discount packages are available. Ask about fun and exciting events for adventure enthusiasts of all ages throughout the season!

> i The oldest continuous hang-gliding competition in the country is held at Jockey's Ridge State Park. Kitty Hawk Kites sponsors the **Annual Hang Gliding Spectacular and Air Games**, which began in 1973. Visit kittyhawk.com/event/hang-gliding-spectacular/about/ for more information.

KITE FLYING

Kite flying is not what it used to be. Thanks to modern technology, today it's an adventurous, interactive activity, even a competitive sport. And the Outer Banks is the perfect place to try your hand at it, since one of the top kite stores in the world, Kitty Hawk Kites, is here. There are plenty of open spaces to fly kites on the Outer Banks, though Jockey's Ridge State Park in Nags Head is the absolute best because it offers acres unobstructed by power lines and trees.

FLYING SMILES KITES, Corolla Light Town Center, Corolla; (252) 453-8442; flyingsmileskites.com. A small but very well-stocked kite store right across from the Currituck Lighthouse and the grounds of the Whalehead Club. The staff is pleasant, professional and very knowledgeable.

KITTY HAWK KITES, US 158, MP 13, Nags Head; (252) 441-4124; kitty hawk.com. Offering an enormous range of kites, from the backyard variety to competition style (which comes with an instructional video), the Kitty Hawk Kites Jockeys Ridge Crossing store is the largest and most complete kite store on the Outer Banks. The staff is knowledgeable about what they sell, and they can help you pick out just the right kite for your skill level. In addition to lessons and repairs, they offer kite-making workshops in summer. There are several locations of Kitty Hawk Kites on the Outer Banks, but the Nags Head location across from Jockey's Ridge has the largest selection. This company hosts several kite-flying events throughout the year, including the annual Outer Banks Stunt Kite Competition and Festival at Jockey's Ridge in October. See the **Annual Events** chapter for more kite events.

MOVIE THEATERS

On some steamy summer afternoons or those rainy Saturday nights, there's no better place to be than inside a dark, air conditioned movie theater, catching the latest flick with a companion. First-run movies are offered at most Outer Banks theaters. Popcorn, candy, and sodas are, of course, sold at all movie houses.

Corolla

COROLLA MOVIES, 815 E Ocean Trl., Monterey Plaza; (252) 453-2999; corollamoviebistro.com. Small four screen multiplex next to the Corolla Food Lion. Open Seasonally.

Kill Devil Hills

RC THEATRES, US 158, MP 6½; (252) 441-5630; rctheatres.com. This multiplex cinema houses 10 screens. Films are shown seven days a week in season from 2 p.m. until midnight. On summer days when the weather is bad, the theater adds a rainy day showing at 11 a.m.

Roanoke Island

PIONEER THEATRE, 113 Budleigh St., Manteo; (252) 473-2216; face book.com/Pioneer-Theatre-Manteo-NC. The nation's oldest theater operated continuously by one family, the Pioneer is filled with nostalgia and smells of just-buttered popcorn. And it's been showing flicks since 1934. For the inexpensive admission price—and the old-fashioned feel of the place—it can't be beat. Even the popcorn, sodas, and candy are a great deal. The Pioneer is open year-round. All movies start at 8 p.m. daily, and ticket prices are very reasonable. Listings change weekly on Friday; call for a synopsis of the current show or check the Facebook page. See the **Attractions** chapter for more information.

NATURE TRAIL HIKES

The Outer Banks is home to several diverse ecosystems that house a wide variety of wildlife. If you love nature, you'll love the many self-guided nature trails that allow you to see the diversity of the Outer Banks up close. You can hike in wildlife refuges, across sand dunes, and through maritime forests. The National Park Service offers some guided walks; call (252) 473-2111 or visit nps.gov/caha for more information.

Corolla

AUDUBON WILDLIFE SANCTUARY, Pine Island. An unmarked trail leads through this 2,600-acre wildlife sanctuary, a protected habitat for birds, deer, rabbits, and a variety of plants. Park at the Sanderling Inn to access the 2.5-mile soundside path through a portion of the sanctuary. There are two viewing platforms along the trail that overlook the Currituck Sound.

CURRITUCK BANKS TRAIL. About three quarters of a mile past the village of Corolla heading north, NC 12 takes a 90 degree bend to the right. At that bend there is a small parking lot that that is the trailhead to explore the Currituck Estuarine trails. There is a gate that leads to a boardwalk. The gate must remain closed at all times. The Corolla Wild Horse herd does come into the reserve from time to time and the horses must be kept away from the heavily traveled areas of Corolla.

Crossing wetlands and swamp and bordered by towering pine trees the boardwalk is a very easy half mile stroll to Currituck Sound. The view at the end is wonderful so bring a camera.

A little more adventurous, but still a very easy walk through the woods, is the three quarter mile Maritime Forest Trail. Look for some steps with a sign marking the trail on the right side of the boardwalk about 200 yards from the gate. A good pair of sandals—not flip-flops—or walking shoes is fine for this trek. Eight years of age and up, should be fine be able to navigate the path. The trail, marked by blue-topped posts, winds through the forest, passing through one of the most spectacular groves of live oak on the Outer Banks. Squirrels are abundant and there are lots of birds around.

In spring, summer, and fall, insect repellant is a necessity.

Kitty Hawk

KITTY HAWK WOODS. The two easiest trailheads to find are at the end of Birch Lane on the east side of the Reserve and the Ridge Road Trailhead. Ridge Road is off Tillett Street which connects with the Woods Road. Go to the end of Tillett and turn right at the Austin Cemetery. Turn Right again onto Ridge Road. Go to the end of Ridge. The wooden barrier is the entrance to Kitty Hawk Woods. The Ridge Road Trail is a loop trail that connects with the Barlowe Trail.

The Birch Trail is about a mile and a half long. It is not a loop trail, so you will return on the same path. Birch Lane is off US 158 about a half mile past the end of the Wright Memorial Bridge.

All of the paths are an easy walk. There may be some dead fall requiring a little bit of a scramble, but there are no real barriers to stop anyone. Suitable for children 10 and older. Bug repellant will be needed.

Nags Head

JOCKEY'S RIDGE STATE PARK. Climbing the tallest sand dune on the East Coast is a challenging hike, but two nature trails wind through the lower regions of the dune. The Soundside Nature Trail is an easy 45-minute walk, and the Tracks in the Sand Trail is a 1.5-mile walk. Start at the state park visitor center at MP 12 in Nags Head.

NAGS HEAD WOODS ECOLOGICAL PRESERVE. Part of the Nature Conservancy, Nags Head Woods is a preserved maritime forest with diverse flora and fauna. There are more than 5 miles of trails through forest, dunes, swamp, and pond habitats. Some of the trails are surprisingly rugged. You'll also see 19th-century cemeteries. For maps and start locations, go to the visitor center at 701 West Ocean Acres Dr. in Kill Devil Hills or call (252) 441-2525.

Roanoke Island

FREEDMEN'S TRAIL. This 2-mile trail commemorates the history of the Freedmen's Colony, a Roanoke Island community that provided a safe haven for freed slaves during the Civil War. Access to the trail is near the Elizabethan Gardens entrance, and exhibits are at the end of the trail on Roanoke Sound. Call the National Park Service for information at (252) 473-5772.

MARSHALL AND GUSSIE COLLINS WALKWAY. Located at the Dare County Government Complex off Old US 64, the Collins Walkway is a tribute to a prominent African-American couple whose children donated the land the complex now occupies. There are two components to the trail—a short fitness trail and a longer two mile trail.

The three mile trail is not too exciting at first, passing behind government buildings, but it soon enters overhanging trees and parallels an old canal. The trail winds its way to the sound and underneath the Virginia Dare Bridge, eventually coming to the Outer Bank Visitors Bureau Visitor's Center. The trail eventually finds its way to the Coastal Studies Institute.

The trail is packed dirt and quite wide. Suitable for almost anyone.

THOMAS HARIOT NATURE TRAIL, Fort Raleigh. This trail winds through a heavily wooded area from the Fort Raleigh National Historic Site to Roanoke Sound. Along the way are several interpretive markers with Hariot's descriptions of Roanoke Island in the 16th century. Call the Fort Raleigh National Historic Site at (252) 473-5772 for information.

Mainland

ALLIGATOR RIVER NATIONAL WILDLIFE REFUGE. Two trails lead through this refuge. Sandy Ridge Wildlife Trail starts at the south end of the dirt Buffalo City Road. The trail, a half mile out and a half mile back, has footpaths and a boardwalk. Creef Cut Wildlife Trail starts on US 64 at the intersection with Milltail Road. A kiosk with parking marks the trailhead. It's also a half mile out and back. Additionally, it has a fishing dock, an overlook, and a boardwalk. Both trails are wheelchair accessible. Call (252) 473-1131 for information.

Bodie Island

BODIE ISLAND DIKE TRAIL AND POND TRAIL. Starting at the Bodie Island Lighthouse, two trails wind through marsh and wetlands to the sound. Call the light station at (252) 441-5711 for information.

Pea Island

PEA ISLAND NATIONAL WILDLIFE REFUGE. North Pond Trail starts behind Pea Island Visitor Center and leads hikers on a half-mile, 30-minute walk around the refuge. The quarter-mile Salt Flats Trail starts at the north end of North Pond Trail. These are favorite walks for birders year-round, but especially in late fall and winter when migrating swans, ducks, and geese winter here. Call (252) 987-2394 for information.

Hatteras Island - Buxton

BUXTON WOODS NATURE TRAIL. Starting at Cape Point Campground, this 0.75-mile trail leads through maritime forest, across dunes, and into freshwater marshes. Small plaques along the way explain the fragile maritime forest eco system.

A flock of red-winged blackbirds and two brown cowbirds perch on a snag in the Pea Island National Wildlife Refuge. Joesboy/GettyImages

Ocracoke Island

HAMMOCK HILLS NATURE TRAIL. This 0.75-mile trail, about a 30-minute walk, leads through the salt marsh and forest. The trailhead is north of the village on NC 12; signs direct you to it. Call the Ocracoke Island Visitor Center at (252) 928-4531 for information.

Portsmouth Island

PORTSMOUTH ISLAND. This ghost-town island is accessible only by boat, but once you get there you'll find numerous trails that lead you on a fascinating exploration of this island, past abandoned but restored buildings. A 2-mile-long trail leads from the village to the beach through the heart of the island. Call Cape Lookout National Seashore for information at (252) 728-2250.

TENNIS

Many cottage rental developments throughout the Outer Banks have private tennis courts for their guests. If you don't own a racquet or left yours back on the mainland, you can rent one by the day or week from Ocean Atlantic Rentals (see the "Weekly & Long-Term Cottage Rentals" section in the **Accommodations** chapter). Outdoor public tennis courts include the following free courts:

KILL DEVIL HILLS. Two hard-surface courts are located near the Kill Devil Hills Fire Department at MP 6 on US 158, and four hard-surface courts are beside the Kill Devil Hills Water Plant on Mustian Street.

NAGS HEAD. A public court is off US 158 at MP 10½.

PINE ISLAND RACQUET CLUB, NC 12, between Corolla and Duck; (252) 453-8525. Home to the Outer Banks' only indoor tennis courts, Pine Island is 2.5 miles north of the Sanderling Inn. It is open to the public year-round for recreational play, and several tournaments are held each season. Three hard-surface courts are under a vaulted roof for air conditioned or heated comfort, while two clay courts and two platform tennis courts are outdoors. Restroom, locker, and shower facilities are included. Pine Island also has two ball machines, a radar gun for timing serves, and a videotape analysis machine to help improve your game. Tennis pro Rick Ostlund and his assistant Betty Wright teach clinics for adults and children and offer individualized instruction at any skill level. The pro shop sells racquets, clothes, and tennis accessories and provides stringing services. Reservations are suggested for both indoor and

RECREATION

outdoor courts. Pine Island is open every day but Christmas from 9 a.m. off-season and 8 a.m. in season.

ROANOKE ISLAND. Courts are available at Manteo High School on Wingina Avenue and at Manteo Middle School on US 64/264 after school hours.

HATTERAS ISLAND. Courts are available at Cape Hatteras School on NC 12 in Buxton after school hours.

Fishing

If fishing is your passion, these barrier islands should be enough to send you reeling. Situated as we are in the Atlantic, not only do we have fabulous close-range ocean and inlet fishing but we're so close to the Gulf Stream and its bounty that offshore trips are just as popular. Half-day and full-day charters are available year-round, or if you're a seasoned boater with an ocean-worthy vessel, you can make the trip yourself. If you're looking to spend only a couple of hours angling, you can surf fish along nearly 100 miles of wide, sandy beaches, or you can wet a line at any one of a number of fishing piers—and that's just covering the ocean. Our sound waters are home to numerous finned species, and interior freshwater ponds are stocked with fish. Outer Banks angling is the stuff of which dreams are made.

OVERVIEW

The International Game Fish Association lists 92 world records for fish caught in Outer Banks waters, though some of those are now retired. These record holders include a 405-pound lemon shark caught off of Buxton, a 67-pound amberjack caught in Oregon Inlet, a 41-pound bluefish, and a 72-pound red drum landed off Hatteras. A 348-pound bluefin tuna was caught in Hatteras waters as well, along with record—size black sea bass, Spanish mackerel, oyster toadfish, bigeye tuna, kingfish, and sheepshead landed in waters from Kill Devil Hills to Ocracoke. Even if you don't tip the scales with a record-breaking catch, you're bound to fill your coolers with anything from albacore to wahoo. Depending upon the season, where you fish, and your choice of bait, you'll also find speckled trout, gray trout, flounder, striped bass (or rockfish), black drum, largemouth bass, tautog, cobia, a variety of pan fish, and the big attraction, billfish.

You might think that the variety here draws expert anglers, hence the great catches. Chances of a good catch are enhanced by physical conditions existing here that don't exist anywhere else. And that's no fish story! We outline these characteristics in the offshore section that follows.

Another factor that hugely influences the catch is our charter fleets. Many consider the local sportfishing boats, called Carolina boats, the most beautiful in the world, and these vessels house the complete package of brains, talent, and beauty. Our experienced captains are without peer, and their charter mates will awe you with their knowledge, their skill, and the manner in which they work. Some mates move as if their actions are choreographed: simultaneously working lines, assisting members of the fishing party, keeping the captain apprised

of catches in progress, arranging poles, gaffing fish, and encouraging you to keep reeling when it feels as if your arm just won't manage another revolution. A good mate is worth his or her weight in gold.

While anyone who's ever gone fishing knows you can't predict catches, the local charter boat captains know what species may be in the area, and they will guide you. Charters leave the docks for inshore and offshore fishing every day that the weather permits. When you call to book a boat, you may find it hard to decide what kind of trip to choose unless you've fished before. Booking agents at each marina will help you.

In the following sections we describe offshore and inshore angling, backwater, surf, fly, and pier fishing. Offshore trips generally leave the docks at 5:30 a.m. and return no later than 6 p.m. Inshore trips are half-day excursions that leave twice daily, generally at 7 a.m. and again around noon. Intermediate trips can last all day but generally don't travel as far as the Gulf Stream.

PERMITS

If you decide to fish without a guide or charter captain, the North Carolina Division of Marine Fisheries (800-682-2632) is a wealth of information. It's your resource for all available licenses, including recreational, commercial gear, and standard commercial licenses. A license to land flounder is available only through this Morehead City office. The division publishes an annual recreational-fishing handbook, the *North Carolina Coastal Waters Guide for Sports Fishermen*, a comprehensive guide to licenses, limits, and sizes. The helpful staff will also direct you to the appropriate contacts for obtaining federal permits for tuna and other controlled species.

For information on freshwater fishing permits and regulations, you'll need to contact the North Carolina Wildlife Resources Commission in Raleigh. The number for hunting and fishing licenses is (919) 662-4370. A regulations digest is available at sporting goods stores and tackle shops. Call either Wildlife Resources or the North Carolina Division of Marine Fisheries for information on motorboat registration. Official weigh stations are listed toward the end of this chapter.

OFFSHORE FISHING

The Outer Banks is famed as the Billfish Capital of the World. The Outer Banks waters are home to an incredible number of billfish—white and blue marlin and sailfish. These fighting fish are caught from spring through early fall, with peak catches for blue marlin in June and peak catches for white marlin and sailfish in August and September. To protect the species, billfish are almost always caught and released. You still get bragging rights for your released fish, though; the mate flies one flag per released billfish on the outriggers of the boat so everyone at the dock sees how many your party reeled in that day.

Next to billfish, some of the most pursued Gulf Stream fish are the yellowfin tuna and bluefin tuna. Other fish you're likely to catch are bigeye tuna, blackfin tuna, dolphinfish (mahimahi), king mackerel, wahoo, and mako shark.

The majority of Outer Banks captains who lead the way to offshore fishing grounds have been working these waters for years. Many are second- and third-generation watermen. They generally choose the daily fishing spot depending on recent trends, seasons, and weather. Expect to pay $900 to $1,500 for six people to charter a fishing excursion. Bluefin tuna trips cost a bit more. Gulf Stream charters leaving from Hatteras marinas tend to be less expensive than those near Oregon Inlet.

At about 50 miles wide and a half mile deep, the Gulf Stream has temperatures that rarely drop below 65 to 70 degrees, providing a comfortable habitat for a variety of sea life. The Gulf Stream flows at an average rate of 2.5 mph, at times quickening to 5 mph. This steady flow carries millions of tons

> i Always dress in layers for an Outer Banks fishing trip. Cold mornings have been known to transform into a warm afternoon on many fall and winter days. Of course, the opposite is also true, and gales and thunderstorms notoriously appear out of nowhere.

> **i** A fishing license is required to fish anywhere on the Outer Banks, including up to 3 miles offshore. If you are younger than age 16, you are exempt. July Fourth is a free fishing day in North Carolina. No license is required, but recreational size and possession limits are still enforced.

of water per second, continually pushing along sea life in its path, including fish, microscopic plants and animals, and gulfweed. Gulfweed lines the edge of the Gulf Stream when winds are favorable, creating a habitat for baitfish. You can pull up a handful of vegetation and find it teeming with miniature shrimp and fish. Anglers fish these "grass lines" as well as the warm-water eddies that spin off from the Gulf Stream. These warm pockets, which vary in size from 20 to 100 miles long by a half mile to a mile wide, are sometimes filled with schools of dolphin, tuna, and mako shark. The Gulf Stream passes closest to the North American continent at Cape Hatteras and is about 30 miles off the Outer Banks as it does so. It takes about two hours to get there from Oregon Inlet, and about an hour and a half from Hatteras Inlet, depending on the prevailing winds and the speed of your boat.

Catch-and-release fishing for bluefin tuna has anglers from across the globe traveling to Hatteras Island to partake in a bonanza that revived winter offshore charter fishing along the Outer Banks. In 1994 captains began noticing a massive congregation of bluefin tuna inhabiting the wrecks about 20 miles from Hatteras Inlet. The quantity of bluefin available and the frequency with which they bite are phenomenal. Bluefin fishing takes place on the southern Outer Banks, with trips leaving from Hatteras and Ocracoke marinas. Charter boats that ordinarily dock on the northern Outer Banks make their home base on Hatteras during the bluefin months. Many motels on Hatteras Island gladly stay open year-round to accommodate bluefin anglers.

Bluefin tuna weighing 200 to more than 800 pounds have been caught in these waters. These giants are a federally protected species, so anglers almost always must release them. Restrictions state that during bluefin tuna season anglers may keep one fish from 27 to 73 inches per boat per day. The length of the tuna season is determined annually by the National Marine Fisheries and is contingent on overall poundage caught.

Offshore fishing charters accommodate six people. If your party is shy of six, many times the booking agents or captain can hook you up with another small party. Anglers are expected to bring their own food and drinks on the trips. Coolers for any fish you want to take home can be left in your car at the dock to save room on the boat. Fish-cleaning facilities are available at all docks, and fish-cleaning services (for a fee) are available at most. Bring sunscreen and seasickness remedies. All bait, tackle, instruction, and advice are included in the price of your charter. Mates work for tips, so be sure to tip them at least 15 percent and up to 20 percent of the cost of your trip.

If you really love offshore fishing, consider entering one of the fishing tournaments listed in the **Annual Events** chapter. If you're not up for Gulf Stream fishing but want to see the fish, show up at these docks at about 4 p.m. to watch the boats unload their catches. You'll see Mahi-mahi, tuna, wahoo, cobia, and others, but no billfish since those are catch-and-release species.

INSHORE & SMALL-BOAT FISHING

Inshore opportunities strike the fancy of the novice or expert angler. Inshore generally refers to inlet, sound, lake, river, and some close-range ocean fishing on a boat.

Inshore captains generally book half-day trips but also offer intermediate all-day trips to take you farther out. If you're interested in bluefish, Spanish mackerel, cobia, king mackerel, bonito, trout, flounder, croaker, or red drum, book trips from virtually any marina. Half-day trips are a little easier on the pocketbook.

Spanish mackerel are a mainstay of the area. Ocracoke Island captains begin looking for them in late April and typically enjoy catches through late October. Farther north on the Outer Banks, Spanish mackerel usually arrive the first or second week in May, depending on the water temperature.

If it's flounder you're after, you can find these flat fish in both Hatteras and Oregon Inlets, in clear water. Anglers drift bottom rigs on medium-light spinning tackle. Croakers are found in the sounds around deep holes, oyster rocks, and sloughs.

Outer Banks anglers enjoy fishing for rockfish (also called striped bass or stripers) year-round. They are fun to catch and make a great-tasting dinner.

The ocean season for stripers is open year-round, but limits vary according to season. Though stripers are present in our waters year-round, the sound inhabitants are protected by restrictions. Since the sound fishing season fluctuates, call a tackle shop for up-to-date regulations. If you want to catch and release, go at it anytime.

When a cold snap hits the Chesapeake Bay area, stripers migrate down past Corolla into Oregon Inlet. November is one of the best months to fish for them around the Manns Harbor Bridge that connects Roanoke Island to the East Lake community. Anglers also fish in the winter for stripers behind Roanoke Island in East and South Lakes.

Currently a keeper must be a 12-inch total length minimum. Call your local tackle shop for more information.

Charter and commercial fishing boats share dock space at Wanchese Harbor.

OFFSHORE & INSHORE CHARTERS

To book offshore and inshore charters, contact one of the marinas listed here. You can request a certain boat and captain or let them offer you one. All of these marinas represent reputable, licensed captains. Call at least a month ahead, but earlier if you know your schedule. Fishing trips continue year-round. If everything is booked, ask to be put on a waiting list; somebody might cancel. You should know that it is the captain's call on whether to go out in inclement weather. Always defer to the captain's judgment. Prices are for full-day trips, unless specified otherwise.

Bodie Island

OREGON INLET FISHING CENTER, NC 12, Bodie Island; (252) 441-6301; oregon-inlet.com. The Oregon Inlet charter fishing fleet is a historic landmark on the Outer Banks. Most of the 45 sportfishing boats in this marina were locally made and have the famous Carolina flared bow. Some of the Outer Banks' most seasoned captains fish from this marina and have done so since it opened in the 1960s. Seven boats offer near-shore and intermediate trips from Oregon Inlet Fishing Center. Inlet intermediate trips of 5 to 10 miles are available.

Roanoke Island

PIRATE'S COVE YACHT CLUB, Nags Head–Manteo Causeway, Manteo; (252) 473-3906; fishpiratescove.com. Pirate's Cove is a world-class fishing center known for its boats, captains, and large-purse tournaments. By far the most modern marina on the Outer Banks, its prices reflect its high quality. Twenty-two sportfishing boats operate out of this marina, taking guests to the Gulf Stream or for an inshore adventure. Booking is centralized through the marina. Pirate's Cove Yacht Club is about a 15- to 20-minute boat ride from Oregon Inlet, the northernmost ocean-sound inlet on the Outer Banks. The Gulf Stream is about a two-hour ride from the inlet. Pirate's Cove is the central booking agent for five inshore boats. Trips run year-round. Pirate's Cove sponsors several fishing tournaments each year; see the **Annual Events** chapter.

TIDELINE CHARTERS, Thicket Lump Marina, Wanchese; (337) 660-1814. The 34-foot custom Carolina boat and 20-foot boat take full- and half-day inshore and intermediate trips.

Hatteras Island

ALBATROSS FLEET, Foster's Quay, Hatteras Village; (252) 986-2515; albatrossfleet.com. The Albatross Fleet of Hatteras, established by Capt. Ernal Foster in 1937, was the first charter fishing operation on the North Carolina coast. The original boat, the *Albatross*, still takes anglers to the Gulf Stream. The *Albatross* was designed by Foster to perfectly accommodate offshore fishing parties, and it was built across the sound in Harkers Island. The fleet now consists of three boats, all named *Albatross*, and is now operated by Foster's son, Ernal Foster Jr., who began working as a mate on his father's boat in 1958. The *Albatross I, II,* and *III,* all 44 feet, dock at Foster's Quay. One-hour evening cruises are available daily at 6 pm.

FREE AGENT SPORT FISHING CHARTERS, Oden's Dock, Hatteras; (252) 216-6765; freeagentsportfishing.com. Capt. Rick Caton has long been fishing the Outer Banks waters, both inshore and offshore, and offers a wide variety of trips. Year-round you can charter sound-fishing trips with Caton, who specializes in catching striped bass. He'll take you fly fishing or light-tackle fishing for trout, puppy drum, flounder, striped bass, and bluefish. Everything you need is furnished. Caton's inshore trips are offered on the 42-foot *Free Agent*. Caton also conducts shrimping and crabbing trips, inshore Spanish mackerel trolling trips, and light-tackle bottom fishing over wrecks for triggerfish and black sea bass. Or you can choose to anchor and chum for sharks, cobia, and king mackerel. Call for more information.

HATTERAS HARBOR MARINA, NC 12, Hatteras Village; (252) 986-2166; hatterasharbor.com. This marina represents about 20 vessels that take anglers to the Gulf Stream via Hatteras Inlet. The Gulf Stream is about a 90-minute boat ride from Hatteras Inlet. Inshore fishing trips are chartered year-round from this marina on one of six 24- to 26-foot boats. Half-day trips are available.

HATTERAS LANDING MARINA, NC 12, Hatteras Village; (252) 986-2077; hatteraslanding.com. Hatteras Landing Marina represents eight offshore fishing boats. Call for current pricing. If you don't have a full party, Hatteras Landing can put one together for you if you're willing to wait on standby.

ODEN'S DOCK MARINA, NC 12, Hatteras Village; (252) 986-2555; odensdock.com. The chaser sport fishing charter boat operates out of Oden's Dock and takes anglers offshore for a day of fishing. Oden's books inshore charters on five 22-foot boats and a 24-foot that each handle four people. These boats fish in the sound only. A larger 42-foot headboat operates in the sound or ocean. Guides are available.

TEACH'S LAIR MARINA, NC 12, Hatteras Village; (252) 986-2460; teachslair.com. Twenty-five boats operate out of Teach's Lair. Bluefin trips are popular. Teach's Lair books full day offshore charters and inshore charters on morning or afternoon half-day trips. Morning trips run from 7 a.m. to noon, and afternoon trips run from 12:30 to 5:30 p.m.

Ocracoke Island

ANCHORAGE INN & MARINA, NC 12, Ocracoke Village; (252) 928-6661; theanchorageinn.com. Four boats offer full-day offshore charters out of this marina. Full-day trips cost around $900 to $1,200. These boats use Ocracoke Inlet when heading to the Gulf Stream. Sunset trips and night fishing charters are also offered.

OFFSHORE & INSHORE HEADBOAT FISHING

Headboat fishing can give you a great fishing experience without the expense of chartering a private boat. Several large boats take parties into the intermediate waters (in the ocean, though not as far as the Gulf Stream) all day, while others ply the inshore waters for half days. Ocean trips typically track bottom species, such as black sea bass, triggerfish, tilefish, amberjack, snapper, tautog, grouper, and occasionally small sharks. The species vary slightly from north to south. Generally on these trips you're dropping a line down over artificial and natural reefs and wrecks, not trolling. Inshore trips ply the sounds and inlets and sometimes go several miles offshore to the wrecks on calm days. The trips usually yield croaker, trout, spot, flounder, sea mullet, blow toads, and pigfish. There is one headboat, the *Country Girl* out of Pirate's Cove, which takes trips to the Gulf Stream.

Headboats are built to accommodate a multitude of passengers, each person paying "by the head," hence the name. Open deck space from bow to stern holds anglers comfortably, and sometimes there is an enclosed cabin area. The boats are generally between 60 and 75 feet long and can hold up to 50 anglers. All gear and bait are supplied. All you have to bring is food, drinks, and sunscreen. Some boats provide snacks and drinks, so you should check when making reservations. You don't even need a fishing license. If you're new to fishing, the mates will help you with everything from baiting your hook to identifying your catch. Be sure to dress in layers if you're fishing any time other than summer. Mornings and evenings can be cool, even when days are warm.

Inshore headboat trips are the most suitable choice for families with young children, mainly because they're shorter. Deep-sea trips are full-day trips that can be as long as 8 to 10 hours, and the captain will not turn around except in a real emergency. Seasickness is not an emergency. Inshore trips are typically a half day. Watch the kids carefully on the boats. The decks are often slippery, so you should enforce a no-running policy. Plus these boats carry large crowds of people and fishing gear. Getting hooked can ruin a trip. That said, headboats are great places to teach children how to fish for a very small amount of money. You often see dolphins, birds, turtles, and sometimes whales on these trips.

Bodie Island

MISS OREGON INLET, Oregon Inlet Fishing Center, NC 12, Bodie Island; (252) 441-6301; oregon-inlet.com. *Miss Oregon Inlet* is a 65-foot headboat that offers half-day inshore fishing trips for around $36 per person or $26 for kids age 6 and younger. In early spring and fall, the boat makes one trip per day (except Sunday), leaving at 8 a.m. and returning at 12:30 p.m. From Memorial Day through Labor Day, there are two trips: 7 to 11:30 a.m. and noon to 4:30 p.m. On Tuesday and Friday try a twilight cruise from 5:30 to 7 pm. Buy tickets one day in advance, if possible, because the boat often fills up.

Roanoke Island

CRYSTAL DAWN and *COUNTRY GIRL*, Pirate's Cove Yacht Club, Nags Head–Manteo Causeway, Manteo; (252) 473-5577; crystaldawnheadboat .com. The *Crystal Dawn* is a 65-foot, 2-story vessel offering inshore (inlet and sound) bottom-fishing trips from May through October. The boat holds up to 55 passengers. All bait and tackle are provided, but you have to bring your own snacks and drinks. In peak season (Memorial Day to Labor Day), trips run from 7 a.m. to noon or 12:30 to 5 p.m. The rest of the time, the boat heads out from 8 a.m. to 1 p.m. *Crystal Dawn* also takes sightseeing trips in the evenings.

Country Girl heads offshore from 5 to 35 miles, depending on the weather and the fishing. This is a full-day trip, lasting from 7 a.m. to 4:30 p.m. Older children and teenagers are welcome, but younger children are not. *Country Girl* offers trips from May through October.

Hatteras Island

MISS HATTERAS and *CAP 'N CLAM*, Oden's Dock, NC 12, Hatteras Village; (252) 986-2365; odensdock.com. The *Miss Hatteras* headboat ties up at Oden's Dock in Hatteras Village and operates from February through November. She offers half-day fishing trips on Monday, Tuesday, and Thursday from 8 a.m. to noon, and Tuesday and Thursday from 1 to 5 p.m. On Wednesday, Friday, Saturday, and Sunday, she offers full-day bottom-fishing trips from 6:30 a.m. to 4:30 p.m. The boat accommodates 45 people. In late October and early November, she offers full-day king mackerel fishing trips. All gear is included in the cost of the trip, and a snack bar is on board. In the summer, when the *Miss Hatteras* is booked, Oden's Dock also offers the *Cap 'N Clam*, a 40-person-capacity headboat that conducts half-day, inshore sound, and inlet fishing trips. These trips run Monday through Saturday from 8 a.m. to noon and 1 to 5 p.m. The *Cap 'N Clam* is also host to Eco Tours on Tuesday and Friday, Pirate Tours for the family, and Dolphin Tours. Call for current rates.

THE STORMY PETREL II, Hatteras Marina. The *Stormy Petrel II* is a 61-foot boat built to accommodate up to 10 passengers. What makes her unique among all Outer Banks boats, is she is the only craft traveling to the Gulf Stream on birding trips. The Gulf Stream is the non-breeding ground for petrels and shearwaters, birds that only return to land to breed. Captain Brian Patteson is an international recognized expert for his work in taking scientists on birding expeditions to the Gulf Stream: He's also a heck of a charter captain when it comes to finding fish.

MARINAS

The Outer Banks is dotted with many marinas with slips, boat ramps, gas and diesel fuel, tackle, and supplies. Almost all offer fishing charters as well. We've listed the fishing opportunities available at marinas in the **Offshore & Inshore Headboat Fishing** category in this chapter. For information pertaining to slip rental, see the **Getting Here, Getting Around** chapter; and for information on amenities offered to boaters, such as boat ramps, gas, and supplies, see the **Water Sports** chapter.

BACKWATER FISHING

Fishing the backwaters means fishing the more-protected inland sounds, rivers, and lakes, either brackish or freshwater. The Croatan Sound, between Roanoke Island and the mainland, is a popular fishing spot for striped bass, also known as stripers or rockfish in these parts. Striper fishing is a year-round sport on the Outer Banks, though you can keep those caught in the sound only at certain times of the year. The Manns Harbor Bridge is renowned for its striper activity. Stripers congregate at the bridge, feeding around the pilings. They also feed over oyster bars located near the bridge. Be on the lookout for diving gulls and terns, which is a good identifying marker of the location of stripers. Both sides of the bridge have public parking and access for waders, but the western side has a marina with a boat-launch ramp. The Croatan Sound Bridge, just beyond the Manns Harbor Bridge, has proven itself as a striper-attracting structure, so you should try both bridges.

Backwater fishing also includes the Alligator River and South and East Lakes. You can troll, spin cast, bait cast, or fly fish year-round in the backwaters. You'll find an interesting mix of freshwater and saltwater species, including crappie, striped bass, largemouth bass, flounder, bream, sheepshead, drum, perch, croaker, spot, catfish, and trout. It all depends on the season.

If you'd like a guide, there are a few that offer backwater services. The fishing is so laid-back that you might find the guide throwing in a line with you. Since these waters are more protected and less prone to harsh offshore winds, you can often fish here when you can't elsewhere. This is a nice alternative to ocean fishing, and it's a good choice for families. Bring your camera. You might spot birds, deer, and bears on land and alligators in the water.

You don't have to hire a guide, though. You can launch your own boat from any number of local ramps (see the **Water Sports** chapter) or contact a tackle shop or marina for information.

> i When booking a fishing trip, ask about cash discounts. Occasionally charter captains will save you some money if you pay without swiping a credit card or debit card.

CUSTOM SOUND CHARTERS, Oden's Dock, Hatteras; (252) 986-2201; facebook.com/customsoundcharters. Light-tackle backwater trips are taken on the *Iron Will*, an 18-foot center-console. Capt. Rick Caton books trips on this boat in the spring and fall. Call for prices.

PHIDEAUX TOO, Manns Harbor; (252) 473-3059. Capt. V. P. Brinson uses a 150-hp Pathfinder to get you to the fish. Brinson offers spin-casting, fly rod, bait-casting, and trolling charters in lakes, sounds, and rivers. Fish for rockfish, trout, red drum, flounder, bass, bream, crappie, and perch. Call for prices.

FLY FISHING

The fly-fishing bug on the Outer Banks started in the 1960s and 1970s, when a few well-known fly anglers and locals cast flies into the surf for bluefish and were quite successful. In 1979 Chico Fernandez fly fished the Outer Banks, catching a white marlin. In 1981 he set an International Game Fish Association Fly Rod record with a 42-pound, 5-ounce red drum on a 12-pound tippet. Since then anglers have slowly discovered the Outer Banks' varied fly-fishing opportunities. Fly-fishing magazines and television shows now regularly feature the Outer Banks and its fly-fishing guides.

Fly anglers fish in the same places conventional anglers do. Fly anglers catch dolphin, tuna, and marlin in the Gulf Stream. They catch amberjack, mackerel, albacore, and cobia on inshore wrecks. They reap pompano and bluefish in the surf and stripers in the sounds. The most successful and accessible fly fishing is in the sounds, where you'll find speckled trout, stripers, red drum, bluefish, and Spanish mackerel.

It can be difficult to learn to fly fish the Outer Banks, especially the vast Pamlico and Roanoke Sounds. Hiring a guide is the quickest way to learn the area. If you prefer to go on your own, ask for advice at local tackle shops.

> **i** If you're going fishing without a local captain or guide, check on current fishing regulations before embarking on your trip. Size and bag limits change frequently, and fines for illegal fish can be substantial.

FLAT OUT FLY-FISHING & LIGHT-TACKLE CHARTERS, Oregon Inlet; (252) 449-0562; outerbanksflyfishing.com. Capt. Brian Horsley and Capt. Sarah Gardner are true insiders when it comes to Outer Banks fly fishing. Both halves of this fly-fishing duo are guides and well-known fishing writers.

Horsley's *Flat Out* and Gardner's *Fly Girl* dock at Oregon Inlet Fishing Center. They run near-shore fly-fishing/light-tackle charters from April through November, though they move both boats to Harkers Island on the southernmost Outer Banks during October and November for false albacore fishing. They fish the Pamlico, Roanoke, and Croatan Sounds for speckled trout, bluefish, puppy drum, little tunny, flounder, and cobia.

OUTER BANKS WATERFOWL, Kitty Hawk; (252) 261-7842; outerbanks waterfowl.com. Capt. Vic Berg runs sound and inlet fly- or spinning-tackle fishing trips. Everything you need is included, or if you like, you can bring your favorite tackle. Berg also offers instruction on fly or surf fishing. Family and group rates are available for lessons. Berg is also an experienced hunting guide who leads hunting trips that can yield many species of waterfowl. A typical bag of 10 ducks can contain seven different species. Berg's blinds are located between Oregon Inlet and Pea Island and have proven their success for more than 45 years. He also offers swan-hunting trips and is an outstanding bird carver.

SURF FISHING

Surf fishing is a popular Outer Banks pastime for the competitor or amateur alike. While there are miles of beach from which to cast a line, experienced local anglers say a surf caster's success will vary depending on sloughs, temperature, currents, and season. One of the hottest surf-casting spots on the Outer Banks is Cape Point, a sand spit at the tip of Cape Hatteras. Anglers often stand waist deep in the churning waters, dutifully waiting for red drum to strike.

About nine months out of the year, anglers can fish for red drum on the Outer Banks. The best time to catch big drum is mid-October through mid-November. During this period large schools of drum are feeding on baitfish called menhaden that migrate down the coastline. Cape Point is the hot spot for drum, but it tends to be a very crowded place to fish. A good second choice is the beach between Salvo and Buxton. But in the fall you can catch them from Rodanthe down to Hatteras Inlet. From mid-April through about the third week in May, red drum show up around Ocracoke Inlet, both in the ocean and shallow shoal waters at the inlet's mouth and also in the Pamlico Sound.

Serious drum anglers fish after dark for the nocturnal feeders. Insiders prefer a southwesterly wind with an incoming tide and water temperatures in the low 60s. Big drum are known to come close to the surf during rough weather. Puppy drum (or juvenile drum) are easier to catch than the adult fish. They show up in the surf after a northeast blow in late summer or early fall. Anglers use finger mullet with success as well as fresh shrimp (and we do mean fresh). Red drum are a regulated fish, both in size and limit. Call your local tackle shop for more information. If you're interested in learning more about red drum tag-and-release programs, call the Division of Marine Fisheries at (252) 473-5734 or (252) 264-3911.

There's a lengthy list of fish regularly caught at Cape Point. Common species include dogfish, bluefish, pompano, striped bass, and Spanish mackerel as well as bottom feeders such as croaker, flounder, spot, sea mullet, and both gray and speckled trout. More uncommon are tarpon, cobia, amberjack, jack crevalles, and shark weighing several hundred pounds.

Shoaling that takes place off Cape Hatteras makes Cape Point a haven for baitfish, and the influence of the nearby Gulf Stream and its warm-water jetties also contribute to excellent fishing. The beach accommodates many four-wheel-drive vehicles, and during peak season (spring and fall) it's packed with anglers. If you want to try fishing Cape Point, take NC 12 to Buxton and look for signs to vehicle access ramp 43. (For more information about driving on the beach, please see the **Getting Here, Getting Around** chapter.)

A section on surf fishing would not be complete without discussing bluefish. For years anglers enjoyed the arrival and subsequent blitzes of big bluefish during the Easter season and again around Thanksgiving. During a blitz, big blues chase baitfish up onto the beach in a feeding frenzy. This puts the blues in striking distance of ready surf casters. It's a phenomenal sight to watch anglers reel in these fat and ferocious fish one after the other. Anglers line up along the shore like soldiers, and many a rod is bent in that telltale C-shape, fighting a bluefish. Some days you can see a sky full of birds hovering, waiting to feast on the baitfish that the bluefish run toward the shore for.

The last few years the blues have not blitzed like they used to. As with most species, population figures (or at least landings) tend to rise and fall in cycles; perhaps they're tending toward a low point in the pattern. Maybe the big bluefin tuna, which feed on bluefish, are taking over these days, but blitz or not, you can usually catch some bluefish in the surf or in greater numbers offshore.

> **i** For a taste of offshore fishing from the comfort of your own sofa, tune in to *Wicked Tuna: North vs. South*, running on the National Geographic channel. Anglers compete from NC's Outer Banks and Gloucester, MA, to find out who can hook the most tuna. Check the National Geographic channel for air times.

PIER FISHING

Pier fishing is a true Outer Banks institution and has delighted anglers young and old for decades. The appeal is obvious: low cost and a chance to fish deeper waters without a boat. The variety of fish available also lures anglers. Depending on the time of year, you can catch croakers, dogfish, rockfish, spot, sea mullet, red drum, cobia, and occasionally a tarpon, king mackerel, sheepshead, or amberjack.

Bait and tackle are sold at each pier, or you can rent whatever gear you need. Avid anglers usually come prepared, but newcomers to the sport are always welcome on the pier, and staff are more than willing to outfit you and offer some fishing tips. Pier fishing is a good way to introduce kids to the sport. Many Outer Banks locals spent their youth on the pier soaking in know-how and area fishing lore. For instance, Garry Oliver, who owns the Outer Banks

Pier in South Nags Head, spent many a summer day at the Nags Head Fishing Pier when he was a lad. Today Garry is a member of an award-winning surf-casters team.

The Outer Banks has no oceanfront boardwalks, but the piers more than make up for it. The smells of salt air and creosote-treated lumber greet you as you walk the wide planks over the ocean water. Looking down between the cracks, you see the waves crashing beneath you. You don't have to fish to appreciate the piers. For a small fee you can just walk out on the piers to enjoy the vantage points.

AVALON FISHING PIER, NC 12, Kill Devil Hills; (252) 441-7494; avalonpier.com. Avalon Pier, in the heart of Kill Devil Hills, was built in the mid-1950s and is 705 feet long. The pier has lights for night fishing, a snack bar, a bait and tackle shop, ice, video games, and rental fishing gear. A busy place in season, the pier is open 24 hours a day. The pier house is open from 6 a.m. until midnight. The pier is closed December through mid-March. People with disabilities are admitted free.

AVON FISHING PIER, NC 12, Avon; (252) 995-5480; avonfishingpier .com. Avon Fishing Pier has a reputation for being a hot spot for red drum. The all-tackle world-record red drum, weighing in at 94 pounds, 2 ounces, was caught about 200 yards from the pier in 1984, and the record holds to this day. The pier opens at the beginning of April and remains open through Thanksgiving. Purchase or rent your fishing supplies here, buy sandwiches and drinks, and pick up nautical gifts, including T-shirts and sand mirrors.

JENNETTE'S PIER, NC 12, MP 16½; Nags Head; (252) 255-1501; ncaquariums.com/jennettes-pier. With a mantra of "Fishing, Family and Fun," Jennette's Pier tries to offer something for everyone. There's world-class fishing, unique educational programs and excellent opportunities for sightseeing from the 1,000-foot-long fishing pier, which was re-opened in 2011 after a complete renovation. In the past three seasons, anglers have caught plenty of cobia, big bull red drum, puppy drum, speckled trout, gray trout, monster bluefish, tailor blues, Spanish mackerel, king mackerel, sea mullet, flounder, a dolphin fish (Mahi-mahi) and more. Anglers can find everything they need for a day of fishing inside the pier house. Purchase a rod and reel combo, or rent one by the day for $10 (photo ID required). There's plenty of bait, rigs, lures, line and other fishing gear for sale as well as drinks, snacks and souvenir items. The pier has a blanket license for all anglers, so individuals do not need their own license. A daily fishing pass is good all day and night until the pier closes; call for hours as they change with the seasons. The pier staff offers a variety of fishing classes from family fishing to advanced fishing. Learn how to jig or pin-rig fish, attend a surf fishing workshop, or try the popular "Catch It, Clean It,

Part of the North Carolina Aquarium System, Jennette's Pier reaches 1,000 feet into the Atlantic Ocean creating great conditions for anyone fishing from the pier.

and Cook It." A handful of fishing tournaments are held throughout the year. Jennette's Pier is a state-of-the-art educational center and features wide, clean public beaches, free parking, and a bath house with outdoor showers. The pier is open year-round and is designed to be "clean and green."

KITTY HAWK FISHING PIER, NC 12, MP 1, Hilton Garden Inn, Kitty Hawk; (252) 261-1290. This privately owned pier was upgraded in 2008 as an amenity for guests staying at the Hilton Garden Inn. Anglers not staying at the Inn may also fish here. Check with Hilton Garden Inn for availability.

NAGS HEAD FISHING PIER, NC 12, MP 12, Nags Head; (252) 441-5141; nagsheadpier.com. This is one of the most popular fishing piers on the Outer Banks. It is 750 feet long and has its own bait and tackle shop. Enjoy night fishing, game tables for the kids, and a restaurant. The Pier House Restaurant features fresh seafood and wonderful views of the ocean. The restaurant serves breakfast, lunch, and dinner. (See the **Dining** chapter for more information.) The pier closes in December and reopens in March or April, depending upon whether the fish are biting. It is open 24 hours during the season.

OUTER BANKS PIER AND FISHING CENTER, NC 12, MP 18½, South Nags Head; (252) 441-5740; fishingunlimited.net. This 650-foot ocean pier was originally built in 1959 and rebuilt in 1962 after the Ash Wednesday storm. Owner Garry Oliver has all you need in the bait and tackle shop for a day of fishing along this stretch of beach. A 300-foot sound fishing and crabbing pier is also available on the Nags Head–Manteo Causeway. The piers are open 24 hours a day from Memorial Day until mid-October and closed from Thanksgiving through Easter. Call for rates. Snack at the pier's on-site oceanside deli.

RODANTHE FISHING PIER, NC 12, Rodanthe; (252) 987-2323; rodanthepierllc.com. After massive poundings by Hurricanes Dennis and Floyd, this pier collapsed in 1999. Even the land on which the pier house stood disappeared due to storm erosion. The land was refilled and in 2000 the pier reopened, a little farther back from its original location. The pier house sells drinks, snacks, sandwiches, tackle, and bait. The pier and pier house are open every day in the summer, 6 a.m. to 12 midnight from Memorial Day to Labor Day and 6 a.m. to 10 p.m. the rest of the season. The Rodanthe pier is closed January 1 through April 1.

> **i** When buying waders or boots, always buy them one-and-a-half sizes larger than your shoe size. The larger size will enable you to slip them off in the event that you step in a slough or fall overboard.

BAIT & TACKLE SHOPS

Full-service tackle shops are scattered from Corolla to Ocracoke. They are good sources for not only rods, reels, bait, and other fishing equipment and accessories, but also for tips on what's biting and where. You'll find bait and tackle at all Outer Banks fishing piers and most marinas, too. Just about every department store and general store on the barrier islands carries some sort of fishing gear, and many shops also offer tackle rental. You can ask for guide information at any one of the following shops.

Duck

BOB'S BAIT & TACKLE, NC 12; (252) 261-8589; bobsbaitandtackle.com. Stop into Bob's if you're looking for advice on where to catch the really big one. The old building is left over from Duck's early days, when a soundside dock out back was the distribution point for shiploads of fresh ocean fish. The shop carries a good supply of rods, reels, bait, and tackle. Bob's also books offshore charters and provides a hunting and fishing guide service.

Close-up

Citation Fish

Citation fish are caught in the waters off the Outer Banks every year. The North Carolina Division of Marine Fisheries manages the North Carolina Saltwater Fishing Tournament, which recognizes outstanding angling achievement. The tournament runs year-round. Other than charter boat captains and crews for hire, everyone is eligible for a citation fish award. Eligible waters include North Carolina sounds, surf, estuaries, and the ocean. This tournament is for the hook-and-line angler; use of electric or hydraulic equipment is not allowed. There is one award per species, and all fish must be weighed in at an official weigh station. Anglers receive a certificate after the close of the tournament. There is no registration fee. Following is a list of the area's weigh stations, where you can pick up a species list and receive rules for the tournament. Citations are also awarded for the catch and release of some species.

OFFICIAL WEIGH STATIONS

Corolla
- TW's Bait & Tackle, NC 12; (252) 453-3339

Duck
- Bob's Bait & Tackle, NC 12; (252) 261-8589

Kitty Hawk
- TW's Bait & Tackle, US 158, MP 4; (252) 261-7848

Kill Devil Hills
- Avalon Fishing Pier, NC 12, MP 6; (252) 441-7494

Nags Head
- Nags Head Fishing Pier, NC 12, MP 12; (252) 441-5141
- Outer Banks Pier & Fishing Center, NC 12, MP 18½; (252) 441-5740
- TW's Bait & Tackle, US 158, MP 10½; (252) 441-4807
- Whalebone Tackle, Nags Head–Manteo Causeway; (252) 441-7413

Manteo

- Pirate's Cove, Nags Head–Manteo Causeway; (252) 473-3906
- Salty Dawg Marina, Manteo, NC; (252) 473-3405

Oregon Inlet

- Oregon Inlet Fishing Center, NC 12, 8 miles south of Whalebone Junction; (252) 441-6301

Rodanthe

- Hatteras Jack, NC 12; (252) 987-2428
- Mac's Tackle & Island Convenience, NC 12; (252) 987-2239

Salvo

- Fishin' Hole, NC 12; (252) 987-2351

Avon

- Frank & Fran's Fisherman's Friend, NC 12; (252) 995-4171

Buxton

- Dillon's Corner, NC 12; (252) 995-5083
- Red Drum Tackle Shop, NC 12; (252) 995-5414

Frisco

- Frisco Rod & Gun, NC 12; (252) 995-5366
- Frisco Tackle, NC 12; (252) 995-4361

Hatteras Village

- Hatteras Harbor Marina, NC 12; (252) 986-2166
- Hatteras Island Fishing Pier, NC 12; (252) 987-2322
- Oden's Dock, NC 12; (252) 986-2555
- Pelican's Roost, NC 12; (252) 986-2213
- Teach's Lair Marina, NC 12; (252) 986-2460
- Willis Boat Landing, 57209 Willis Ln.; (252) 986-2208

Ocracoke

- Anchorage Inn & Marina, NC 12; (252) 928-6661
- O'Neal's Dockside Tackle Shop, NC 12; (252) 928-1111
- Tradewinds, NC 12; (252) 928-5491

Kitty Hawk

TW'S BAIT & TACKLE, US 158, MP 4; (252) 261-7848; twstackle.com.
TW's Bait & Tackle, next to the 7-Eleven in Kitty Hawk, is a great place to find the right stuff for your fishing adventure. Owner Terry "T. W." Stewart has been in business since 1981 and can sell you what you need, including ice and live bait. TW's also books inshore and offshore charter fishing trips. There is another location in Corolla (252-453-3339) at the Food Lion Shopping Center, but it's closed during January and February. The Kitty Hawk location stays open year-round. TW's has a Nags Head store at milepost 10½; call (252) 441-4807. The Nags Head location is open all year also.

Kill Devil Hills

STOP 'N' SHOP CONVENIENCE & DELI, NC 12, MP 8½; (252) 441-6105; stopnshopobx.com. Located on the Beach Road across from the Kill Devil Hills beach access, Stop 'N' Shop has about anything you might need for a day of fishing or a day at the beach. This is a full-service tackle shop, with fishing and beach items that include bait, tackle, local information, beer, ice, gas, and rental equipment. A surprising amount of goods are stocked for anglers, and you can pick up a sandwich from their popular deli. Stop 'N' Shop is open seven days a week year-round.

Nags Head

FISHING UNLIMITED, Nags Head–Manteo Causeway; (252) 441-5028; fishingunlimited.net. Fishing Unlimited specializes in fresh bait and is a full-service tackle shop. You can purchase live bait, custom rigs, and lures here as well as crabbing supplies, snacks, and drinks. Services include 16-foot outboard and 20-foot pontoon boat rentals. Fish or crab from the 300-foot Roanoke Sound pier. Rods and reels also available for rent. The shop is open from Easter until early December.

OCEANS EAST OBX, Nags Head–Manteo Causeway; (252) 441-7413; fishoceanseast.com. Oceans East is a full-service tackle shop offering ice, fresh bait, tackle, and reel repairs for Shimano, Tiagra, and TLD brands. The store is open year-round.

Hatteras Island

FISHIN' HOLE, NC 12; (252) 987-2351. Operating on the Outer Banks since 1976, The Fishin' Hole is a full-service tackle shop that sells live bait, tackle, beach supplies, groceries, and T-shirts. Rod and reel repairs for Daiwa, Penn, and other brands are available here. It's an official weigh station for the

North Carolina Beach Buggy Association. The shop is open from the end of March through mid-December.

FRANK AND FRAN'S FISHERMAN'S FRIEND, NC 12; (252) 995-4171; frankandfrans.vendecommerce.com. A full-service tackle shop and headquarters for the local Red Drum Tournament held every October, Frank and Fran's is an emporium of fishing gear. This is another official weigh station for the state and the North Carolina Beach Buggy Association.

DILLON'S CORNER, NC 12; (252) 995-5083; dillonscorner.com. Stop here for an assortment of tackle, including custom rods and bait. The shop also carries a wide selection of gifts, T-shirts, and lighthouse replicas (see the **Shopping** chapter). The shop offers rod repairs and has gas pumps. Dillon's Corner is open all year but has shorter hours in winter.

RED DRUM TACKLE SHOP, NC 12; (252) 995-5414; reddrumtackle.com. Get the latest in fishing information and select gear at Red Drum Tackle Shop. It offers everything you need in the way of custom rods, bait, and tackle, plus reel repairs. They're a Penn warranty center and official weigh station for the state, the North Carolina Beach Buggy Association, and the Cape Hatteras Anglers Club.

FRISCO ROD & GUN, NC 12; (252) 995-5366; friscorodandgun.com. Frisco Rod & Gun is a one-stop shop for everything you need for hunting or fishing trips. The owner calls it his "hobby gone wild." You'll find inshore and offshore fishing equipment, fly-fishing gear, custom rods, guns, ice, bait, tackle, and one of the biggest and best selections of knives you'll ever see. They also offer rod and reel repairs and can help you find hunting or fishing guides. Taxidermy services can be arranged. Camping supplies, name-brand outdoor apparel, Sperry footwear, T-shirts, groceries, gas, and convenience items round out the offerings.

FRISCO TACKLE, 52570 NC 12; 252-995-3229; friscotackle.com. Tackle, fishing, clamming, and crabbing equipment and great advice. Convenience store on premises.

Ocracoke Island

O'NEALS DOCKSIDE TACKLE SHOP, NC 12; (252) 928-1111. O'Neal's offers fresh and frozen bait as well as fishing, marine, and hunting supplies and can furnish you with any license you need. They are a full-service tackle shop and offer tackle rentals. These folks have been in business for more than 20 years and are official North Carolina Wildlife and Marine Fisheries agents. If you have any questions on official regulations, stop here.

TRADEWINDS, NC 12; (252) 928-5491; fishtradewinds.com. Tradewinds is a one-stop tackle shop that can supply all your fishing needs, including fresh and frozen bait, tackle, clothing items, and plenty of good advice about fishing. The shop also offers tackle rentals and rod and reel repair. Tradewinds is an official North Carolina weigh station and is open seven days a week from March through December.

FISHING REPORTS

The *ReelFisher News* is a free, quarterly tabloid available at retail outlets throughout the Outer Banks; it has folksy fishing editorials plus a directory to area piers, ramps, marinas, and weigh stations.

Online Resources

Almost every charter boat captain posts fishing reports, but there are a few that we have consistently found to be the best. These are not, by any means the only ones.

FRISCO ROD & GUN, fishingreport.friscorodandgun.com. Focus is mainly on Hatteras Island with some mention of what's happening up north. Short, but good resource for fishing south of Oregon Inlet.

JENNETTE'S PIER, ncaquariums.com/jennettes-pier-fishing-report. Brief and to the point, but if they're biting at Jennette's Pier, they're probably biting at every pier.

OUTER BANKS FISHING PIER, fishingunlimited.net/fishing-report. One of our favorites. Captain Garry gives a verbal report. Very accurate and inclusive.

TW'S BAIT & TACKLE, twsbaitandtacklefishingreport.com. With three stores, TW's is the largest bait and tackle shop on the Outer Banks. Their fishing reports are inclusive and fun to read with some pictures from time to time.

Golf

Whether you're a scratch golfer or a duffer, you'll find play to suit your game and style on or near the Outer Banks. Part of the pleasure of golf almost everywhere is in the lushness of the environment, but few locations outside of this area offer the astounding ocean-to-sound views you'll find at many courses along these barrier islands. Such distraction might not be good for your game, but it'll do wonders for the soul!

In this section you'll find golf courses from Corolla to Hatteras Island, plus courses on the Currituck mainland just north of the Wright Memorial Bridge. We've also included an excellent course in Hertford that's only an hour's drive from the heart of the Outer Banks.

Golfers have it made during the off-season and shoulder seasons. Accommodations are a bargain from the fall through the spring, and many hotels, motels, and cottage rental companies package special golf vacations. Depending on the season you can usually plan a visit on the spur of the moment if you want to play at off-peak times. The temperatures on the Outer Banks remain fairly moderate throughout the year. A day in January might bring temperatures of 60 degrees or higher, so keep an eye on the weather and your clubs close at hand. To avoid disappointment, call for tee times at your course of choice before your visit; more and more golfers are discovering the Outer Banks in the off-season.

All the regulation courses in the following section are semi-private, meaning the public can pay to play, and all welcome beginners and newcomers. Yardage and par figures are based on men's/white tees.

GEETARISM/GETTYIMAGES

REGULATION & EXECUTIVE COURSES

THE CAROLINA CLUB, US 158, Grandy; (252) 453-3588; thecarolina club.com. More and more Outer Banks golfers are discovering the courses on the Currituck mainland, and the Carolina Club, designed by Russell Breeden, is one of the nicest of the bunch. Located in Grandy, the course is just 13.5 miles past the Wright Memorial Bridge, about a 20-minute drive from Kitty Hawk. The 7,000-yard, par 72 course has, according to the southeastern director of the US Golf Association (USGA), "among the finest putting surfaces in the eastern US." Indeed, the Carolina Club management prides itself on its high level of course conditioning, slick bent-grass greens, and plush Tifway Bermuda fairways. Five sets of tees allow you to match your game to an appropriate level of challenge. On this course you will encounter wetlands, woodlands, water, and bunkers galore.

There's a snack bar on the premises, plus a pro shop. Rental clubs and carts are available. Individual and group lessons are offered. Greens fees, including cart, are a good value, but they change monthly so call for accurate prices. Youth rates are available. Tee times are booked up to three months in advance. The course is open all year.

THE CURRITUCK CLUB, NC 12, Corolla, (252) 453-9400; thecurrituck club.com. When the Currituck Club opened in 1997, Golf magazine named it one of the "Top 10 You Can Play" and in 1999 *Golf Digest* ranked it as one of the top 25 courses in North Carolina, a great compliment for a young course in a renowned golfing state. This 6,885-yard, par 72 course is situated on 600 acres of pristine wetlands along Currituck Sound, surrounded by luxurious homes in the Currituck Club resort community. The natural beauty of this course makes it one of the most peaceful golfing spots around. Prominent golf architect Rees Jones designed the stunningly scenic links-style course with respect for the wildlife and waterfowl that populate the area. While protecting their habitats, he offers golfers a course set amid dunes, wetlands, and marsh fringes. From the rolling dunes golfers enjoy views of the Atlantic Ocean and Currituck Sound. The course features a full driving range. Lessons are offered year-round, along with weekly clinics by PGA professionals. Golf schools take place from June through August on Tuesday, Wednesday, and Thursday from 9 to 11 a.m. Junior golf school is offered on Thursday from 5 to 7 p.m. Rates include golf cart rental and vary according to the season. The clubhouse includes a restaurant, a bar and lounge with full ABC permits, a pro shop, locker rooms, bag storage, and a private members' lounge.

DUCK WOODS COUNTRY CLUB, 50 Dogwood Trl., Southern Shores; (252) 261-2609; duckwoodscc.com. Duck Woods is the club to play on windy days, since it provides more shelter than the soundside clubs. This 18-hole,

6,161-yard, par 72 course was built in 1968. Designed by Ellis Maples, Duck Woods features a traditional layout with tree-lined fairways. Shots must be placed with care, especially on the par 5 14th hole, where water dissects the fairway. Water comes into play on 14 holes. You might want to warm up before your round; the course begins with a 481-yard par 5 and ends with a 506-yard par 5. While the club accommodates 900 members, it accepts public play year-round. Nonmembers can take advantage of the driving range and putting green on the day of play only. Target greens and a practice bunker are available. Duck Woods' pro shop is complemented by the presence of the golf pro on hand. Club rentals are available. Members enjoy clubhouse and locker room privileges and the bar and restaurant.

Riding is mandatory for nonmembers. Booking is accepted a week in advance for members and two days in advance for nonmembers. Call for more information. Greens fees vary.

THE GOLF CLUB AT EAGLE CREEK, US 168, Moyock; (252) 232-9901; eaglecreekgolfing.com. If you're willing to drive a ways, The Golf Club at Eagle Creek offers a great bargain for Outer Banks golfers. The course, opened in 1999 and renamed in 2011, is just south of Moyock on US 168, about 50 miles from the Outer Banks on the mainland and about 5 miles south of the Virginia state line. The course is fun and enjoyable, not overly difficult; so if you're looking for a good-time game, come here. Mill Run is a great course for beginners. Course architect James Overton Sr. designed the 6,651-yard course to take advantage of the natural terrain and to provide challenging play for golfers of all levels. Mill Run is relatively flat and plays somewhat like a links-style course, though it's nowhere near the ocean or sound. It does offer some challenges with wind, ponds, and woods. Bunkers are still being added to the course. The signature hole is number 17, a par 3 with the carry over water. Greens are in tip-top shape. A driving range, practice putting green and chipping green, and lessons are available. Walking is allowed here. The pro shop is well equipped, and the on-site Hackers Grill serves breakfast and lunch.

HOLLY RIDGE GOLF COURSE, US 158, Harbinger; (252) 491-2893; cathyjohnstonforbes.com. Holly Ridge Golf Course is 1.5 miles north of the Wright Memorial Bridge in Harbinger. The front nine wind through a peaceful forest of native trees and picturesque ponds, while the more open back nine are affected by winds. Holly Ridge has a full-length, fully lighted grass practice area and putting green. LPGA major champion Cathy Johnston Forbes teaches golfers of all levels. Private lessons and group clinics are available, as are private lessons with video analysis. The pro shop carries apparel, accessories, and equipment, and the staff helps with selecting the right clubs. Walking is allowed on this course. Pull carts, golf clubs, and, of course, golf carts are available to rent. Greens fees are a good value here, and they vary throughout the year, so call ahead. Juniors may play for half price but must have a valid driver's license to operate a cart.

KILMARLIC GOLF CLUB, US 158, Powell's Point; (252) 491-4220; kilmarlicgolfclub.com. This beautiful very challenging course is just 1 mile north of the Wright Memorial Bridge in Powells Point. Designed by Tom Steele and designated as an official nature preserve, its natural beauty is only one of its attractions. Situated on 605 acres of maritime forest and sprawling wetlands yet kept in consistent tournament condition, Kilmarlic was chosen to host the 2004 and 2009 North Carolina Open. Individual and group lessons are offered by appointment.

NAGS HEAD GOLF LINKS, Seachase Dr., Nags Head; (252) 389-9079; nagsheadgolflinks.com. This soundside 18-hole Scottish links-style course is in the Village at Nags Head off US 158 at milepost 15½. Architect Bob Moore left most of the natural setting intact, and the 6,100-yard, par 71 course is a real beach beauty. Golfers enjoy idyllic views of Roanoke Sound from nearly every hole. With the sound to the west and the ocean to the east, wind plays a significant role here. It doesn't take but one quick gust of wind to blow your ball off course on the 221-yard 15th hole, a lengthy par 3. The green is fronted by a pond. All but four holes are affected by water here. Nags Head Golf Links pros are on hand and invite you to try this mercurial course. *Golf Digest* called the holes along the sound "among the most beautiful in the eastern US," and went on to say that "Nags Head Golf Links is the longest 6,100 yards you'll ever play." The same journal awarded the course 4½ stars. Cart and greens fees vary, and starting times may be reserved up to one year in advance. Seniors pay special off-season rates. A nine-hole scramble is played June through August late Sunday afternoon; call to sign up. Enjoy good food and excellent views of Roanoke Sound from the Links Grill, which is open for lunch only. Nags Head Golf Links also has a bar, golf shop, driving range, putting green, and rental clubs. The course is open every day, except Christmas, from sunrise to sunset. Call for more information.

THE POINTE GOLF CLUB, US 158 East, Powell's Point; (252) 491-8388; thepointegolfclub.com. "Golfer's heaven" well describes this 5,911-yard, par 71, 18-hole championship golf course on the mainland. Both the recreational golfer and the professional will find a challenge on this verdant course created by Russell Breeden. Breeden's unique design features soundfront views from wooded and links-style holes with gentle mounds and slopes. This was the first course in the country to feature A1 bentgrass greens, a new disease-resistant dense grass. It's no surprise because the folks at Pointe are grass experts. Pointe owner Keith Hall is the president of United Turf. The course sports a traditional design, with water hazards coming into play laterally on 15 holes. The signature hole is number 6, a 457-yard par 4 with a carry over wetlands, a blind shot to the fairway, water, bunkers, and slopes to the right. You can fine-tune your game on the driving range, in the practice bunker, or on the full-size putting green. The Pointe offers a full-service pro shop headed by resident golf pro Doug Kinser. Other amenities include a clubhouse, carts, lessons, sales, and rentals. The Pointe Restaurant, which serves breakfast and lunch, has views of the 9th green and the 10th tee. Walking is allowed after noon for greens-fee pass holders, October 1 through May 24. Greens fees vary, so it's a good idea to call for information. Annual golf packages are offered through Outer Banks Golf Getaways (800-635-1559) and Outer Banks Golf Packages (800-916-6244); accommodations packages are available through area rental companies. The golf course is located 3.5 miles north of the Wright Memorial Bridge. Call for tee times up to a month in advance.

SEA SCAPE GOLF LINKS, Eckner St., Kitty Hawk; (252) 261-2158; sea scapegolf.com. Keep your eye on the ball and not the view on this 18-hole, links-style championship course. You get a real taste of Outer Banks beauty with water vistas from almost every hole, especially from the elevated ninth tee. Sea Scape is cut into Kitty Hawk's maritime forest, just off US 158 East at milepost 2½. Designed by Art Wall, the 6,052-yard, par 72 course features bent-grass greens and fairways, which are fairly wide. Sea Scape will test your ability with five par 3s and five par 5s. Scheduled golf clinics are offered for all ages from June through August. Sea Scape offers club fitting, rental clubs, and a driving range, a bar, restaurant, and fully stocked pro shop. Pro Danny Miller is available to discuss your game or the course. Sea Scape Bar and Grill has a wide variety of good food available. Walking is not allowed and golfers may only wear soft spikes. Greens fees range from $50 to $100, including the cart. Call ahead for tee times, especially if you plan to play during the summer (there's no established rule, but we were informed that eight months in advance isn't too soon). The course is open every day except Christmas from 7:30 a.m. until dark.

THE SOUND GOLF LINKS, 101 Clubhouse Dr., Hertford; (252) 426-5555; soundgolflinks.com. Tucked within Albemarle Plantation, the Sound is a 6,504-yard, par 72, 18-hole course. It's also a world-class golfing and boating community at the tip of the Albemarle Sound near Hertford. The beautiful 12,000-square-foot clubhouse overlooks the water. Owner and designer Dan Maples stamped his signature here. As with all Maples-designed courses, you get a break on the par 4s and 5s, but the par 3s are extremely difficult. It's a target golf course with a few similarities to a links course. Fairways are narrow, and marsh must be carried frequently. It's a fair course overall but a tough one from the back tees. On the 7th and 13th holes, the landing areas are extremely small. Both are par 4s. A golf pro is available here. The clubhouse includes a golf shop and restaurant, the Soundside Grille, which serves lunch and dinner. A driving range and putting green are also available. The marina, available to the public, is the largest in the area. Walking is restricted, so call for details. Tee times may be booked up to nine months in advance. The course is a little over an hour's drive from Kitty Hawk. Call for greens fees.

MINIATURE GOLF COURSES

No beach vacation is complete without the timeless activity of miniature golf. More than a dozen mini golf courses adorn the Outer Banks from Corolla through Hatteras Island. Themed fairways featuring African animals, circus clowns, and strange obstacles await even the most amateur club-swinging families. Small children enjoy the ease of some of these holes, and even skilled golfers can get into the par 3 grass courses that have been growing in numbers over recent years.

You can tee off at most places by 10 a.m. Many courses stay open past midnight for night owls to enjoy. Several of these attractions offer play-all-day packages for a single price. Almost all mini golf courses operate seasonally, and since they are all outside, their openings are weather dependent.

Corolla

THE GRASS COURSE, NC 12; (252) 453-4198; grasscourse.com. Offering the Outer Banks' first natural-grass course, these soundside greens are open seven days a week throughout the summer season from 10 a.m. to 11 p.m. The 18-hole course includes par 3s, 4s, and 5s. The undulating hills winding around natural dunes provide intriguing challenges for beginning and better golfers. The course is open from April to October and at Thanksgiving and Christmas. The Grass Course sells hot dogs and barbecue.

Kill Devil Hills

PARADISE GOLF, US 158, MP 5½; (252) 441-7626. More challenging than the usual mini golf fairways, this natural-grass site includes two 18-hole, par 56 courses. Most holes are 110 feet from the tees. The courses are open from 10 a.m. until midnight daily during summer. For one price, you can play all day.

PROFESSOR HACKER'S LOST TREASURE GOLF, US 158, MP 7½; (252) 480-0142; losttreasuregolf.com. Lost Treasure Golf features two 18-hole courses situated among five waterfalls illuminated with different colors at night. Kids love the little train that carts them up to the first hole and through a series of caves and mines. Professor Hacker, a fictional adventurer, tells his story about gold and diamond expeditions that kids read about as they play. Lost

Treasure Golf is open April through November. Hours are 9 a.m. to 11 p.m. daily in the summer and are decreased accordingly in the off-season.

Nags Head

GALAXY GOLF, NC 12, MP 11; (252) 441-5875; facebook.com/Galaxy -Golf. Aliens, flying saucers, and outer space objects surround 36 lighted holes of mini golf at this popular old school Outer Banks course on the Beach Road. Galaxy Golf is open on weekends in April, early May, September, and October and daily throughout the summer. In-season hours are 9 a.m. to midnight. Children younger than four with a paying adult play free. The price doesn't change after dark as it does on many mini golf courses.

JURASSIC PUTT, US 158, MP 16; (252) 441-6841. Life-size models of dinosaurs from the Jurassic period hover over and among Jurassic Putt's greens, delighting kids and adults alike. Two 18-hole courses wind through caves and streams and around the dinosaur models. Jurassic Putt is open daily from mid-March until November. Hours are 9 a.m. to midnight. Call or stop by for rates.

MUTINY BAY ADVENTURE GOLF, US 158, MP 16; (252) 480-6606; obxfamilyfun.com. Get your swagger on at this pirate-themed golf course. The enormous pirate ship sets the tone here. There is also an arcade and sweet shop on site. Next door is the sister thrill stop, Full Throttle Speedway.

Hatteras Island

FRISCO MINI GOLF AND GO-KARTS, NC 12, Frisco; (252) 995-6325. This 18-hole championship miniature golf course is a little more challenging than the average mini golf game, though all levels of players will enjoy the experience. Waterfalls splash amid the well-manicured course, and children feed goldfish. There are also two go-kart tracks, a concession stand, and an arcade on the premises.

UNCLE EDDY'S FROZEN CUSTARD AND 18 HOLE MINI GOLF, 46878 NC 12, Buxton; (252) 995-4059. Homemade frozen custard and miniature golf.

GOLF

Water Sports

Water is the Outer Banks' biggest draw. Everywhere you look on the Outer Banks there's wet, wonderful H20—the deep, blue Atlantic Ocean; the wide, shallow Currituck, Croatan, Roanoke, and Pamlico Sounds; brackish bays and estuaries teeming with wildlife; thick, sopping marshes; and dark, man-made canals sluicing through the islands. And everywhere you look there are people on or in the water. Whether it's on a surfboard, a kiteboard, a sailboard, a Jet Ski, a kayak, or just in a bathing suit, everyone eventually finds his or her way to the water. Numerous water-sports establishments happily accommodate anyone's wish to get wet.

In this chapter we will give you a rundown of water sports and a list of places to rent or buy equipment and take lessons. We list prices to give you a general idea of how much things cost, but be aware that prices are subject to change.

BOATING

From small skiffs to luxurious pleasure boats, there is dock space for almost every type of boat on the Outer Banks. Most marinas require advance reservations. Space is extremely limited on summer weekends, so call as soon as you make plans to visit the area. Prices vary greatly, depending on the dock location, amenities, and type of vessel you're operating.

If you don't own your own boat, you can still access the sounds, inlets, and ocean around the Outer Banks by renting powerboats from area outfitters. Most store owners don't require previous boating experience. If you leave a deposit and driver's license, they'll include a brief boating lesson in the rental price. Whether you're looking to lease a craft to catch this evening's fish dinner or want to take an afternoon cruise, you can find a vessel to suit your needs at a variety of marinas. Slow-going pontoon boats are popular with vacationers because they're easy to handle and accommodate a crowd of boaters. Prices range from $15 an hour to more than $100 per day, depending on the type of boat. Some places require a two-hour or more minimum. Most accept major credit cards. See the **Recreation** chapter for charter and boat tour information.

Public Boat Launch Ramps
Find free public launch ramps at these locations:

- Whalehead Club in Corolla

- Soundside end of Wampum Drive in Duck

- Bob Perry Road on Kitty Hawk Bay in Kitty Hawk

- Avalon Beach off Bay Drive in Kill Devil Hills (small boats only)

- Washington Baum Bridge on Nags Head–Manteo Causeway, opposite Pirate's Cove

- Thicket Lump Marina near Thicket Lump Lane in Wanchese

- Foot of the bridge leading to Roanoke Island Festival Park in Manteo

- Oregon Inlet Fishing Center

- Oceanside end of Lighthouse Road in Buxton

- Frisco Cove in Frisco

- Between Cedar Island/Swan Quarter ferry docks on Ocracoke Island

Marinas & Dock Space

The following Outer Banks marinas offer services to boaters, such as fuel, bait and tackle, ice, supplies, and weighing stations. If you're interested in dockage at a marina, see the **Getting Here, Getting Around** chapter. If you're interested in chartering a boat at one of these marinas, see the **Fishing** section.

ANCHORAGE INN & MARINA, NC 12, Ocracoke; (252) 928-6661; the anchorageinn.com. Right in the heart of Ocracoke on Silver Lake, Anchorage Marina has 35 slips accommodating boats up to 120 feet long. Diesel fuel and gas are available. The marina is open year-round with no limit on the length of stays. The dock-side sMacNally's Raw Bar is next door, and Anchorage offers bike rentals and small-boat rentals. Boaters have swimming pool and shower privileges.

DOCK OF THE BAY, Bob Perry Rd., Kitty Hawk; (252) 255-5578; dock ofthebayobx.com. This fuel dock and convenience shop is a welcome service to boaters on the northern beaches. Dock of the Bay is easily accessed by boat from Kitty Hawk Bay. It offers ice, gas and diesel fuel, snacks and drinks, fishing tackle, and bait. Fishing and crabbing are allowed on the docks as well. It's located at the end of Bob Perry Road, on the Loving Canal at Hog Island, past the Dare County boat landing.

HATTERAS HARBOR MARINA, NC 12 and Gulfstream Way, Hatteras; (252) 986-2166; hatterasharbor.com. This marina accommodates boats up to

68 feet for a day, month, or year. Call for in-season rates and annual charges. Hatteras Harbor also has five apartments available for customers to rent. A full-service deli and ship's store are located at the marina. Diesel fuel is available. Hatteras Harbor is open year-round, and its public laundry facilities are open 24 hours a day.

HATTERAS LANDING MARINA, NC 12, Hatteras Village; (252) 986-2205; hatteraslanding.com. Hatteras Landing offers a complete ship's store with tackle, fresh and frozen baits, lures, sportswear, and a market with beer, ice, and groceries. Gas and diesel fuel are available. Hatteras Landing has fully metered slips, laundry facilities, bathrooms, and a fish-cleaning service. It's open year-round.

MANTEO WATERFRONT MARINA, 207 Queen Elizabeth Ave., Manteo; (252) 305-4800; townofmanteo.com/marina. Located within walking distance of restaurants, a movie theater, a bookstore, and retail shops, this marina has 53 slips and accommodates boats up to 130 feet. Air conditioned heads and showers are available, as well as laundry facilities, a picnic area with gas grills, e-mail access, and rental cars. Fuel is not available. Both 30-amp and 50-amp power is on-site. Block and cube ice are sold on-site. Ask about weekend packages and sailing and fishing charters. Manteo Waterfront Marina is open all year.

NATIONAL PARK SERVICE SILVER LAKE DOCK, Ocracoke Village; (252) 928-4531. There's a two-week limit on summer stays, and dock space is assigned on a first-come, first-served basis. Open year-round, except no water is available in the winter season. If no ranger is on-site when you arrive, pay at the visitor center across the street.

ODEN'S DOCK, NC 12, Hatteras Village; (252) 986-2555; odensdock .com. Oden's Dock has a deep draft that accommodates vessels up to 65 feet. Of the 27 slips at the marina, 20 are deep draft. Reservations are suggested during the peak season. A seafood market and Breakwater Island Restaurant are at Oden's Dock. Diesel fuel and gasoline are sold at the ship's store, along with bait, tackle, food, and beverages. Showers are available during business hours, and fish-cleaning facilities are also available for anglers. One headboat and a charter fishing fleet dock here. Oden's is open year-round. Hours vary during the off-season. Please call ahead for details.

OREGON INLET FISHING CENTER, NC 12, Bodie Island; (252) 441-6301; oregon-inlet.com. The closest marina and fuel dock to Oregon Inlet, Oregon Inlet Fishing Center is on the north side of the Marc Basnight Bridge, about 10 miles from Nags Head. The fishing center accommodates anglers with gas and diesel fuel and a well-stocked bait and tackle shop that opens at 5 a.m.

The tackle shop carries a complete line of surf, inshore, and deep-sea fishing equipment, plus drinks, snacks, coffee, hot dogs, T-shirts, ice, sunscreen, sunglasses, and other items. The boat ramp at Oregon Inlet Fishing Center, with five concrete ramps, is one of the nicest in the area, with plenty of parking for vehicles and trailers. Restroom and trash facilities are on-site.

PIRATE'S COVE YACHT CLUB, Nags Head–Manteo Causeway, Manteo; (252) 473-3906; fishpiratescove.com. This full-service marina is known for its good service and many amenities. It offers a fuel dock with gas and diesel fuel, and diesel is now available at every slip. An on-site restaurant, Pirate's Cove Dockside Restaurant, serves lunch and dinner. Professional fish-cleaning staff is on hand at the dock, or do it yourself at the facilities. The dock master's office monitors marine radio channels 16 and 78. Pirate's Cove is open year-round. For boat-ramp access head across the street to the site just under the west side of the Washington Baum Bridge. This site has concrete ramps and plenty of parking for vehicles with trailers.

TEACH'S LAIR MARINA, NC 12, Hatteras Village; (252) 986-2460; teachslair.com. This year-round, full-service marina has 95 slips accommodating boats up to 65 feet. Two launching ramps are also located at the marina. Teach's Lair has a bathhouse, dry storage, and a ship's store. Fuel (diesel and gasoline), oil, and tackle are all available at the store. A headboat, charter fishing fleet, and two dive boats dock here. Parasailing adventures leave from the marina.

THICKET LUMP MARINA, Thicket Lump Rd., Wanchese; (252) 473-4500. This family-owned and -operated, 28-slip marina rents dock space to pleasure and fishing vessels up to 45 feet by the day, week, month, or year. A ship's store and tackle shop are at the marina, and both gas and diesel fuel are available. Thicket Lump offers inshore and offshore charters; call for information. The marina is open throughout the year.

> **i** The extra-long parking spaces near boat ramps are for vehicles pulling boat trailers. These are the only spaces for them to park and unload or load their boat. Vehicles with no trailers should be parked in the normal-size spots.

Boat Rentals

If you don't own a powerboat but want to explore the vast waters of this region, rent one. Lots of places, even marinas or rental services, rent boats. Following are some reliable sources for motorboats.

A small motor boat idles in the marshes on Ocracoke Island.
EIFEL KREUTZ/GETTYIMAGES

ANCHORAGE MARINA, NC 12, Ocracoke; (252) 928-6661. Anchorage Marina rents 16- to 24-foot skiffs for half days, whole days, and weekly. Call for rates. The marina is on Silver Lake and is open year-round.

CHARLIE'S BOAT RENTALS, 25628 NC 12, Waves, (252) 489-0048; charliesboatrentals.com. Renting everything from wave runners to 22-foot-long pontoon boats. Some age restrictions apply.

JET SKIS AND OTHER PERSONAL WATERCRAFT

If you feel a need for speed and enjoy the idea of riding a motor-powered vehicle across the water, Outer Banks businesses rent personal watercraft by the hour. Personal watercraft (PWC) are most known and referred to by their brand names—Sea-Doo, Jet Ski, and WaveRunner. No experience is necessary to ride these powerful boatlike devices, although a training session is a must if you've never before piloted a PWC. Unlike landlocked go-karts and other speedy road rides, there are no lanes on the open sound or ocean. But that doesn't mean you should ride with reckless abandon. With more and more people riding PWCs, it is imperative that each person practice responsible and safe riding.

PWCs are akin to motorboats with inboard motors that power a water pump. Like other motorized boats, however, PWCs are loud and are dangerous if you are not extremely cautious and aware. Most rental places include brief instructions and sometimes even a video on how to handle WaveRunners, Jet Skis, and Runabouts.

Most rental shops are on the sound side of the Outer Banks, where the water's surface is generally slicker and depths are much shallower. A few PWC outlets let you take the vessels into the ocean. There shore break and offshore waves challenge experienced Jet Ski drivers. Watch out for surfers, swimmers, dolphins, turtles, sharks, and birds—and other Jet Ski drivers who might not see you coming.

Those who own their own PWCs can launch their craft at public boat ramps. Be aware, however, that PWCs are banned in certain areas of the Outer Banks. The National Park Service does not allow the launching of PWCs anywhere in Cape Hatteras National Seashore. The town of Southern Shores requires PWC launchers to get a permit from the police department. To get this permit you must show proof of insurance and that you have taken a boating-safety course. You must stay at least 400 yards offshore in Southern Shores. In Nags Head PWCs must stay at least 600 yards offshore and away from piers. Ocracoke Island forbids the use of PWCs.

> **i** Know the rules of the water before you operate a boat! Observe no-wake signs and slow down for smaller craft so that your wake doesn't swash them. Sail craft always have the right-of-way. When you pass through a channel, the red markers should be on your left as you're moving out to sea and on your right as you're coming in. Use this mnemonic device—Red on Right Returning—to remember which side of the channel to stay on.

Renting Personal Watercraft

New PWCs sell for $5,000 to $13,000. Several Outer Banks rental shops sell used PWCs for cheaper prices at the end of the summer. You'll probably need a trailer to haul these vessels behind your vehicle.

Shops from Corolla to Hatteras Island rent PWCs by the half hour. Price wars occasionally result in very low prices. More powerful models are generally more expensive. Additional charges sometimes apply for extra riders. PWCs also can be rented by the hour, day, or even week at some places.

CAUSEWAY WATERSPORTS, 7649 S. Virginia Dare Trl., Nags Head; (252) 441-8875; causewaywatersportsobx.com. Jet skis and pontoon boats, just about every type of watercraft can be rented here.

COROLLA WATER SPORTS, Timbuck II Shopping Village, Corolla; (252) 453-6900; corollawatersports.com. At this store you can rent Wave-Runners and kayaks. Also go parasailing, play miniature golf, and shop in the retail store. Call for rates and more information. Corolla Water Sports is open May through October.

HATTERAS WATERSPORTS, NC 12, Salvo; (252) 987-2306; hatteraswater sports.com. Hatteras Watersports rents WaveRunner personal watercrafts. The store is on the soundside, across from the Salvo Volunteer Fire Department.

KITTY HAWK SURF COMPANY, 12, Monterey Plaza, Corolla, (252) 453-3685; 1216 Duck Rd., Duck, (252) 261-8787; 3933 S. Croatan Hwy., Nags Head, (252) 441-6800; NC 12, Waves Village, Rodanthe, (252) 987-2528; 58848 Hatteras Landing, Hatteras, (252) 986-1446; khsurf.com. Kitty Hawk Surf Company rents WaveRunners by the half hour and hour. Call for prices and more information. Water bikes, paddleboats, kayaks, and parasailing are also offered through this iconic store. Kitty Hawk Surf Company is open from early spring through fall. The Nags Head location at milepost 13 at Jockey's Ridge Crossing stays open longer.

KITTY HAWK WATERSPORTS, US 158, MP 16, Nags Head; (252) 441-2756; kittyhawkwatersports.com. This complete store rents WaveRunners by the half hour and hour. The store is on the sound in Nags Head, so launching is easy. Water bikes, paddleboats, stand-up paddleboards, windsurfers, and kayaks are available for purists. Call for prices.

NOR'BANKS SAILING CENTER, NC 12, Duck; (252) 261-7100; norbanks.com. Nor'Banks Sailing Center rents WaveRunners and Sea-Doo jet boats. It is open spring through fall.

RAD KITE & JET SKI RENTALS, 24202 NC 12, Rodanthe; (252) 489-0451; radkiteandjetskirental.com. Jet ski rentals and tours as well as kiteboarding lessons.

RODANTHE WATERSPORTS AND SHORELINE CAMPGROUND, NC 12; (252) 987-1431; watersportscampground.com. This soundfront campground and watersports operation rents WaveRunners, as well as surfboards, bikes, kayaks, and sailboats.

Jetpaks and More

OUTER BANKS JETOVATOR, 40181 Bonito Rd., Avon; (252) 305-3394; outerbanksjetovator.com. Jetovartor and hoverboard lessons. Riding a

Jetovator is a bit like riding a bike with a powerful stream of water shooting out the back of it. Very highly recommended.

OUTER BANKS JETPAK & FLYBOARD, Manteo; (877) 359-8447; kitty hawk.com. A lot of fun trying to master how to fly a JetPack. Booked through Kitty Hawk Kites.

KAYAKING & CANOEING

The easiest, most adaptable, and most accessible water sports available on the Outer Banks—kayaking and canoeing—are activities people of any age can enjoy. The lightweight paddlecraft are maneuverable, glide almost anywhere along the seas or sounds, and afford adventurous activity as well as silent solitude. They're also relatively inexpensive ways to tour uncharted waterways and see sights not observable from shore.

In recent years more than a dozen ecotour outlets have opened on the barrier islands. Stores offer everything from rent-your-own kayaks for less than $40 a day to guided, daylong, and even overnight tours around uninhabited islands. With no fuel to foul the estuaries, no noise to frighten wildlife, and no

Kayaks (in all colors and sizes) are available to rent at shops on every island.
Joe_Potato/GettyImages

need for a demanding skill level, kayaks and canoes offer a sport as strenuous or as relaxing as you want it to be.

Unlike the kayaks used in whitewater rivers, kayaks on the Outer Banks are either the sit-on-top style from 7 to 10 feet long, or specifically designed for flat water paddling. They're molded in brightly colored plastic, are light to carry to a launch site, and are manufactured in one- and two-seat models. A double-blade paddle and a life jacket are the only other pieces of equipment needed, and these are included with rentals and lessons.

Canoes are heavier and harder to get into the water, but slightly more stable than kayaks. However, with their high sides, they can be more difficult to maneuver in windy conditions. They seat two or three people and include a more sheltered hull to haul gear or picnic lunches. Single-blade paddles, usually two per boat, are needed to maneuver this traditional watercraft.

These sports lend themselves to solitary enjoyment just as easily as group fun. Thrill seekers can splash kayaks through frothy surf in the Atlantic or paddle past the breakers and float alongside schools of dolphin. For more tranquility, kayakers and canoeists can slip slowly through mysterious, marshy creeks at the isolated Alligator River National Wildlife Refuge, explore narrow canals that bigger boats can't access, or slip alongside an uninhabited island in the middle of the shallow sound. There are historical tours around Roanoke Island, nature tours through maritime forests, and self-guided trails with markers winding through a former logging town called Buffalo City on the Dare County mainland.

Rentals

CAUSEWAY WATERSPORTS, 7649 S. Virginia Dare Trl., Nags Head; (252) 441-8875; causewaywatersportsobx.com. Kayaks, SUPs, just about every type of watercraft can be rented here.

COROLLA EXPLORATIONS, 1118 Corolla Village Rd., Corolla; (252) 453-9872; coastalexplorations.com. Corolla based outfitter offering tours and kayak rentals. Also rents SUPs.

DUCK VILLAGE OUTFITTERS, NC 12, Waterfront Shops, Duck; (252) 261-7222; duckvillageoutfitters.net. These folks will take you wherever you want to go in a kayak. Their preplanned tours are ocean kayak dolphin tours and scenic tours through the estuaries of Kitty Hawk Nature Preserve, Kitty Hawk Bay, and Ginguite Creek. Two-hour soundside tours are offered, both single and double kayaks are available. Rentals are also offered. Tours are conducted daily in the warm seasons, but call in the off-season and one of the enthusiastic guides will take you out. The shop is open all year.

HATTERAS ISLAND BOARDSPORTS, NC 12, Avon; (252) 995-6160; hiboardsports.com. Rent a kayak (single or double) touring for the sound or a surf kayak for the ocean. Choose from a variety of styles and makes. Rent for a half day, a whole day, three days, or a week. HIB delivers, or you can pick up the gear yourself.

KITTY HAWK KITES, Queen Elizabeth St., Manteo; (252) 473-2357; kittyhawk.com. Kitty Hawk Kites rents kayaks from its location, which is right on Shallowbag Bay in downtown Manteo. Ecotours through Shallowbag Bay and surrounding canals are given throughout the day. The tours last about one and a half hours. Sunset and moonlight tours are also available.

KITTY HAWK KITES KITEBOARDING CENTER, Waves Village Resort, NC 12, Rodanthe; (252) 987-2528; wavesvillage.com. This huge retail store offers everything you need for kiteboarding. There is ample space to set up, and pros are on hand to help you with your skills. Enthusiasts can rent before buying gear. Warm showers and a restaurant are also on the premises.

KITTY HAWK SURF COMPANY, NC 12, Monterey Plaza, Corolla, (252) 453-3685; 1216 Duck Rd., Duck, (252) 261-8787; 3933 S. Croatan Hwy, Nags Head, (252) 441-6800; NC 12, Waves Village, Rodanthe, (252) 987-2528; 58848 Hatteras Landing, Hatteras, (252) 986-1446; khsurf.com. Kitty Hawk Surf Company's water sports operation offers a selection of sound tours from Corolla to Hatteras, in addition to sea and surf kayak lessons. No experience is necessary, and tours include all necessary equipment, including single and tandem kayaks, paddles, and life jackets. Tours are offered around Kitty Hawk Woods, Manteo and Roanoke Island, Alligator River, and Pea Island. Sunset tours, dolphin tours, lighthouse tours, and tours with historical narration are offered. Tours range from one hour to more than two hours. Long, specialty tours are available; see the website for more information. Sea, surf, and touring kayaks as well as a selection of personal sailboats are available for sale, including Escape boats and the WindRider Trimarans. Special programs for kids are available in summer months. Equipment can be rented by the hour, day, or week.

NOR'BANKS SAILING CENTER, NC 12, Duck; (252) 261-7100; norbanks.com. Single as well as tandem kayaks are available for sale or rent here. Open May through October.

OCEAN ATLANTIC RENTALS; 40809 NC 12, Avon, (252) 995-5868; 103 A Corolla Light Town Center, Corolla, (252) 453-2440; 1194 Duck Rd., Duck, (252) 261-4346; 2001 S. Croatan Hwy, Kill Devil Hills, (252) 441-7823 (showroom); oceanatlanticrentals.com. Huge selection of rental equipment. The kayak and watersport rentals may be the largest on the beach. Ocean and surf kayaks, as well as tandem and single seat for the sounds. Very good selection of SUPs as well.

RIDE THE WIND SURF SHOP, NC 12, Ocracoke; (252) 928-6311; surf ocracoke.com. Ride the Wind offers four two-and-a-half-hour kayak tours (the Sunrise, the Midday, the Sunset, the Full Moon) of Pamlico Sound and the surrounding estuarine waters every day in spring, summer, and fall, weather permitting.

Any size group can be accommodated with advance notice. The fee includes kayak, life jackets, and a four-page plastic field guide to area fish, shellfish, and fauna. Call for prices. Reservations are strongly suggested during summer.

KITEBOARDING & WINDSURFING

Springtime on the Outer Banks brings a specific annual migration, mostly from Canada and the northern United States. Tourism officials estimate that as many as 500 wind enthusiasts a week arrive at the Outer Banks in spring and fall. Dozens of other visitors try the sport for the first time while vacationing in Dare County.

Owing to our position in the Atlantic, plus the area's prevailing winds, shallow sounds, and temperate weather, Hatteras Island is a sailboarding mecca on the East Coast. When the wind whips just right, hundreds of sails soar along the sound and ocean shores, skimming over the salty water like bright butterflies flitting near the beach.

Kiteboarding and Windsurfing are not easy sports, although once you get the hang of them, they are one of the most intoxicating experiences imaginable. It's clean and quiet and just as easily lends itself to solitary excursions as it does to group outings. With the proper equipment, sailboarders glide into a sunset or cruise more than 40 mph across choppy breaks. On the Outer Banks sailboarders can usually find some wind to ride year-round. Windsurfing is permitted any place you can set your sails, except lifeguarded beaches. This sport truly allows the rider to feel a part of the natural surroundings—and it's an incredible rush to fly with the wind.

Kiteboarding is the latest rage among sailboarders, wake boarders, and surfers alike. The Outer Banks is widely recognized as one of the top places in the world to kitesurf because of the ever-present wind and shallow sounds. Kitesurfers favor the Pamlico Sound off Hatteras Island because it is so wide and has few obstructions to the kite lines. Some daredevil types also kitesurf in the ocean.

Kiteboarding does offer significant advantages over windsurfing: The gear is much more portable, you can do it in a wider range of winds (even low winds), and most people say it's much easier to learn. However, windsurfing is safer. Kitesurfing is a dangerous sport, though it's hard to perceive that danger when you're watching from the shore. The amount of wind power behind the kite is enormous.

For this reason you cannot simply rent a kite and board at the local outfitters and go on your merry way. You must attain a basic level of certification before you are allowed to rent or buy kitesurfing equipment, and some outfitters don't rent the gear at all, saying the risks are just too great.

Kitty Hawk Kites Kite Surfing School does rent equipment, but only to people who have completed their Professional Air Sports Association-certified training courses through Kitty Hawk Surf Company in Nags Head. It takes about four hours of training to become certified, and then you are able to rent gear. The amount of training time depends on your previous kiting skills. If you're not familiar with kite physics, trainers suggest that you practice with a trainer kite until kite-steering techniques become ingrained.

If you want to buy kitesurfing gear, the whole setup will cost you $1,500 or more. If you want to watch or compete in kitesurfing, check it out at popular spots, the Canadian Hole between Avon and Buxton, or at milepost 15 or 16 on the sound in Nags Head. Nags Head's soundside beaches also provide areas that are great for sailboarding. The sounds are shallower than at Canadian Hole, and thus safer for beginners. The town of Nags Head has a soundside access at milepost 16 with plenty of parking. Jockey's Ridge State Park's soundside access area also provides parking and a small beach for launching sailboards. In Duck most people launch on the sound. There are dozens of launch areas on the soundside all along the Outer Banks.

On particularly windy days, you'll see kiteboarders sailing the waves on the ocean. Watching these sailors is a wondrous sight that's likely to inspire the thrill seekers in your party.

Shops & Lessons
Whether you're looking for a lesson, need a sail or a fin of a different size, or want advice, more than a dozen shops stock windsurfing and kitesurfing supplies, and many provide instructors in season.

HATTERAS ISLAND BOARDSPORTS, NC 12, Avon; (252) 995-6160; hiboardsports.com. For windsurfing and kiteboarding equipment, new or used, for sale or to rent, visit Hatteras Island Boardsports. Instructors teach all levels, catering to your specific needs, particularly with private lessons. The shop stocks casual clothing for the beach and to wear at home. Kayaks, kayak tours, and other watersport needs are served here. The shop is open all year; call for hours.

HATTERAS ISLAND SAIL SHOP, NC 12, Waves; (252) 987-2292. On the soundfront, this windsurfing shop was opened in 1996 by the owners of Hatteras Island Surf Shop, which is 250 yards south. They offer sales, rentals, and lessons. Owner Barton Decker says the sailing site is the largest grassy rigging area on the Outer Banks with a sandy beach launch. With about 150 new and used boards in stock, the store also has necessary accessories in its complete inventory. Windsurfing lessons are available as well as rentals. Kiteboarding lessons are offered;

Close-up

Canadian Hole

Wide-open sky, unobstructed by trees and skyscrapers, hovers over a ridge of sand. The wind blows from every direction, sweeping sometimes gently, sometimes with excited fury, across the island from sea to sound or sound to sea. Welcome to Canadian Hole.

Hatteras Island's Canadian Hole, so named for all of our visitors from the far north, has often been touted in international windsurfing circles as one of the continent's best sailboarding spots. Formed in the early 1960s, Canadian Hole was created after a storm cut an inlet across Hatteras Island, just north of Buxton, and workers dredged sand from the sound to rebuild the roadway. Dredging activities carved troughs just offshore in the Pamlico Sound. The deep depressions, which extend well beyond 5 feet, help create ideal conditions for sailboarders. Additionally, Canadian Hole flanks one of the barrier islands' narrowest landmasses. The walk from ocean to sound is less than five minutes, enabling sailboarders to easily switch between the two bodies of water.

Besides the sound and the Atlantic, Canadian Hole's amenities include a 100-space paved lot in which to park big vans and trailers, toilets and showers, a phone booth, and trash cans. The beach at Canadian Hole is much wider than other soundside stretches of sand—it's about 50 yards wide and accommodates sunbathers, coolers, and plenty of spectators.

Long before sailboarders and kiteboarders arrived in droves at Canadian Hole, Hatteras Island's local fishermen toiled night into day, day into night, plying fish from the salt- and freshwater sound. Arriving upon the shore, they toted their boats and fishing equipment, crossing the island at one of its narrowest locations to the Atlantic's beach.

Some days their journey took them from the ocean to the sound at this place, dubbed "the Haulover." The crossing was frequently made here between Avon and Buxton, where the ocean has met the sound in past storm rages and will do so again one day.

For now Canadian Hole is available for wind and water lovers to use. It is a privilege granted by the National Park Service, which holds jurisdiction over the land as part of Cape Hatteras National Seashore. Americans, Canadians, and indeed people of the world come here to sail across the shining seas known as the prime windsurfing and kitesailing spot on the United States' East Coast.

The place has a smell of its own, dusted by wind, sun, and island brush, wetted with rain and salt spray. At times windriders wait in a quiet hush, lazily aware, keen to every movement of the wind. When the wind picks up, the scurry begins. Dashing across the parking lot, board over head, squeezing between cars, trucks, and vans, sailboarders in wet suits head to the shallow sound while new arrivals find a parking space, scope the scene, assess the wind speed, and follow suit.

The spot attracts visitors from Canada seeking warm water and air often accompanied by steady wind. The drive is accomplished in a day or two, consuming 16 to 20 hours from eastern locales, with eager anticipation pushing the wind lovers south.

A few resident sailboarders remember when the sport was new and first brought to the island in the early 1970s. One or two wet-behind-the-ears windsurfing pioneers ventured into the shores meeting the Graveyard of the Atlantic, where shoals and unpredictable shifting conditions wrecked more than 1,000 ships.

Enthusiasts soon determined that windsurfing in the safer sound is fun, not only for beginners but for intermediate and advanced wind sailors as well. At times, hundreds of sails flit about, dancing upon the sparkles.

Some brave and skilled sailors carry their boards and sails across the highway, over the dune, and ride the waves into the Atlantic. The experience, if successful, is surreal, intoxicatingly beautiful. But many a daredevil has been smashed by the surf and "denied" entry or has been swept along in a wicked current or lost equipment and pride, which is renewed in the next great session. More and more dedicated enthusiasts become wave sailors, enticed by the never-ending challenges and thrills.

Now kiteboarding has found its perfect spot. Those with kites rather than sails park along the sound in the sand and sail where the water is definitely shallow, away from the crowd of windsurfers, at Kite Point. Kite Point is just south of the Hole but part of the same park.

Despite the rise of windsurfing, followed by the rise of kiteboarding, the water is the same, and so is the wind. It's beautiful and free. Whether holding a sail or a kite, sailors smile, tasting freedom, keeping the feeling forever and ever.

no rentals are available. Stand-up paddleboards (SUPs) and kayaks can be rented or purchased here. The store closes in January and February.

KITTY HAWK KITES KITEBOARDING CENTER, Waves Village Resort, NC 12, Rodanthe; (252) 987-2528; wavesvillage.com. This huge retail store offers everything you need for kiteboarding. There is ample space to set up, and pros are on hand to help you with your skills. Enthusiasts can rent before buying gear. Warm showers and a restaurant are also on the premises.

KITTY HAWK WATERSPORTS, US 158, MP 16, Nags Head; (252) 441-2756; kittyhawkwatersports.com. Dealing in windsurfing on the Outer Banks for more than 20 years, Kitty Hawk Watersports was one of the first windsurfing operations on the barrier islands. At its site on Roanoke Sound, the center is open almost all year-round and offers windsurfing instruction in spring, summer, and fall. With a two-hour lesson, instructors guarantee you'll start skimming the Roanoke Sound on your own. Call the number listed for rates. Kitesurfing lessons are available, but rentals are not. Wind- and kitesurfing equipment is also for sale.

OCEANAIR, NC 12, Avon; (252) 995-5000; oceanairsports.com. With private access to Pamlico Sound, this widely respected store was opened in 1988 as Windsurfing Hatteras by a group of dedicated local sailboarders. Now known as OceanAir, the operation offers windsurfing and kitesurfing lessons and clinics every year for both beginners and advanced students. The clinics are staffed by some of the best kite- and windsurfing talent around. Lessons come with guaranteed success for beginners. Windsurfing lessons include all equipment and on-water instruction. Windsurfing boards and rigs can be rented at the site. Kiteboarding lessons are offered by highly qualified instructors. Kitesurfing gear is not available for rent. Call for rates on renting surfboards, body boards, kayaks, Hobie Cats, and other fun-inspired items. OceanAir stocks everything you could possibly need for wind- or kiteboarding.

RAD KITE & JET SKI RENTALS, 24202 NC 12, Rodanthe; (252) 489-0451; radkiteandjetskirental.com. Jetski rentals and tours as well as kiteboarding lessons.

REAL KITEBOARDING, NC 12, Waves; (252) 995-4740; realwatersports .com. REAL Kiteboarding is a full-service kiteboarding center that offers gear and instruction. With home bases on Hatteras Island and Puerto Rico, they offer instruction in many areas of the East Coast. Three-day Kite Camps are offered on Hatteras Island in spring, summer, and fall, and after one of these intense camps, you'll certainly be ripping. Less-expensive lessons require less time but still cover basic skills. Kids' camps are also offered.

PARASAILING

If you've always wanted to float high above the water beneath a colorful parachute, adventures await at various locations along the Outer Banks. Although a boat pulls from below, allowing the wind to lift you toward the clouds, you don't get wet on these outdoor trips over the sounds unless you want to. You take off and land on the back of the boat. Riders soar with the seagulls above whitecaps and beach cottages. People of any age, without any athletic ability at all, enjoy parasailing and find it one of their most memorable experiences. And it's safe, too; unbreakable ropes are standard.

Corolla

COROLLA WATER SPORTS, NC 12; (252) 453-6900. Parasailing trips are offered at heights from 400 to 1,400 feet above the Currituck Sound. Call ahead for reservations and rates. Parasailing is offered in the spring, summer, and fall.

Duck

NOR'BANKS SAILING CENTER, NC 12; (252) 261-7100; norbanks .com. Specializing in single, tandem, and triple flights, this was one of the original parasailing locations on the Outer Banks. All vessels that give you your ride are Coast Guard-inspected and are able to take passengers up 400 to 1,400 feet. Parasailing is available from May through October.

Nags Head

CAUSEWAY WATERSPORTS, 7649 S. Virginia Dare Trl.; (252) 441-8875; causewaywatersportsobx.com. Single, double, or triple flights 250- to 500-feet.

KITTY HAWK WATERSPORTS, US 158, MP 16; (252) 441-2756; kitty hawkwatersports.com. Parasailing captains from Kitty Hawk Watersports can get you high. Uplifting experiences are offered daily from April through November. These 8- to 15-minute flights allow you to float at 400 to 1,400 feet; cost depends on how high you want to fly.

SAILING

Sir Walter Raleigh's explorers first sailed along these shores more than four centuries ago. Private sailboat owners have long enjoyed the barrier islands as a stopover while en route along the Intracoastal Waterway. Many sailors have also dropped anchor beside Roanoke or Hatteras Islands—only to tie up at the docks permanently and make Dare County their home.

Until recently you had to have your own sailboat to cruise the area waterways. Now shops from Corolla through Ocracoke rent sailboats, Hobie Cats, and catamarans to weekend water enthusiasts. Others offer introductory and advanced sailing lessons. Some take people who have no desire to learn to sail on excursions across the sounds aboard multipassenger sailing ships. Ecotours, luncheon swim-and-sails, and sunset cruises have become increasingly popular with vacationers. From 40-passenger catamarans sailed by experienced captains to piratelike schooners carrying up to six passengers to single-person Sunfish sailboats, you can find almost any type of sailing vessel you desire on these barrier islands.

If you've never sailed before, don't rent a boat and try to wing it. Winds in this area are trickier than elsewhere and either increase in intensity or shift direction without a moment's notice. If you get caught in a gale, you could end up miles from land if you don't know how to maneuver the vessel. A two-hour introductory lesson is worth the minimal investment to learn basic sailing skills such as knot tying, sail rigging, and steering.

Sailors with basic on-water experience manage to navigate their way around the shallow sounds. All boat passengers should always wear a life jacket.

Sailboat Cruises, Courses & Rentals
Prices for sailboat cruises depend on the amenities, length of voyage, and time of day. Midday trips sometimes include lunches or at least drinks for passengers. Some sunset tours offer wine, beer, and appetizers. Almost all of the excursions let people bring their own food and drink aboard, and some even accept dogs on leashes. Special arrangements can also be made for disabled passengers. Prices generally range from $30 to $60 per person. If you'd like to book a boat for a private charter for you and your friends, some captains also offer their services along with the sailboats, beginning at $50 per hour per vessel.

Lesson costs, too, span a range, depending on how in-depth the course is, what type of craft you're learning on, and whether you prefer group or

i Famous for its wind and water, the Outer Banks is hoping to become established as a sailing destination and hub. The annual average wind speed is 12 knots, and when combined with the clean accessible waterways, the Outer Banks has an opportunity to become a premier sailing destination. SAIL NC is a newer organization on the Outer Banks that entices sailors to choose the Outer Banks as a destination for competitive and leisure sailing. Their maiden event, ISAF International A-Class Catamaran Race, is held in June. Events will be added each year as the organization grows. Check SAILNC.org for scheduling and information.

WATER SPORTS

individualized instruction. Costs start at $10 and go to $50 per person. Call ahead for group rates for more than four people in your party.

If you'd rather rent a craft and sail it yourself, Outer Banks outfitters lease sailboats by the hour, day, or week. Deposits generally are required. Costs range from $25 to $60 per hour and $50 to $110 per day. Most shops accept major credit cards.

COROLLA WATER SPORTS, NC 12, Timbuck II Shopping Village, Corolla; (252) 453-6900; corollawatersports.com. Corolla Water Sports rents day sailers and catamarans, also kayaks, WaveRunners and parasailing adventures. Call for rates.

HATTERAS ISLAND SAIL SHOP, NC 12, Waves; (252) 987-2292; hatterasislandsurfshop.com. Catamarans, day sailers, and Hobie Cats are available for rent by the hour at this extension of the Hatteras Island Surf Shop. Kayaks and other ocean vessels are also available to rent. Sound access is on-site. Lessons are offered. Call for more information. The sail shop is closed in January and February.

KITTY HAWK KITES, NC 12, Duck, (252) 261-4450; NC 12, Island Shops, Avon, (252) 995-6060; kittyhawk.com. Kitty Hawk Kites, rents the WindRider Trimaran, a stable sailing vessel, for hourly and daily rates. The lightweight Escape, a less destructible and more portable version of the Sunfish, is also available for rent or sale. The Escape is equipped with a Windicator, which sets the sail by measuring wind speed and direction. WindRider Trimarans are also available to rent in Corolla. Call (252) 453-3685.

Avon location of Kitty Hawk Kites rents WindRider Trimaran sailboats, probably the easiest boats to learn to sail on. KHK also offers kayak rentals.

KITTY HAWK WATERSPORTS, US 158, MP 16, Nags Head; (252) 441-2756; kittyhawkwatersports.com. Kitty Hawk Watersports rents day sailers and catamarans from its soundside Nags Head location. This is a great place to learn to sail on a not-too-windy day. The sound is wide with few hazards to look out for—except Jet Skiers and other watersports enthusiasts. Stand-up paddleboards and kayaks are also available here.

NOR'BANKS SAILING CENTER, NC 12, Duck; (252) 261-7100; norbanks.com. In recent years Duck has become one of the Outer Banks' busiest sailing hubs and is among the easiest places in the area to learn to sail or take a calm cruise. Nor'banks offers lessons and is particularly effective working with kids. Rent day sailers and catamarans hourly, by the half day, or daily. Open May through October.

SCUBA DIVING

Although cloudier and cooler than waters off the Florida Keys and the Caribbean Islands, offshore areas along the Outer Banks offer unique scuba diving experiences in the Graveyard of the Atlantic. The area owes its moniker to the more than 1,000 shipwrecks (at least 200 named and identified) whose remains rest on the ocean floor from Corolla to Ocracoke. Experienced divers enjoy the challenge of unpredictable currents while exploring beneath the ocean's surface. From 17th-century schooners to World War II submarines, wreckage lies at a variety of depths in almost every imaginable condition.

Some underwater archaeological shipwreck sites are federally protected and can be visited but not touched. Others offer incredible souvenirs for deepwater divers: bits of china plates and teacups, old medicine and liquor bottles, brass-rimmed porthole covers, and thick, handblown glass that's been buried beneath the ocean for more than a century. If you prefer to leave history as you find it, waterproof cameras bring back memorable treasures from the mostly unexplored underwater world.

Sharks, whales, dolphins, and hundreds of varieties of colorful fish also frequent deep waters around these barrier islands. The northernmost coral reef in the world is off Avon. Submerged Civil War forts are scattered along the banks of Roanoke Island in much shallower sound waters.

Dive-boat captains carry charter parties to places of their choosing. Some shipwrecks have become popular with scuba divers and are among the most frequently selected sites. The freighter *Metropolis*, also called the "Horsehead Wreck," lies about 3 miles south of the Currituck Beach Lighthouse off Whalehead Beach in Corolla, 100 yards offshore and in about 15 feet of water. This ship was carrying 500 tons of iron rails and 200 tons of stones when it sank in 1878, taking 85 crewmen to a watery grave. Formerly the federal gunboat *Stars and Stripes*, which served in the Civil War, this is a good wreck to explore in the off-season. If you have a four-wheel-drive vehicle, you can drive up the beach and swim out to this shipwreck site.

Off the shores of Kill Devil Hills, an unidentified tugboat rests about 300 yards south of Avalon Pier, approximately 75 yards off the beach, in 20 feet of water. Two miles south, the Triangle Wrecks—*Josephine, Kyzickes*, and *Carl Gerhard*—sit about 100 yards offshore, about 200 yards south of the Sea Ranch Motel, in about 20 feet of water. These vessels sank in 1915, 1927, and 1929, respectively. You can access these wrecks by boat or swim from the beach.

Nags Head's most famous dive site is the USS *Huron*, a federal gunship that sank in 1877, taking 95 crewmen to the bottom. This wreck is about 200 yards off the beach at MP 11, resting in an estimated 26 feet of water with many salvageable artifacts. The tugboat *Explorer* is nearby.

Long known as the East Coast's most treacherous inlet, Oregon Inlet rages between Bodie Island and Hatteras Island. It's infamous for the hundreds of ships—and scores of lives—that it has claimed through the ages. The liberty ship *Zane Grey* lies about a mile south of this inlet in 80 feet of water. A German sub sank northeast of the inlet in 100 feet of water in 1942. The *Oriental* has been sitting about 4 miles south of Oregon Inlet since sinking in 1862; its boiler is visible above the surf. Most of these dive sites can be accessed only from boats.

About a mile north of Rodanthe Fishing Pier, 100 yards offshore, the *LST 471* lies in only 15 feet of water. This ship sank in 1949 and is accessible by swimming from shore. Nearby off Rodanthe, about 22 miles southeast of Oregon Inlet, the tanker *Marore* is approximately 12 miles offshore. It sank when torpedoed in 1942 and lies in about 100 feet of water.

Experienced deepwater divers enjoy the *Empire Gem*, a British carrier that sank in January 1942, torpedoed by a German U-boat. This shipwreck sits about 17 miles off Cape Hatteras in 140 feet of water and was one of the first vessels to go down in these waters in World War II. It, too, must be reached by boat.

Dive Shops

OUTER BANKS DIVING AND CHARTERS, NC 12, Hatteras Village; (252) 986-1056; outerbanksdiving.com. Offering daily dives on Gulf Stream wrecks for individuals and groups, Outer Banks Diving and Charters specializes in family and group outings. Dive trips are made on *Bayou Runner*, a 42-foot US Coast Guard–certified vessel, which is docked at Teach's Lair Marina, 1 mile from the dive shop. This full-service facility is open year-round and has equipment sales, full rental gear, tank fills, and Nitrox.

ROANOKE ISLAND OUTFITTERS AND DIVE CHARTERS, 627 US 64, Manteo; (252) 423-1257; roanokeislandoutfittersanddivecenter.com. One of the first and most respected dive shops on the Outer Banks. Offers lessons and complete equipment rental. Takes dive trips to the wrecks and into shallow waters. Offers advanced classes and certifications.

SURFING

Warmer than New England waters and wielding more consistent waves than most Florida beaches, the Outer Banks' surf is reputed to have the best breaks on the East Coast. Local surfing experts explain that since we are set out farther into the ocean in deeper waters than most other coastal regions, our beaches pick up more swells and wind patterns than any place around. Piers, shipwrecks, and offshore sandbars also create unusual wave patterns. Along with those swells, the Outer Banks has the added bonus of sharp drop-offs and troughs right offshore, which make the waves break with more power and force.

WATER SPORTS

An October swell and no wetsuit needed. Any time is a good time to go surfing on the Outer Banks but fall is considered by many to be the best.

The beaches from Corolla through Ocracoke are some of the only spots left that don't have strict surfing regulations: As long as you keep yourself leashed to your board and stay at least 300 feet away from public piers, you won't get a surfing citation.

The best surfing is from late August through November in hurricane season, when swells from storms are likely to roll toward shore. However, winter nor'easters can kick up waves 8- to 10-feet high. There's a lot of chop and it is absolutely not for beginners, but experienced surfers, grab your drysuit and paddle out. Midsummer is traditionally the worst time for surfing. On small summer waves it's more fun to surf a longboard.

Since the beaches are getting increasingly crowded with summer surfers, some folks understandably don't want to reveal their favorite wave-catching locales. And breaks, which are affected by shifting sandbars, change every year. After fall hurricane season and winter nor'easters, no one really knows which breaks subsided or where they reappear. It takes some looking around in the spring to find new breaks and relinquish old ones.

Piers always make for good breaks because of the sandbars that form around them. In Corolla there is a good break on the beach in front of the Corolla Light swimming pool. You can't park there unless you're staying in the resort, so park at the south ramp road next to the lighthouse and walk up the beach. Swan Beach in the four-wheel-drive area is also good. Kitty Hawk Pier in Kitty Hawk and Avalon Pier in Kill Devil Hills each boast ample parking and pretty good waves. Also check out the area around First and Second Streets in Kill Devil Hills. Nags Head Pier is a good spot, but also check out the beaches north and south of there, especially around milepost 13. Jennette's Pier consistency has one of the best breaks around.

When swells come from the south, Hatteras Island beaches have the best waves. If you don't mind hiking across the dunes with a board under your arm, Pea Island and Coquina Beach both have waves worth the walk. Rodanthe has always been a popular destination, and its name sparks fond recognition with surfers all over the world. If there are waves you'll have no trouble spotting the area because you'll see hundreds of surfers squeezing into wet suits along the roadside. The surf is just a short hop over the dunes from the road. The ramps north and south of Salvo are also worth a try. Ramp 34, just north of Avon, is another location, as are the turnout north of Buxton, ramp 49 in Frisco, Frisco Pier, and the public beach access area between Frisco and Hatteras Village.

> **i** Though good surf breaks tend to form around fishing piers, it's illegal to surf within 300 feet of a pier—for the surfers' own protection, of course.

The best and biggest waves by far roll in around the original site of Cape Hatteras Lighthouse. Here at Cape Point, the beaches jut closest to the Gulf Stream and face in two directions, doubling the chances for good conditions. Concrete and steel groins jut out into the Atlantic, though, so beware of being tossed into these head-bashing barriers.

Surf Reports

Local radio station WVOD 99.1 offers a daily surf report at 8:45 a.m. For an online surf report, visit surfchex.com or surfreport.corollasurfshop.com, or check out surf-cams for the following location websites: Hatteras Lighthouse (surfline.com) or Avalon Pier (avalonpier.com).

Most surf shops have an even more up-to-the-minute pulse on the surf, but not all provide a formal "surf line" service. Following is a list of numbers to call for the daily wave report. Most shops give the scoop only on the portion of the beach in their geographical area.

Surf Shops

Ranging from sublime to specialized to hip, the Outer Banks is inundated with surf shops—hot spots for wave riders of all ages and skill levels. Each summer surf shop managers post competition schedules for beginners through surfing-circuit riders near the storefronts. Most shops stock gear, and many offer instruction during the season. The following list highlights some favorites of Outer Banks surfers.

CAVALIER SURF SHOP, NC 12, MP 13½, Nags Head; (252) 441-7349; cavaliersurfshop.com. This classic shop, the only one on the Beach Road, has been in business since the 1960s. The family-run operation is dedicated to the surfing lifestyle. Cavalier rents a variety of surfboards, boogie boards, and skimboards, plus gloves, booties, and wet suits. They also rent umbrellas, chairs, and rafts for long beach days. Surfboard rental is available. When you're not in the surf, rent a surf video for excitement. New and used boards are for sale, and Cavalier also sells boards by consignment. You'll also find a huge collection of stickers and sunglasses, watches, and clothing for men and women.

COROLLA SURF SHOP, NC 12, Monterey Plaza, Corolla; (252) 453-9283; corollasurfshop.com. Corolla Surf Shop is a full-service shop with boards, lessons, sales, repairs, and rentals. The store also has a full line of new surfboards for sale (more than 100 boards are in stock). A good stock of used boards is available for purchase, along with new skateboards, skimboards, and body boards. The store carries a full skateboard department, clothing, shoes, shades, and jewelry. Check out the surfer's museum too! Surf lessons include all of the equipment for a two-hour lesson. Up to five people take lessons together. Special needs surf lessons are available for ages 9 and up. Rentals are available on a daily and weekly basis. The shop is the home of the Nalu Kai Surf Museum, a free exhibit of 15 collectible surfboards and other surfer memorabilia. Corolla Surf Shop is open year-round. Winter hours vary.

DUCK VILLAGE OUTFITTERS, NC 12, Waterfront Shops, Duck; (252) 261-7222; duckvillageoutfitters.net. With surfboards and body boards, Duck Village Outfitters is surf-shop central for Duck. Surfing lessons are offered daily during the summer season. The shop conducts kayak tours every day in the summer and has a large assortment of rentals and retail items, including bikes, wet suits, fishing equipment, kayaks, and ocean toys.

> **i** Waves look good for body surfing? Be sure that the waves are not breaking right on shore. There is a steep rise at the edge of the water and body surfers risk broken bones if the water breaks at the edge of the beach. Try surfing farther out in the open water.

HATTERAS ISLAND BOARDSPORTS, NC 12, Avon; (252) 995-6160; hiboardsports.com. Just as the name suggests, this surf shop has boards—pick from all styles of surfboards (including custom designs), skimboards, and body boards. Wet suits and surf clothing are sold as well.

HATTERAS ISLAND SURF SHOP, NC 12, Waves; (252) 987-2296; hatterasislandsurfshop.com. Veteran surfers Barton and Chris Decker have operated Hatteras Island Surf Shop since 1971. They expanded their ventures to include windsurfing. The surf shop offers new and used equipment, rentals, and lessons. It sells surfboards, balsa boards, longboards, body boards, ocean toys, kayaks, and in-line skates. Wet suits, surfwear, beach clothing, and bathing suits are also for sale in this no-nonsense surf shop. The shop closes in January and February.

NATURAL ART SURF SHOP, NC 12, Buxton, (252) 995-5682; surfinthe eye.com. Natural Art specializes in both custom-made surfboards and a full line of handmade surf wear for men, women, and kids. The shop also carries shoes, wet suits, skatewear, and videos. The surfboards are shaped by owner Scott Busbey in a separate shop in the backyard. Busbey has gained a national reputation for his beautiful craftsmanship and reasonably priced boards. Rent surfboards, boogie boards, and wet suits here.

i When you're surfing or kayaking in the ocean waves, look out for your fellow surfers and for swimmers. Do not cut across the path of someone actively riding a wave. Courteously ask swimmers to move down the beach a bit if they're swimming in the best breaks.

THE PIT SURF SHOP, US 158, MP 9, Kill Devil Hills; (252) 480-3128; pitsurf.com. The Pit bills itself as a "surf hangout." The setup includes a 3,000-square-foot surf shop that covers all board sports—surfing, body boarding, skimming, and skateboarding. Owners Steve Pauls and Ben Sproul, both devout surfers, sell a large selection of new, used, and custom boards, including the locally made Gale Force boards, plus a selection of wet suits and related accessories. All boards are available for sale or rent. Surf lessons and camps are offered in the summer months for groups or individuals. Lessons run about two hours and include board rental and a T-shirt.

RIDE THE WIND SURF SHOP, NC 12, Ocracoke; (252) 928-6311; surf ocracoke.com. In business since 1985, Ride the Wind features two floors of merchandise, ranging from the latest contemporary surf gear to casual, comfortable clothing and footwear for men and women. Ride the Wind rents surfboards, body boards, wet suits, and practically all Outer Banks water sports equipment, except windsurfing items. Surfboards can be rented here. The shop is open seven days a week from March through December and is closed for the winter. Ride the Wind also offers outfitting trips to Portsmouth Island and a surf and kayak day camp for kids. Beginner surf lessons are available for adults and kids.

RODANTHE SURF SHOP, NC 12, Rodanthe; (252) 987-2412; rodanthe surfshop.com. Rodanthe Surf Shop owners Randy Hall and Debbie Bell moved to the southern Outer Banks to surf, and the shop evolved naturally from their lifestyle. A hands-on, no-frills operation, the shop sells only the boards it makes, Hatteras Glass Surfboards, along with surfing equipment and surfer lifestyle clothing. Get a true surfing experience by renting a real fiberglass board here. The shop is closed Thanksgiving through March.

SECRET SPOT SURF SHOP, US 158, MP 11, Nags Head; (252) 441-4030; secretspotsurfshop.com. No secret to surf enthusiasts, Secret Spot is one of the old-timers of the barrier islands' surf scene and claims to have the most boards available. Packed with the best of contemporary and classic boards and favorite surfwear, the store prides itself in catering to both younger and older surfers. The business has manufactured its own surfboards since 1977; the shop opened five years later. A full line of shortboards, longboards, and custom and used boards are available, along with a selection of wet suits. Surfboards can be rented and lessons are available. Call the shop or visit the website for surf reports. Secret Spot also sells items for women and girls, including sundresses, T-shirts, bathing suits, shorts, shoes, and accessories. The skate store has a full selection of skateboard paraphernalia, including decks, trucks, wheels, and accessories.

WAVE RIDING VEHICLES, US 158, MP 2, Kitty Hawk; (252) 261-7952; waveridingvehicles.com. Carrying top-of-the-line surfboards, apparel, and accessories since 1967, WRV focuses on what the owner calls "the godfather of water sports"—surfing. This year-round shop also sells skateboards and snowboards. It's one of the largest full-service surf shops on the barrier islands. WRV is also the biggest surfboard manufacturing company under one label on the

i Don't know how to surf, and not sure you want to learn? Try purchasing a boogie board and you'll still have big fun on the waves. No instruction is necessary; only good swimming skills and a board are required.

East Coast. The company produces private-label surfwear, which is sold from Maine to Florida and overseas. Surfboards rent daily and weekly.

WHALEBONE SURF SHOP, US 158, MP 10, Nags Head; (252) 441-6747; whalebonesurfshop.com. Surfer-owned and -operated, Whalebone boasts that it has been in business since the 1960s. Major brands of surfboards, and the best of the smaller brands, are available at this well-stocked store. Surfboard rentals are available for trials. The store is open year-ound, but hours vary so call ahead.

Annual Events

The beach isn't just for summer anymore. The Outer Banks has become a favorite destination for visitors year-round, providing those vacationing during less crowded times with a selection of activities to enjoy when life slows a bit.

When it comes to annual events on the Outer Banks, the environment and history are on our side. We have our time-honored cornerstones that draw national audiences, including the festivities each December commemorating the anniversary of humankind's first powered flight and the annual celebrations that revolve around Virginia Dare's birthday. Our environment is the calling card for national surfing championships, windsurfing and kiteboarding competitions, hang-gliding events, and world-class fishing tournaments.

The Outer Banks Forum (252-202-9732) offers musical performances, dramas, and comedies in the off-season. The Bryan Cultural Series (bryan culturalseries.org) brings top flight classically trained musicians to the Outer Banks, as well as, artists and authors. Look to the Theatre of Dare (252-473-1825) for comedy and drama performances in the off-season. The Dare County Arts Council (252-473-5558) sponsors a variety of performing and visual arts events throughout the year. Check out the **Arts & Culture** chapter for other options.

Check outerbanks.org/events for recently added activities.

THROUGHOUT THE YEAR

DON AND KATHARINE BRYAN CULTURAL SERIES, bryancultural series.org. Created through a generous behest from Don Bryan, artist, veteran, community leader and Mayor of Nags Head, the Bryan Cultural Series brings a variety of events to the Outer Banks. One of their most popular events is the annual Surf & Sound Concert Series that brings string quartet to various Outer Banks locations in August. The BCS has also sponsored lectures from best-selling authors and brought the NY Gilbert and Sullivan Players to the Outer Banks.

OUTER BANKS FORUM FOR THE LIVELY ARTS, (252) 202-9732; outerbanksforum.org. The Outer Banks Forum organizes six varied arts performances a year, bringing world-class performers to this remote stretch of the world. Since 1983 the forum has scheduled these performances from October through April, making the off-season months brighter for many folks. The forum seasons are filled with interesting and wide-ranging selections, including bluegrass, opera, and folk tales. Most performances are held in the First Flight

High School auditorium. Weather permitting the Virginia Symphony last performance of the season is held outdoors at Roanoke Island Festival Park. The Virginia Symphony is usually scheduled in April. Starting time is at 7:30 p.m.

THE THEATRE OF DARE, (252) 261-4064; theatreofdare.org. The Theatre of Dare was established in 1992 with a grant from the Outer Banks Forum. Its members bring quality live theater to the Outer Banks by taking part in all phases of production, such as directing, set design, and performing. The Theatre of Dare produces three main stage productions a year from fall to spring. TOD embodies the true spirit of community theater by welcoming amateur and professional thespians alike.

The organization thus far has produced hits such as *Arsenic and Old Lace*, *Steel Magnolias*, *The Odd Couple*, *Peter Pan*, *Bell Book and Candle*, *The Gin Game*, and *Little Women*. The Theatre of Dare performances are held at COA in Manteo. Adult tickets are usually around $13 and kids are around $8. For more information about membership, volunteering, auditions, or production dates, call the number listed here.

JANUARY

FRANK STICK MEMORIAL ART SHOW, Old Courthouse, Manteo; (252) 473-5558; darearts.org. This art show has been held in late January through early February every year since 1978 and features the work of more than 160 artists. If you want to submit work, you must be at least 18 years-old and a Dare County resident or a member of the Dare County Arts Council, which sponsors the show. The evening reception is eagerly anticipated, and local artists and patrons flock to the gallery to view the newest offerings from the art world. But don't be shy; the event welcomes visitors to partake of the sights, sounds, and tastes of the evening. If you can't make the reception, stop by during the month of February and view this always exciting and innovative exhibit. It's a fun show, and the reception becomes an annual get-together for locals and visitors alike.

FEBRUARY

ELIZABETHAN RENDEZVOUS CABARET, Pamlico Jack's Pirate Hideaway; (252) 473-1061. This seven-course gourmet feast includes musical entertainment and dramatic interpretations. Tickets are about $100 per person and include food, wine, and beer.

MARCH OF DIMES SIGNATURE CHEF'S AUCTION, Hilton Garden Inn, Kitty Hawk; (240) 432-1994; hrsigchef.com/outer-banks. Fans of fine dining, fine wine, auctions, and entertainment will want to attend the March of Dimes Signature Chef's auction held in late February. Get your tickets early, this is a popular event that sells out.

MARCH

PRICELESS PIECES PAST & PRESENT QUILT EXTRAVAGANZA, Roanoke Island Festival Park Art Gallery, Manteo; (252) 475-1500. If you love quilts and the fabric arts, you'll love this popular annual show. The show features old and new quilts made by or belonging to Dare County residents. There are also demonstrations. It's held throughout the month of March.

ST. PATRICK'S DAY PARADE, NC 12, Nags Head; (252) 441-4116; kellysrestaurant.com. The St. Patrick's Day Parade is held the Sunday before St. Patrick's Day every year. The parade begins around the Nags Head Fishing Pier at MP 12 on the Beach Road and proceeds north to about MP 10. Reputed to be one of the largest parades of its kind in North Carolina, the event is fun for the whole family. Float participants throw candy, so wear something with pockets! Kelly's serves free hot dogs and sodas after the parade and celebrates with an evening of live entertainment. All events are free.

Since 1989, Mike Kelly's St. Patrick's Day Parade has brought a sense of whimsy and laughter to the Outer Banks.

OUTER BANKS WEDDING EXPO, First Flight High School, Kill Devil Hills; outerbanksweddingassoc.org. The largest wedding event on the Outer Banks takes place every year in early to mid-March. More than 1,000 brides and families attend the Saturday and Sunday exhibit and meet with many of the businesses on the beach that cater to the local wedding industry. Foods can be sampled from caterers; photographers display their work; and musicians play samples of their music throughout the day. A fashion show and a drawing for an all-expenses-paid wedding top off the event.

TASTE OF THE BEACH, various places from Corolla to Manteo; (252) 202-8837; obxtasteofthebeach.com. Four days of food, dining, and fun. At the finest independent restaurants all over the beach, partake in wine tastings, cooking classes, and more. Top-notch eateries compete for awards, and the event culminates in a grand tasting. This event grows each year and has become quite popular. Get tickets early; check the website for details.

APRIL

ANNUAL EASTER EGGSTRAVAGANZA, Kitty Hawk Kites, US 158, MP 12, Nags Head; (252) 441-4124; kittyhawk.com. This event is held at Kitty Hawk Kites in Nags Head, with the specific date dependent on when Easter falls. Kids enjoy chalk coloring contests, a variety of games, and an Easter candy dig on the premises. Small fries get a kick out of meeting KHK's fuzzy brown mascot, Wil-Bear Wright. All activities are free.

ANNUAL OUTER BANKS BIKE WEEK, Outer Banks Harley-Davidson, US 158, Harbinger; US 158, MP 13, Nags Head; (252) 338-8866; outer bankshd.com. Rumbling into town, motorcyclists explore the Outer Banks for bike week the third week of each April. More than a few riders comb the area on their bikes during the festivities. Included in the fun are poker runs, bike shows, beauty contests, beer belly and tattoo contests, music, and official party sites named for each night.

EASTER EGGSTRAVAGANZA, Elizabethan Gardens, US 64, Roanoke Island; (252) 473-3234; elizabethangardens.org. Spring over to the Elizabethan Gardens and participate in this festive event. Hundreds of Easter eggs are hidden among the 40,000 blooms. Bunnies, Easter hat competitions, and more.

EARTH DAY CELEBRATION, North Carolina Aquarium at Roanoke Island; (252) 473-5121; ncaquarium.com. Each year the Earth Day celebration on the Outer Banks encourages a large subset of the community to participate in activities recognizing and education participants about environmental awareness. Admission to the aquarium is free on Earth Day (April 22). From 11 a.m. until 3 p.m.

EARTH FAIR OBX, UNC Coastal Studies Institute, Wanchese; (252) 473-1607; csi.northcarolina.edu. On the Satuday closest to Earth Day, the UNC Coastal Studies Institute hosts an open house of science and family fun! This event offers various ongoing activities, and the chance to learn about many local organizations while exploring the facility.

FLYING PIRATE HALF MARATHON, Kitty Hawk to Nags Head; (252) 255-6273; flyingpiratehalfmarathon.com. This popular event is held in mid-April. Runners take off in Kitty Hawk and complete the course in the maritime forest in Nags Head.

MAY

BRITISH CEMETERY CEREMONY, British Cemetery Rd., Ocracoke Island; (252) 928-3711. This ceremony commemorates the 1942 sinking of a British ship. On May 11 of that year, the HMS *Bedfordshire*, a trawler stationed off Ocracoke to protect our shores during World War II, was torpedoed and sunk by a German submarine. All on board perished, and only four bodies were recovered. Island residents buried these men, and every year in early May on the Friday closest to the anniversary of the sinking, the US Coast Guard holds a service to honor them. The service is free. (See the **Attractions** chapter for more information.)

HANG GLIDING SPECTACULAR, Jockey's Ridge State Park, US 158, MP 12, Nags Head; (252) 441-4124; kittyhawk.com. Spectators and participants cover the dunes at the park every year to attend the longest-running hang-gliding competition in the country (held for over 40 years), Pilots from all over the world compete in a variety of flying maneuvers, including an aerotow competition. Beginner hang-gliding lessons are given. The event is sponsored by Kitty Hawk Kites, and a free admission street dance and an awards ceremony add icing to the cake. Annual inductions to the Rogallo Hall of Fame (Southern Shores local Francis Rogallo was the beloved father of the Flexible Wing Flyer—the prototype for the modern hang glider) close the ceremony. Hang glider pilots with a Hang One rating or above are eligible to compete. The public is invited to view the event for free. Participants pay an entry fee.

HATTERAS VILLAGE OFFSHORE OPEN, Hatteras Harbor Marina, NC 12, Hatteras Village; (757) 287-4932; hatterasonmymind.com. Anglers contend for cash prizes as they fish to catch and release the biggest billfish. A meat fish category is included for the largest tuna, dolphin, and wahoo caught daily.

The three-day fishing tournament is sponsored by the Hatteras Village Civic Association. This is a Governor's Cup–sanctioned event, and it's the kickoff tournament in the Governor's Cup challenge. All competitors must enter Level 1 for $700; three additional levels—Level 2 at $800, Level 3 at $500, and Level 4 at $1,000—are not mandatory. Fishing begins at 8 a.m., and lines come out of the water promptly at 3 p.m. Festivities with food and drink are usually held each evening, and the event closes with an awards banquet. The tournament is open to the public.

INTERNATIONAL MINIATURE ART SHOW, Seaside Art Gallery, NC 12, MP 11, Nags Head; (252) 441-5418; seasideart.com. Artists from all over the world compete for cash prizes in this exhibition of miniature art. Past shows have seen more than 600 works from 38 states and 12 countries. The work includes paintings, sculpture, and drawings of all styles. The art is on view for the month of May.

MOLLIE FEARING MEMORIAL ART SHOW, Old Courthouse, Manteo; (252) 473-5558; darearts.org. This exhibition, sponsored by the Dare County Arts Council, is open to all artists, and cash awards are given. It is held throughout the month of May and is open for public viewing. Call for membership, reception, and entry information.

MUSTANG SPRING JAM, Whalehead Club, Corolla; mustangmusic festival.com. This righteous music festival benefits the Corolla Wild Horse Fund and the Mustang Outreach Program helping young musicians to hone their performance skills. It also is known as one of the most fun spring events on the beach! Held in mid-May on a Saturday and Sunday from 1 to 10 p.m., festival-goers hear great tunes, eat fantastic food, and help the horses and young musicians. Kids 12 and under free; tickets around range from $20 to $30. VIP Tickets are also available.

OUTER BANKS BLUEGRASS FESTIVAL, Roanoke Island Festival Park, Manteo; bluegrassisland.com. This four day celebration of all things bluegrass music is one of the largest around. Headliners in the past include Rhonda Vincent and the Rage who has made an appearance at every OBF to date, Steep Canyon Rangers, Joe Mullins & The Radio Ramblers, Seldom Seen and more. An outdoor concert the setting is beautiful and the music divine.

YUENGLING NAGS HEAD WOODS 5K RUN, Nags Head Woods Ecological Preserve, Ocean Acres Dr., Kill Devil Hills; nagsheadwoods5krun.org. Folks from all walks of life run side-by-side through Nags Head Woods in this annual event, held on the second Saturday in May. The run is limited to the first 400 runners registered. For entry fees and tickets, visit the website.

JUNE

DARE DAY FESTIVAL, Downtown Manteo; (252) 475-5629. This is the quintessential small-town family event. Dare Day, held the first Saturday of June, is a much-loved local tradition that celebrates the wonderful county of Dare. You'll find locals, visitors, politicians, children, and just about everybody you can think of coming out to enjoy the day in downtown Manteo. Dare Day features arts and crafts booths, lots of food (including in-season soft-shell crabs), national and local musical entertainment, kids' activities, games, rides, and much more. A free concert is held at Roanoke Island Festival Park in the pavilion. All of Festival Park's sites, including the *Elizabeth II*, are free on this day. This event is as "local" as it gets.

HATTERAS MARLIN CLUB BILLFISH TOURNAMENT, Hatteras Marlin Club, off NC 12, Hatteras Village; (252) 986-2454; hatterasmarlin club.com. The Hatteras Marlin Club Billfish Tournament, going strong since 1959, offers a week of competition fishing and entertainment to participants and their guests. Teams head for offshore waters looking to catch the biggest billfish or meat fish, including blue marlin, tuna, dolphin, and wahoo. Evenings are filled with socials that include entertainment, cocktails, appetizers, and dinner. The tournament is for members and anglers invited by the tournament committee. Call for registration fee information.

Before you leave home, check outerbanks.org/calendar_of_events for recently added happenings on the Outer Banks. It's a great resource for new celebrations happening on the islands.

ROGALLO KITE FESTIVAL, Jockey's Ridge State Park, US 158, MP 12, Nags Head; (800) 334-4777; kittyhawk.com. This two-day annual festival celebrates kites of all sizes and shapes. Fly a kite on the dunes and enjoy nightly entertainment at Kitty Hawk Kites. Exhibitions, demonstrations, and kids' activities are all a part of this event.

TEA WITH THE QUEEN, Waterside Theatre, Roanoke Island; (252) 473-2127; thelostcolony.org. Have an audience and enjoy tea with Queen Elizabeth I and her royal court at Waterside Theatre, the same spot where *The Lost Colony* performs in the evening. A backstage tour is included. Held Thursdays, June through August; advance reservations are required. Ticket prices are $22 for adults, $11 for children 7 to 18.

UNDER THE OAKS ARTS FESTIVAL, The Whalehead Club, Corolla; whalehead.com. Enjoy this annual outdoor art show on the waterfront grounds of Currituck Heritage Park. This festival features the unique talents of over 100 quality artists using a wide variety of media, plus musical entertainment, local food, wine tasting, concessions, an art auction, and children's activities. Admission is free. $5 parking donation requested.

JULY

ANNUAL WRIGHT KITE FESTIVAL, Wright Brothers National Memorial; US 158, MP 8, Kill Devil Hills; (252) 441-4124; kittyhawk.com. This mid-July family event involves kite flying for all ages and also includes free kite-making workshops, stunt kite demos, and children's games. The event, sponsored by Kitty Hawk Kites and the National Park Service, has been held every year since 1978. You can watch for free. Adults are invited to participate in kite contests. Call for fees.

Sponsored by Kitty Hawk Kites, the Wright Kite Festival occurs annually in July.

DUCK ANNUAL 4TH OF JULY PARADE, Duck; (252) 255-1234; townofduck.com. ABC News named this parade as one of the top 10 best small town 4th of July celebrations. It has to be experienced to be appreciated. The parade is sometimes held on July 3, so incoming traffic of arriving guests will not create a bottleneck in this small town (call ahead). At 9 a.m. the parade winds its way from Scarborough Lane, up Clover Way to Christopher Drive. After the parade, a community social is held at Duck Town Park. Loads of patriotic garb recommended.

FIREWORKS FESTIVAL AND FAIR, The Whalehead Club, NC 12, Corolla; (252) 453-9040; visitwhalehead.com. The historic hunt club is the backdrop for the fireworks and fair which begin at 6 p.m. and run to 11 p.m. The Currituck County Board of Commissioners and the Corolla Business Association host this event. Expect fun, food, live musical entertainment, and, of course, pyrotechnics galore. Admission is free.

KILL DEVIL HILLS INDEPENDENCE DAY FIREWORKS, Avalon Pier, MP 6, Kill Devil Hills. There is something magical about watching the celebration of our nation's birth at the edge of a continent. Best viewing is anywhere on the beach within a mile of the pier. Even a bit farther away will still give a good show. Expect heavy traffic after the light show.

MANTEO INDEPENDENCE DAY CELEBRATION, Manteo; (252) 473-1101; townofmanteo.com. Activities run from 1 to 9 p.m. and include a Wacky Tacky Hat Contest, children's games, food and other concessions, musical entertainment, and a street dance from 6 to 9 p.m., when a fireworks display begins. The event is free.

NAGS HEAD INDEPENDENCE DAY FIREWORKS, Nags Head Pier, MP 11.5, Nags Head. Best viewing is anywhere on the beach within a mile of the pier (or even a bit farther away). Expect heavy traffic after the light show.

SAND SCULPTURE CONTEST, Ocracoke Village; (252) 928-7689. This artistic endeavor kicks off Fourth of July festivities on the island. Kids and adults are welcome to participate in the early-morning event. You can work alone or in groups. Past events have seen sand transformed into turtles, jumping dolphins, pirates, mermaids, and ships. The contest is free. Call for times and location.

AUGUST

ALICE KELLY MEMORIAL LADIES-ONLY BILLFISH TOURNAMENT, Pirate's Cove Yacht Club, Nags Head–Manteo Causeway, Manteo;

(252) 473-6800; pcbgt.com. The tournament, sponsored by Pirate's Cove since 1989, honors the memory of local fishing enthusiast Alice Kelly, who died in her 30s from Hodgkin's disease. Kelly was a high-spirited woman whose love for fishing inspired many local women to try (and fall in love with) the sport. Women form teams and arrange for charter boats to carry them out to sea. The tournament occurs in mid-August. The entry fee is $500 per boat.

ANNUAL PIRATE'S COVE BILLFISH TOURNAMENT, Pirate's Cove Yacht Club, Nags Head–Manteo Causeway, Manteo; (252) 473-6800, fish-piratescove.com. Pirate's Cove Yacht Club has hosted a billfish release tournament every August since 1983. Contenders fish for several days to catch and release the largest billfish. A meat fish (tuna, dolphin, and wahoo) category, in which a prize is awarded for the largest catch, adds to the fun. The tournament is an official part of the NC Governor's Cup Billfish Series and occurs mid-month. Call for entry fee information.

NATIONAL AVIATION DAY, Wright Brothers National Memorial, US 158, MP 8, Kill Devil Hills; (252) 441-7430; nps.gov/wrbr. Explore planes galore at this free mid-August event. Aviation enthusiasts enjoy viewing about 25 different types of single-engine aircraft ranging from the antique to modern-day models. The schedule is not firm until a few days before the event so weather conditions can be taken into consideration. Past events have included a flyover with US Air Force and Navy planes, jets from Langley Field, and the Blue Angels. The day's festivities include free admission to the memorial and special talks given throughout the day.

NEW WORLD FESTIVAL OF THE ARTS, Manteo; (252) 473-2838; townofmanteo.com. This mid-August event brings downtown Manteo alive with art every year. The outdoor two-day show features more than 80 artists showcasing fine art and crafts, including pottery, jewelry, paintings, and more. Outdoor booths and tents line the historic waterfront, attracting visitors who return each year looking for their favorite artists; free admission.

OUTER BANKS PIRATE FESTIVAL, Kitty Hawk Kites, MP 12½, Nags Head; (252) 441-4124; kittyhawk.com. Hark, all ye little buccaneers! Aaaaarrgh, it's pirate week on the Outer Banks in mid-August. Community events throughout the week culminate at the Nags Head Kitty Hawk Kites location. Entertainment, reenactments, games, stories, and pirate appearances top off the week.

SURFING FOR AUTISM, Jennette's Pier, Nags Head; surfingforautism .org. Second Saturday of August. One of the most amazing feel good days of the year. Experienced surfers of the Outer Banks community take kids across

All Summer Long

Acoustic Sunset, Sanctuary Vineyards/Cotton Gin, 6957 Caratoke Hwy, Jarvisburg; (252) 491-2387; sanctuaryvineyards.com. Not strictly on the Outer Banks but close enough that this wonderful Thursday evening free concert is worth checking out. Held beneath the towering pines on the north end of the Cotton Gin just 11 miles north of the Wright Memorial Bridge, Acoustic Sunset is a perfect family outing. Picnic tables, wine from Sanctuary Vineyards, which is part of the Cotton Gin and of course, wonderful music.

Artrageous Art Extravaganza, Dare County Arts Council, Dowdy Park, Nags Head; (252) 473-5558; darearts.org. Artrageous, started in 1990, is a community art festival and auction sponsored by the Dare County Arts Council in May. Children and adults are invited to spend Saturday painting, weaving, and creating various arts and crafts. All art supplies are provided. Listen to local musicians young and old, eat tasty food, and witness art in the making by professionals. Artists sell their wares. This event does not require an admission fee. Average price for booth activities is $1.

Chicamacomico Lifesaving Station, NC 12, Rodanthe; (252) 987-1552; chicamacomico.net. Summer programs at the Chicamacomico Lifesaving Station run June through August. Monday: Behind the scenes stories on the filming of *Nights in Rodanthe*; Tuesday: America's Forgotten Heroes; Most Wednesdays: Traditional Hatteras Cooking (small fee); Thursday: Beach Apparatus Drill, Friday: Hence the Phrase word game.

Duck Town Park, NC 12, Duck; (252) 255-1286; townofduck .com. Throughout June, July, and August, a variety of programs are held at Duck Town Park. Check the website or call the above number for more information on these programs. Bring a hat and a blanket or beach chair to this lovely setting.

First Friday, downtown Manteo; roanokeisland.net. Visit the waterfront and downtown Manteo the first Friday of the month April through December. The waterfront comes alive with music, artisans, magicians, and more. 6 p.m. until 9 p.m.

Kitty Hawk Kites Kids Day, Corolla, Nags Head, Waves, and Hatteras; (252) 441-4124; kittyhawk.com. This free event is held on Tuesday (except in Nags Head and Waves, on Wednesday) June through August. Kids can make and fly a kite, try their hands at yo-yos, have their faces painted and—best of all—demo the latest toys.

Roanoke Island Festival Park Children's Theater, Roanoke Island Festival Park, Manteo; (252) 475-1500; roanokeisland.com. Roanoke Island Festival Park is an interactive family cultural site. Each year in June and early July, a Children's Theater Program is presented. A series of plays and shows catering to the 5-to-12 set run for one week and are performed by various theater companies from across the state. Showtimes are typically 10:30 a.m. Tickets are $5.

The Lost Colony, Waterside Theatre, Manteo; (252) 473-3414; thelostcolony.org. *The Lost Colony* is a theatrical presentation of a 400-year-old mystery performed on the actual location of the historic event. It is presented from the end of May through the third week of August at 8 p.m. Backstage tours and picnics are available with a reservation before the show. Call the box office or visit the website for details. Other presentations are performed at 2 p.m. on Wednesday and Thursday. More information appears in the **Attractions** chapter.

Whalehead Club Wednesday Wine Festival, Whalehead Club, Corolla; (252) 453-9040; visitwhalehead.com. Held July, August, and September, come enjoy North Carolina wines and wines from around the world each Wed. A $25 admission fee not only admits you to the sampling areas, but you also may keep the souvenir glass, listen to popular local musical groups, sample food from local vendors, and take a complimentary tour of the Whalehead Club. 3 until 7 p.m. Leashed pets welcome.

the entire spectrum of autism into the surf to help them ride some waves. Hard to tell who gets the most out of it—the kids, the surfers or the parents.

VIRGINIA DARE BIRTHDAY CELEBRATION, Fort Raleigh National Historic Site Visitor Center; US 64/264, Roanoke Island; (252) 473-2127. This event, held August 18, commemorates the birth of Virginia Dare, the first English child born in the New World. The celebration features a daylong series of special happenings. Past events featured performances by members of the cast of *The Lost Colony* and demonstrations of arms from that period in history. Call the National Park Service for details. This event is free. The Elizabethan Gardens, right next to Fort Raleigh, honors Virginia Dare's birthday by offering reduced admission to the gardens on this day; cake and ice cream are served.

WAVE RIDING VEHICLES HURLEY OBX PRO, Jennette's Pier, Nags Head; (252) 261-7952; wrvobxpro.com. Talent from all over the world competes at one of the largest pro surfing events on the East Coast for a $30,000 prize. Held last weekend of August or early September. Check site for details. Corresponding events held in the evening throughout the community.

SEPTEMBER

DAY AT THE DOCKS—A CELEBRATION OF HATTERAS WATER-MEN, Hatteras Village; dayatthedocks.org. In mid-September, visit Hatteras Village to view the commercial and charter fleets anchored in the Hatteras waters. Displays, boat skills, demonstrations, and competitions kick off the day. Maritime games for kids will be available throughout the day, as well as fun activities like crab races and meaningful releasing of the doves at the invocation ceremony. Participants enjoy the live music and the educational tent. Fresh local seafood will be featured in the chowder cook-off and cooking demonstrations. The event takes place from 10 a.m. until 5 p.m.

ESA EASTERN SURFING CHAMPIONSHIPS, Jennette's Pier, Nags Head; outerbanks.surfesa.org. Competition is open to Eastern Surfing Association members only, but it's an exciting and free spectator event. Watch as surfers grab their boards and head to the ocean to pit their skills against the waves and their fellow competitors. First and last weekends in September; check the website for exact date.

HATTERAS VILLAGE CIVIC ASSOCIATION SURF FISHING TOUR-NAMENT, Hatteras Village Civic Center, NC 12, Hatteras Village; (252) 986-2579; hatterasonmymind.com. Since 1982 surf-fishing fans have met the third week in September for this tournament. Over 90 teams fish for eligible species including drum, bluefish, trout, and more. Call for registration fees and information.

THE LOST COLONY WINE AND CULINARY FESTIVAL & GRAND TASTING, The Lost Colony, 1409 National Park Dr., Manteo; (252)-473-2127; tlcwinefest.com. A two-day event featuring wind and beer tasting on The Lost Colony grounds. The setting is spectacular with Roanoke and Croatan Sounds as a backdrop. The Vintner's Dinner is a must do to the event as some of the finest Outer Banks chef's team up to create a culinary masterpiece that pairs with classic wines.

OBX BREWTÄG, Outer Banks Event Site, MP 16, Croatan Hwy, Nags Head; (252) 441-1719; obxbrewtag.com. Leave it to the fun crew at Kitty Hawk Kites to come up with another innovative, fun-packed celebration like OBX Brewtäg. Twenty-five teams will compete to defy gravity and launch into the air a half-barrel keg. Judged on distance and enthusiasm of teams, this event is fun for all ages. While teams compete, festival-goers can visit the KidZone, enjoy live music, and sample local food. A North Carolina Brew Haus will be on site for the beer lovers in the crowd.

OBX PRIDEFEST, various locations; obxpridefest.com. A three-day LGBTQ festival. Daytime events are very family friendly. Evening events not so much.

OBX TRIATHALON, Dare County Regional Airport, Manteo; (252) 255-6273; obxtriathalon.com. Swim, bike, and run in this event held in early September, which brings athletes from near and far to compete in this unique coastal environment. The event features half distance, sprint, and Olympic distance challenges.

OUTER BANKS FOOD TRUCK SHOWDOWN, Soundside Event Site, Nags Head. Grab your appetite and get ready to try some of the best fast food you have ever had as food trucks from the Outer Banks and surrounding communities compete for best in show. Held the first weekend after Labor Day.

SURFALOROUS FILM FESTIVAL, Dare County Arts Council, Old Dare County Courthouse, Manteo; darearts.org. An eclectic blend of surf movies and art. Some of the movies are surprisingly good and are shown outdoors at various locations. A multi-day event.

OCTOBER

ANNUAL DUCK JAZZ FESTIVAL, Duck Town Park, (252) 255-1286; townofduck.com. Dig that groovy beat at Duck Town Park's annual jazz festival. Several acclaimed bands will perform at this free festival held the second Sunday in October from 11 a.m. until 5 p.m. Bring a blanket and enjoy some great music. Local businesses in Duck hold events in conjunction with this hot and hip festival.

KELLY'S/PAMLICO JACK'S CHARITY GOLF TOURNAMENT, US 158, MP 15, Nags Head; Currituck Club, Corolla; (252) 441-4116. Six-person teams play 18 holes for charity during late October. Proceeds benefit the Outer Banks Community Foundation. Fees per team generally run around $500.

MUSTANG ROCK & ROAST, Mike Dianna's Grill Room, Corolla; mustangmusicfestival.com. A two-day event featuring food and music. The first day is a BBQ cook-off; the second day is an oyster roast. Throughout both days some of the finest rock, blues and fusion bands around perform. A must do for anyone with a taste for BBQ, oysters, and great music. Proceeds benefit the Corolla Wild Horse Fund and the Mustang Outreach Program helping young musicians to hone their performance skills.

Since 2007 the Duck Jazz Festival has given visitors and residents two days of great music in a beautiful setting. This is a free event.

NAGS HEAD SURF FISHING CLUB INVITATIONAL TOURNAMENT, Nags Head; nagsheadsurffishingclub.org. The Nags Head Surf Fishing Club's tournament has been active since 1951! Team fishing can be booked solid for years. But participants are welcome to fish the individual tournament held in mid-October on Saturday from 8 a.m. to noon.

OUTER BANKS HOMEBUILDERS ASSOCIATION'S PARADE OF HOMES, from Corolla to South Nags Head and Manteo; (252) 449-8232. Planning on building a home or looking for some design inspiration? The OBHA opens new and remodeled homes to the public for this event being held early October. It costs $15 to tour about 18 participating homes. Proceeds are donated to local charities.

OUTER BANKS STUNT KITE COMPETITION, Wright Brothers Memorial, MP 8, Kill Devil Hills; (252) 441-4124; kittyhawk.com. Entrants compete on the Eastern League Circuit of the American Kiting Association, held the last weekend in September. The program features novice, intermediate, and expert challenges as well as workshops and demos. Kids enjoy making kites. Music, kite-ballet competitions, and team train competitions highlight the sanctioned event. Registration and competition fees are charged to competitors.

RED DRUM TOURNAMENT, Frank and Fran's Fisherman's Friend, NC 12, Avon; also ramps 23-38, Avon; (252) 995-4171; ncbbaonline.com. Two hundred anglers fish the surf and try to catch the largest red drum during this late October event, sponsored by the popular Avon tackle shop. Fees are about $100 per person. Limited space is available for this three-day tournament.

NOVEMBER

ADVICE 5K ANNUAL TURKEY TROT, Duck, (252) 255-1050; advice5 .com. Pump up your Thanksgiving Day appetite with an early-morning 5K run. This annual, non-sanctioned 3.1-mile run starts behind Scarborough Lane Shops in Duck and ends at the Red Sky Cafe/Village Wine Shop, where everyone gathers for a raffle and to see the winners. The top male and female runners win a pumpkin pie. This is a lively event. Walkers and runners are welcome, and no one is expected to take it too seriously. Register early by calling the number above, or register in person at the Red Sky Cafe on the Wednesday before Thanksgiving Day. There is no race-day registration.

ALL SAINTS EPISCOPAL CHURCH CHRISTMAS BAZAAR, 40 Pintail Trl., Southern Shores; (252) 261-6674; all-saints-eastcarolina.org. Expect to be wowed on the Friday and Saturday before Thanksgiving, when All Saints Episcopal Church becomes a Christmas shopper's paradise. Fine art, hand-painted home accessories, custom jewelry, artful Christmas decor, and more are available at this annual event. Delicious baked goods are prepared just in time to serve for Thanksgiving. Also popular are the frozen, chef-prepared entrees ready to stock your freezer. You'll find truly wonderful gifts in all price ranges. This event is not to be missed!

BOB BERNARD CAPE HATTERAS ANGLERS CLUB INDIVIDUAL SURF. The Cape Hatteras Anglers Club sponsors a one-day individual surf-fishing tournament in mid-November. Registration is held at the Cape Hatteras Anglers Club in Buxton, and fishing takes place from 8 a.m. to noon. Prizes are awarded. Adult, junior, and youth competitions are held.

CHICAMACOMICO LIFESAVING STATION CHRISTMAS LIGHTING, NC 12, Rodanthe; (252) 987-1552; chicamacomico.com. This classic lifesaving station looks absolutely stunning when decorated for the holidays with lights, greenery, and ribbons. In late November when the building is decorated in its finery, the folks at Chicamacomico have a daylong celebration and open house.

ISLAND FARM ISLAND FOODWAYS, US 64/264, Roanoke Island; (252) 473-6500. During the weekend after Thanksgiving, Island Farm interprets fall food traditions and shares how Roanoke Islanders prepared for winters during the 1850s. Activities such as hearth cooking, food preservation, ox-drawn wagon rides corn shucking, and shelling are included. Bring a nonperishable food item for the food pantry and receive $1 off admission.

KITES WITH LIGHTS, Jockey's Ridge State Park, Nags Head; (252) 441-4124; kittyhawk.com. Stunt kites are strung with lights, creating a magical, multicolored nighttime scene. The kites fly sky high, dancing to traditional Christmas carols. Climbing up Jockey's Ridge at night is fun, especially when you're treated with a show like this at the top. Christmas carols, hot apple cider, and cookies add to the festivities. This event is held in late November. It's free and begins at sunset.

MANTEO ROTARY INSHORE SLAM, Pavilion at Pirate's Cove, Manteo; (252) 473-4268; rockfishrodeo.com. Participants fish in the sound or ocean from 6 a.m. to 3 p.m. and bring one fish back to the weigh station. Participants compete for the largest fish in four categories; stripers, flounder, puppy drum, and speckle trout. Trophies are given to the top four winners in the ocean and sound categories, and the top winner can win up to $5,000. All nonfishing events and the weigh-in are held at the Pavilion at Pirate's Cove. Registration, a social hour, and an anglers' rule meeting are held Friday night. Saturday it's fishing, the weigh-in, and an awards dinner. Manteo Rotary, the sponsor of this event, uses the profits to give college scholarships to local youth.

OBX MARATHON AND HALF MARATHON, Kitty Hawk and Jockey's Ridge State Park; obxmarathon.com. The second Sunday in November brings runners from all over the country to the OBX Marathon. Runners begin in Kitty Hawk and journey by the Wright Brothers National Memorial, through Nags Head Woods maritime forest, and across the scenic Washington Baum Bridge to finish on Roanoke Island. Participants in the half marathon will take off at Jockey's Ridge State Park and follow the same route from that point. Four thousand slots are available, and the total purse for both events is $17,200. Prizes, music, food, medals, and T-shirts follow the event. Proceeds benefit the Dare Education Foundation and the Outer Banks Relief Foundation.

WINGS OVER WATER FESTIVAL, many Outer Banks locations, (252) 216-9464; wingsoverwater.org. Wings Over Water is a six-day celebration of the Outer Banks' wonderful wildlife and wildlands, held the third week of October. It offers a number of activities for those who want to learn more about this enchanting natural area. You select the field trips, programs, and seminars that interest you the most and then get an inside look at the various ecological settings and wildlife of the Outer Banks. For example, go on guided bird-watching trips at Pea Island National Wildlife Refuge, kayak or canoe into a salt marsh, attend a photography or art seminar, or motor out to the waters of the Gulf Stream. There is such an enormous list of activities that this is only the tip of the iceberg. All programs charge a moderate fee. For information or to register for the event, call the number above or visit the website, where there's an online registration form.

DECEMBER

GRAND ILLUMINATION AT THE ELIZABETHAN GARDENS, off US 64, Roanoke Island; (252) 473-3234; elizabethangardens.org. The first weekend in December is a time of wonderment and magic in the Elizabethan Gardens. Teams of designers light the gardens into a glowing paradise of winter enchantment. Over one million lights are used to create an enchanting experience.

HATTERAS CHRISTMAS PARADE, Hatteras Village. Quintessentially small town and perfect. Parade route is from the Oden Docks to Eagle Pass Road. Local businesses and ordinary citizens create floats for the parade. One or two bands and of course Santa rides at the end of the parade in a fire truck. Mid-December.

LIGHTING OF THE TOWN TREE AND CHRISTMAS PARADE, Manteo; (252) 473-2133. Manteo and Dare County get ready for the holidays over the first weekend in December with events for the whole family. On Friday the big town tree, right on the waterfront next to the Tranquil House Inn is lit about 6:30 p.m. The event is accompanied by carols, a Yule log, cake, and hot chocolate. It's a good place to gather and get in the holiday spirit. On Saturday morning, a hometown parade rambles through downtown Manteo.

OUTER BANKS HOTLINE'S FESTIVAL OF TREES, (252) 473-5121. Since 1988 this popular auction and fundraiser has taken place in early December. Businesses and individuals donate fully decorated Christmas trees and other holiday items to be auctioned and delivered to buyers. Proceeds benefit Hotline's crisis intervention program and needy families in the area. Past trees have been decorated with dinner and wine certificates, hand-woven tapestry wear and accessories, and even a fishing-gear tree. The festive event includes several days of celebrations. Call the Hotline office for location and ticket information.

ROANOKE ISLAND CHRISTMAS WEEKEND, Historic Manteo; (252) 473-5548. Get an inside peek at some of Manteo's finest homes on this festive tour. The Elizabethan Gardens and the Island Farm are included on the route. This magical event is sponsored by the Manteo Preservation Trust.

Held the first Friday of December every year, the town of Manteo tree lighting is a perfect small town celebration, featuring choir performances from local schools and churches, speeches, and of course Santa.

TOWN OF DUCK CRAB POT CHRISTMAS TREE LIGHTING, Duck; townofduck.com. A little bit wacky, but very much in the spirit of the season. The Christmas tree is made up of crab pots stacked in a pyramid. A wonderful community event that includes free hot chocolate and coffee, cookies, and pastries. The Duck Santa Claus arrives by fire truck and may be the best around. First Saturday after Thanksgiving.

WRIGHT BROTHERS ANNIVERSARY OF THE FIRST FLIGHT, Wright Brothers National Monument; US 158, MP 8, Kill Devil Hills; (252) 441-7430. On December 17, 1903, Wilbur and Orville Wright made their first successful flights before a handful of local residents. This event is celebrated every year on December 17, in the exact place where those flights occurred. Antique and technologically advanced planes fly overhead as the monumental accomplishments of the Wright brothers are recalled. Speakers generally include military personnel, local dignitaries, and individuals who have dedicated their lives to the advancement of flight technology. A portrait of the year's induction to the First Flight Society is unveiled. There is no charge.

APPENDIX: Living Here

In this section we feature specific information for residents or those planning to relocate here. Topics include real estate and retirement.

Real Estate

There's a certain feeling that many of us get when we cross a bridge to the Outer Banks. It's excitement mixed with awe, blended with the spirit that something wonderful might happen at any moment. It's also a feeling of coming home. Any visitor to these shores who has that feeling should know one thing: It only gets stronger, and it makes leaving increasingly difficult. When you get that feeling, you know that it's time to look at Outer Banks real estate.

It's the desire to belong here, as much as the desire to own here, that puts the ink on all those real estate contracts. Before you take up a pen, however, realize that no matter how much experience you have buying and selling real estate in other areas, you need a deep understanding of the Outer Banks and its unique real estate market in order to make a sound decision. There's a lot to learn about seasonal versus residential neighborhoods, coastal and wetlands regulations, investing in an income-producing property versus buying a second home, buying an existing home versus building—you get the picture. It's not unusual for real estate agents to work with prospective buyers for two or three years before it all comes together. Then again, you may find exactly what you want on your first day out looking.

So if you're serious about buying on the Outer Banks, begin by reading this chapter, and when you're done, consider that you've learned just enough to be dangerous. Do two things: (1) Start interviewing real estate professionals, and (2) begin collecting and reading everything you can get your hands on that will help you decipher the real estate market. An excellent book on the subject is Jeff Scott's book, *Living the Dream*. Although written more than 20 years ago, Jeff's knowledge of the market and his observations are still relevant and useful. Subscribe to the local newspapers and get to know the areas, the issues, and the prices. Search the Internet and pick up the free real estate magazines. Smart buyers begin performing this due diligence well before they're ready to make a purchase.

Understanding the Local Market

As you learn about the Outer Banks, you'll come to understand that the market varies quite a bit by township and by proximity to water. Nowhere is the old adage about location, location, location more important than here on the Outer Banks. The rules of supply and demand apply, period. The closer to the ocean, the greater the demand—and nothing is more precious than an oceanfront lot. Bear in mind that all oceanfront lots aren't created equal. The shoreline along the entire East Coast is in a constant state of flux. With such a dynamic scenario, some areas of the beach will experience erosion, some will experience accretion, and it's all subject to change. There's always an element of risk in owning property in a coastal environment.

The priciest real estate on the Outer Banks is in Corolla, where the newer oceanfront homes sell for up to $7 million. Still, there are many excellent, established neighborhoods in other areas of the Outer Banks where you can buy a cottage for around $320,000 and still walk to the ocean. This chapter touches upon the flavor of the various sections of the beach; for more information on townships, see the **Area Overview** chapter.

Working with a Real Estate Agent

Whether you decide to buy an existing home or build your own, a good real estate agent can supply you with the information you need to make a smart decision and can save you a great deal of time and, very often, money. You are wise to enlist the services of a knowledgeable agent when you buy real estate on the Outer Banks given the uniqueness of the market economics and the local environment.

Interview a few agents before you decide with whom you'd like to work. Ask around for referrals. It's important for you to know that any real estate agent or broker can represent your interests, but be careful to select an agent with expertise in the communities in which you're most interested. Generally you're better off working with an agent whose office is located near your preferred areas. An agent who understands the market in Corolla probably won't be quite as knowledgeable of markets in Hatteras or Manteo.

Real estate agents and brokers are licensed by the State of North Carolina and are subject to its laws and regulations. A Realtor is an agent or broker who also belongs to the Board of Realtors, represented in our area by the Outer Banks Association of Realtors. What sets a Realtor apart from any licensee is the Realtor Code of Ethics, a set of stricter rules of conduct to which members subscribe, and access to the Multiple Listing Service, the most comprehensive database of properties for sale. For a listing of local Realtors, contact the Outer Banks Association of Realtors, PO Box 1070, Kill Devil Hills, NC 27948; (252) 441-4036; outerbanksrealtors.com. This organization represents more than 900 Realtors on the Outer Banks.

When you choose an agent or broker, technically you're entering into an agreement not only with that agent but also with the agent's firm. You'll need to decide whether you want exclusive representation from a buyer's agent, whether you're content to work with the seller's agent, or whether under certain circumstances you'll allow your buyer's agent to represent both you and the other party to the transaction, which makes your agent a "dual" agent. There are specific rules governing these relationships, and all agents and brokers are required to explain these rules at the first substantive contact with a prospective client or customer. You will be asked to sign an agency agreement; make sure you understand your options and your obligations to your agent as well as her or his obligations to you. Most agents collect their fees from the proceeds of the sale, but this is not always the case. Make sure you understand the compensation arrangement before you commit to an agent. According to North Carolina statute, even if an agent does not represent you, the agent must still be fair and honest and disclose to you all material facts that the agent knows or reasonably should know.

A conscientious, hardworking agent or broker will supply you with extensive information on the market—including comps (comparable properties currently listed and recently sold), neighborhood amenities and covenants, and financing options—and will be conversant in the pros and cons of building your own versus buying an existing home. She or he can also help you estimate the costs of ownership and what you might expect to realize in terms of income if you decide, as many owners do, to rent your home to others.

At the end of this chapter are listings of real estate companies and the areas they specialize in. Along with some community listings, we've supplied contact information for the developer, but do be aware that you don't have to work with the developer or the developer's agent directly; you should feel free to use your own buyer's agent if that's your preference.

Building Your Own

If you decide to build, your agent can help you choose a building contractor, or you can ask for a list of members from the Outer Banks Homebuilders Association, 105 West Airstrip Rd., Kill Devil Hills, NC 27948; (252) 449-8232, obhomebuilders.org.

If you decide to build your own home, first be clear about its intended use: Do you want a second home, rental property, or year-round residence? Your answer will determine where you build and the style of home. If you're designing for the rental market, you'll have to keep in mind not only your preferences but those of others as well. Talk with your builder and property managers to learn the features that will make your home a popular rental. You'll be wise to listen to their advice.

Ask your builder to not only show you floor plans but also take you through other houses he or she has built. (If you do this in the off-season, you'll have a better chance of viewing homes, for they will probably be vacant. Understandably, property managers try not to interrupt their guests' summer vacations.) If your goal is to achieve the maximum income, ask a property manager whose firm represents a lot of homes in your area to show you the most popular rentals in their inventory, but be careful to focus on homes similarly located to the lot you've selected. You can't compare income on an oceanfront to income on a house four rows back from the ocean.

You'll want to familiarize yourself with the building codes and regulations unique to our area, including regulations relating to environmental protection set by the North Carolina Coastal Management Authority (CAMA).

Throughout the process, keep in mind that your intended use of the property will dictate its design and construction. A home intended for weekly rental is usually substantially different in design from a home intended for year-round residential use. Wandering through open houses and model homes is a fun and informative way to refine your ideas before you begin to set them down on paper.

TIMESHARING

Timesharing is a deeded transaction under the jurisdiction of the North Carolina Real Estate Commission. A deeded share is $\frac{1}{52}$ of the unit property being purchased (one week of a year). This deed grants the right to use the property in perpetuity. Always ask if the property you're inspecting is a deeded timeshare because there is such a thing as undeeded timeshares—these give the right to use a property, but the property reverts to the developer in the end.

What you buy in a time-share is the right to use a specific piece of real estate for a week per year. The weeks are either fixed at the time of sale or rotate yearly. Members trade their weeks for different time slots at a variety of locations around the world. Qualifying for the purchase of a timeshare unit can be no more difficult than qualifying for a credit card, but be aware of financing charges that are higher than regular mortgages.

Most timeshare resorts on the Outer Banks are multifamily constructions with recreational amenities varying from minimal to luxurious and sometimes include the services of a recreational director. Timeshare units usually come furnished and carry a monthly maintenance fee. Tax advantages for ownership and financing are not available to the purchaser of a timeshare.

Many time-share ventures offer "free weekends"—you agree to a sales pitch and tour of the facilities in exchange for accommodations. Listen, ask questions, and stay in control of your money and your particular situation. If you get swept away, you'll only have five days to change your mind, according to the North Carolina Timeshare Act that governs the sale of timeshares.

It is best to keep the purchase of timeshares in proper perspective; your deeded share only enables you to vacation in that property during a designated time period each year for as long as you own that share. This makes timeshare very different from other potential investments.

All real estate investment decisions require thorough research and planning, and timeshare is no exception. Timeshare salespeople are licensed (to everyone's advantage) and earn commissions. Some great arrangements are out there, while others are not so good. Check thoroughly before buying. Several Outer Banks companies specialize in timesharing. The following list includes some of these.

BARRIER ISLAND OCEAN PINES, NC 12, Duck; (252) 261-3525; oceanpinesresort.com. Ocean Pines offers timesharing opportunities featuring oceanfront one- and two-bedroom condominiums. Amenities include an indoor pool, tennis courts, whirlpool tubs, and, of course, the beach.

BARRIER ISLAND STATION, NC 12, Duck; (252) 261-3525; ocean pinesresort.com. Barrier Island, one of the largest timeshare resorts on the Outer Banks, is on a high dune area of ocean-to-sound property. These are multifamily units of wood construction.

There is an attractive, full-service restaurant and bar with a soundside sailing center, in addition to the beach. A full-time recreation director is on board for a variety of planned activities and events. Indoor swimming, tennis courts, and other recreational facilities round out a full amenities package. This is a popular resort in a just-as-popular seaside village.

BEACHWOODS RESORT BY DIAMOND RESORTS, 1 Cypress Knee Trl., Kitty Hawk; (252) 261-4610; beachwoods.com. Beachwoods Resort is a multifamily vacation ownership resort set in a maritime forest. The 100 acres of private land sport a million-dollar sports complex featuring an indoor pool, free weights, circuit training, and aerobic and massage facilities. Shoot pool or play table tennis in the game room. Condominiums have one, two, or three bedrooms. The community is near two shopping centers.

DUNES SOUTH BEACH AND RACQUET CLUB, NC 12, MP 18, Nags Head; (252) 441-4090; dunesouth.com. Townhome timesharing at this resort features two- and three-bedroom units with fireplaces, washers and dryers, and whirlpool tubs. The 20 units are mostly oceanfront; the remaining units are oceanside. A pool, tennis court, putting green, and playground make up the recreational amenities.

OUTER BANKS BEACH CLUB, NC 12, MP 9, Kill Devil Hills; (252) 441-6321; outerbanksbeachclubresort.com. The round, wooden buildings of the Outer Banks Beach Club were the first timesharing opportunities built and sold on the Outer Banks. The 160 units include oceanfront and oceanside units, plus clubhouse units across the Beach Road, near the clubhouse and its indoor pool. There are two outdoor pools in great oceanfront locations. One-, two-, and three-bedroom units have access to whirlpools, tennis courts, and a playground. There is a full-time recreation director offering a variety of activities and games.

OUTER BANKS RESORT RENTALS, Croatan Centre, MP 13½, Nags Head; (252) 441-2134; outerbanksresorts.com. This company deals exclusively with timeshares, handling rentals and resales at all the timeshare complexes on the Outer Banks. All the units this company represents are furnished and self-contained, and all have swimming pools.

SEA SCAPE BEACH AND GOLF VILLAS, US 158, MP 2½, Kitty Hawk; (252) 261-3837. There are plenty of recreational opportunities here: tennis courts, three swimming pools, an indoor recreation facility, an exercise room, and a game room. The villas are next to the Sea Scape golf course. The two-bed, two-bath units are of wood construction, and they are on the west side of US 158. Sea Scape offers a unique opportunity for timeshare ownership and an active rental program.

REAL ESTATE SALES FIRMS

Following are some Outer Banks real estate sales companies, their locations, and contact information. While this list is not all-inclusive, it is representative of reputable real estate sales companies on the Outer Banks. Most, if not all, of these companies are members of the Outer Banks Association of Realtors.

BEACH REALTY & CONSTRUCTION/KITTY HAWK RENTALS, 790-B NC 12, Corolla; (252) 453-3131; beachrealtync.com. Steve Blaisdell is one of the expert consultants at Beach Realty, which handles real estate sales, rentals, and construction. The firm represents property from Carova to South Nags Head. Other locations are at 1450 NC 12, Duck, (252) 261-6600; US 158, MP 2, Kitty Hawk, (252) 261-3815, (800) 849-9888; and US 158, Kill Devil Hills, (252) 441-1106.

BRINDLEY BEACH VACATIONS, Corolla, 1023 Ocean Trl., Corolla; 1213-C Duck Rd., Duck; 3719 N. Croatan Hwy, Kitty Hawk; (877) 642-3224. Specializes in properties north of Oregon Inlet.

COVE REALTY, between NC 12 and US 158, MP 14, Nags Head; (252) 441-6391, (800) 635-7007; coverealty.com. Cove represents Nags Head and South Nags Head and specializes in Old Nags Head Cove.

DOLPHIN REALTY, NC 12, Hatteras Village; (252) 986-2562, (800) 338-4775; dolphin-realty.com. This company provides real estate properties in the villages of Avon, Buxton, Frisco, and Hatteras for buyers and sellers on Hatteras Island.

HARRELL AND ASSOCIATES, US 158, MP 7, Kill Devil Hills; (252) 441-7887; harrellandassociates.com. This company specializes in property throughout Dare County, including commercial and residential listings, plus many condominiums.

HATTERAS REALTY, NC 12, Avon; (252) 995-5466, (800) HATTERA; hatterasrealty.com. Hatteras Realty covers residential and commercial lots and homes on Hatteras Island.

JIM PERRY & COMPANY, Executive Center, US 158, MP 5½, Kill Devil Hills; (252) 441-3051, (800) 222-6135; jimperry.com. Jim Perry represents properties in all areas of the Outer Banks.

JOE LAMB JR. & ASSOCIATES, REALTORS, US 158, MP 2, Kitty Hawk; (252) 261-4444, (800) 552-6257; joelambjr.com. Joe Lamb represents properties from northern Corolla to South Nags Head.

KARICHELE REALTY, 66 Sunset Blvd., Timbuck II Shopping Village, NC 12, Corolla; (252) 453-4400, (800) 453-2377; karichele.com. Karichele covers properties from the Virginia line to Nags Head.

KITTY HAWK LAND COMPANY, US 158, Kitty Hawk; (252) 261-2131, (800) 488-0738; kittyhawklandcompany.com. Kitty Hawk Land Company has been in the real estate business for more than 50 years. KHL is credited with developing Southern Shores, Spindrift on the Currituck Outer Banks, WatersEdge on Colington Island, Sea Pines and Oceancrest in Duck, and the Currituck Club in Corolla. They offer properties within these developments, as well as select listings of outside properties on the Outer Banks.

MIDGETT REALTY, NC 12, Rodanthe; (252) 987-2350; midgettrealty .com. Midgett Realty represents properties on the southern end of the Outer Banks. Other locations are at NC 12, Avon, (252) 995-5333; and NC 12, Hatteras Village, (252) 986-2841, (800) 527-2903.

NAGS HEAD REALTY, US 158, MP 10½, Nags Head; (252) 441-4311, (800) 222-1531; nagsheadrealty.com. Nags Head Realty represents property from Corolla to Oregon Inlet.

OCRACOKE ISLAND REALTY, NC 12, Ocracoke; (252) 928-6261, (252) 928-7411; ocracokeislandrealty.com. Ocracoke Island Realty represents Ocracoke Island properties.

OUTER BANKS BLUE, 3732 N. Croatan Hwy; (252) 255-1220, (844) 557-3463; outerbanksblue.com. Properties throughout the Outer Banks.

OUTER BANKS VACATION REALTY, US 158, MP 2½, Kitty Hawk; (252) 261-5500, (866) 884-0267; outerbanksvacations.com. Properties from Kitty Hawk to South Nags Head are offered through Outer Banks Vacation Realty.

OUTER BEACHES REALTY, NC 12, Waves; (252) 987-1102, (800) 627-3750; outerbeaches.com. Outer Beaches Realty specializes in properties throughout Hatteras Island. Other locations are at NC 12, Avon, (252) 995-6041, (800) 627-3150; and NC 12, Hatteras, (252) 986-1105, (888) 627-3650.

PIRATE'S COVE YACHT CLUB, Nags Head–Manteo Causeway, Manteo; (252) 473-1451, (800) 762-0245; pirates-cove.com. The realty arm of Pirate's Cove Yacht Club represents properties in this boating paradise.

RIGGS REALTY, Austin Building, 1152 Ocean Trl., NC 12, Corolla; (252) 453-3111; riggsrealtycorp.com. Riggs specializes in northern beach land and home properties, especially in the four-wheel-drive areas like Swan, North Swan, and Carova Beach. Riggs Realty has 30-plus years of real estate experience.

SOUTHERN SHORES REALTY, NC 12, Southern Shores; (252) 261-2000, (800) 334-1000; southernshores.com. Southern Shores Realty represents properties from Corolla to Nags Head.

STAN WHITE REALTY & CONSTRUCTION, 812 Ocean Trl., Corolla; (252) 453-3161, (800) 753-6200; builderouterbanks.com. Stan White represents properties from Corolla to Hatteras Village. Other locations are at US 158, MP 10½, Nags Head, (252) 441-1515, (800) 753-9699; and NC 12, Duck, (252) 261-2224, (800) 992-2976.

SCOTT TEAM REALTY, The Marketplace, 5535 N. Croatan Hwy, Kitty Hawk; (252) 261-1500; scottrealtyobx.com. A small but highly respected realty company. Jeff Scott's book, *Living the Dream,* is an excellent resource.

SUN REALTY, US 158, MP 9, Kill Devil Hills; (252) 441-8011; sunrealty .com. This realty represents properties throughout the Outer Banks. Other locations are at NC 12, Corolla, (252) 453-8811; NC 12, Duck, (252) 261-4183; US 158, Kitty Hawk, (252) 261-3892; NC 12, Salvo, (252) 987-2755; and NC 12, Avon, (252) 995-5821.

SURF OR SOUND REALTY, NC 12, Rodanthe; (252) 987-1444, (800) 237-1138; surforsound.com. Surf or Sound represents properties from Rodanthe to Hatteras Village. Another location is at NC 12, Avon, (252) 995-6052.

TWIDDY & COMPANY, NC 12, Duck; (252) 261-8311, (800) 342-1609; twiddy.com. Twiddy represents properties from Carova through Kitty Hawk. Another location is at NC 12 and Second St., Corolla, (252) 453-3325, (800) 579-6130.

VILLAGE REALTY, US 158, MP 14½, Nags Head; (252) 480-2224, (800) 548-9688; villagerealtyobx.com. Village Realty represents properties from Corolla through South Nags Head.

Retirement

When some people dream of retirement, they might picture themselves strolling along stretches of deserted beaches on a mild winter afternoon. Perhaps later they would enjoy a round of golf with friends on an award-winning course, followed by a good meal at one of many area restaurants. Sound too good to be true? It's possible right here on the Outer Banks. But beware, this isn't your normal retirement community! The retirees here eagerly pursue an active lifestyle, participating in the many activities the beach has to offer. Many seniors also enjoy working with the public, filling a spot in the workplace through retail sales or other tourist-oriented jobs. As for fun activities, the senior centers offer all kinds of group trips and classes.

If you're thinking of retiring to the Outer Banks, you're in good company. Each year it seems that more retirees are lured to these barrier islands by some sort of siren call. Moderate winters (remarkably quiet due to the small year-round population) provide for a tranquil environment, and 90-plus miles of broad, soft-sand beaches might figure into the equation as well. North Carolina is now the third most attractive state to retirees, after Florida and Arizona.

These are retirement locations that tend to attract baby boomers and early retirees who are seeking relatively remote areas on the water where outdoor recreation is an integral part of life. Options for any type of dwelling abound all along the Outer Banks. If you're looking for a seaside mansion in a gated community, you'll find it. And if your tastes lean more toward a bungalow in the woods or to a traditional three-bedroom home with a yard, you'll find those, too.

OVERVIEW

If you're looking for property, check out the **Real Estate** and **Area Overview** chapters before you start shopping. For information on our community's senior services, read on.

Seniors are encouraged to participate in the Outer Banks Senior Games sponsored by Dare County Older Adult Services. But be warned, these senior athletes are a dedicated and talented bunch, capable of putting much younger athletes to shame. This is a year-round program to promote health and fitness for Dare County residents age 55 and older. Competition events include track and field, bicycle racing, swimming, tennis, bowling, golf, softball and football throwing, basketball shooting, archery, shuffleboard, billiards, horseshoes, and croquet. Medal winners automatically qualify to compete at the North Carolina Senior Games in September. Besides athletics, there is a Silver Competition for the visual and performing arts. See the listings in the **Annual Events** chapter under April, or call the Thomas A. Baum Center, (252) 441-1811, for more information.

> ℹ You don't have to limit yourself to the senior centers to socialize. Cultural arts nonprofit groups such as the Theatre of Dare, Dare County Arts Council, and Outer Banks Forum offer plenty of opportunities for you to volunteer your time and offer your expertise. See the **Arts & Culture** chapter for more information.

SENIOR CENTERS

FESSENDEN CENTER, NC 12, Buxton; (252) 995-3888. The Fessenden Center offers services and programs for county residents and property owners of all ages, although you must be age 55 or older to participate in the older adult activities for free. However, the center schedules activities, such as aerobic classes, for adults of all ages for various fees.

The building has a gym with a basketball court. The center operates as a senior center and a site for youth athletic activities. The gym is open from 3 to 5 p.m. Monday through Friday. You can enjoy basketball and volleyball as well as fishing, believe it or not. Throw a line in the creek off the back deck—chances are you'll snag a puppy drum (juvenile channel bass).

The full-service kitchen/conference room is available for preparing meals. Every second and fourth Thursday of the month, seniors attend a luncheon. The second Thursday lunch is prepared at the center by seniors; the fourth Thursday lunch is a covered-dish affair. Funds for the lunches are provided by Festivities, a volunteer senior group that raises money by running the center's concession stand at athletic functions. Seniors contribute a $1 donation if they are able. The kitchen/conference room does double duty as a county meeting facility.

The center also sports an activity room, a sitting room, and a library. Seniors are invited to hone their skills at the outdoor tennis courts or play with grandchildren at the on-site playground. The soccer and baseball fields give them plenty of room to stretch or jog.

Adults can participate in organized step aerobics, toning and stretching, abdominal exercise, tae kwon do, tai chi, walking, basketball, and dance. Take Spanish or sign language classes; attend seminars, workshops, and classes on fire safety, cardiac rehabilitation, credit fraud, nutrition, home decorating, quilting, and painting; or take cultural arts trips to shows and parks outside the area. Minimal fees are attached for supplies ($5 to $10).

Transportation is available through the center's coordinator by calling the center's main number. Shopping trips are scheduled for seniors and disabled adults with transportation problems. Rides are available to medical appointments and out-of-town hospitals and doctors' offices in Norfolk and Chesapeake, Virginia, as well as Elizabeth City, Nags Head, and Greenville, North Carolina.

The Fessenden Center is open Monday through Friday from 8:30 a.m. to 5 p.m. and weekends for youth and special activities.

THOMAS A. BAUM CENTER, 300 Mustian St., Kill Devil Hills; (252) 441-1181. The Thomas A. Baum Center is named after a Dare County native who was a pioneer in ferry transportation. His daughter, Diane Baum St. Clair, arranged for the town of Kill Devil Hills to purchase the land, known locally as the Baum Tract, on very generous terms. Dare County bought a section of the land, which today is home to the senior center, water plant, library, two public schools, the local chamber of commerce, and the town's administration and water departments.

The senior center was dedicated in 1987. The 10,000-square-foot-plus building houses the senior center and the county's older adult services. A handful of paid staff and countless senior volunteers operate the center, which is the hub for senior activity north of Hatteras Island. Dare County residents or property owners who are age 55 or older may use the center for free; if you are younger than age 55 but your spouse meets the age requirement, you also may use the center.

The facility includes a multipurpose room with a stage where the center's drama group, Center Front, performs various productions annually. The Outer Banks Senior Chorus, which performs two concerts per year, also uses this room for practice sessions. The Baum Center is home to the Wright Tappers, a seniors tap dancing group, and the Dare Devils, the official cheerleaders for the Outer Banks Senior Games. Line- and square-dance groups round out the foot-tapping activities. And going hand in hand with its name, the multipurpose room does double-duty for aerobic classes three days a week.

A full-service kitchen is used for social functions and fundraisers such as the popular annual eat-in or take-out spaghetti supper. The center does not offer daily lunches on the premises.

Head to the lounge to chat, relax, or read a paperback book borrowed from the center's honor system library. Adjacent to the lounge is the game room, where you can play bridge weekly, work puzzles, play cribbage or canasta, or sit in on seminars in history, tax aid, or health education, to name a few. The center also hosts support group meetings for such organizations as the Outer Banks Cancer Support Group and the Amputee Coalition of Coastal Carolina. Twice a month seniors gather at the center for an afternoon movie with popcorn.

If you're an outdoor lover, eat lunch on the deck or watch for resident deer and foxes. Five picnic tables and various chairs encourage relaxation or conversation. The nearby yard is host to a football target that tests throwing accuracy, horseshoe pits, and spin-casting targets. Outer Banks Senior Games contenders practice discus and shot put as well as archery using bales of hay for targets.

The recreation room comes alive as competitors play a leisurely game of billiards, table tennis, or shuffleboard. There's plenty of elbow room in this spacious area, complete with three pool tables, two Ping Pong tables, and several huge shuffleboard games. Coffee is available in the kitchenette just off the recreation room, and cups are in the cabinet. Donations are welcome. Bring your lunch and store it in the refrigerator or heat it in the microwave.

Off the rec room is a craft room complete with two sinks, a projector, storage space, seven tables with four chairs each, and a sewing machine. Check the center's newsletter, *Senior Soundings*, for craft courses and special activities that take place in this room. The newsletter comes out by the 15th of the month and is available at both county senior centers and the three public libraries.

The center has an information and referral room where you can sign up for programs on preparing healthful food, bird watching, growing perennials, and acrylic painting. Some activities have a small supplies fee; scholarships are available. A wall of pamphlets cover topics such as taxes, health, and fire safety. Countywide information is available via the computerized Senior Connection information and referral system. Questions on Alzheimer's disease, in-home services, marriage licenses, and the like can be answered by using this program staffed by trained volunteers.

A small computer room is set up with Internet connections. An exercise suite features a treadmill, a rowing machine, and four stationary bicycles, and a staff exercise specialist offers regular exercise programs.

Seniors can take advantage of the center's 20-seat conference room complete with a telephone and white marker board. Community groups also use this space from time to time.

The senior center plays a vital role in providing transportation for elderly and disabled Dare County residents. A paid staff member is on hand at the

i The local chapter of SCORE (Service Corps of Retired Executives) provides free counseling on business matters such as putting together a marketing plan, starting a business, compiling financial statements, computerizing an office, obtaining small business loans, and expanding business plans. Weekly sessions are held on Tuesday at the Outer Banks Chamber of Commerce in Kill Devil Hills. For more information call the chamber of commerce: (252) 441-8144.

RETIREMENT

center to schedule free rides to doctor appointments and hospitals in Chesapeake and Norfolk, Virginia, as well as Greenville, North Carolina. The transportation volunteer needs 24 hours' notice.

Rides also are available for shopping trips and getting to and from the center and to the nutrition site at Mount Olivet United Methodist Church in Manteo, where lunch is served Monday through Friday. Seniors are asked to make a $1 donation, but it's not mandatory. Menu selections may include herb-baked chicken with mixed vegetables and rice pilaf or spaghetti with a tossed salad. Two-percent milk and dessert top off the meal. The meals are prepared off the premises by the Columbia 4-H center. A day's notice is all they need to make sure the food count is correct. If you can't make it to the luncheon, home delivery is available.

The Baum Center is open Monday through Friday from 8:30 a.m. until 5 p.m. and for special functions.

SENIOR SERVICES

HELPING HAND, Manteo Police Department, 410 Ananias Dare St., Manteo; (252) 473-2069. Working from a list of voluntary participants, Manteo officers check on more than 70 elderly or disabled citizens twice a week in person or by phone to make sure they are healthy and their needs are being met. The town list is divided among the officers, who prefer to go in person but telephone from time to time. Participants include seniors, disabled individuals, and persons who live alone. This program is particularly useful in a community like the Outer Banks, where storms occasionally threaten the coast and require residents to evacuate. Officers are in such close contact with the community that they are able to alert homebound individuals in the event of a weather emergency. If you're interested in being on the Helping Hands list, call the police department. Anyone there will give you more information on this free service.

LITTLE GROVE UNITED METHODIST CHURCH MONTHLY LUNCHEON, NC 12, Frisco; (252) 986-2149. Little Grove usually has a luncheon the third Thursday of the month for anyone interested in food and fellowship. The luncheon includes singing and storytelling that begins at 11:30 a.m. Call the above number on the Monday before the third Thursday of the month to reserve your space. Donations are appreciated.

Index